CONTENTS

PART FOUR   REMEDIES IN CONTRACT LAW

PREFACE

The tradition of the common law is to enunciate principles of law through the decisions of the judges in actual cases. While the enactment of a written Constitution, and the consequences which have flowed from that event, have to some extent diluted our dependence on the common law type of judicial system, the decision of a judge on a novel point of law argued on actual facts continues to present the most fruitful source of legal principles. To understand the law in any particular area, it is necessary to study the previously decided judgments of the courts.

Because these are found in a diverse number of law reports, many old or unavailable, the practitioner and the student need an accessible method of reaching these cases. This difficulty is further compounded by the absence in the law reports of many of the important decisions. The answer is the casebook: a collection of the relevant cases under a single cover. By judicious editing of each judgment with a short synopsis of the facts, followed by a clear statement of the actual decision, a two-fold effect is achieved. First, the principle of law is expounded in each case and secondly, the subject locks together into a cohesive body of law.

A casebook generally complements a textbook though in contract law a clear understanding of the subject can be gleaned from sole study of the case law. It is a feature of contract law that the legislature has rarely intruded and has left to the courts the development of the subject. Thus the reader can rely on the casebook without the nagging doubt that some statute has dented the authority of the case law.

This is the first occasion that a casebook on Irish contract law has been compiled. It may come as a surprise to some—particularly to those who unduly harp on cases from other common law jurisdictions—that our case law contains judgments as varied and wide ranging as it does and as this book illustrates. It seems that in legal matters, as in many other aspects of Irish life, we tend to acknowledge the outside influence and ignore the Irish one. I hope that this book helps to reverse that trend.

I must express my appreciation to the Librarian of the King's Inns, Jonathan Armstrong (and his staff), and to the Librarian of the Law

Society, Margaret Byrne (and her staff) for their assistance. A special word of thanks to Bridget Lunn for her considerable editorial expertise.

I wish to thank the Incorporated Law Reporting Council of Ireland for permission to reproduce extracts from the *Irish Reports* and to the Round Hall Press for permission to reproduce excerpts from the *Irish Law Reports Monthly*. My thanks are due to the judges, both past and present for permission to reproduce their endeavours.

Brian Doolan
Law Library, Four Courts, Dublin
July 1989

ABBREVIATIONS

A.C./App.Cas.	Appeal Cases
All E.R.	All England Reports
B./BB.	Baron/Barons
C.	Chancellor
C.B.	Chief Baron
Ch.	Chancery
Ch.App.	Chancery Appeal
Ch.D	Chancery Division
C.J.	Chief Justice
Eq.	Equity
I.L.R.M.	Irish Law Reports Monthly
I.L.T.R.	Irish Law Times Report
I.R.	Irish Reports
Ir.Ch.Rep	Irish Chancery Reports
Ir. C.L.	Irish Reports—Common Law
Ir. C.L.R.	Irish Common Law Reports
I.R.Eq.	Irish Reports—Equity
Ir.Jur.Rep.	Irish Jurists Reports
Ir.L.R.	Irish Law Reports
J./JJ.	Mr Justice/Miss Justice
L.C.	Lord Chancellor
L.C.J.	Lord Chief Justice
L.J./L.JJ.	Lord Justice/Lord Justices
L.R. H.L.	Law Reports—House of Lords
L.R.Ir.	Law Reports Ireland
L.T.	Law Times
M.R.	Master of the Rolls
P.	President of the High Court
Q.B.D.	Queens Bench Division
S.C.	Court of Sessions—Scotland
Sol. Jo.	Solicitors' Journal
unrep.H.C.	unreported judgment of the High Court
V.C.	Vice Chancellor
W.L.R.	Weekly Law Reports

TABLE OF CASES

PART ONE

FORMATION OF CONTRACT

A contract is an agreement giving rise to obligations which are enforced or recognised by law. A contract exists when legally capable persons have reached agreement, or where the law considers them to have reached agreement. A valid contract attaches rights and obligations to each of the parties.

For a contract to be legally valid, and therefore binding on the parties, it must be possessed of three essentials, which are (1) agreement, (2) an intention to be contractually bound, and (3) consideration.

CHAPTER 1.

AGREEMENT

The first essential of a valid contract is the agreement between the parties. Where disputes arise it is necessary to discover whether an agreement was in fact reached. This is done by a close examination of the negotiations surrounding the transaction. The courts seek to discover whether the parties were *ad idem*: agreeing on the essential point: *Megaw v Molloy* (Case 1), *J.L. Smallman Ltd v O'Moore* (Case 2) and *Collins v O'Brien* (Case 3).

To assist the courts in resolving the question as to whether there is, or is not, agreement, the courts sub-divide the inquiry into whether there was an offer by one party and an acceptance by the other party.

An offer exists where the offeror undertakes to be contractually bound should a proper acceptance be made by the offeree. To constitute an effective offer the terms must be unconditional, clear and certain: *Russell & Laird Ltd v Hoban* (Case 4), *Central Meat Products Ltd v Carney* (Case 13) and *Tansey v College of Occupational Therapists Ltd* (Case 5).

A mere quotation is not an offer: *Boyers & Co. v Duke* (Case 6).

But a quotation coupled with the words 'subject to immediate acceptance' has been held to constitute a valid offer: *Dooley v T.L. Egan & Co. Ltd* (Case 7).

An offer can be made to an individual, or to a group of individuals: *Billings v Arnott & Co.* (Case 16), or to the world at large: *Kennedy v London Express Newspapers Ltd* (Case 15).

An offer must be distinguished from a mere invitation to treat. The latter has been defined as a first step in negotiations which may, or may not, be a prelude to a firm offer being made by one of the parties: *Minister for Industry and Commerce v Pim Bros. Ltd* (Case 8).

Unless and until an offer is communicated to the offeree by the offeror it is invalid: *Wilson v Belfast Corporation* (Case 9). A party may qualify the offer in some way and until that condition is fulfilled there is no agreement: *Kelly v Irish Nursery & Landscape Co. Ltd* (Case 10).

An acceptance exists when the offeree unqualifiedly accepts the offer made by the offeror: *Tully v Irish Land Commission* (Case 11). The acceptance must correspond exactly with the terms of the offer: *Swan v Miller* (Case 12). An 'acceptance in principle' may not constitute an acceptance: *Central Meat Products v Carney* (Case 13).

An acceptance must, as a general rule, be communicated to the offeror by the offeree though there are two exceptions to this rule: the first is where the proper acceptance is by post: *Sanderson v Cunningham* (Case 14), and the second is where the offer contains a term which provides that complete performance by the offeree constitutes a sufficient agreement: *Kennedy v London Express Newspapers Ltd* (Case 15).

An offer continues in existence until it is terminated by lapsing, rejection or revocation. An offer may be withdrawn at any time before its acceptance. But once a valid acceptance is made by the offeree the offeror is bound by it and cannot subsequently withdraw it: *Billings v Arnott & Co.* (Case 16).

Once agreement is reached between the parties it is not open to one of them to unilaterally introduce additional terms: *Ryle v Minister for Agriculture* (Case 17). But the introduction of an additional term may be accepted by the other party: *Wheeler & Co. Ltd v John Jeffrey & Co.* (Case 18).

Case 1. Megaw v Molloy
Court of Appeal (1878) 2 L.R.Ir. 530

A corn-broker, on the plaintiff's instruction, offered for sale by auction a quantity of grain which it was claimed came from a ship called the *Emma Peasant*. A sample of grain was shown to the defendant. By accident the sample was of a superior grain taken from another of the plaintiff's ships, the *Jessie Parker*. The defendant agreed to purchase the grain but on learning the true position refused to complete the sale. The plaintiff sued for damages for breach of contract.

Held that as the plaintiff intended to sell one bulk and the defendant to buy another, the parties were not *ad idem*. The claim was dismissed.

Ball L.C.:

The plaintiff employed a broker to sell maize for him. The maize he intended to sell had been imported in a ship called the *Emma Peasant*. The plaintiff had also other maize imported in a ship called the *Jessie Parker*. Both were stored in the same building. The maize from the *Jessie Parker* was superior to the maize from the *Emma Peasant*. By accident on the morning of the sale, a sample was taken from the cargo of the *Jessie Parker*, not from that of the *Emma Peasant*. The auctioneer believed the sample to have been taken from the proper bulk; so believing he, at the sale, exhibited it. The defendant made the highest bid at the auction, and was afterwards offered from the cargo of the *Emma Peasant* the quantity he had bid for—it was re-sold; and the action is to recover the loss upon the re-sale, when compared with the price bid by the defendant.

The defendant pleads that he did not contract; and the substantial objection raised to the case of the plaintiff is, that the purchaser and the vendor were not dealing in respect of the same matter. Whether this is so or not must, we think, depend upon what passed at the auction. I take this from the evidence of the auctioneer, who was himself examined. He says: 'I had conditions of sale . . . They were read out by me at the auction. I do not know whether the defendant was then present. The defendant bought lots 6, 7, 8, and 9—in all, 200 quarters, at 26*s*. 9*d*. I signed the sale. A sample was produced. I made the usual statement about it, viz., that it was a true sample, but that we did not guarantee it, and were not to be responsible.'

The conditions of sale made no mention of the maize to be sold having come by the *Emma Peasant*. Other witnesses prove the bags which held the sample had on them the words, 'ex *Emma Peasant*'. This is all the allusion to the cargo as connected with that ship which I can find to have been made during the auction. The defendant says that at the auction he saw the sample produced; that it was spilled out of a bag, and was sound American maize.

Now what meaning would the auctioneer's words naturally convey to an intending purchaser in reference to the sample? He said it was a true sample, but he did not guarantee it. I apprehend this would be understood—'The sample is taken from the bulk to be sold, but I do not guarantee that it is a perfect representation of its general quality. I guarantee that it has been taken, not that it has been fairly taken, from it.'

Then what did the purchaser buy? Something of which that sample had been part—he bought that bulk out of which this sample had been taken—he knew of nothing else. What did the vendor intend to sell? Not that bulk out of which the sample had been taken, but a wholly different commodity which had come by the *Emma Peasant*. The vendor and purchaser were therefore not dealing for the same subject-matter. There was misapprehension as to the very substance of the thing in contract, not as to any quality or incident or merit or demerit of it—*error in corpore.*

It is not the case of a seller and purchaser intending to sell and buy the same horse with a misapprehension as to his soundness, but of the seller intending to sell one horse and the buyer to bid for another, and not at the time of the treaty discovering the difference in the identity. A dealing, where the parties are not intending the same subject-matter, evidently cannot be an agreement . . . On the true nature of the transaction as it existed it appears to me that there was no contract.

May C.J., Christian and Deasy L.JJ. delivered concurring judgments.

Case 2. J.L. Smallman & Co. Ltd v O'Moore
High Court [1959] I.R. 220

Two persons carried on a partnership business. In September 1954 the partners decided to terminate the partnership and to operate the business as a limited company. The plaintiff had supplied the partnership prior to the formation of the company and continued, as it is thought, after its formation, to supply goods to the partners, who intended to purchase such goods on behalf of the company. The plaintiff sued the partners for the price of the goods.

Held that there was no binding contract as the parties were not *ad idem.*

Davitt P.:

. . . This is an action for the balance of the price of goods sold and delivered. The plaintiff alleges a contract of sale with the defendants. In my opinion it has not established such a contract. Unless I am to assume fraud on the part of the defendants, which has neither been alleged nor proved, it is, I think, reasonably clear that the parties were not *ad idem.* The plaintiff believed it was supplying the goods to the partnership while the defendants believed they were being supplied to the company. The only contract which can be spelt out of the circumstances is that the company, which accepted and used the goods, is under the obligation to pay for them.

Case 3. Collins v O'Brien
High Court [1981] I.L.R.M. 328

The parties made an oral agreement for the letting of land for grazing, on the eleven months system, which was to commence on 23 March. The plaintiff believed, having regard to the custom in that part of the country, that the letting was to terminate on 31 December, whereas the defendant believed it was to terminate on 22 February of the following year. The plaintiff, in January, demanded that the defendant vacate the land, which he did on 7 February, and sued for the use and occupation of the land from 1 January to 7 February. The defendant counterclaimed for the loss of the use and enjoyment of the land from 7 to 22 February.

Held that the parties were never *ad idem*. The court approached the case on a *quantum meruit* basis and awarded damages to the defendant for the lost 15 days of grazing.

Doyle J.:

. . . Usually the agreement is, however, reduced to writing which embodies dates for the commencement and termination of the period of grazing. In the present case . . . the plaintiff decided on a clearance sale of her cattle and farm implements by public auction and on the letting of the grazing of her 46 Irish acres. The date of the auction, which was 23 March 1979, was an unusual date for the commencement of a grazing letting. . . . In the present case there is nothing in writing as to when the letting was to end. The conclusion to which I have come is that the plaintiff thought the term was from 23 March 1979 until 31 December 1979. The defendant believed that it was from 23 March 1979 until 22 February 1980. The parties were thus, never *ad idem* and so there was no contract between. In those circumstances I have to ask myself: what would a court of equity allow? I approach the case as if on a claim for *quantum meruit*. If the defendant had taken the grazing from a date in or about the middle of January 1979 to end on 31 December of that year the price for the grazing would be £162 per acre. The plaintiff has not discharged the onus of proof which rested on her to show that, in the circumstances, the term ended on 31 December 1979. The defendant enjoyed the grazing only from 23 March 1979 to 7 February 1980 when he was forced to vacate the lands. He lost 15 days grazing and I will give him a decree on his counterclaim for £315 being 15 days at the agreed figure of £21 per day.

Case 4. Russell & Laird Ltd v Hoban
Court of Appeal [1922] 2 I.R. 159

The plaintiff's traveller at a business interview with the defendant gave him a sale note, which was subject to confirmation, for some goods. This note was not signed by the defendant. Some days later the plaintiff sent the defendant a contract note confirming the sale note but with some variations. The defendant wrote to the plaintiff cancelling his order and subsequently refused to accept delivery of the goods on the ground that there was no completed contract between the parties.

Held that the sale note and contract note did not constitute a contract between the parties in that the offer was conditional which was not accepted by the defendant.

Ronan L.J.:

. . . I have come to the conclusion that there was no contract in this case. The materials on which I base my judgment are the documents plus the evidence of the . . . traveller for the plaintiff. His business was to go round the country soliciting orders for it. He kept a book which he describes as an 'order book'; and his account of the transaction here is: 'I met defendant; I talked to him about buying forward oatmeal. The defendant said he would buy forty tons . . . The defendant said he would like if we could manage it that we should deliver in six separate deliveries. I could not promise; I thought only two deliveries were possible, and I told him that. He said if we could not do six he would take two. I made him the sale subject to the usual confirmation from head office.' That is the account from which we are asked to infer that on that occasion a final contract was concluded between the traveller, on behalf of the plaintiff, and the defendant. The traveller says he made the sale . . . 'subject to the usual confirmation from head office.' Surely, if the man is telling the truth, that is not an unconditional sale. It is only a sale subject to confirmation by head office. As if to make the matter plain, the traveller says: 'I wrote out sale note from order book and handed carbon copy to the defendant. I forwarded order to Dublin. When I returned to Dublin I wrote letter of 6 November.'

Counsel for the plaintiff says if the first document be taken, apart from this conversation, and apart from the other documents in the case, there is an absolute contract. It is always open to parties to show that notwithstanding the terms of a document there was, in fact, no contract. This traveller is supposed to have drawn up in the interest of his employers a contract which would have bound them, but would not have bound the other party. The idea of this man making a contract which would bind his employers and did not bind it is too grotesque for belief.

On 18 October the plaintiff made its first communication from the head office to the defendant in the following terms: 'With reference to the order given to our traveller, we are today in receipt of a cable enabling us to accept same. We have accordingly much pleasure in handing you contract note herewith, and shall be pleased to receive your further orders.' How can it be contended that there was a contract when these people wrote that letter? If they had written, 'We hereby accept it,' and the order had been signed by the defendant, that would be all right; but no order had been signed by the defendant. All this shows that the traveller never intended the first document to be a contract. The contract note enclosed with the letter of 18 October from the head office used these words: 'We confirm having this day sold you subject to safe arrival,' etc. That is a complete departure from the terms of the sale note of 12 October. The terms of the original document provided for 'December and January shipment from mills' and for 'cash orders 7 days from date of invoice.' The terms of the contract note are: 'December and January seaboard shipments and net cash in seven days.' The concluding words of the contract note were: 'If this sale note be retained beyond three days after this date, it will be held to have been accepted by the buyer.' No man can impose such conditions upon another. The document is conclusive evidence against the parties who sent it, that it was an offer which required acceptance.

In my opinion it is conclusively proved that there was never any contract between the parties . . .

Case 5. Tansey v College of Occupational Therapists Ltd
High Court, unreported, 27 August 1986

The plaintiff wished to study occupational therapy and she applied to a college recognised by the defendant which provided a course of tuition and training designed to prepare students for the defendant's diploma. The defendant was solely an examination body and offered a diploma which was highly regarded. The plaintiff was offered a place in the college in August 1978 on a course which was to commence in October of that year. The defendant's manual, prepared and published in April 1977, provided that it was the normal policy to allow two retakes of each part of the examination. In April 1977, the defendant altered the regulations by providing that henceforth students should have the right to one retake only. This amendment was only to apply to students commencing their studies in October 1978. A circular to this effect was sent to the college in which the plaintiff had enrolled and it was placed on the notice board. The 1977 manual was distributed to students only after their admission to the college and the plaintiff was given a copy of the 1977 manual without an amendment slip containing the amended examination rule. In meetings of teachers and students in May 1980 this amended rule was explained. The plaintiff sat and passed a number of subjects but failed one on two occasions. She applied to retake this subject for a second time but this request was refused. The plaintiff sued the defendant for breach of contract.

Held that the plaintiff had not proved that she offered or the defendant accepted any offer by the plaintiff to take the diploma course on terms which exclusively included the regulations contained in the unamended 1977 manual. The action was dismissed.

Murphy J.:
___

First, it is contended that the relationship between the plaintiff and the defendant is founded upon a contract which confers legally enforceable rights on the plaintiff. As the agreement (if any) between the plaintiff and the defendant related to the admission of the plaintiff to the course of studies approved by the defendant rather than the regulation of the conduct of students subsequent to their admission the matter is one—or so the plaintiff would contend—of general law and not a domestic matter which might, in the case of an appropriate institution, be dealt with by a visitor. The case of *Casson v University of Aston in Birmingham* (1983) was cited as persuasive authority in support of this proposition.

Secondly, that the contract was made in the month of November 1978 by the plaintiff offering herself as a student for the defendant's diploma course and the defendant by their agents, St Joseph's College, and their officials handing to the plaintiff the defendant's manual for the course.

Thirdly, that the acceptance of the plaintiff's offer was on the terms and conditions and subject to the regulations contained in the manual actually handed to the plaintiff and did not include any alterations thereof which were not at the time brought to her attention.

Fourthly, that the plaintiff was not given that degree of notice of the amendment contained in the circular pinned to the college notice board which would be appropriate having regard to the nature of that condition. It was contended that the alteration was in the nature of a restrictive condition and accordingly that clear notice thereof should have been given to the plaintiff.

Fifthly, that the contract having been made by the acceptance of the plaintiff as a student, no alteration in the terms of that contract could be made without the plaintiff's consent and that any notice or advice purporting to make such a change was ineffective (see *Olley v Malborough Court Ltd* (1949)).

Sixthly, that the plaintiff was entitled to damages for breach of contract which would reflect the income which she might have earned had she been permitted to re-sit her examination in psychiatry, duly passed it and then practised as an occupational therapist as against the income which she did in fact earn as a montessori teacher, notwithstanding the doubt which must exist as to whether she would indeed have succeeded in the examination. In support of that proposition reliance was placed on the decision of the late Mr Justice Dixon in *Hawkins v Rogers* (1951).

On behalf of the defendant it was accepted that there was a contractual relationship between it and the plaintiff but only insofar as it related to the setting and correcting of individual examinations. It was the defendant's contention that such contracts arose and arose only as and when the plaintiff applied in writing to the defendant to sit the various exams constituting the diploma course and on the acceptance of those applications by the defendant. The defendant also accepted that there was a contract between the plaintiff and St Joseph's College for the provision of training and tuition. In particular the defendant contends that no contract was entered into between the plaintiff and the defendant in the year 1978. On its behalf it was said that it made no offer to the plaintiff and received no offer from her. Less still was one accepted. It was emphasised that the defendant did not know of the existence of the plaintiff at any time before she applied in 1979 to sit her Group 1 examination. To the argument that St Joseph's College acted as the agents of the defendant it was pointed out that the evidence made it clear that St Joseph's College was an autonomous body which exercised their own discretion as to what students they would take in and indeed their own judgment as to what students they might expel.

I am unable to accept that a contract between the defendant and the plaintiff came into existence at the time, in the manner or on the terms for which the plaintiff contends as aforesaid. One would like to think that a student in the plaintiff's position would have some guarantee that significant changes would not be made in the structure of the course which she was pursuing or the fundamental regulations governing it after she had embarked thereon. No doubt to some extent this is achieved by the sense of responsibility actually displayed by the defendant in the present case and hopefully exercised by similar bodies in other cases.

Contractual obligations derive from agreement made between two or more parties under which one promises or undertakes with the other the performance of some action. Ordinarily the existence of an agreement presupposes an offer by one party to perform the action on certain terms and the acceptance of that offer by the other. Logical analysis would suggest that the offer must be communicated to the person for whom it is intended and in turn his/her acceptance must likewise be communicated to the offerer. In the absence of such communication, whether expressed or implied, there would not be that meeting of minds which is implicit in the concept of any agreement. It must be recognised, however, that the innumerable authorities dealing with the law of contract and academic analyses of those decisions over many years reveal refinements of this analysis and apparent exceptions to it. Nevertheless, it seems to me that the case made on behalf of the plaintiff must be examined with a view to identifying the offer and acceptance constituting the alleged agreement.

The celebrated case of *Carlill v Carbolic Smoke Ball Co.* (1893) is authority for the propositions first that an offer may be made to the world at large even though a contract can only be made with identified persons. Secondly, that such an offer may be accepted by the performance of a particular condition prescribed in the offer and thirdly, that as notification of acceptance is required for the benefit of the person who makes the offer he may, if he thinks it desirable to do so, dispense with such notice. Accordingly one could envisage circumstances in which an examining body might communicate to the public at large the terms in which they were offering a series of examinations and expressly or by implication inviting interested persons to accept that offer by undertaking a specified course of study. However, that is not the present case. The plaintiff was not aware of any offer made by the defendant prior to the commencement of her studies and accordingly her application to St Joseph's and their admission of her as a student could not constitute acceptance of any offer by the defendant herein. Even if the position were otherwise this approach would be of no avail to the plaintiff—as her counsel fully recognised—because the terms and conditions on offer from the defendant at that time provided only for one automatic retake of failed examinations. Again it would not be sufficient for the plaintiff to argue that on her admission as a student of St Joseph's the defendant thereby accepted an offer from her simply to take the exams which they proffered. To succeed in this case the plaintiff must establish the existence of a contract which incorporates the particular provision entitling her as of right to a second repeat of her examinations. In the circumstances of the present case it has to be contended either that the plaintiff should be seen as making an offer to take the defendant's course on such terms as it would prescribe and that the defendant accepted that offer by permitting or authorising St Joseph's College as their agents to hand to the plaintiff the manual containing the terms prescribed herein—or, alternatively, that the presentation of the manual by St Joseph's to the plaintiff constituted an offer and that some conduct by the plaintiff—perhaps continuing with her course of studies—constituted acceptance of that offer. Counsel on behalf of the plaintiff did not pursue the second of these alternatives recognising, no doubt, the difficulty in establishing any action which could be interpreted as acceptance.

There are two formidable difficulties to be overcome in establishing the case on which the plaintiff does rely. First, it is difficult to conceive of an acceptance which would itself prescribe conditions. Ordinarily a communication in the course of negotiations leading to a contract which contains conditions not previously agreed by the party to whom the communication is addressed will fall to be treated as a new or counter offer rather than an acceptance. Secondly the plaintiff's argument was criticised on the basis that if the offer permitted the defendant to establish the terms, conditions or regulations governing the contract, there was no justification for assuming that these provisions would not be subject to alteration. However, perhaps the best way of presenting the defendant's counter argument is to say that the plaintiff did not prescribe the production of the manual as the means of accepting any offer made by her and there is no internal evidence in this manual and nothing in the conduct of the officials of St Joseph's college by whom it was distributed to suggest that the circulation of the manual amongst the students was intended to constitute acceptance of a contract either by St Joseph's College or by the defendant. I believe that this objection to the plaintiff's argument is well founded. The manual contains for the greater part a large body of information in relation to the medical and surgical conditions relevant to the study of occupational therapy. The information with regard to examinations is obviously important but there is nothing in its presentation to suggest that the communication of this information by the officials of a recognised college should constitute acceptance of an offer by potential students.

I am not to be taken as laying down any principle that conditions or regulations made by an examining body—be it the defendant or any such body—could not be made part of a legally binding contract. Indeed it is possible that a successful argument could have been made to the effect that the amended rules of the defendant did form part of such a contract. All that can be said in relation to the present case is that the plaintiff has not proved that the plaintiff offered or the defendant accepted any offer by the plaintiff to take the diploma course on terms which included and included only the regulations contained in the unamended 1977 manual.

In these circumstances it seem to me—not without some regret—that the plaintiff's claim must fail.

Case 6. Boyers & Co. v Duke

King's Bench [1905] 2 I.R. 617

The plaintiffs wrote to the defendant seeking the lowest quotation for a quantity of goods. The defendant replied stating quantity, price and time of delivery. The plaintiffs replied accepting the quotation, sought a further quotation for other goods, and enclosed the names of two trade references. When the defendant realised he had underestimated the price he refused to supply the goods at the price quoted. The plaintiffs sued for breach of contract.

Held that the defendant's letter was not an offer to sell, but merely a quotation of terms on which the plaintiffs might offer an order. The plaintiff's letter in reply was in the nature of an offer of an order, and not an acceptance of an offer. Since there was no completed contract between the parties the action was dismissed.

Madden J.:

The defendant in this case was asked for a 'quotation'. Now the word 'quotation' is capable of different meanings according to the connection in which it is used, but there is a common idea underlying them all, that of notation or enumeration. The things quoted may be passages in an author, the prices of specific articles, or the terms upon which work is to be done. In the case before us both parties agree that the documents before us must be read and construed, giving the words the ordinary meaning which they bear in the English language, having regard to the subject-matter to which they relate; for neither party has contended that evidence should have been taken as to the use of the word 'quotation' in mercantile transactions.

A quotation might be so expressed as to amount to an offer to provide a definite article, or to do a certain work, at a defined price. But the ideas of a quotation, and of an offer to sell, are radically different. The difference is well illustrated by the case of *Harvey v Facey* (1893). There, to a telegram in these terms, 'Will you sell us B.H.P.? Telegraph lowest cash price,' the answer was returned, 'Lowest price for B.H.P., £900.' The inquirer telegraphed, 'We agree to buy B.H.P. for £900 asked by you.' An exceptionally strong judicial committee of the Privy Council, in a judgment delivered by Lord Morris, held that the statement, or quotation, of the lowest price at which a definite thing will be sold, does not import an offer to sell.

The principle on which this case was decided applies with a greater force to mercantile transactions than to an application for a statement of the price of a single parcel of land. It is a matter of common knowledge that quotations of prices are scattered broadcast among possible customers. Business could not be carried on if each recipient of a priced catalogue offering a desirable article—say a rare book—at an attractive price, were in a position to create a contract of sale by writing that he would buy at the price mentioned. The catalogue has probably reached many collectors. The order of one only can be honoured. Has each of the others who write for the book a right of action? Wholesale dealers have not in stock an unlimited supply of the articles the prices of which they quote to the public at large. This stock usually bears some proportion to the orders which they may reasonably expect to receive. Transactions of the kind under consideration are intelligible and businesslike, if we bear in mind the distinction between a quotation, submitted as the basis of a possible order, and an offer to sell which, if accepted, creates a contract, for the breach of which damages may be recovered.

These observations seem to apply with special force to a quotation furnished by a manufacturer, in the position of the defendant, stating the terms on which he is prepared to work, as to price and time for completion. He may receive and comply with many applications for quotations on the same day. If his reply in each case can be turned into a contract by acceptance, his looms might be burdened with an amount of work which would render it impossible for him to meet his engagements. In my opinion, a merchant, dealer, or manufacturer, by furnishing a quotation, invites an offer which will be honoured or not according to the exigencies of his buisness. A quotation based on current prices usually holds good for a limited time. But it remains a quotation, on the basis of which an offer will not be entertained after a certain date. I have arrived at this conclusion irrespective of the terms of the letter of 3 March, as to which I will only say that it suggests to my mind that the writer knew well that he was giving an order, not accepting an offer for sale.

Lord O'Brien L.C.J. and Gibson J. delivered concurring judgments.

Case 7. Dooley v T.L. Egan & Co. Ltd
High Court (1938) 72 I.L.T.R. 155

The defendant made inquiries by postcard as to the plaintiff's ability to supply it with specified goods. The plaintiff forwarded a quotation which was for immediate acceptance and subject to change without notice. To this the defendant replied by ordering more goods than were quoted for. The plaintiff replied by accepting that order. The defendant refused to accept the goods when ready and the plaintiff sued for their price.

Held that the plaintiff's quotation was in the nature of an offer and that the defendant's order was not an unqualified acceptance but a counter offer which had been accepted by the plaintiff.

Meredith J.:

. . . The defendant carries on business in Cork as traders in and distributors of medical and surgical instruments and hospital equipment. It appears that in June 1937 the defendant received enquiries as to their ability to supply medical instrument cabinets of the type described in the surgical manufacturer company's catalogue. The defendant then made enquiries by a postcard, which is not forthcoming, as to the ability of the plaintiff to supply them, the defendant, as distributors, with the articles specified under the title in the catalogue and in reply to this enquiry they received a quotation in the form of a letter dated 22 June 1937. The terms of this letter are important and are as follows:

John Dooley,
General Sheet Metal Works,

Messrs. T.L. Egan and Co. Ltd.,
9 Lavitt's Quay,
Cork.

Quotation

Dear Sir(s),

I thank you for your esteemed enquiry of the 18th inst. and I have much pleasure in submitting my quotation as follows:—

Description.   Price.

Six Sterilizing Drums as per Specification supplied £3 17 6 each less 25%
One Instrument Cabinet similar to No. B9558 in the Surgical
Manufacturer Company's Catalogue   £18 0 0 less 25%

Awaiting the favour of your valued order and assuring you of my best attention at all times,

I am, dear Sir(s),
Yours faithfully,
John G. Dooley.

Delivery 3–4 weeks.   Terms Nett M/A.

All quotations for Copper, Monel Metal, Stainless Steel, Tin and Brass Goods are given subject to Market Fluctuations without notice. All quotations are for immediate acceptance only and are subject to change without notice. The delivery of all orders accepted by me shall be contingent upon strikes, fires, accidents, delays of carriers and other causes unavoidable or beyond my control. I will not be responsible for damages due to any delays whatever. Clerical errors are subject to correction. Orders accepted by me cannot be countermanded without my consent and upon terms which will indemnify me against all loss.

The sentence in the letter 'All quotations are made for immediate acceptance only and are subject to change without notice' is important and was largely dealt with in the argument. To this letter the defendant replied immediately by letter dated 24 June in which it said:

We enclose herewith order for two cabinets and trust that you can let us have delivery as soon as possible, if possible round 23 to 28 July. We have to cancel order for sterilizing drum at the moment as we have to submit another quotation.

The Order referred to is in a printed invoice. It is directed to the plaintiff and simply specifies:

'2 Instrument Cabinets similar to No. B9558, Surgical Manufacturing Company's catalogue at £18 0 0 each less 25%.

C.E.'

To this the plaintiff replied by letter dated 25 June 1937, which I will read later.

The whole question at issue is whether the letter of 22 June was an offer which defendant company accepted by their letter of 24 June, or the latter letter was an offer to purchase, which was accepted by the plaintiff's letter of 26 June. The plaintiff argued that this quotation of 22 June was not really an offer, but only a statement of terms on which the party was ready to discuss the question of sale. I was referred to the case of *Boyers v Duke* (Case 6). In the argument a good deal was made out of the sentence in the

'Quotation': 'All quotations are made for immediate acceptance only and are subject to change without notice.' The interpretation that I put upon that was this 'quotation' was an offer subject to immediate acceptance; but that if it were not accepted immediately it became subject to contingencies which made it vague and if it was not accepted immediately the decision in *Boyers v Duke* (Case 6) would apply. But assuming that it is definite as to one instrument cabinet and one only then I do not regard it as indefinite in any way unless indeed it might be argued that these contingencies as to strikes might make it indefinite. I will therefore take this 'Quotation' to be a definite offer. The question then arises as to whether this offer was definitely accepted by the defendant's order of 24 June accepting two instrument cabinets. I think that matter may be disposed of by looking at it in the same way as the Court of Appeal looked at the case of *Wheeler v Jeffrey* (Case 18).

Let us suppose that when plaintiff got the order for two cabinets he had replied 'I have only quoted for one. I have one nearly ready. It is part of a large number I had made for another order and I have no difficulty in supplying one at the price quoted and within the time specified, but as labour conditions have changed and prices are different I am unable to supply two.' If the plaintiff had replied in this way the other party could say: 'But I want two cabinets, and as you say you can only supply one I'll enquire elsewhere.' Under those circumstances the application for two could not be regarded as the acceptance of the offer.

In this case subsequent correspondence showed that it did not matter to the plaintiff whether he supplied one or two; but those circumstances cannot affect the construction of the correspondence. Accordingly I hold that the order of 24 June was not an unqualified acceptance, but another offer which was accepted by the plaintiff's letter of 25 June which said:

Dear Sirs,

I thank you for your valued order of the 24th inst., for two Instrument Cabinets, and have great pleasure in placing the work in hands immediately and shall let you have delivery as soon as possible. Again thanking you for your esteemed order and assuring you of our best attention at all times.

> I am,
> Yours faithfully,
> John G. Dooley.

Therefore I am of opinion that this letter from Dublin was the acceptance of the offer . . .

Case 8. Minister for Industry and Commerce v Pim Bros. Ltd
High Court [1966] I.R. 154

The defendant, retail drapers, displayed on its premises a notice attached to goods indicating both the cash price and the weekly repayments if purchased on credit. The defendant was prosecuted with having displayed an advertisement in contravention of the hire-purchase code.

Held that the notice placed on the goods, indicating the information that it did, was not an offer for sale but an invitation to treat with an indication that credit facilities, not specified, would be available. The prosecution failed.

Davitt P.:

> . . . What the defendants were really charged with was displaying an advertisement relating to goods *offered* for sale, by way of hire-purchase agreement or credit-sale agreement, which failed to include certain statements required by the Order. Before one could determine whether the advertisement related to goods offered for sale by way of hire-purchase agreement or to goods offered for sale by way of credit-sale agreement one would have to decide whether it related to goods offered for sale at all; in other words, whether the advertisement constituted an offer by the defendants to sell the coat. In one sense it could be described as an offer to sell. In popular terms the coat could properly be said to be on offer to the public. In the strictly legal sense, however, the advertisement was merely a statement of the cash price at which the defendants were prepared to sell the goods, with an indication that certain credit facilities, the exact nature of which were unspecified, would be available. This would not constitute an offer to sell which could be made a contract of sale by acceptance: *Harvey v Facey* . . . (see p. 12 for facts of this case).

Case 9. Wilson v Belfast Corporation
Court of Appeal (1921) 55 I.L.T.R. 205

The corporation passed a resolution in September 1914 to the effect that half wages would be paid to their employees who joined the forces; it was during the First World War. Without the corporation's authority this resolution was publicised in the press. In October, a second resolution was passed limiting this offer to such persons as were in the corporation's service on 5 August 1914, which was not publicised in the press. Subsequent to these resolutions the plaintiff's husband entered the corporation's service and later joined the army. He was killed in action and his widow sued to recover an amount of half wages due from the date of his enlistment to the date of his death.

Held that the September resolution was not intended as an offer and that its publication in the newspapers did not constitute a communication. Any offer there may have been had been revoked by the second resolution as regards persons not then in the corporations's employment. Since the terms of the second resolution did not form part of the deceased's terms of employment, he was not entitled to avail of them, and the action was dismissed.

O'Connor L.J.:

The plaintiff's case must be based on the corporation's resolution of 1 September. The King's Bench decided that the resolution referred only to persons in the employment of the corporation at the time, and I am of the same opinion. The resolution of 1 October put the matter beyond all doubt by limiting its application to those persons who were in the corporation's service on 5 August. The deceased entered their employment three months later than the alleged contract. I say there was no such contract. Even if the original resolution embraced his class there was no contract. Was there an offer? Was it meant to be an offer? There was no intention to make the resolution an offer. Of necessity, it had to be public. Neither was there any communication. The reporter puts the resolution into the press: its publication is not authorised by the corporation, and could not be prevented by them. Before the deceased joined the army a new resolution had been passed. Even if he saw the first resolution, and did not see the second, it makes no difference to him. He had no right to assume that the corporation's resolutions are unalterable: they may change from day to day. Therefore, no contract at all was made.

Case 10. Kelly v Irish Nursery & Landscape Co. Ltd.

Supreme Court [1983] I.R. 221

When sending to the plaintiff's solicitor a contract in duplicate for the sale of defendant's land the defendant's solicitor stated that no agreement enforceable at law was to be created 'until exchange of contracts had taken place'. The plaintiff's solicitor accepted that term. The plaintiff signed these contracts as did the defendant but one was not returned to the plaintiff. When the defendant failed to complete the contract the plaintiff sued for specific performance.

Held that there was no enforceable contract as no exchange of contracts had taken place. The action was dismissed.

Kenny J.:

The defendant's second defence is that there was an express condition in the correspondence that no contract would come into existence until contracts were exchanged between the solicitors. The plaintiff admits that no exchange of contracts took place. The letters relied on as creating this condition are the letter of the 14 July 1978, from the defendant's solicitor to the plaintiff's solicitor and that of the 28 November 1978, between the same two solicitors. I think that the letter of the 28 November may be ignored. While we do not know the exact date when the contract bearing date 6 October 1978, was signed, it was certainly signed in October and so the letter of 28 November must have come into existence after the contract was signed and could not import a condition as to exchange into the contract.

The letter of 14 July 1978, from the defendant's solicitor to the plaintiff's solicitor contains this paragraph: 'It must be understood that no agreement enforceable at law is created or intended to be created until exchange of contracts has taken place.' It was argued by the plaintiff that this condition has been waived but I see nothing (in the correspondence, the conduct of the parties, or the evidence) which amounts to a waiver. The agreement itself did not contain any clause dealing with exchange, but that is not a waiver.

In my opinion, the effect of the paragraph in the letter of 14 July 1978 was that no enforceable contract between the plaintiff and the defendant ever came into existence because there was no exchange of contracts.

O'Higgins C.J. agreed and Walsh J. delivered a concurring judgment.

Case 11. Tully v Irish Land Commission
High Court (1963) 97 I.L.T.R. 174

The plaintiff, attending a public auction where some of the defendants' property was for sale, had a friend make bids on his behalf. The auctioneer announced that the reserve price was reached and one further bid was made. On the auctioneer's failure to get further bids he knocked the property down to that bidder. A memorandum attached to the conditions of sale was signed on behalf of this bidder. One condition provided that the highest bidder should be the buyer, and should any dispute arise as to the bidding the property should be again put up for sale at the last undisputed bid. The plaintiff immediately claimed that his agent had made the highest bid and required the auctioneer to put up the property for sale again, which the auctioneer refused. The plaintiff sought a declaration that since he was the highest bidder there was a contract between him and the defendants, and an injunction to restrain the defendants from vesting the property in the party on whose behalf the memorandum had been signed.

Held that the conditions of sale were an offer which could be accepted so as to create a contractual relationship between the seller and the highest bidder at the auction. A contract was concluded when the property was knocked down by the use of the traditional hammer, or when some indication was given to the persons at the auction that the property had been sold. The plaintiff was not entitled to the relief sought as he only disputed the bidding after the property had been knocked down, after a contract had been concluded.

Kenny J.:

. . . I think that clauses 2 and 3 of the conditions of sale were an offer which could be accepted by bidding at the auction and that they could constitute a contract between the vendor and the highest bidder at the auction; this view seems to me to be in accord with legal principle and to be supported by the better authorities. Counsel have cited the views of some eminent writers of text-books to establish that this view is incorrect; the passages cited shew some confusion between the two contracts which may be involved. When property is put up for sale, and is sold, a memorandum is signed by the purchaser, there is a contract for the sale of the property to the person who has signed the memorandum. The clauses of the conditions of sale which relate to what may happen before the purchaser signs the memorandum are capable of being an offer in connection with a different contract, a contract to which the *Statute of Frauds* does not apply and which may be accepted by bidding at the auction.

All the witnesses who gave evidence said that the conditions of sale were read before the bidding began; the bidding was clearly made on the terms of and by reference to them. When giving evidence, the plaintiff admitted that he did not attend the auction because of the conditions of sale, and he said that he would have gone in any event. It was argued by counsel for the defendants that the plaintiff could not rely on the conditions of sale as an offer as he did not attend the auction because of them. But the conditions of sale were read before the bidding began and the biddings were made by reference to them and they were capable of being an offer.

It has also been argued that clause 2 of the conditions could not constitute an offer because the offeror (the vendor) cannot know the person who has accepted the bid and with whom the contract is made. This contention ignores the many cases in which it has been held that a person who had performed conditions published by another has thereby accepted the offer made by the publication even though his identity was not known. There is a contract when the conditions of a competition are published and somebody complies with the terms which entitles them to a prize. In most cases there is no difficulty about ascertaining the person who was the highest bidder and I do not see any ground, in principle, why it should be held that these conditions and the bidding at the auction were not capable of creating a contract between the vendor and the person who made the highest bid. When conditions of sale are read, those relating to the conduct of the auction (such as clause 2) amount to an offer and the bidding is an acceptance. It has been suggested that this view leads to absurdity as it would have the result that the vendors were making an offer to everybody in this country but the offer which is made by the reading of the conditions of sale and the making of bids is an offer made by the owner of the lands who puts them up for sale to those who attend the auction and bid . . .

This conclusion seems to me to be supported by all the better authorities. Counsel for the plaintiff based his case on the decision in *Warlow v Harrison* (1858). But the matter had been considered before then by Lord Cottenham L.C. in *Robinson v Wall* (1847). In that case property was put up for sale by auction without reserve and was sold; it was subsequently discovered that the vendor had arranged with a friend that bids would be made to raise the price. The purchaser then brought proceedings to be relieved from his contract. Lord Cottenham decided that the purchaser was entitled to succeed as a number of fictitious bids had been made. In the course of his judgment he said:

Now, that a sale by auction, announced to be without reserve, where there has been a bidding on the part of the vendor for the purpose of keeping up the price, cannot be enforced against the purchaser, was decided by Sir John Leach in the case of *Meadows v Tanner*. Although that was the only case referred to, and the only one that I am aware of in which this particular question has arisen and been decided, it depends in fact upon the same principle as that numerous class of cases in which questions have been raised as to the effect of employing puffers at a sale. They all turn upon this, whether the course pursued by the vendor is or is not in violation of the contract which he enters into with the public as to the mode in which he offers the property for sale; and, in any case in which it is clear that the course pursued has not been consistent with that contract, a court of equity will treat the sale as contrary to good faith on the part of the vendor, and will refuse to enforce it.

There being, then, no doubt upon the law, the only question is whether that which took place in this case was or was not a violation of the contract proposed to the public, namely, that the property should be sold 'without reserve'. . . . When a property is offered for sale without reserve, the meaning, and the only meaning that can be attached to it is that, if the bidders—the public—who choose to attend the sale, whoever bids the highest shall be the purchaser; that the biddings shall be left to themselves, and that there shall be no bidding on the part of the vendor. And it is not without reserve, the biddings are not left free from the interference of the vendor, if any means or contrivance, it matters not what, be resorted to for the purpose of preventing the effect of open competition. I consider, therefore, the term 'without reserve' to exclude any interference on the part of the vendor (or, which is the same thing, of those who come in under the vendor), which can, under any possible circumstances affect the right of the highest bidder to have the property knocked down to him, and *that*, without reference to the amount to which that highest bidding shall go.

It seems to me that the judgment of the Lord Chancellor assumes that the publication of the conditions to the public and the making of bids are together capable of constituting a contract. A similar view was taken in *Warlow v Harrison* . . .

In the well known *Carlill v Carbolic Smoke Ball Co.* (1893) Bowen L.J. said:

It was also said that the contract is made with all the world—that is, with everybody; and that you cannot contract with everybody. It is not a contract made with all the world. There is the fallacy of the argument. It is an offer made to all the world; and why should not an offer be made to all the world which is to ripen into a contract with anybody who comes forward and performs the condition? It is an offer to become liable to any one who, before it is retracted, performs the condition, and, although the offer is made to the world, the contract is made with that limited portion of the public who come forward and perform the condition on the faith of the advertisement. It is not like cases in which you offer to negotiate, or you issue advertisements that you have got a stock of books to sell, or houses to let, in which case there is no offer to be bound by any contract. Such advertisements are offers to negotiate— offers to receive offers—offers to chaffer, as, I think, some learned judge in one of the cases has said. If this is an offer to be bound, then it is a contract the moment the person fulfils the condition. That seems to me to be sense . . .

In *Johnston v Boyes* the plaintiff sent his agent to bid at the auction and the agent who was the highest bidder was not allowed to sign the contract. The plaintiff then brought an action claiming damages for breach of the contract arising out of the clause in the conditions of sale that its highest bidder should be the purchaser. The judgment of Cozens Hardy J. contains the following passage: 'The plaintiff complains that by the defendants' direction Mr Johnston was not allowed to sign the contract, and the property was sold to some one else for £4,950, and the plaintiff claims damages on this footing. In point of law I think such an action can be maintained. A vendor who offers property for sale by auction on the terms of printed conditions can be made liable to a member of the public who accepts the offer if those conditions be violated: see *Warlow v Harrison* and the recent case of *Carlill v Carbolic Smoke Ball Co.*. Nor do I think that the *Statute of Frauds* would afford any defence to such an action. The plaintiff is not suing on a contract to purchase land: she is suing simply because her agent, in breach of the first and second conditions of sale, was not allowed to sign a contract which would have resulted in her becoming the purchaser of the land. I think this conclusion results from the decision of the Exchequer Chamber in *Warlow v Harrison*.' The cases which have been cited as authorities for the view that clause 2 of the conditions of sale in this case is not an offer capable of being accepted are not decisions to this effect . . .

I am therefore of opinion that clauses 2 and 3 of these conditions were an offer which could be accepted so as to create a contractual relation and that there was a contract between the defendants and the highest bidder at the auction, the contract being that the highest bidder should be the purchaser and that if any dispute arose as to any bidding the property would be put up for sale at the last undisputed bidding.

The next matter argued related to the time when a sale takes place where there is a public auction: it was submitted that the contractual obligation to put the property up for sale at the last undisputed bidding ended when the property had been knocked down to the purchaser. I think that the conditions of sale showed that the sale took place when the property was knocked down by the auctioneer. Clause 3 provided 'the purchaser shall immediately after the sale pay to the auctioneer a deposit of £25 per cent on the amount of the purchase money and there pay to the auctioneer his fees on the said price' and it contained a provision for signature of the memorandum.

As these matters were to be done 'immediately after the sale' the sale must have taken place before any of them were done and it follows, I think, that the sale took place when the property was knocked down to the highest bidder provided that the offer was over the reserve price. The contract for sale which comes into existence when the property is knocked down may not be enforceable because of the provisions of the *Statute of Frauds* but the absence of the memorandum in writing does not prevent a valid contract coming into existence . . .

A contract is therefore concluded when property is knocked down either by using the traditional 'hammer' or, as in this case, by giving some indication to the public attending the auction that the property has been sold. On that construction of the conditions of sale the contract made between the vendor and the highest bidder was that if any dispute arose as to any bidding before the property was knocked down, the property would be again put up for sale at the last undisputed bidding. In this case the auctioneer held the property at the last bidding for nearly five minutes and then knocked it down to highest bidder. The dispute as to the person who made the last bidding first arose after the property had been knocked down to highest bidder. In my opinion the plaintiff's claim fails on this ground as there was not any breach of contract by the defendants.

Case 12. Swan v Miller
Court of Appeal [1919] 1 I.R. 151

The plaintiff's agent sent a telegram to the defendant's agent offering a stated sum as the purchase price of certain premises. The defendant's agent replied by telegram, after communicating with the defendant, stating that his principal accepted the sum offered plus £50 annual ground rent. A letter containing the same terms was written by the defendant's agent to the plaintiff's agent. The plaintiff sought specific performance of the contract when the defendant refused to complete the sale in accordance with the plaintiff's offer.

Held that the telegram and letter from the defendant's agent to the plaintiff's agent was not an unconditional acceptance of the offer contained in the telegram from the plaintiff's agent by reason of the inclusion of the new term relating to the payment of rent.

O'Connor L.J.:

C. [the plaintiff's agent] sent a telegram to H. [the defendant's agent] on 17 November 1917, in the following terms: 'Offer you £4750 for Maxwell Buildings. C.' H. replied on the same day: 'Dear Mr. C., I received your wire, 'Offer you £4750 for Maxwell Buildings,' which I forwarded to my London firm, advising them to take, and wire acceptance. Ground rent is £50, as stated, but other particulars you can verify. Yours sincerely, J.W.H.' H. communicated the offer by letter on the same day to the defendant, who wired him on the 19th: 'Accept four thousand five hundred net, plus fifty pounds ground rent' (this £4500 being the net sum after providing for H.'s commission). On receipt of this wire, H. writes to C. on the 19 November 1917, as follows: 'Dear Mr. C., My principal [the defendant], has wired me accepting your offer of (£4750) four thousand seven hundred and fifty pounds, plus £50 annual ground rent, for building at present tenanted at Maxwell Street. Yours sincerely, J.W.A.H.' Later, namely on the 22nd, the defendant repudiated the proposal.

That is the whole story, so far as written offer and acceptance are concerned. Is any enforceable contract made out from them? I think not. In the first place, on the face of the documents themselves there is no unconditional acceptance. The offer was £4750 simpliciter; the alleged acceptance was £4750 plus £50 annual ground rent. That is a vital difference.

Ronan L.J. concurred and Sir James Campbell C. dissented.

Case 13. Central Meat Products Ltd v Carney
High Court [1944] Ir.Jur.Rep. 34

In the course of negotiations between the plaintiff and another company, of which the defendant was a director, for the supply of prepared meat, that company wrote to the plaintiff a letter outlining its proposals and a second letter setting out the proposals with greater precision, which included an undertaking by the directors to supply as many cattle as possible to the plaintiff, and a guarantee not to supply any firm other than the plaintiff without the plaintiff's consent. The plaintiff agreed to accept these terms 'in principle'. When the other company began to supply other firms the plaintiff sought an injunction to compel that company to abide by the agreement.

Held that no enforceable contract existed between the parties in that the letters from the other company did not constitute an offer because of the absence of essential details and, even if a valid offer had been made, the acceptance 'in principle' was tantamount to a refusal of that offer.

Overend J.:

. . . The question is: Is there in existence an enforceable contract between the parties?

The first of these five letters is dated 25 September 1943, and is from the other company to the plaintiff. This letter was apparently written after a discussion between the parties, and it merely set out an outline of the proposition which they had been discussing, but does not constitute an offer.

From its terms it will be seen that the other company was proposing to 'guarantee to supply the plaintiff with all the cattle which they obtain for canning purposes'. This seems to me to be a very vague term. No number of cattle is stated, and the proposal is subject to the parties coming to agreement as to two matters namely: alterations in price and an alteration in an insurance scheme.

This was followed by a second letter of 28 September from the other company to the plaintiff . . . Then comes the material clause by which the directors of the other company 'individually and collectively' agree to supply as many cattle as possible to the plaintiff, and 'guarantee on no account to supply meat to any other Dublin or provincial canner without the consent of the plaintiff.'

This would mean, no doubt, as many cattle as could be supplied, but there is nothing specific about the number, or the price, or the quality, and in my opinion, in the absence of these essential details, this letter cannot be regarded as a final offer. In addition, it is important to note that the capacity of the plaintiff to purchase cattle is limited by law as a result of a Government quota.

A third letter, bearing the same date and written by the plaintiff to the other company is relied upon as an acceptance of the offer said to be contained in one or both of the preceding letters. The proposal for the supply of boned meat already made, however, related only to the companies concerned and not to any individual director, and accordingly this third letter of the 28 September, in which the plaintiff merely accepted 'in principle' the proposals made to them, making that limited acceptance itself subject to conditions, was tantamount to a refusal to accept the offer, and was hardly even a counter offer. It was little more than an invitation to further discussions.

Then came the joint letter of the same date signed by all of the directors of the other company except one, which reiterates the proposals already outlined in the earlier letters. But this very document, which is relied upon by the plaintiff as constituting an acceptance and thereby completing the contract, shows that there was no proposal for the supply of boned meat made at any time by any of the individual directors as such. This letter, which is on the company's notepaper, clearly does not establish an agreement by each of the signatories personally to be bound to the plaintiff in the terms of the proposals set out in the long letter written earlier on the same day to which I have referred.

Accordingly in my opinion there is here no contract capable of enforcement at law between the plaintiff and the defendant.

Case 14. Sanderson v Cunningham
Court of Appeal [1919] 2 I.R. 234

The plaintiff, carrying on business in Dublin, made a proposal through brokers in Dublin for a policy of insurance which was transmitted to the defendant in London. A policy was issued and posted from London to the brokers for delivery to the plaintiff. The plaintiff, who was not personally aware of the conditions in the policy, argued that the contract was not completed until he had, after the receipt of the policy from the brokers, signified his acceptance.

Held that the brokers had full authority from the plaintiff to negotiate on his behalf, that the conditions usually contained in such a policy were well known to the brokers, that the plaintiff received the precise form of policy for which he had bargained, and that the contract was completed by the signing and posting of the policy in London.

O'Connor L.J.:

It was admitted at the bar that the brokers were agents for the plaintiff for the purpose of negotiating a policy of insurance in respect of their commercial motor vehicles. Certain arguments have been adduced for the purpose of showing some limitation of the brokers' authority. It may be that the brokers had no authority without the plaintiff's consent to close a bargain in respect of a policy, but in my view that consideration is not material and does not help the plaintiff. For certainly, it was the brokers' duty and business to look out for a suitable policy for their client, to convey such knowledge as they had or could obtain for their client, and to advise their client generally as to the transaction. Another matter is equally clear, that the brokers were perfectly aware of what a dreadnought policy was, what it contained and what it did not contain; they had been in touch with these policies from 1912; and before the transaction was finally closed they actually had for a month in their possession a policy which was made out for an erroneous number of cars.

On 22 May 1916, the plaintiff, presumably after receiving advice from the brokers, signed a proposal. That proposal set forth the risks to be covered, the premium to be paid, and the nature of the policy that was required, namely, a dreadnought policy. It is argued that the plaintiff did not know what were the conditions on such a policy. That may be so; but he had all the means of knowledge, for he had the expert broker at his elbow to advise him. Is not the truth of the transaction this, that the plaintiff, knowing nothing as to the insurance policies, employed brokers who knew everything about them, trusted the brokers to choose a suitable policy, and having obtained the brokers' advice, ordered a certain policy? If that be so, the discussion as to whether the plaintiff did or did not know the conditions seem to me futile. He cannot be heard to say that he did not know the contents of the policy, including, of course, the conditions endorsed on the policy. The proposal so signed was posted to London; the policy of insurance, in accordance with the proposal, was signed in London; and it was duly posted to Dublin, to the brokers acting on behalf of the plaintiff. In my opinion, it is clear in these conditions that the contract was made in England . . .

It was suggested on behalf of the plaintiff that the policy was not in conformity with the terms set forth on p. 2 of a booklet of which the proposal formed part; and that that being so, the policy was a mere offer which was accepted in Ireland by the payment of the premium or by acquiescence. The answer is twofold—first, that when the plaintiff signed the proposal, the proposal was not attached to the booklet, which indeed had not been seen by the plaintiff; and secondly, that the policy was in all respects in accordance with the plaintiff's instructions and proposal, and indeed with the booklet, which merely indicated, in a general way and in popular language, the nature of the risks insured.

It will be noted that I base my decision on a very narrow point, namely, that an Irish firm proposed in Ireland for a specific policy of insurance, with the terms of which the firm were actually or constructively familiar, and that this proposal was accepted (and a contract established) by the signing in England of such a policy as proposed for, or by the posting of such policy in England, addressed to the agent in Ireland for the plaintiff. If the brokers had not been agents for the plaintiff *quoad* the receipt of the policy, different considerations might have arisen, but it has not even been argued that that is the case here. For example, if they had instructions from England not to deliver the policy (which would be the usual way of indicating acceptance of the proposal) until the premium was paid, an argument might have been advanced that the payment of the premium, and not the signing of the policy, concluded the bargain. When that case arises, we shall deal with it; but it is far removed from the present case.

Sir James Campbell C. and Ronan L.J. gave concurring judgments.

Case 15. Kennedy v London Express Newspapers Ltd
Supreme Court [1931] I.R. 532

The defendant, owners of a newspaper in England which circulated in Ireland, published an advertisement of a free accident insurance for the benefit of their 'registered readers' in one of their issues. A registered reader was one registered in the books of the newspaper as having given to a registered newsagent a signed order for the newspaper and as receiving it daily from such newsagent. The plaintiff's wife was a registered reader and when she was accidentally killed, the plaintiff claimed the sum payable under the insurance scheme. It was admitted that the deceased had fulfilled the first requirement but a dispute arose as to whether she had continued to receive the newspaper daily. The question arose whether the dispute should be resolved by arbitration or by legal proceedings.

Held that the dispute should be resolved by arbitration but that the defendant was bound not to raise any question of fraud or other matter challenging the existence or validity of the contract.

Kennedy C.J.:

. . . The defendant, the London Express Newspaper Ltd., which is an English company, publishes in England a newspaper known as *The Daily Express*, which, it appears, has a certain circulation in Ireland. The issue of the paper of 1 January 1929, contained an advertisement under the following headings, prominently displayed:
> *Daily Express Free Insurance, 1929.*
> Great benefits for husband and wife. New children's benefit. Every kind of fatal accident covered. No need to re-register if you have registered after April 25, 1922.
. . . Immediately following the statement of the benefits offered there was a number of paragraphs headed 'Conditions', and introduced by a proviso as follows:
> Provided always that the whole of this undertaking is subject to the following conditions, which are the essence of the contract, viz., that (unless otherwise stated):
> (a) A registered reader must be duly registered in the books of the *Daily Express* as having given to a newsagent since April 25, 1922, a signed

order for the *Daily Express*, and be receiving the *Daily Express* daily from such newsagent, or be a postal subscriber to the *Daily Express*, receiving the paper direct from the publishers. Registration must be effected by such reader forwarding to the *Daily Express* a signed registration coupon duly completed. Such reader must immediately notify the *Daily Express* by letter or postcard of any change of address and/or newsagent . . .

At the foot of this advertisement there was a 'Registration Form' in two parts, one of which the reader was directed to hand to his newsagent or bookstall agent, requesting that the *Daily Express* be delivered or reserved for him until further notice; the other part was a coupon to be posted, addressed to the '*Daily Express* Registration Department' in London, and contained blank spaces in which the reader's name and address and the name and address of the newsagent were to be written, and it also contained the following declaration by the reader: 'I have sent an order form to my newsagent, and I enclose a stamped addressed envelope for your acknowledgment of my registration. Please register me as a regular reader for the benefits of your free insurance in accordance with the full conditions published in the *Daily Express*, January 1, 1929.'

Mrs Catherine Kennedy, wife of the plaintiff, duly filled up the registration forms with her own name and address, and, as her newsagent, the name and address of Mrs Madden of Clonmel. She gave the form of order for delivery of the paper to Mrs Madden, and she posted the coupon form to the '*Daily Express* Registration Department' in London, where it is admitted to have been received on 7 January 1929, and from whose files it was produced in court. On or about 7 January 1929, the defendant sent to Mrs Kennedy a document described in an endorsement as 'Certificate of Registration.' Upon the front of the 'Certificate' there was also endorsed the following note:

The manager of the *Daily Express* Insurance Department is in receipt of the registration form from the above-named, who has accordingly been registered as a regular reader for the purpose of the free accident insurance, the benefits and conditions of which are as printed overleaf, or as published from time to time in the *Daily Express*.

. . . Mrs Catherine Kennedy was killed accidentally on 3 August 1930, by a bus, at Arran Quay, in the City of Dublin, whereupon her husband, the plaintiff, made a claim for the amount payable under . . . the free insurance scheme, as set out in the newspapers to which I have referred. The plaintiff on 5 August 1930, gave notice of the claim to the [insurance corporation] at their London office, as provided by condition (*e*).

On 3 September the insurance corporation replied to the plaintiff by letter of that date, stating that they had completed their inquiries, and that, from the result of their investigations, it did not appear that the deceased was in receipt of the *Daily Express* daily, as required by condition (*a*) of the coupon. The corporation stated that, as the condition had not been fully complied with, they were unable to entertain the claim.

. . . It is admitted that Mrs Kennedy fulfilled the first requirement, viz., that of registration and of giving an order for delivery of the paper to her daily, but the defendant says (as the corporation also said) that she did not continue, after some date in 1930 prior to the fatal accident, to be 'receiving the *Daily Express* daily,' and it was not questioned on the plaintiff's part that, on ceasing to take the paper daily, she would by the terms of the contract go out of benefit under the insurance scheme. The plaintiff, on the other hand, avers that he is in a position to prove that she never ceased to receive the paper daily up to her death. There is the dispute, and the only dispute between the parties. It is a simple question of fact as to whether the deceased lady continued to perform the contract on her part. Counsel for the defendant expressly disclaims any suggestion of fraud, and has undertaken to raise no such question. He expressly admits that the contract was made, and confines the case on the defendant's part to the single issue—whether, in fact, the late Mrs Kennedy ceased, prior to the accident, to fulfil the second requirement of condition (*a*) by not continuing to receive the paper daily. The ground upon which the application was made to stay the action was that the dispute on this question between the plaintiff and the company is a dispute which must be submitted to arbitration, pursuant to clause (*n*) of the conditions set out in the 1930 contract . . .

Counsel for the defendant admits the existence of a valid contract (i.e., the contract of 1930, under which the claim is made), and disclaims any charge of fraud; but he says that a dispute has been raised as to a matter relating to the insurance, viz., the continuance by Mrs Kennedy of daily receipt of the paper up to the accident, and that the award of an arbitrator is by the contract a condition precedent to liability. A dispute upon a simple question of fact exists between the parties, and by the terms of the admitted contract an award upon that dispute is a condition precedent to liability under the contract, but the jurisdiction of the courts of [this country are] not ousted. The dispute is not a trivial one, nor is there any suggestion that it has not been raised by the company with *bona fides*, and it is within the scope of the submission to arbitration. In these circumstances, I am of opinion that the action ought to be stayed to allow of the dispute being determined by an award in an arbitration to be held in London according to the Irish statutes applicable to, and regulating the procedure of, arbitration, the company being bound not to raise in such arbitration any question of fraud or any other matter going to the root of the existence or validity of the contract, which for the purpose of such arbitration is to be taken as admitted . . .

FitzGibbon and Murnaghan JJ. concurred.

Case 16. Billings v Arnott & Co. Ltd
High Court (1946) 80 I.L.T.R. 50

The defendant posted a notice offering employees who joined the Defence Forces (it was during the Second World War) one half of their salaries up to a specified limit. When the plaintiff, an employee, informed his supervisor of his intention to avail of this offer he was informed he could not do so as another employee from his department had joined and he could not then be spared. Nonetheless the plaintiff joined the Defence Forces and on the defendant refusing to pay him in line with the offer he sued for the amount.

Held that the action must succeed as the defendant could not properly plead revocation once the plaintiff had accepted the offer.

Maguire J.:

The defendant published a notice on 7 June 1940. It appears that this notice follows a minute of the company passed on 6 June 1940. This was a very generous gesture on the part of the company. Notice was published in good faith and it is a pleasant feature of the case that there is no suggestion that it was not in good faith or that there was an absence of good faith on the part of the plaintiff. When the notice was published certain employees availed themselves of it and on 16 August 1940, plaintiff informed his director, of his intention of joining the Defence Forces, he having been at one time trained as an officer. It is common case that the interview was of short duration and that plaintiff announced his intention of joining the Defence Forces. Most of the time seems to have been taken up by the director trying to dissuade plaintiff from joining. It is also common case that plaintiff indicated clearly that he had made up his mind. The director believes that he told plaintiff that he did not come within the section but plaintiff denies this. I am satisfied that the director is doing his best to give an accurate account but he is a very busy man and I am not satisfied that I am to rely on his recollection. Where there is a conflict of evidence I feel obliged to rely on the evidence of plaintiff without any reflection on the director.

There was an inducement to the employees to join the Defence Forces. The notice I find is unconditional, with no reservation to allow a refusal to release any employee. I cannot take the view that it was a mere declaration of intention. It is a clear expression of what the company would do. Acceptance was then completed when the plaintiff joined the Defence Forces and intimated his intention of so doing on 16 August 1940. On that view a contract was completed under which the defendant undertook to pay the plaintiff the allowance. There was no provision in the notice published that the managing director had power to decide to whom the allowance was to be paid. I am satisfied that the money claimed is due and accordingly I give judgment for the plaintiff for the sum claimed, with costs.

Case 17. Ryle v Minister for Agriculture
Circuit Court (1963) 97 I.L.T.R. 127

The parties entered into a contract under the bovine tuberculosis eradication scheme, on terms set out in forms issued by the defendant. The contract provided that should the plaintiff submit his cattle for free testing, the defendant would pay the plaintiff specified sums in certain circumstances. Later amending regulations were issued which altered the payments under the scheme. When the defendant failed to pay the sums due under the original contract the plaintiff sued to recover them.

Held that the plaintiff was entitled to succeed in that a binding contract was created between the parties and its terms could not be altered unilaterally by the defendant's introduction of amending measures.

Judge O Briain:

In my opinion there was clearly a contract between the plaintiff and the defendant in this case, either in the form of an offer by the defendant to the plaintiff and the latter's acceptance by signing the form of application, or on the other hand, an offer by the plaintiff to the defendant by signing the said form and the acceptance by the defendant in the form of the granting of free tests and the payment of the headage grant on the four reactor cows sold to a licensed cannery.

Having entered into the contract, the plaintiff was bound by its terms and had to comply with those terms at the risk of being sued for breach of contract. The plaintiff was at no time bound to enter into the contract but having done so, both parties were bound by its terms.

While the contract was entered into in February 1960, it is submitted by counsel for the defendant that the contract was altered in August of that year by the introduction of amending measures . . . In other words, counsel submits that, having entered into the contract, the defendant could alter it unilaterally. In my view the defendant is bound by the same rule of law as a private individual and he could not, in law, alter the contract without the agreement of the other party thereto.

Case 18. Wheeler & Co. Ltd v John Jeffrey & Co.
Court of Appeal [1921] 2 I.R. 395

In the course of correspondence the plaintiff agreed to act as agents for the defendants, a Scottish firm. There was no reference made to the date on which the agency was to commence until the plaintiff wrote that it agreed to carry on the agency from the 1 July 1921, to which the defendants replied that they noted with pleasure that the plaintiff was agreeable to carry on the agency from that date. When the defendants failed to observe the contract the plaintiff sued for damages.

Held that the introduction of the new and material term with regard to the commencement of the agency had been accepted by the defendants.

Sir James Campbell C.:

The facts are not in dispute. They turn upon correspondence between the defendants in Scotland and the plaintiff in Belfast, and the purport of that correspondence was to endeavour to arrive at terms under which the plaintiff would act as agents for the sale of the defendants' beers in West Africa. The parties appear to have come to terms rather quickly, but ultimately, on 10 June 1911, the plaintiff wrote to the defendants: 'Under the circumstances we think your attitude is a reasonable one, and we will agree to carry on your agency as from the 1 July next on the terms and conditions specified in our joint correspondence.' If it had left out the words 'as from the 1 July next,' and had simply agreed to carry on the agency on the terms specified in the joint correspondence, the question then would have been what was a reasonable time in connection with the starting of the agency; and if the parties did not agree upon that, it would have to be determined by the court. In reply to the plaintiff's letter the defendants wrote: 'We are in receipt of your favour of 10th inst., and note with pleasure that you are agreeable to carry on the agency for our . . . beers for West Africa as from the 1st prox. on the terms and conditions stipulated in our joint correspondence.'

It is said that that was not an acceptance of the offer that the agency was to start from 1 July; that it was merely a notification in reference to an already completed agreement. I think it is impossible to construe it in that way, because it is admitted that it would have been open to the defendants to have said, 'No, we cannot agree; the 1 July would not suit us.' And if it was open to them to reject, was it not a new and material term of the contract? The acceptance of that new and material term was by letter written in Scotland . . .

Here a new and material term was certainly introduced, and that new and material term was not accepted until the letter, written by the defendants on 12 June in Scotland, was posted.

Ronan and O'Connor L.JJ. concurred.

CHAPTER 2.

INTENTION TO BE
CONTRACTUALLY BOUND

The intention to be contractually bound is the second essential ingredient of a valid contract. It follows that where there is no intention to be legally bound there is no enforceable contract: *Mackey v Jones* (Case 19) and *Rogers v Smith* (Case 20).

Case 19. Mackey v Jones
Circuit Court (1959) 93 I.L.T.R. 177

The plaintiff worked on his uncle's farm for a number of years without receiving wages. The plaintiff claimed that his uncle verbally agreed to make a will leaving the plaintiff the farm. The uncle subsequently made a will bequeathing the farm to another relative. After his uncle's death the plaintiff sued his uncle's personal representative for specific performance of the alleged contract.

Held that there was no binding contract to leave the farm to the plaintiff but only a statement of intention to do so which did not amount to a contract and the claim was dismissed.

Judge Deale:

The principal claim in this action is for a declaration that the defendant, the personal representative of the deceased, holds in trust certain lands of the deceased, to which he has succeeded as such personal representative. This claim is based on the alleged oral contract made about the year 1943 between the deceased and the plaintiff, who was then about fourteen years of age. The alleged contract arose from a conversation which took place in January 1943, between the plaintiff's mother and the deceased, and from acts of what are alleged to be part performance by the plaintiff. On 17 March 1943, the plaintiff went to the deceased's farm and there lived with him and his wife, doing almost, though not all, the work needed to be done on a small farm such as the deceased had. This is the alleged part performance and it is submitted that a contract to bequeath the lands by will to the plaintiff was thereby made and performed. If this conversation created a contractual relationship between the parties, certain difficult legal questions arise as to its effect, but if it did not then the only question is what is the right of the plaintiff to be paid for the work done.

In my opinion, there was no contract to leave the lands to the plaintiff, and, indeed, no contract of any kind arose out of the conversation. The conversation, in my opinion, amounted to nothing more than a statement of intention or wish by the deceased; the words of the deceased relied on are worth repeating: 'He (the plaintiff) could have the place when he (the deceased) was done with it.' And on another occasion the deceased said by way of affirmation of the alleged contract: 'You need not give him pocket-money. I will give him anything he wants. He can have the place when I am done with it.' In my opinion, a reading of these words makes it plain that no promise was made and it is unnecessary to dwell on the point . . .

(See also Case 29, regarding privity of contract.)

Case 20. Rogers v Smith
Supreme Court, unreported, 16 July 1970

The plaintiff's father was a licenced moneylender. After his involvement in an accident he transferred the business to the son, the plaintiff. This was subject to the express proviso that he could retain a certain sum weekly from the business and discharge his mother's house-keeping expenses out of the profits. The plaintiff was then a tradesman in employment. The plaintiff took no benefit from the business. When the father died he left the business by will to the plaintiff. The plaintiff continued to pay his mother a weekly sum and to discharge the expenses of the house. By this time the plaintiff was married and living elsewhere. Shortly after the father's death the mother received a bill for the father's hospital expenses. Around that time a conversation took place between mother and son. It was alleged by the plaintiff that his mother said that 'any money I owe you when I am dead and gone you will probably take it from the estate' and that these words amounted to a legally enforceable agreement. After his mother's death the plaintiff sought to reclaim from her estate the sums he had given to her together with those he had expended on her house.

Held that the parties did not intend to enter into a contract having legal consequences and the action should be dismissed.

Budd J.:

. . . I intend to confine myself to considering whether any legally enforceable contract was entered into by the plaintiff and his mother. This will involve not only whether a clear agreement can be shown to have been arrived at but also whether it was the intention of mother and son to have entered into an arrangement of a legally binding nature at all.
. . . Counsel for the defendant stressed the necessity in law that an agreement alleged to constitute a contract in law should not leave uncertainty as to its effect or doubt as to its intention. If authority for his proposition is required it seems to me to emerge clearly from the words used by Lord O'Hagan in his judgment in *Madison v Alderson* stating his

reasons for concluding that an agreement relied on in that case could not have been enforced. He states:

I do not see that a bargain so obscure in its terms, so uncertain in its effect, and so doubtful in its intention, could have been properly enforced.

Counsel further submitted that there was likewise a necessity to show that a bargain had been made between mother and son as distinct from some supposition as to what would probably occur or might happen. Lord Blackburn, in the case above referred to, clearly indicated the necessity when he stated that the evidence in the case was such from which a contract would not have been found by the jury if it had been explained to them that 'to make a contract there must be a bargain between both parties'.

It was further submitted that the matter of the intention of the parties to the alleged contract requires particular attention in this case. These parties were mother and son, and if an agreement can be spelt out of the conversation between them, it was contended that the surrounding circumstances and the words used lead to the conclusion that the parties did not intend that any agreement which could be said to have been come to, was to have legal consequences and to be enforceable but was rather of a purely family nature not intended to have such consequences. The learned Chief Justice in the course of his judgment has referred to passages from the judgments of Scrutton L.J. in *Rose & Frank Co. v J.R. Crampton & Bros. Ltd* (1923) and Atkin L.J. in *Balfour v Balfour* (1919) which are highly relevant on this point. It clearly emerges from these passages that in social and family matters agreements may be come to which do not give rise to legal relations because such a consequence is not the intention of the parties and in family matters, an intention to remain free of legal obligations will be readily implied whereas in business matters the opposite result would ordinarily follow.

What was said, in the conversation between the plaintiff . . . and his mother is relied on by the plaintiff as constituting a valid contract for repayment of the moneys in question. It was claimed that the agreement would have the practical effect of entitling him to retain out of the moneys now in his hands as administrator, the amount of the moneys paid to his mother or expended on her behalf after the death of the plaintiff's father. The plaintiff's evidence as to those conversations is to be found . . . in the transcript.

Q. You had a conversation with her?
A. Yes.
Q. When about was that?
A. I know the first time this was when she got a hospital bill for £300 and it shook us.
Q. After your father died?
A. It came very close after that. My father died and we realised I had to take it out of what was there. She realised that if it was taken out of

the business it would weaken to such an extent that I would have to
go somewhere else. She said the best thing you can do is to get it out
of the way and she said any money I owe you when I am dead and
gone you will probably take it from the estate and give up the job
and run the business. That was the first time it happened.

A further account of the conversation was given in the plaintiff's cross-
examination. The relevant portions are as follows:

Q. What did your mother say? What did she say would happen after her
death?

A. I told you she simply said on these occasions, I told her the business
was not good enough and on one occasion she said, 'When I am
dead and gone you will be able to claim anything you may have
spent on me.'

The plaintiff stated further that he could not remember the exact words.
He was then asked:

Q. What do you think she meant?

A. I think she meant that she felt the reason why I was working from
eight o'clock in the morning until eleven at night was in order to
keep her going. I think she would not (*sic*) be necessary to keep her
going any longer that I would be able to take things easier, that I
would be able to give up my job, and that would be financed, that
by getting anything I might have given her.

He was then asked to repeat the words she said:

I think she thought that when I would no longer have to keep her that
then I would reach a stage when I could give up my job . . . and devote
my full time to the business, with possibly the help of money from her
estate that I had paid to her. I am saying what I think she meant. I am
not saying what I think she said.

The nature of the conversations between the mother and son must be
viewed and considered in the light of the background of the family life of
the parties and the surrounding circumstances.

It is to be noted that the arrangement as to paying his mother £4 a week
for housekeeping and the payment of the outgoings on [the house] was not
a new arrangement made for the first time just after his father's death.
Similar payments were made during the father's lifetime. The plaintiff
agreed that it was his father's intention that he should look after him and
his mother. The gist of his evidence was that he continued to make the
payments in the same way as before his father's death. He also agreed that
he would have continued to make the payments to her whether or not she
had said that when she was dead and gone he would be able to claim
anything he might have spent on her. Here we have the position that the
mother's statements relied on by the plaintiff were made in the course of
conversations relating to family affairs and, in my view, the above facts
and the surrounding circumstances deposed to by the plaintiff indicate that
the payments and disbursements previously made had been of a voluntary

nature as part of the family arrangements and that they were not made as the result of any contractual agreement. The evidence is that they carried on as before and in those circumstances the proper inference to draw is that the payments and disbursements were continued on the same voluntary and non-contractual basis. Further investigation into the evidence reinforces my view.

Business agreements intended to have legal consequence are usually preceded by some discussion as to the terms thereof and some type of bargaining generally takes place. Further, while I do not say that express words of offer and acceptance must be proved it must be shown that it can be inferred from the evidence that what was said, viewed in the light of the surrounding circumstances, amounted to offer and acceptance, or put more colloquially that a bargain was made.

There is no evidence as to any discussion as to the terms of an agreement or of any manner of bargaining before the words relied on as creating a contract were spoken. The conversations deposed to do not convey to me with any clarity that the parties arrived at any bargain or agreement. Furthermore, the evidence as to its terms was of a vague and uncertain nature.

It is to be noted that part of the words used by the plaintiff's mother on the occasions relied on by the plaintiff as showing that an agreement was arrived at that he was to be repaid the money given to her as an allowance or expended on her behalf were 'any money I owe you when I am dead and gone you will probably take it from the estate and give up the job and run the business'. These words are not appropriate to indicate that any agreement and bargain had been come to between the parties intended to bind the mother's estate but are rather the statement of a supposition as to what would probably occur. It is to my mind also not clear what was meant by 'any money I owe you'. It is of course suggested that the reference was to the allowance made to the mother and to the payments made in connection with the house but since the date of the conversation is placed as being at the time when the bill from the hospital was received, which is stated to have arrived shortly after the father's death, it would seem highly improbable that such allowance or payments, the bulk if not all of which were paid well after the father's death, could have been the moneys in the contemplation of the parties. There is further no stipulation as to how long the payments were to continue to be made. If it were not to be for the mother's lifetime it would appear that the son would have committed no breach of the alleged agreement by stopping payments and the agreement could not then have been enforced against him. The absence of any stipulation as to the period over which the payments were to continue indicates further the uncertainty as to the terms of the alleged agreement.

Having regard to the background to the conversations between the plaintiff and his mother and the indefiniteness of the evidence both as to the making of any binding agreement and as to its terms the plaintiff has, in my view, failed to establish his case. There is also, in my view, no sufficient evidence of the intention of the parties to enter into a contract having legal consequences . . .

Ó Dálaigh C.J. gave a concurring judgment and FitzGerald J. dissented.

CHAPTER 3.

CONSIDERATION

The third essential ingredient of a valid contract is consideration. Consideration has been judicially defined as either some right, interest, profit or benefit accruing to one party, or some forbearance, detriment, loss or responsibility given, suffered or undertaken by the other party. It is a complete defence in an action in contract to prove that no consideraton was given: *McCoubray v Thomson* (Case 21). But the slightest consideration, such as the forbearance to enforce a legal right, is sufficient: *Barry v Barry* (Case 22) and *Commodity Broking Co. Ltd v Meehan* (Case 23).

Should one party agree to waive, or abandon, contractual rights against another party, that waiver or abandonment must be supported by consideration. Otherwise it is not binding and the party who has waived or abandoned these rights may have a change of heart and later seek to enforce these rights by action: *Drogheda Corporation* v *Fairtlough* (Case 24).

Case 21. McCoubray v Thomson
Common Pleas (1868) I.R. 2 C.L. 226

A party possessed of land transferred it to the defendant in consideration of which the defendant undertook to pay the plaintiff a sum of money. When the defendant failed to pay over the money the plaintiff sued for it.

Held that the claim must be dismissed because no consideration moved from the plaintiff to support the defendant's promise.

Monahan C.J.:

No express promise is made to the plaintiff; and if a promise is to be implied, it would appear to be rather to the party from whom the consideration moved. It is true that in the note to *Lampleigh v Braithwait* it is stated that if the plaintiff had intervened in the *agreement* it is sufficient; but on examining *Tipper v Bicknell* and the other cases which counsel for the defendant has cited in support of that proposition, it will be found that in each of them something was done by the plaintiff, that some part of the consideration moved from him.

O'Hagan and Morris JJ. concurred.

Case 22. Barry v Barry
Queen's Bench (1891) 28 L.R.Ir. 45

A father by will devised his farm, subject to certain legacies, to his eldest son, the defendant. One of the legacies was to his younger son, the plaintiff. The executors, in the presence of the plaintiff, asked the defendant would he possess the farm and pay the legacies. The defendant agreed. When the defendant failed to pay, the plaintiff sued and was met with the argument that no consideration moved from the plaintiff.

Held that the plaintiff's forbearance to enforce the legacy out of the farm was sufficient consideration. The claim suceeded.

O'Brien J.:

In this case the facts were that a farmer had two sons; and upon the marriage of one of them (the defendant), part of his farm, with part of his stock, was assigned to two persons in trust for the son. All the family lived together upon the lands till the father's death. By his will, taking no notice of the settlement, he bequeathed the whole lands to the same son, and bound him to pay certain legacies to his other children, amongst the rest £20 to the plaintiff. The terms of the will are considered sufficient either to create a charge of the legacies upon the farm or to amount to a gift of the lands upon the condition of paying them. The executors named in the will who were the same persons to whom the lands were assigned in trust by the settlement, some time after the death of the father, went to the son, and in the presence of the plaintiff asked him whether he would possess the lands and pay the legacies, which I would take to mean nothing more than whether he would prefer to take half the farm under his settlement, or the whole with the charges upon it. He agreed to take the whole farm and pay the legacies. At that time the will was not proved. Afterwards the plaintiff asked the defendant to pay him, and he promised to pay him £12, after a certain fair where he would have cattle to sell. Upon these facts an action was brought by the plaintiff for the £20 . . . Upon the question of law it was contended that there was no contract or consideration on which an action at law could be maintained at all, on the ground that there was no legal consideration at all, or that the plaintiff was a stranger to it . . .

But I am of opinion, if a person has a legacy upon land, and requires the devisee to pay it, and he promises to do so, that there is a consideration on which he can subject himself to liability in an action at law, and that that consideration is properly in the nature of forbearance, the person having the right and the power to enforce, as the plaintiff had, by means of a proceeding against the land or the assets, and it not being necessary, in my view, that the power should be actually used or referred to. There is another ground of consideration on which the plaintiff's claim was put. The assent of the executors to the defendant's possession of the whole of the lands was required, and without a positive act upon their part he was a trespasser. He must be presumed in law, therefore, to have taken possession by means of that positive act, and to that act the plaintiff was a party. In other words he was allowed by the executors, with the plaintiff's consent, to go into possession of property against which the plaintiff had a specific right, and the possession of the assets for a time however short was a benefit in law to the defendant, and might mean the whole loss of the plaintiff's remedy. The statement that he would 'possess' the lands might merely mean that the defendant would elect to take under the will, as against the settlement, but that, with his subsequent promises to pay, was evidence for the jury of a personal contract. For these reasons I consider that we do not, for the sake of honesty, trench upon any rule of law—nor are much affected as to anything but substantial right—in holding that the plaintiff was entitled to judgment.

Holmes and Gibson JJ. delivered concurring judgments.

Case 23. Commodity Broking Co. Ltd v Meehan
High Court [1985] I.R. 12

A company opened an account with the plaintiff. The defendant was the sole beneficial owner of the company. The company traded through the agency of the plaintiff and eventually owed it a considerable sum of money. The defendant acknowledged the company's indebtedness and intimated that the company was insolvent. He said that he would try to repay the debt by monthly instalments. The defendant made a total of two payments. The plaintiff sued the defendant, claiming that there was an agreement with the defendant to indemnify it, and that the plaintiff acting on that agreement forbore to sue the company.

Held that the indemnity was unenforceable as it was not given for consideration. There was neither an express nor implied request to forbear from bringing proceedings. Had there been such request which induced such forbearance that would have amounted to good consideration.

Barron J.:

. . . The final issue is whether there is any consideration for the
defendant's promise. The consideration relied upon by the plaintiff is that
it forbore to sue the company. In the *Alliance Bank Ltd v Broom* (1864)
the defendant who was a customer of the plaintiff bank was asked to give
security for money which he owed to the bank. He agreed to hypothecate
certain goods in favour of the bank. When he failed to do so, the bank
sought to enforce his promise, which he pleaded was given without
consideration. He failed in this plea. It was held that he had by implication
asked the bank to forbear and that he had received a sufficient degree of
forbearance to amount to consideration for his promise. The Vice-
Chancellor Sir. D.R.T. Kindersley said:

> It appears to me that, when the plaintiffs demanded payment of their
> debt, and, in consequence of that application the defendant agreed to
> give certain security, although there was no promise on the part of the
> plaintiffs to abstain for any certain time from suing for the debt, the
> effect was, that the plaintiffs did in effect give, and the defendant
> received, the benefit of some degree of forbearance; not, indeed, for any
> definite time, but, at all events, some extent of forbearance. If, on the
> application for security being made, the defendant had refused to give
> any security at all, the consequence certainly would have been that the
> creditor would have demanded payment of the debt, and have taken
> steps to enforce it. It is very true that, at any time after the promise, the
> creditor might have insisted on payment of his debt, and have brought
> an action; but the circumstances necessarily involve the benefit to the
> debtor of a certain amount of forbearance, which he would not have
> derived if he had not made the agreement.

In *Miles v New Zealand Alford Estate Co.* (1886) director and
shareholder had sold certain property to the company. At a general
meeting, several shareholders complained that the company had overpaid
for the property. To still such criticisms, it was agreed that the company
should pay a minimum dividend and that in any year in which it was not
earned the vendor would make up the difference. He was subsequently
sued on this agreement and it was contended that forbearance by the
company to bring proceedings in relation to the sale was a sufficient
consideration to make the agreement binding. Cotton L.J. in considering
the proofs to establish consideration said:

> Now, what I understand to be the law is this, that if there is in fact a
> serious claim honestly made, the abandonment of the claim is a good
> 'consideration' for a contract; and if that is the law, what we really have
> to now consider is whether in the present case there is any evidence on
> which the court ought to find that there was a serious claim in fact
> made, and whether a contract to abandon that claim was the
> consideration for this letter of guarantee.

Having considered the evidence he said:

> The conclusion at which I have arrived is, that there is no evidence on which we ought to rely that there was in fact a claim intended to be made against the vendor, and, in my opinion, on the evidence before us, we ought not to arrive at the conclusion that there was ever intended to be any contract by the company, much less that there was in fact any contract binding the company that that claim should not be prosecuted, and should be given up.

Fry L.J. accepted the same test and took the view that there was no intention by the company to abandon its claim. He said:

> I think the true result of the evidence is to show that there was an expectation in the mind of the vendor that if he gave this document no proceedings would be taken against him, that there was an expectation in the minds of many of those who were present, if they got this dividend they would take no proceedings; but it appears to me it is not right or competent for the court to turn an expectation into a contract, and that is what I think we should do if we gave effect to this as a valid contract.

Bowen L.J. dissented. He regarded consideration as being any forbearance to sue as a result of the express or implied request of the promissor. He regarded the decision of the trial judge 'as finding that proceedings had been threatened, that the vendor knew that they had been threatened, that he gave the guarantee in order to put an end to them, and that the proceedings were dropped in consequence of his giving that undertaking.' He regarded this as a finding that there has been consideration and in doing so he expressly followed *Alliance Bank Ltd v Broom* (1886). The majority view that there should be an actual agreement to abandon threatened proceedings before there can be good consideration was not followed in later cases.

On similar facts, *Alliance Bank Ltd v Broom* (1886) was approved by the House of Lords in *Fullerton v Provincial Bank of Ireland* (1903). In the same case, the judgment of Bowen L.J. in *Miles v New Zealand Alford Estate Co.* (1886) was cited with approval by Lord Davey.

In *Combe v Combe* (1955) the court had to consider whether there was consideration for a promise by a husband to pay permanent maintenance to his wife upon the dissolution of their marriage. The wife was not paid and after several years sued on the promise. It was held that there was no consideration since she had been entitled at all times to apply to the court for maintenance and such right would have been unaffected by her husband's promise. Accordingly there had been no request to forbear. Denning L.J. said:

> I cannot find any evidence of any intention by the husband that the wife should forbear from applying to the court for maintenance, or, in other words, any request by the husband, express or implied, that the wife should so forbear. Her forbearance was not intended by him, nor was it done at his request. It was, therefore, no consideration.

In the same case Asquith L.J. said:

> Finally, I do not think an actual forbearance, as opposed to an agreement to forbear to approach the court, is a good consideration unless it proceeds from a request, express or implied, on the part of the promissor. If not moved by such a request, the forbearance is not in respect of the promise.

In my view, these cases establish that the better view is that where a request express or implied to forbear from bringing proceedings induces such forbearance this amounts to good consideration. It is not necessary as the majority decided in *Miles v New Zealand Alford Estate Co.* (1886) that there should be an actual agreement not to sue.

The reality of the present case is that when the company was unable to meet its calls the plaintiff took steps to protect itself. So far as the plaintiff was concerned, the company was almost certainly unable to pay. Accordingly, every effort was made to ensure that a promise could be obtained from the defendant that he would pay instead. In the course of events, I can find no implied request by the defendant not to sue the company nor clearly any express request. Nor can I find that the defendant's promise to pay influenced the plaintiff's decision not to sue the company. The plaintiff did not deliberately refrain from suing the company. Had it seemed to it a sensible course to adopt, it would have done so. Its reason for not doing so was not the defendant's promise to pay, but the realisation that it would be a fruitless exercise. If it had been deliberately misled by the defendant, either as to the solvency of the company or into not suing the company by reason of the payments made, the matter might have been otherwise. But there is no evidence to suggest any such calculated conduct on the part of the defendant nor is such a case made. Reluctantly I must hold that no consideration was given for the defendant's promise.

Case 24. Drogheda Corporation v Fairtlough
Queen's Bench (1858) 8 Ir.C.L.R. 98

The plaintiffs in 1820 leased premises to the defendant at a rent £11 per annum. In 1842 under a new lease the plaintiffs reduced the rent to £5 per annum. When the type of lease executed in 1842 was held null and void in unconnected proceedings, the plaintiffs, in 1858, sued for the arrears of rent.

Held that since the lease of 1842, which was to operate as a surrender of the earlier lease, was null and void, the lease of 1820 continued in force with all the rights and incidents attaching to it. The receipts of the reduced rent were not evidence of an agreement to receive that rent in satisfaction of the rent reserved by the lease of 1820 because there was no consideration for such agreement.

Lefroy C.J.:

. . . But, I must further observe, what is the consideration which the corporation received for this agreement? They received a less rent; but, upon the other hand, the tenant was allowed to keep in his pocket the balance of the greater rent. The arrangement may have been for their mutual advantage; but unquestionably no peculiar advantage whatsoever resulted to the corporation. There is no consideration for this alleged agreement; and even if there were a consideration—if a consideration could have been worked out of the circumstances, that consideration should have appeared upon the face of the agreement; for the rule of law is inflexible, that the consideration for an agreement must appear upon the face of the agreement, either expressly or by necessary inference, wherever, under the *Statute of Frauds*, an agreement is required to be in writing. Now, there is no consideration here, express or implied . . . There is, therefore, an utter failure both of evidence of the contract, and also of evidence of the consideration for it, to remove the rule of the common law, that payment of a less sum cannot be a satisfaction of a greater liquidated sum, unless there is some further advantage accompanying the payment, and that advantage must be a reasonable one, and must appear upon the face of the agreement . . .

O'Brien and Hayes JJ. concurred.

CHAPTER 4.

DOCTRINE OF EQUITABLE ESTOPPEL

Promissory estoppel arises where one party to a transaction makes to the other a promise, which is intended to create legal relations between them, and that other party acts upon the promise to his detriment. The party making the promise will not be allowed to act inconsistently with that promise: *Cullen v Cullen* (Case 25) and *Revenue Commissioners v Moroney* (Case 26).

Case 25. Cullen v Cullen
High Court [1962] I.R. 268

Relations between a husband and wife had been strained for some years. The wife won a mobile house in a competition which she gave to her son. He offered it to his father, who was living separate from his wife, but the offer was refused. The son prepared a site for the house on his own land. His mother thought it more suitable to have it erected on lands owned by her husband and she sought her husband's permission to do so. He replied that since he intended transferring the lands to her, she could erect the house where she liked. As a result the son erected it on his father's land rather than his own. Among various reliefs, in legal proceedings, sought by the husband was an injunction to restrain his son from trespassing on his lands.

Held that the plaintiff was estopped by his conduct from asserting any title to the site on which the house was erected.

Kenny J.:

. . . I am of opinion, however, that the plaintiff is estopped by his conduct in giving consent to the erection of the house when he knew that the house had been given to his son and that the plaintiff cannot now assert any title to the site on which the house has been erected. There was a representation by him that he consented to this and that representation was acted on by his son who spent £200 at least in erecting the house and gave considerable amount of his time to this work. It seems to me that the principle stated by Denning J. in *Central London Property Trust Ltd v High Trees House Ltd* (1947) [this case is explained on p. 47] and affirmed by the same judge when he was a Lord Justice of Appeal in *Lyle-Meller v Lewis & Co. (Westminster) Ltd* (1956) applies to this aspect of the case and that the plaintiff cannot withdraw the permission which he gave for the erection of the house on the lands . . . and cannot now assert a title to the site on which the house stands or to the house. While the estoppel created by the plaintiff's conduct prevents him asserting a title to the site, it does not give his son a right to require the plaintiff to transfer the site to him: if I had jurisdiction to make such an order I would do so, but I do not think I have. However, neither the plaintiff nor any person claiming through him can now successfully assert a title to the lands on which the house is built by any proceedings and, at the end of the twelve-year period from the date when the erection of the bungalow commenced, his son will be able to bring a successful application under [statute] for his registration as owner.

Case 26. Revenue Commissioners v Moroney
High Court [1972] I.R. 372

The father of the defendant assigned by deed certain premises to himself, the defendant and the defendant's brother in consideration of a stated sum. The deed contained a receipt clause. However, the parties never intended that any purchase price should be paid and, despite the receipt clause, none was ever paid. After the father's death the plaintiffs claimed that two-thirds of the purchase price was a debt due to the father's estate.

Held that the plaintiffs' claim depended on whether the deceased could have successfully sued for any part of the purchase price. The representations of the deceased before the execution of the deed were such as would have prevented him, by promissory estoppel, from enforcing any right to the purchase money under the deed. Accordingly, the plaintiffs' claim failed.

Kenny J.:

. . . This doctrine first appeared in *Hughes v Metropolitan Railway Co.* (1877) which was a claim that a lease be forfeited on the ground that the lessee was in breach of a covenant to effect certain required repairs within six months from the date on which the lessee received from the lessor a notice specifying the defects. The landlord gave notice of the breaches on 22 October 1874, and the tenant's solicitors wrote that the repairs would be commenced immediately but that they proposed to postpone them until they heard whether the landlord wished to purchase the tenant's interest. The landlord's solicitors replied asking whether the tenant was the owner of other adjoining property and was willing to give immediate possession of it and stating that, when they had this information, their client would consider whether he would acquire the tenant's interest. The attempt to negotiate a settlement broke down on 31 December and the question in the case was whether the six months ran from that date or from 22 October, for the repairs had been carried out within the period of six months from 31 December. The case was decided before the law was altered by s. 14 of the *Conveyancing Act 1881*. In the course of his speech the Lord Chancellor, Lord Cairns, said:

> . . . it is the first principle upon which all courts of equity proceed, that if parties who have entered into definite and distinct terms involving certain legal results—certain penalties or legal forfeiture—afterwards by their own act or with their own consent enter upon a course of negotiation which has the effect of leading one of the parties to suppose that the strict rights arising under the contract will not be enforced, or will be kept in suspense, or held in abeyance, the person who otherwise might have enforced those rights will not be allowed to enforce them where it would be inequitable having regard to the dealings which have thus taken place between the parties.

Lord Justice Bowen in *Birmingham & District Land Co. v London & North Western Railway Co.* (1888) showed that the principle was not confined to forfeiture cases but was of general application. He said:

> . . . if persons who have contractual rights against others induce by their conduct those against whom they have such rights to believe that such rights will either not be enforced or will be kept in suspense or abeyance for some particular time, those persons will not be allowed by a court of

equity to enforce the rights until such time has elapsed, without at all events placing the parties in the same position as they were before.

The doctrine got little attention in the textbooks until it was revived in striking fashion by Mr Justice Denning (as he then was) in *Central London Property Trust Ltd v High Trees House Ltd* (1947). In that case the landlords had let a block of flats for 99 years at an annual rent of £2,500. The tenants found difficulty in letting them and in 1940 the landlords agreed to reduce the rent to £1,250. There was no consideration given for this nor was any period for the reduction agreed. From then the tenants paid the reduced rent until September 1945, when the landlords demanded the full amount of £2,500 and the arrears for the period during which the lower rent had been paid. Mr Justice Denning held that the rent of £2,500 could not be recovered for any period before September 1945. In the course of his judgment he said:

> There has been a series of decisions over the last fifty years which, although they are said to be cases of estoppel are not really such. They are cases in which a promise was made which was intended to create legal relations and which, to the knowledge of the person making the promise, was going to be acted on by the person to whom it was made, and which was in fact so acted on. In such cases the courts have said that the promise must be honoured . . . The courts have not gone so far as to give a cause of action in damages for the breach of such a promise, but they have refused to allow the party making it to act inconsistently with it.

In *Combe v Combe* (1951) the same judge said that the doctrine 'only prevents a party from insisting upon his strict legal rights, when it would be unjust to allow him to enforce them, having regard to the dealings which have taken place between the parties.' These cases were discussed by Viscount Simonds in *Tool Metal Manufacturing Co. Ltd v Tungsten Electric Co. Ltd* (1955) in which he said that the gist of the equity lies in the fact that one party has by his conduct led the other to alter his position; this aspect was emphasised by Mr Justice McVeigh in *Morrow v Carty* (1957); see also *Cullen v Cullen* (Case 25) and *Inwards v Baker* (1965).

In *Ajayi v R.T. Briscoe (Nig.) Ltd* (1964) the advice of the Privy Council, given by Lord Hodson, was that the doctrine is confined to cases where the representation relates to *existing* contractual rights. Lord Hodson said: 'Their Lordships are of opinion that the principle of law as defined by Bowen L.J. has been confirmed by the House of Lords in the case of *Tool Metal Manufacturing Co. Ltd v Tungsten Electric Co. Ltd* where the authorities were reviewed and no encouragement was given to the view that the principle was capable of extension so as to create rights in the promisee for which he had given no consideration. The principle, which has been described as *quasi estoppel* and perhaps more aptly as *promissory estoppel*, is that when one party to a contract in the absence of fresh consideration agrees not to enforce his rights, an equity will be raised in favour of the other party. This equity is, however, subject to the qualifications (1) that the other party has altered his position, (2) that the promissor can resile from his promise on giving reasonable notice, which need not be a formal notice, giving the promisee a reasonable opportunity of resuming his position, (3) the promise only becomes final and irrevocable if the promisee cannot resume his position.' This, if correct, would conclude this case in favour of the plaintiffs as any promissory estoppel arises here because the parent before the deed was signed represented by his conduct and by what he said to his sons that he would not require payment of any part of the 'purchase' price. Until the deed was signed, there were no legal relations to be effected.

   In my view there is no reason in principle why the doctrine of promissory estoppel should be confined to cases where the representation related to existing contractual rights. It includes cases where there is a representation by one person to another that rights which will come into existence under a contract to be entered into will not be enforced. This is the way in which the doctrine is stated at p. 627 of Snell's *Principles of Equity* (26th edn 1966) which has the considerable authority of having had Mr Megarry (as he then was) as one of its co-editors: 'Where by his words or conduct one party to a transaction makes to the other a promise or assurance which is intended to affect the legal relations between them, and the other party acts upon it, altering his position to his detriment, the party making the promise or assurance will not be permitted to act inconsistently with it.' It seems to me that the parent represented to his sons that he would never seek payment of any part of the consideration of £16,000 and that they acted on this by signing the assignment. Each of them altered his position to his detriment because by signing each took on a legal liability to pay two-thirds of the consideration which they would not otherwise have assumed. Although they got the benefit of the interest in the joint tenancy, it seems to me to be probable that if they had refused to sign the deed in the form in which it was they would have got this without payment. The assumption of the legal liability created by the deed was in my opinion sufficient to raise the equity against the parent and the representation has become final because the sons cannot be restored to their original position unless the view is taken that there never was a debt. This equity does not affect the rights of other parties who would be entitled to rely on the deed, but this does not assist the plaintiffs. Their claim can succeed only if the parent would have succeeded in a claim against his sons.

   In my view the plaintiffs' claim fails because the parent would not have got judgment against the sons for any part of the 'purchase' price if he had sued them for it . . .

The Supreme Court (Ó Dálaigh C.J., Walsh and Budd JJ.) dismissed the plaintiffs' appeal without discussing this doctrine. (See also Case 46 regarding the construction of a contract.)

CHAPTER 5.

PRIVITY OF CONTRACT

The doctrine of privity of contract means that a contract cannot, as a general rule, confer rights or impose obligations arising under it on any person except the parties to that contract: *Murphy v Bower* (Case 27), *Clitheroe v Simpson* (Case 28) and *Mackey v Jones* (Case 29). But the courts of equity developed a general exception to this doctrine of privity of contract by the use of the concept of the trust: *Drimmie v Davies* (Case 30).

Case 27. Murphy v Bower
Common Pleas (1866) I.R. 2 C.L. 506

The plaintiff undertook construction work for a railway company. The railway company employed the defendant as an engineer to supervise the work. The construction contract stipulated that the defendant would issue certificates as work was completed, thereupon entitling the plaintiff to payment. When the defendant refused to certify the work the plaintiff sued him.

Held that the action should be dismissed on the ground that there was no privity of contract between the plaintiff and the defendant.

Monahan C.J.:

. . . It therefore appears that the engineer was not a party to the original agreement between the plaintiff and the company; and that the alleged duty of the defendant to give a certificate, so far as it exists, arises from the simple fact that he was employed by the company as their engineer to superintend their works. The question then arises, whether the defendant has rendered himself liable to plaintiff's action by merely refusing to give his certificate, though aware that the plaintiff, had done everything to entitle himself to it, and how far the matter would be affected by the fact of his being actuated by a fraudulent motive in withholding such certificate, or having done so in collusion with the company.

The argument for the defendant is, that since the duty of the engineer to give a certificate arises, if at all, out of a contract, the plaintiff, not being party to it, cannot maintain an action for its breach, and this argument is equally applicable, whether the contract out of which the duty arises is a contract between the engineer and the company, or, as has been suggested, between the railway company and the plaintiff assuming them to have contracted on the part of their engineer, that he, as their employee, should do his duty, and give such certificate.

It was also contended on the part of the plaintiff that, inasmuch as the defendant has taken upon himself the duty of engineer, it might be inferred that he had expressly contracted with the plaintiff to perform his duty as such engineer; but the answer to this suggestion is, that, if any such contract was intended to be relied on, it should have been stated that such a contract was in fact entered into; the consideration for that contract should have been also stated, and it would have been then competent for the defendant to traverse the alleged consideration. If the contract was an express contract between the railway company and the plaintiff, by which the railway company contracted that their engineer should do his duty properly, there is no doubt but that a right to maintain an action against the railway company would have accrued to them upon the engineer's default; but some cases have been referred to in which it has been decided that, where the foundation of the right of action is rested upon contract, no one can maintain an action who is not a party to the contract. In *Alton v Midland Railway Co.* an action was brought by the employer of a commercial traveller for the loss of the services of his servant, who, it was alleged, had taken his railway ticket in the usual way, and, while proceeding upon his journey thereunder, sustained injuries through the negligence of the company. There was no doubt but that if no contract had existed between the injured man and the company—if, for instance, he had been walking upon the line, and had been injured through the default of the company—his employer would have been enabled to recover damages for the loss of his services; nevertheless the court held that the action having been in fact founded upon the contract between the traveller and the company to carry him to the place for which he had obtained a ticket, the action could not be maintained by one who was not a party to that contract . . .

Keogh, O'Hagan and Morris JJ. concurred.

Case 28. Clitheroe v Simpson
Common Pleas (1879) 4 L.R.Ir. 59

A father conveyed property to his son by deed in consideration for the son's agreement to pay a sum of money to his sister. The sister's personal representative sued the brother for the money which remained unpaid at the sister's death. The action was defended on the ground that there was no privity of contract between his sister and himself, or between the personal representative and himself.

Held that since there was no privity of contract between the plaintiff and defendant the action must be dismissed.

Morris C.J.:

We have no doubt that the defence to the statement of claim must be allowed. The statement of claim does not purport to be founded upon any equitable rights or liabilities between the parties. It is founded on contract upon the deed. But the deed is not one between the defendant and the plaintiff, or his sister. It is a deed between their father and the defendant. It has been contended that there may be circumstances which would make the defendant a trustee for his sister: if so, they should have been stated. I do not suggest that there are circumstances. But that is not the case that is made. The case that the defendant meets by his defence is simply an action of contract on a deed to which he is a stranger, and grounded on the deed. The defence must be allowed.

Lawson and Harrison JJ. concurred.

Case 29. Mackey v Jones
Circuit Court (1959) 93 I.L.T.R. 177

The plaintiff worked on his uncle's farm for a number of years without receiving wages. The plaintiff claimed that his uncle verbally agreed to make a will leaving the plaintiff the farm. The uncle subsequently made a will bequeathing the farm to another relative. After his uncle's death the plaintiff sued his uncle's personal representative for specific performance of the alleged contract.

Held that if there was any binding agreement it was between the plaintiff's mother and the deceased. There being no privity of contract between the parties, the action should be dismissed.

Judge Deale:

. . . even if the words did amount to a promise and if the whole conversation could bind the deceased in a contractual manner, there is a further difficulty in the plaintiff's way. He was not a party to the proposal. He was not consulted about it and in no way considered the matter; he was simply told by his mother to go to his uncle's farm and he obeyed. Of course, it may be said that at the age of fourteen years he could do little else, being under the control of his parents, but that does not mean that he was a party to any contract that could be implied from the conversation. Any young boy can make a contract if it is for his benefit; but before he can be said to contract, it must be shown that the affirmation of the contract resulted from acceptance by him of an offer. Here, in my opinion, he did not accept the offer, if offer it was; he obeyed his mother's orders and that was not enough to create the relationship of contracting parties between the deceased and himself. The first part of the claim fails . . .

(See also Case 19, regarding the intention to create legal relations.)

Case 30. Drimmie v Davies
Court of Appeal [1899] 1 I.R. 176

A father and son agreed by deed to enter into a business partnership for five years. It was agreed, *inter alia*, that should the father die during the partnership's continuance the son would pay annually to his brothers and sisters certain sums of money. The father died within the five years and when the son refused to pay the annuities the executors of his father's estate, and his brothers and sisters, brought an action to enforce payment of the annuities.

Held that the executors, as representing one of the contracting parties were entitled to succeed in the action against the other contracting party. The brothers and sisters were entitled to succeed on the ground that the equitable doctrine, that the party for whose benefit the contract had been entered into had a remedy against the person with whom it was expressed to be made, was to be applied.

FitzGibbon L.J.:

We are all satisfied that this appeal must be dismissed on plain and simple grounds, and in so doing we are not to be understood as entertaining any doubt of the liability of the defendant to maintain his younger brothers and sisters in accordance with the terms of his agreement. The agreement of 25 June 1895 was made between father and son; being under seal it did not require valuable consideration to support it, but even if it did, there was, in my opinion, valuable consideration for it in the fact that the defendant got a share in the business during his father's life, and the right of succession to it on his father's death. *Facio ut facias* is just as good consideration as *do ut des*; the deed of partnership contained covenants binding both father and son, and it was a contract for valuable consideration on both sides. That being so, the parties to it could enforce it; and the only defence is that the present plaintiffs cannot maintain the action, and that the parties for whose benefit it was intended cannot sue for the relief which it purports to provide for them.

The clause in question mentions the death of the senior partner as the time when it was to come into operation. It was, therefore, a contract which was not intended to die with the contracting party himself, and the benefit of it passes to the executor. It is a very reasonable and ordinary contract that, in the event of the death of the senior partner during the partnership, the junior partner, continuing the business, should pay to each of the three daughters of the senior partner a yearly sum of £40 for a period of seven years, but should any of the daughters be married or settled in life prior to the death, or within seven years subsequently, then the liability of the junior partner was to cease; he was further to pay to his two younger brothers, from the death of his father, if the partnership should be then existing, a sum of £15 a-year each until majority, but in no event for more than seven years from the father's death.

The first question is—whether the executors can sue? I can see no reason to doubt that they can sue at common law. It is said that there is no remedy, because this is not an action for the benefit of the assets. But it is an action to recover money, under a contract made with the deceased, for the benefit of members of his family who cannot help themselves, and who have natural claims on him and on his assets. It is the same as the common contract which a man makes with an insurance company for payment of an annuity, or a lump sum, to his widow or to his children, after his death. We find a similar and mutual contract on the opposite side of this very deed, for in the event of the death of the junior partner, the senior partner agreed to pay to his widow and children £75 a-year for seven years, if the senior partner continued to practise as a dental surgeon . . .

It was said that this was not a common law action. But the *Judicature (Ireland) Act 1877* has assimilated the procedure at law and in equity, and if the executor can recover the arrears, he is entitled to a declaration of his right to recover them, and such a declaration would involve the disposition both of what had accrued due, and also of any future instalments that might hereafter be recovered. Upon these grounds the executor, as representing one of the two contracting parties, is, in my opinion, entitled to succeed in this action against the other. There is ample authority to show that if the executors had received this money, they would be bound to apply it for the use of the children . . .

There is a passage in the judgment of Bowen L.J., in *Gandy v Gandy*, which contains sufficient to sustain the decree which we propose to make in the present case. That was the case of a separation deed, by which the husband covenanted to pay an annuity to the trustees for the use of the wife and two eldest daughters, and also to maintain the two youngest daughters. One of the latter subsequently brought an action against the trustees, and her father who refused to maintain her after she reached the age of sixteen. Bowen L.J. said:

> Whatever may have been the common law doctrine, if the true intent and true effect of this deed was to give to the children a beneficial right under it, that is to say, to give them a right to have these covenants performed, and to call upon the trustees to protect their rights and interests under it, then the children would be outside the common law doctrine, and would, in a court of equity, be allowed to enforce their rights under the deed.

The decree will be for the specific performance of this agreement by the defendant. But the rights of the plaintiffs, and the liability of the defendant, cannot stop by paying what is due up to the present time; the order must provide for future instalments.

If the law was unable to give effect to this agreement, I do not see how anyone could secure an annuity for his wife and children out of the profits of a business.

Walker and Holmes L.JJ. delivered concurring judgments.

CHAPTER 6.

FORM OF A CONTRACT

As a general rule no particular form is required in the making of a contract. A contract may be in writing, be verbal or be implied from conduct. The form of the contract is a matter to be decided by the parties though in some instances the law demands a particular form.

Contracts unsupported by consideration must be by deed. Some contracts, such as bills of exchange, assignments of copyright, the transfer of shares in a company and hire-purchase agreement, must be in writing.

Other contracts need only be evidenced in writing. The *Statute of Frauds (Ireland) 1695* provides that no action can be brought with regard to the contracts within the statute unless the agreement or some memorandum or note is in writing signed by the person to be charged or his or her agent. Section 2 is fully set out on page 73. The first category of which contracts need to be evidenced in writing is contracts of guarantee: *Fennell v Mulcahy* (Case 31). The second category is contracts made in consideration of marriage. Since these have fallen into disuse the old cases are excluded. The third category of such contracts, in which there has been considerable litigation, is for the sale of any interest in land. One or two cases are sufficient to clearly illustrate how liberally the courts have interpreted this statutory provision: *McQuaid v Lynam* (Case 32).

The fourth category of contracts which need to be evidenced in writing is contracts not to be performed within a year of their making: *Tierney v Marshall* (Case 33), *Farrington v Donoghue* (Case 34) and *Naughton v Limestone Land Co. Ltd* (Case 35).

Case 31. Fennell v Mulcahy
Exchequer (1845) 8 Ir.L.R. 434

The plaintiff landlord distrained the goods of his tenant. In consideration of his withdrawing the distress the defendant undertook verbally to pay the amount of the rent due. The distress was withdrawn and when the defendant failed to pay the sum agreed the plaintiff sued and was met with the defence of the *Statute of Frauds*.

Held that this was an undertaking to pay the debt of another and since it had not been reduced to writing it was void under the *Statute of Frauds*.

Pennefather B.:

. . . By the common law, a consideration is necessary to support an action on any promise, but for that consideration it is enough if any advantage or benefit result to the party making the promise, or any loss or detriment to the party to whom the promise is made. The *Statute of Frauds* has, in this regard, altered the common law; and the common law definition of consideration will no longer answer. The statute was not passed to nullify that which was already void as a *nudum pactum*, but it was passed to avoid, in certain cases, a promise where, independently of that statute, sufficient consideration did exist. The statute provides 'that no action shall be brought whereby to charge the defendant upon any special promise to answer for the debt, default or miscarriage of another, unless the agreement upon which such action is brought be in writing.' Now, if in every case where a promise made to be answerable for the debt of another, founded on a consideration arising from a loss or inconvenience resulting to the person to whom the promise is made, be held good within the statute, it is quite obvious that the statute would have no operation, and would be a mere dead letter. Some line of distinction, therefore, must be taken, different from what the common law had already done. Now, I apprehend that it will be found upon an examination of the cases, that the rule to be extracted for them is, that there must be some benefit or advantage arising to the defendant himself, who makes the promise, or something to be done by the promisee in consideration of the promise, excepting in the case where the original demand is discharged in consequence of the promise, as in the case of *Goodman v Chase* (1818); but, if the other cases, where the debt continued, be properly examined, it will be found that the promiser was not liable in any case where the consideration for the promise was only a detriment resulting to the plaintiff, with the exception of the case in *3 Espinasse*: but as to that case, the observations made on it fully show there were ample reasons for maintaining it on other grounds, grounds for considering it an original undertaking and promise by the defendant, and grounds for considering that the property had got into his possession; and either ground might have fully maintained that decision. *Williams v Leper* has never been overruled, but there is a clear distinction between it and the present case.

In this case no advantage resulted to the defendant, the promiser; nor was there any discharge of the original debt, though it might have been suspended; for we must take it, that the property here was restored to the tenant. I conceive it is governed by the statute, and does not fall within any of the exceptions I have mentioned.

Brady C.B., and Lefroy B. gave concurring judgments and Richards B. concurred.

Case 32. McQuaid v Lynam and Lynam
High Court [1965] I.R. 564

The defendants built a house on which the plaintiff, wishing to purchase it, paid a deposit and received a receipt. At the same time a form of application to a building society for a loan was partly filled in and the second named defendant's name was inserted as builder. Subsequently the form was completed and the plaintiff signed it. The plaintiff paid a further sum of money which was also receipted. Before he paid the latter sum he was told by the defendant that the house could not be sold as freehold but would be leased and the purchase price would be reduced accordingly and he agreed to this. When the defendant refused to complete the sale the plaintiff sued for specific performance.

Held that the application to the building society did not constitute a note or memorandum sufficient to satisfy the *Statute of Frauds* as it was signed by the plaintiff only but that the first receipt and the application to the building society could be read together and thus constituted a sufficient note or memorandum. Since the variation was from a freehold to a leasehold it was essential that the duration of the lease and the rent to be enforceable must be agreed in writing. Therefore the contract was not enforceable and the action was dismissed.

Kenny J.:

. . . The first submission by the plaintiff's counsel in connection with the *Statute of Frauds* was that the application to the building society which was written by the second-named defendant was a sufficient memorandum or note of the oral contract. The application contains all the terms of the oral contract which was made on the 4 September 1963, and the name of the defendants but it was not signed by them or either of them unless the writing in of 'E.J. Lynam' opposite the printed words, 'name of builder,' was a signature. It is settled law that the memorandum or note required by the *Statute of Frauds* may consist of a document which was not intended to be such a note or memorandum but it must, however, be signed by the party to be charged and the signature must have been intended to authenticate the whole document of which it forms a part. This was emphasised by Lord Westbury in *Caton v Caton* (1867) when he said:

> Now, what constitutes a sufficient signature has been described by different judges in different words. In the original case upon this subject, though not quite the original case, but the case most frequently referred to as of the earliest date, that of *Stokes v Moore*, the language of the learned judge is, that the signature must authenticate every part of the

instrument; or again, that it must give authenticity to every part of the instrument. . . . Probably the phrases 'authentic' and 'authenticity' are not quite felicitous, but their meaning is plainly this, that the signature must be so placed as to show that it was intended to relate and refer to, and that in fact it does relate and refer to, every part of the instrument. The language of Sir William Grant in *Ogilvie v Foljambe* (1817) is (as his method was) much more felicitous. He says it must govern every part of the instrument. It must show that every part of the instrument emanates from the individual so signing, and that the signature was intended to have that effect. It follows, therefore, that if a signature be found in an instrument incidentally only, or having relation and reference only to a portion of the instrument, the signature cannot have that legal effect and force which it must have in order to comply with the statute, and to give authenticity to the whole of the memorandum.

The writing of 'E.J. Lynam' by the second-named defendant on the application to the building society was not a signature of that document by the defendants or by either of them as it was not intended to give authenticity to any part of it. The document was intended to be—and was—signed by the plaintiff and the writing of the name of the defendants was intended to give information to the building society. The application is not therefore a memorandum or note in writing of the contract.

The next issue is whether the receipt of 4 September 1963, and the application to the building society, dated 27 September 1963, together constitute such a memorandum or note . . .

I did not have the advantage of hearing any argument on the question whether the receipt of 4 September and the application to the building society, when read together, constitute a memorandum or note in writing of the contract, or on the question whether the application and the receipt of 4 November could constitute such a memorandum or note as counsel for the defendants had not been instructed by their clients that they had given these two receipts. The many cases on the issue whether a number of documents read together can constitute such a memorandum or note in writing show a progressively liberal approach by the courts to this question. I think that the modern cases (*Long v Millar* (1879), *Stokes v Whicher* (1920) and *Timmins v Moreland Street Property Co.* (1957) establish that a number of documents may together constitute a note or memorandum in writing if they have come into existence in connection with the same transaction or if they contain internal references which connect them with each other. But as the memorandum or note considered as a whole must be signed, it would seem to follow that the document which is signed must be the last of the documents in point of time, for it would be absurd to hold that a person who signed a document could be regarded as having signed another document which was not in existence when he signed the first. I think that the correct view on this difficult matter is that stated in the judgment of Romer L.J. in *Timmins v Moreland Street Property Co.*

One of the matters discussed in that case was whether a cheque and a receipt read together constituted a valid memorandum or note and it was argued that the two documents could not unless the document signed by the party to be charged was the later one. On this matter, Romer L.J. said:

> The next point which counsel for the defendant company took was whether the cheque and receipt taken together could form a memorandum having regard to the order in which they were signed. His argument as to that was that although two separate documents can together constitute a memorandum for the purposes of s. 40, the party to be charged must have signed the second of the two; that is to say, if the defendant had signed a document, the plaintiff cannot rely on it in conjunction with a later document signed by himself. This in general must be true. A defendant cannot be bound by a document which he has not signed unless he has in effect incorporated it in the document which he had signed, in which case he would be regarded as having notionally signed both documents; but as he cannot be taken to have incorporated or signed a document which does not exist, the theory is inapplicable except where the defendant has signed the second of two documents on which the plaintiff relies as together constituting a memorandum. If, however, on the same occasion and as part of one and the same transaction—for example, as here, the payment of a deposit under an oral agreement for sale—a vendor and purchaser sit down at a table and respectively write out a receipt and a cheque, then, assuming that these documents between them sufficiently evidence the terms of the bargain, it would be going too far to say that the vendor could not rely on them as constituting a memorandum if the purchaser signed his cheque a few seconds before the vendor signed the receipt. I think it is enough to say that the documents relied on were brought into being more or less contemporaneously for the purpose of furthering a bargain which the party had made,

and in the same case Jenkins L.J. said:

> . . . but I am, on the whole, of opinion that where two documents relied on as a memorandum are signed and exchanged at one and the same meeting as part of the same transaction, so that they may fairly be said to have been to all intents and purposes contemporaneously signed, the document signed by the party to be charged should not be treated as incapable of referring to the other document merely because the latter, on a minute investigation of the order of events at the meeting, is found to have come second in the order of preparation and signing.

The evidence is that on 4 September one half of the application to the building society was filled in by the second-named defendant immediately after the payment of the £800. The remaining half was completed at a subsequent date (probably 27 September). Thus, one half of the application to the building society and the receipt were contemporaneous: in my view, the receipt of 4 September and the whole of the application to the building society should be regarded as having come into existence in such circumstances that the signature to the receipt authenticates the building society application.

The next question is whether the receipt of 4 September and the building society application can be treated together as a memorandum or note. In my view, the reference to the deposit and [the property] and the close connection in time between the two documents enables me to read the documents together. The true principle on this matter was, I think, stated by Jenkins L.J. in *Timmins v Moreland Street Property Co.*, when he said:

> . . . I think it is still indispensably necessary, in order to justify the reading of documents together for this purpose [the provision of a memorandum or note in writing for the purposes of *Statute of Frauds*], that there should be a document signed by the party to be charged which, while not containing in itself all the necessary ingredients of the required memorandum, does contain some reference, express or implied, to some other document or transaction. Where any such reference can be spelt out of a document so signed, then parol [verbal] evidence may be given to identify the other document referred to, or, as the case may be, to explain the other transaction, and to identify any document relating to it. If by this process a document is brought to light which contains in writing all the terms of the bargain so far as not contained in the document signed by the party to be charged, then the two documents can be read together so as to constitute a sufficient memorandum for the purposes of s. 40 of the *Law of Property Act 1925* (an English statute). The laying of documents side by side may no doubt lead to the conclusion as a matter of *res ipsa loquitur* that the two are connected; but before a document signed by the party to be charged can be laid alongside another document to see if between them they constitute a sufficient memorandum, there must, I conceive, be found in the document signed by the party to be charged some reference to some other document or transaction.

If, therefore, the issue in the case be whether there was a sufficient memorandum or note in writing signed by the party to be charged of the agreement made on 4 September, I am of opinion that the plaintiff would succeed. But the agreement made on 4 September was varied by mutual consent on 4 November when the plaintiff and the defendants agreed that the plaintiff would purchase the house by way of lease and that the purchase money would be reduced by £100 and there is no memorandum or note in writing of this variation.

The real problem I think is whether the defendants can successfully contend that the contract of 4 September was varied by mutual agreement when there is a memorandum or note in writing of the contract of 4 September but not of the variation. In any discussion of this problem it is essential to distinguish between the case in which the parties to an agreement intend that agreement to find expression in a written contract and that in which the parties make an oral contract which is intended to be binding. If in the latter case a memorandum or note in writing is required by the *Statute of Frauds*, that memorandum or note does not become the contract. This distinction appears in s. 2 of the *Statute of Frauds* which so far as material provided:

> No action shall be brought . . . upon any contract or sale of lands, tenements or hereditaments, or any interest in or concerning them . . . unless the agreement upon which such action shall be brought, or some memorandum or note thereof, shall be in writing and signed by the party to be charged therewith or some other person thereunto by him lawfully authorised.

The same distinction was emphasised in *Thompson v The King* (Case 39) and in *Law v Robert Roberts and Co.* (1964). (This case is discussed fully on page 87.) In the first type of case, that is, where the parties intend their agreement to find expression in a written document, a subsequent oral variation of the contract is not effective unless it is evidenced by a memorandum or note in writing (see *Goss v Nugent* (1833) and the speech of Lord Atkinson in *British and Beningtons Ltd v N.W. Cachar Tea Co.* (1923). But in the other type of case, where the oral agreement is intended to be the contract, evidence may be given of an agreed variation even if there is a memorandum or note of the contract but not of the variation. This view is supported by the decision of the Court of Appeal in England in *Beckett v Nurse* (1948). In that case the plaintiff claimed specific performance of an alleged agreement for the sale of land and relied on a receipt as the memorandum or note in writing. The Court of Appeal held that the receipt was not the contract and that as the plaintiff was relying on an oral agreement for sale, the defendant was entitled to show that the real bargain between the parties was different from that contained in the memorandum.

In this case the evidence establishes that the oral contract made on 4 September was varied by mutual agreement on a subsequent date. The variation was that the defendants were to sell to the plaintiff not a freehold interest but a leasehold interest, but the amount of the rent to be paid and the date of the commencement of the lease were not agreed: as these were not agreed, there was never a valid contract to sell the property by lease or to grant a lease . . .

Case 33. Tierney v Marshall
Queen's Bench (1857) 7 Ir.C.L.R. 308

The defendant employed the plaintiff as his estate agent at a yearly salary of £20. When £100 arrears of salary were due, the plaintiff also became the defendant's tenant. It was verbally agreed that the plaintiff should retain the annual rent, which was less than his salary, in lieu of salary and the remainder to be applied in part payment of the arrears.

When the plaintiff was dismissed from his position, the defendant sued for the arrears of rent. The plaintiff sought to enforce the verbal agreement and the defendant argued that since it was an agreement which could not be performed within a year of its making it was invalid, having regard to the provisions of the *Statute of Frauds*.

Held that the verbal agreement fell within the *Statute of Frauds* which required such an agreement to be evidenced in writing and that therefore the agreement was unenforceable.

Crampton J.:

The court is unanimously of opinion, that the objection founded upon the *Statute of Frauds* ought to prevail. It appears to me, without going minutely into the case, that this contract was of such a nature as that it could not have been performed within the year. The arrears of salary amounted to upwards of £100, while the annual rent was but £17; and therefore, taking it arithmetically, it was wholly impossible that the contract could have been completed within the year. The intention of the parties, which is what we have to consider, seems to have been that the rent should be annually set off in liquidation of the arrears of the salary . . .

Perrin and Moore JJ. concurred.

Case 34. Farrington v Donohoe
Common Pleas (1866) I.R. 4 C.L. 704

The defendant verbally agreed to maintain a child known to be about five years old until she was able to 'do for herself'. When the defendant failed to honour his commitment the mother of the child sued.

Held that such an agreement came within the *Statute of Frauds* and to be enforceable there needed to be evidence in writing. The fact that the agreement might be determined within the year by the happening of a collateral event, such as the death of the child, did not convert the contract into one which could be performed within the year.

Monahan C.J.:

. . . The jury having found that the agreement was for the maintenance of the child till it was able to maintain itself, the child being between five and six years of age at the time, the question arises, was this an agreement not to be performed within a year? This part of the case has been argued at considerable length. It seems unnecessary to refer to the cases which have been cited, as they were all very carefully considered and commented on in the very recent case of *Murphy v O'Sullivan*, first in the Queen's Bench, and afterwards in the Court of Error, in which both courts held that an agreement to maintain a young person during his life was not an agreement not to be performed within a year, and therefore did not require to be in writing. The ground of that decision was, that the life of the party was an uncertain event which might determine [terminate] within a year, and was not, therefore, within the *Statute of Frauds*, but it was conceded in that case, that if the agreement were to maintain the party till he attained a given age, it would be within the *Statute*, though, of course, determinable by the death of the party, which event might have occurred within the year. So here the agreement to maintain the child till able to maintain itself clearly contemplated an event not to be performed within a year, though, of course, the agreement would have been determined by the collateral event—the death of the child—which might have happened within the year. We therefore are of opinion that the agreement found by the jury required to be in writing . . .

Case 35. Naughton v Limestone Land Co. Ltd
High Court [1952] Ir.Jur.Rep. 18

The plaintiff claimed that the defendant had entered into a verbal contract with him whereby it had agreed that in consideration of his going to England at its request, in order to study and learn underdraining, it would have work available for him on his return for a period of four years. The plaintiff went to England, completed his studies and returned four months later. When the plaintiff sued for wages which he claimed should have been paid while in England the defendant argued that the case fell within the *Statute of Frauds*.

Held that the since the agreement was to be performed in four years and three months it could not be regarded otherwise than as a contract not to be performed within a year. In the absence of any note or memorandum in writing signed by the defendant the agreement was unenforceable.

Dixon J.:

If the *Statute of Frauds* applies to this contract, the defendants have established a good defence. I think the contract alleged is within the Statute. I understand from the plaintiff that he was to go to England, return, and be employed for four years. He went to England, trained there and came back. Counsel says that on the authorities the case is taken out of the Statute since all that the plaintiff had to do was actually done and was intended to be done within the year, that all that the plaintiff had to do was to go to England, learn underdraining for three months, and return.

I cannot accept that that was all he had to do under the contract. He says that he did not regard himself as bound to work for four years. I think the contract necessarily contemplated he was going to work for four years. He could not earn under the contract unless he worked for four years. There was mutuality in this matter, and it was a part of the contract on his side that he would work for four years. The contract cannot be severed or regarded otherwise than as a contract contemplated to extend over one year, to extend four years and three months.

In *Donellan v Read* (1832) there was an existing lease, and over and above that the landlord contracted to do improvements, the tenant to pay an increase of rent. It is clear that it was contemplated by the parties that the landlord would perform his part of the contract within a year. The position in *Donellan v Read* is clearly different from that in the present case. There the landlord had only one specific thing to do. In the present case the parties must necessarily have contemplated that the plaintiff would serve four years.

In my view, the *Statute of Frauds* has to be applied and since the absence of a note or memorandum is a good answer to the claim, I hold that the action should be dismissed.

CHAPTER 7.

TERMS OF A CONTRACT

The contents of a contract are its terms. These determine the limits to which the parties are bound. The terms of a contract may be express or implied. Material statements made by the parties during negotiations leading up to the contract are divided into two. First, there are statements by which the parties intend to be bound. These are often referred to as warranties. Second, there are statements, called mere representations, which may help to induce the making of the contract but which are not intended to be binding. Whether a statement is a warranty or a mere representation is a question of construction in each case.

The parties to a contract may expressly state every term of the contract. Or, the parties may simply agree to the basic purpose of the contract together with a number of its obvious terms and leave the detailed terms to be implied from the surrounding circumstances. The courts when considering whether to imply terms into a contract do so on the basis that they are doing nothing more than the parties themselves would have done had they alerted their minds to the matter. Consequently, in some cases the court will imply a term:

Dundalk Shopping Centre Ltd v Roof Spray Ltd (Case 36) whereas in other cases it will not: *Ward v Spivack Ltd* (Case 37) and *Tradex (Ireland) Ltd v Irish Grain Board Ltd* (Case 38).

There are instances where statute law will imply specified terms into contracts governed by the statute: e.g. *Hire-Purchase Act 1946*, as amended, and *Sale of Goods and Supply of Services Act 1980*.

Case 36. Dundalk Shopping Centre Ltd v Roof Spray Ltd
High Court, unreported, 21 March 1979

The defendant, a specialist in a particular form of roofing, was engaged by the plaintiff to supply and instal a roof on the plaintiff's premises. The roof proved to be faulty. The plaintiff repudiated the contract and sued the defendant for damages.

Held in finding for the plaintiff that it was an implied term that the defendant would use reasonable care and skill in executing the work.

Finlay P.:

. . . There is no doubt that the defendants held themselves out as specialists in a specialist form of roof insulation. I am satisfied that they knew at the commencement of this contract that neither the architect, nor any person working with or on behalf of the main contractors had had previous experience of this particular type of roof insulation which had recently been introduced into Ireland. I am satisfied, therefore, that under the term undoubtedly implied into the contract that they would use reasonable care and skill in the carrying out of their work, they had a duty to provide for and insist upon any special precautions which were required during the course of their work either in the form of work to be carried out by other sub-contractors or by the main contractors or by acts to be refrained from or prohibited in relation to these people . . .

Case 37. Ward v Spivack Ltd
Supreme Court [1957] I.R. 40

The plaintiff was appointed sole agent over a defined area for the sales, on a commission basis, of the defendant's products. It was a term of this verbal contract that commission was to be paid on all orders, with certain exceptions, received by the defendant from customers in the plaintiff's area. No provision was made for payment of commission on the termination of the agency. On its termination by the defendant the plaintiff sought a declaration that a term should be implied in the contract that commission was to be paid, notwithstanding the termination of the contract, on all orders from former customers in his area who did business with the defendant during the period of the agency.

Held that before the court could imply such a term in the contract it would have to be certain that the parties would have agreed to the terms had it been discussed when the contract was being negotiated. To read such a term into the contract would not be to clarify the intention of the parties, unexpressed at the time of contracting, but would in effect be the making a new contract for the parties.

Maguire C.J.:

. . . It is settled law that a term may be implied in a contract to repair what Cheshire and Fifoot, (3rd edn, 1952, at p. 127) calls 'an intrinsic failure of expression'. Where there has been such a failure the judge may supply the further terms which will implement their (the parties) presumed intention and in a hallowed phrase give 'business efficacy' to the contract. 'In doing this he purports at least to do merely what the parties would have done themselves had they thought of the matter. The existence of this judicial power was asserted and justified in *The Moorcock* (1889).' In that case Bowen L.J. explained the nature of the implication in all the cases; he says where they were implied 'the law is raising an implication from the presumed intention of the parties, with the object of giving to the transaction such efficacy as both parties must have intended that at all events it should have.' The test to be applied by the court has been stated by several judges in much the same language.

It will be seen from the language used in so stating the tests that something more is required than the *probability* of which the President of the High Court speaks that the parties must have agreed to the term to be implied had the matter been mentioned. There must be something approaching certainty or as put by Jenkins L.J. in *Sethia (1944) Ltd v Partabmull Rameshwar* (1950) it must be 'clear beyond a peradventure that both parties intended a given term to operate, although they did not include it in so many words.'

Can it be said with the degree of confidence required that the parties must, had the matter been raised, have agreed to the continuance of commission on the basis contended for by the plaintiff. The President came unhesitatingly to the conclusion that it cannot be so said. With this I am in complete agreement. Whatever view one might take had the agency only related to orders obtained from customers introduced by the plaintiff, the fact that the contract was to pay commission on all orders with the exceptions mentioned suggests that the defendant was quite unlikely . . . to agree to the continuance of commission beyond the period of the agency. What had happened with regard to [another agent] supports this view strongly. Furthermore although it might have been a reasonable thing for the defendant to have agreed to continue to pay commission on orders from customers introduced by the plaintiff at least for some time after the termination of the agency I am quite unable to hold as the President does that had the matter been raised the defendant must have agreed. To read such a term into the contract would in my view not be to make clear the intention of the parties unexpressed at the time but would be to make a new contract.

Lavery, Kingsmill Moore, Ó Dálaigh and Maguire JJ. agreed.

Case 38. Tradex (Ireland) Ltd v Irish Grain Board Ltd
Supreme Court [1984] I.R. 1; [1984] I.L.R.M. 471

The defendant agreed to sell a quantity of grain in two lots to the plaintiff. Payment was to be financed by the plaintiff opening letters of credit* in favour of the defendant which were agreed would mature on 1 May. In April, the plaintiff took delivery of the first consignment. On 21 April, the defendant purported to rescind the contract on the ground that letters of credit had not been opened before delivery of the goods. Despite the defendant's action, the plaintiff opened letters of credit in favour of the defendant on 24 April, which could have been drawn on by the defendant from 1 May onwards. The plaintiff brought proceedings for breach of contract.

Held that the court would not imply into the contract a term that letters of credit be opened prior to the date of the first delivery of the goods because such a term was unnecessary to give business efficacy to the contract in view of the fact that the parties had agreed a specific date for the maturing of the letters of credit. The plaintiff was awarded damages.

O'Higgins CJ.:

. . . It goes without question that the courts may in any class of contract imply a term in order to repair an intrinsic failure of expression. This is done to give, as it is said, 'business efficacy' to a contract which would otherwise lack such. The existence of this power was asserted in the well-known case of *The Moorcock* (1889). In that case Bowen L.J. said:
> The implications which the law draws from what must obviously have been the intention of the parties, the law draws with the object of giving efficacy to the transaction and preventing such a failure of consideration

*A *letter of credit* is a form of documentary credit whereby the seller of goods is given a guarantee by a bank acceptable to him that, having delivered the goods he contracted to sell, he will be paid on presentation of stipulated documents.

as cannot have been within the contemplation of either side; and I
believe if one were to take all the cases, and they are many, of implied
warranties or covenants in law, it will be found that in all of them the
law is raising an implication from the presumed intention of the parties
with the object of giving to the transaction such efficacy as both parties
must have intended that at all events it should have. In business
transactions such as this, what the law desires to effect by the
implication is to give such business efficacy to the transaction as must
have been intended at all events by both parties who are business men;
not to impose on one side all the perils of the transaction, or to
emancipate one side from all the chances of failure, but to make each
party promise in law as much, at all events, as it must have been in the
contemplation of both parties that he should be responsible for in
respect of those perils or chances.

This power must, however, be exercised with care. The courts have no role
in acting as contract makers, or as counsellors, to advise or direct what
agreement ought to have been made by two people, whether businessmen
or not, who choose to enter into contractual relations with each other. This
much-quoted passage from the judgment of Bowen L.J. in *The Moorcock*
has been thus referred to by McKinnon L.J. in *Shirlaw v Southern
Foundries Ltd* (1939) as follows:

They are sentences from an *ex tempore* judgment as sound and sensible
as all the utterances of that great judge; but I fancy that he would have
been rather surprised if he could have forseen that these general remarks
of his would come to be a favourite citation of a supposed principle of
law, and I even think that he might sympathise with the occasional
impatience of his successors when *The Moorcock* is so often flushed for
them in that guise.

In the same case the same judge said:

Prima facie that which in any contract is left to be implied and need not
be expressed is something so obvious that it goes without saying; so that,
if, while the parties were making their bargain, an officious bystander
were to suggest some express provision for it in their agreement, they
would testily suppress him with a common 'Oh, of course!'

Can this test be applied in this case? Is it so obvious that the parties
intended as they contracted on 23 March that a week from then a letter of
credit providing for the payment on 1 May of £2.4 million would have
been established in favour of the defendant, at the plaintiff's bank? I
cannot see anything in the circumstances attendant on this contract or in
the manner in which the contract came about to suggest that it was
obviously the intention of the parties that such should be done. Nor can I
see anything in what was said or done or in the circumstances which would
suggest that such a letter should have been opened prior to the drawing of
any barley. The impracticability of doing so, the subsequent actions and
conduct of the parties—all of these suggest to my mind the absence of any
such intention. Further I cannot see that the absence of any term or

agreement as to when the letter of credit was to be opened in any way affected the business efficacy of the transaction: what was required was payment by a bank of the entire purchase money on the due date. This payment date was fixed and the date of the opening of the credit could in no way affect or alter or prejudice this payment.

I am strongly of the view, on reading the evidence, a view which was shared by the learned trial judge, that the plaintiff sought—genuinely—to fulfil their contract, that they never intended to repudiate it and would have abided by any reasonable request made by the defendant as to the date for the opening of the letter of credit. It seems to me that all that can be implied into the contract made by the two contracting parties . . . is that the managing director on behalf of the plaintiff should take reasonable and proper steps to finance the opening of a letter of credit which would mature for payment of £2.4 million on 1 May. If he had been dilatory in securing the transfer of funds to his own company or otherwise acted as if the contractual obligation would not be honoured, there might have been grounds for complaint by the defendant. In my view, in the circumstances of this case, their purported cancellation of the contract on 21 April was unjustified. I would accordingly hold that the plaintiff is entitled to succeed in their action.

Henchy and Griffin JJ. gave concurring judgments, Hederman J. agreed and McCarthy J. gave a dissenting judgment.

CHAPTER 8.

SUBJECT TO CONTRACT

It is common in contracts for the sale of land or premises to find the expression 'subject to contract' used by one party. The courts have given a number of distinct interpretations to this expression and it is difficult to reconcile these conflicting opinions. Some guidance may be obtained by resorting to the rule that each case is decided on its particular facts. Thus the appropriate meaning in any given situation may depend on the circumstances in which the expression is used.

Where the term is used during negotiations between the parties the use of the expression may prevent the conclusion of an enforceable contract: *Thompson & Son Ltd v The King* (Case 39). There has been a difference of judicial view where this expression is first used after an oral agreement has been concluded. In some cases the courts have taken the view that the expression does not prohibit the acknowledg-ment that an enforceable contract exists subject to its being formalised in writing: *Kelly v Park Hall School Ltd* (Case 40). The contrary judicial view has held that the use of the expression 'subject to contract' is inconsistent with the recognition of the existence of a concluded agreement between the parties: *Mulhall v Haren* (Case 41). Where the parties have not reached agreement the use of the expression merely emphasises that no enforceable contract has been concluded: *Carthy v O'Neill* (Case 42).

Case 39. Thompson & Son Ltd v The King

Kings Bench [1920] 2 I.R. 365

The parties were in negotiations for the purchase of some property. A considerable correspondence by letter and telegram took place. In the first of the material telegrams a servant on behalf of the defendant wired to the plaintiff that 'if you had made an offer without a condition which was obviously impossible it would have been accepted subject to contract.' The second telegram contained a similar reply. The plaintiff claimed that the parties had reached a concluded agreement and sought its enforcement.

Held that where an offer and acceptance are made subject to a subsequent formal contract, and if such contract is a condition or term which until performed keeps the agreement in suspense, the offer and acceptance have no contractual force. On the other hand, if all the terms are agreed on and a formal contract is only contemplated as putting the terms in legal shape, the agreement is effectual before and irrespective of such formal contract. On the facts and circumstances in the present case the agreement between the parties was made subject to the execution of a formal contract. The plaintiff's case was dismissed.

Molony C.J.:

. . . It is contended on behalf of the plaintiff that the telegrams of the 24 and 27 May 1919, form a complete and binding agreement, and that the agreement is not the less binding, either because it is expressly stated to be subject to contract, or on account of the subsequent correspondence between the parties.

A large number of cases have been referred to as regards the effect of making an agreement subject to the preparation of a formal contract, but I do not think the general principle is anywhere better stated than it was by Lord Westbury in *Chinnock v The Marchioness of Ely* (1865):

I entirely accept the doctrine contended for by plaintiffs' counsel, and for which they cite cases . . . which establish that if there had been a final agreement, and the terms of it are evidenced in a manner to satisfy the *Statute of Frauds*, the agreement shall be binding, although the parties may have declared that the writing is to serve only as instructions for a formal agreement, or although it may be an express term that a formal agreement shall be prepared and signed by the parties. As soon as the fact is established of the final mutual assent of the parties to certain terms, and those terms are evidenced by any writing signed by the party to be charged, or his agent lawfully authorised, there exist all the materials which this court requires to make a legal binding contract. But if to a proposal or offer an assent be given, subject to a provision as to a contract, then the stipulation as to the contract is a term of the assent, and there is no agreement independent of that stipulation.

This passage was quoted with approval by the Court of Appeal in England in the case of *Rossiter v Miller* (1878), and by Lord Cairns in the same case in the House of Lords, and also by Jessel M.R. in *Winn v Bull* (1877). In the last-mentioned case the defendant entered into a written agreement with the plaintiff to take a lease of a house for a certain term at a certain rent 'subject to the preparation and approval of a formal contract,' and no other contract was ever entered into between the parties. It was held that there was no final agreement of which specific performance could be enforced against the defendant. Jessel M.R., referring to the authorities, states the principle thus:—'It comes therefore to this, that where you have a proposal or agreement made in writing expressed to be subject to a formal contract being prepared, it means what it says, it is subject to and is dependent upon a formal contract being prepared. When it is not expressly stated to be subject to a formal contract, it becomes a question of construction whether the parties intended that the terms agreed should merely be put into form, or whether they should be subject to a new agreement, the terms of which are not expressed in detail. The result is that I must hold that there was no binding contract in this case, and that there must therefore be judgment for the defendant.'

In *Von Hatzfeldt-Wildenburg v Alexander* (1912) Lord Parker (then Parker J.) laid down the same principle in very clear words. He said:

It appears to be well settled by the authorities that if the documents or letters relied on as constituting a contract contemplate the execution of a further contract between the parties, it is a question of construction whether the execution of the further contract is a condition or term of the bargain, or whether it is a mere expression of the desire of the parties as to the manner in which the transaction already agreed to will in fact go through. In the former case there is no enforceable contract, either because the condition is unfulfilled, or because the law does not recognise a contract to enter into a contract. In the latter case there is a binding contract, and the reference to the more formal document may be ignored. The fact that the reference to the more formal document is in words which according to the natural construction import a condition, is generally, if not invariably, conclusive against the reference being treated as the expression of a mere desire.

Upon these authorities it would appear to me to be abundantly clear that there was no binding contract in this case constituted by the two telegrams.

The plaintiff relies upon the case of *Bonnewell v Jenkins*, but in that case Fry J., who tried it originally, and the Court of Appeal both came to the conclusion that there was on the correspondence a simple acceptance of the offer made by the plaintiff, accompanied by a mere statement of an intention that the arrangement should be reduced into a formal contract, and they held that, having regard to the authorities, the letters did constitute a binding contract.

In *Lewis v Brass* the Court of Appeal held that an intimation in the written acceptance of a tender that a contract will be afterwards prepared did not prevent the parties from becoming bound to perform the terms in the tender and acceptance respectively mentioned; but in that case also the court came to the conclusion that the intention of the parties was thereby to enter into an agreement, and that the preparation of the contract was contemplated merely for the purpose of expressing the agreement already arrived at in formal language.

The plaintiff also strongly relies upon the case of *North v Percival*. Where certain 'heads of agreement' had been entered into between a vendor and purchaser, and stated to be expressly 'subject to approval of conditions and form of agreement' by purchaser's solicitor, it was held by Kekewich J. that the 'heads of agreement' constituted a complete contract, and that the clause 'subject to approval,' &c., was not a condition precedent to a complete contract. I agree, however, with the criticism of Parker J. of this case in the case of *Von Hatzfeldt-Wildenburg v Alexander*, where, having stated the rule in the terms which I have already quoted, he said: '*North v Percival* appears to be an exception to this rule; but I doubt whether that case was correctly decided. See the earlier decision of Sir George Jessel in *Winn v Bull*.'

I have hitherto considered the legal aspect of the case on the construction of the two telegrams; but if the subsequent correspondence is referred to, the matter becomes even more clear. There are numerous authorities for saying that although two letters or, as in this case, telegrams standing alone may be evidence of a sufficient contract, yet a negotiation for an important term of purchase and sale carried on afterwards is enough to show that the contract was not complete.

In *Hussey v Horne-Payne* the House of Lords held that where a court has to find a contract in a correspondence, and not in one particular note or memorandum formally signed, the whole of that which has passed between the parties must be taken into consideration, and in that case they decided that, although the first two letters of a correspondence seemed to constitute a complete contract, they were at liberty to come to the conclusion upon the whole of what had passed in letters and conversations that no concluded and complete contract had been established.

In *Bellamy v Debenham*, the last-mentioned case was discussed by North

J., and he came to a conclusion which seems peculiarly applicable to the present case. He said:

> In the present case we find that the vendor's solicitors proposed to introduce into the formal contract terms which they had no authority whatever to introduce, or even to ask for, if they were at variance with the written agreement—which they had no right whatever to ask for, supposing that the letters written in April contained all the terms of the arrangement which had been then definitely arrived at. It is, therefore, a fair argument to say that it is impossible that the parties can have arrived at a concluded agreement when the vendor's solicitors took such a step as they did.

> In my opinion it is clear that the telegrams of the 24 and 27 May 1919, do not in themselves constitute a binding contract; and this conclusion is strengthened by the consideration of the subsequent correspondence, which proceeded on the basis that no concluded agreement had been arrived at, and which shows that the Ministry of Munitions were anxious to have the draft agreement executed, while the plaintiff was endeavouring to negotiate for new terms, which were definitely rejected by the Ministry of Munitions.

Gibson and Gordon JJ. delivered concurring judgments.

Case 40. Kelly v Park Hall School Ltd
Supreme Court [1979] I.R. 340; 113 I.L.T.R. 9

The parties entered into an oral agreement which covered all the essential terms for the sale of land. The first letter, written on behalf of the defendant, acknowledged the oral agreement and stated that the agreed terms were subject to contract. When the defendant failed to complete the sale the plaintiff sought specific performance of the contract and was met with the defence that there was not a sufficient note or memorandum in writing of the contract to satisfy the *Statute of Frauds*.

Held that the oral agreement recorded in the letter was a completed agreement and that nothing further was left to be negotiated. The words 'subject to contract' must be taken to mean that a contract had been made subject to its being formalised in writing. Therefore the letter constituted a sufficient memorandum.

Henchy J.:

. . . The case hangs on whether the letter of 19 December 1977, which I have quoted, constitutes a sufficient memorandum for the purpose of the *Statute of Frauds*. In my opinion it does. It contains not only all the essential terms of the contract but also a recognition that a contract had been made. It says: ' . . . we have agreed terms, subject to contract . . . '. Since the judge [in the High Court], having heard oral evidence, held that the oral agreement recorded in the letter was a completed agreement in the sense that nothing further was left to be negotiated, the words 'we have agreed terms, subject to contract' must be taken to mean that a contract had been made, subject to its being formalised in writing. Therefore, it constitutes a sufficient memorandum . . . [This case is also discussed on p. 84.]

Kenny and Parke JJ. agreed.

Case 41. Mulhall v Haren
High Court [1981] I.R. 364

The parties entered into an oral agreement which covered all the essential terms for the sale of a house. Subsequently a first letter written on behalf of the plaintiff stated that the sale was subject to contract and requested the defendant to forward a contract. When the defendant refused to proceed with the contract the plaintiff sought specific performance of the contract and sought to prove that the correspondence constituted a sufficient note or memorandum in writing as to satisfy the *Statute of Frauds*.

Held that the statement that the sale was subject to contract was inconsistent with the recognition of the existence of a concluded agreement between the parties and prevented that letter, and the subsequent correspondence, from being accepted as a sufficient memorandum or note in writing to satisfy the *Statute of Frauds*.

Keane J.:

. . . There remains the defence under s. 2 of the *Statute of Frauds 1695*, which provides:

No action shall be brought whereby to charge any executor or administrator upon any special promise, to answer damages out of his own estate, or whereby to charge the defendant upon any special promise to answer for the debt, default, or miscarriage of another person, or to charge any person upon any agreement made upon consideration of marriage, *or upon any contract of sale of lands, tenements, or hereditaments, or any interest in or concerning them, or upon any* agreement that is not to be performed within the space of one year from the making thereof, unless the agreement upon which such action shall be brought, or some memorandum or note thereof, shall be in writing, and signed by the party to be charged therewith, or some other person thereunto by him lawfully authorized.

The section is in identical terms to s. 4 of the (English) Statute of Frauds, 1677. With regard to the Act of 1677, the italicised words were repealed in England and replaced by s. 40 of the *Law of Property Act 1925*, which provides:

> No action may be brought upon any contract for the sale, or other disposition of land or any interest in land, unless the agreement upon which such action is brought, or some memorandum or note thereof, is in writing, and signed by the party to be charged or by some other person thereunto by him lawfully authorised.

It has been held in England that s. 40, sub-s. 1, of the Act of 1925 is to be construed in the same manner as was applied to s. 4 of the Statute of 1677 prior to 1926: see *Tiverton Ltd v Wearwell Ltd* (1975).

It was submitted on behalf of the plaintiff that the letters to which reference has already been made, the receipt and the draft contract together constituted a memorandum or note sufficient to satisfy the Statute of 1695. It was submitted on behalf of the defendant that the use of the expression 'subject to contract' in the letters which initiated the correspondence prevented that correspondence, and the documents incorporated therewith, from constituting a sufficient memorandum or note. As I understand this submission, it is based on the proposition that the memorandum or note to which the section refers must be a memorandum or note of the agreement sued upon and, accordingly, it must recognise, either expressly or by implication, the existence of that contract. Since the use of the words 'subject to contract' is inconsistent with the existence of a concluded agreement (the argument runs), the use of that expression in the memorandum or note relied upon prevents it from being a sufficient memorandum or note for the purpose of the statute.

Had this question arisen prior to the decision of the English Court of Appeal in *Law v Jones* (1974), it would have been possible to resolve it with comparative ease. Indeed, I venture to think that, prior to that decision, very few members of either branch of the legal profession in England or Ireland would have thought that a writing which expressly stated that a sale of property was 'subject to contract' could constitute a memorandum or note sufficient to satisfy the *Statute of Frauds*. I believe that the same view would have been taken of a letter from a solicitor which formed part of a chain of correspondence commencing with a letter containing the 'subject to contract' stipulation. A series of authorities in both jurisdictions (commencing with *Winn v Bull* (1877)) had established beyond serious doubt the principle that an oral agreement for the sale of land which was stated to be subject to contract was not enforceable. As a result, it had become a common practice for solicitors, who were acting for parties who had entered into such oral agreements, to commence the correspondence with a letter stating that the sale was 'subject to contract'. Their reasons for doing so were twofold. In the first place, they were conscious of the danger of committing their clients to an open contract for the sale of land by writing a letter which provided the necessary writing to satisfy the statute, a danger which was of particular significance having regard to the complexity of the law of real property. In the second place, they were alive to the possibility that disputes might arise as to the actual terms of the concluded bargain which could only result in expensive litigation.

But while this practice was common, it was by no means universal. Occasions arose, perhaps particularly in the sale of registered land, when the title was so abundantly clear as greatly to reduce the dangers to either party of an open title. There were also occasions on which solicitors, mindful of the fact that their clients had secured good bargains, avoided the use of the phrase 'subject to contract'. In such cases, however, the solicitors frequently used language which indicated that the parties contemplated the execution of a formal agreement. Thus, a solicitor initiating the correspondence, while not stating that the sale was 'subject to contract', might use some expression such as 'please let us have draft contract for approval'. In cases where a dispute arose as to whether, in such circumstances, an enforceable contract existed, the court had to undertake an enquiry as to what was the intention of the parties and, in particular, what was the significance of the fact that they contemplated the execution of a formal agreement. These cases must be carefully distinguished from the cases in which the documents stated that the sale was 'subject to contract'. They are fully reviewed in the judgment of Mr Justice Kenny in *Law v Robert Roberts & Co.* (1964), which was unanimously upheld by the Supreme Court on appeal. They are also reviewed in detail in the judgment delivered by Mr Justice Costello on the 28 July 1977, in *Arnold v Veale* (1979) where the judge was at pains to draw the distinction between the two lines of authority.

One of the earliest statements of the principle that the use of the phrase 'subject to contract' normally indicates that neither party to an arrangement intends to be bound by the terms of the arrangement until they are embodied in a form of contract is to be found in *Winn v Bull*. In that case, the defendant agreed with the plaintiff to take a lease of a house for a certain term at a certain rent 'subject to the preparation and approval of a formal contract'. No other contract was ever entered into between the parties. Jessel M.R. said:

Now with regard to the construction of letters which are relied upon as constituting a contract, I have always thought that the authorities are too favourable to specific performance. When a man agrees to buy an estate, there are a great many more stipulations wanted than a mere agreement to buy the estate and the amount of purchase-money that is to be paid. What is called an open contract was formerly a most perilous thing, and even now, notwithstanding the provisions of a recent Act of Parliament—the *Vendor and Purchaser Act 1874*—no prudent man who has an estate to sell would sign a contract of that kind, but would stipulate that certain conditions should be inserted for his protection. When, therefore, you see a stipulation as to a formal agreement put into a contract, you may say it was not put in for nothing, but to protect the vendor against that very thing. Indeed, notwithstanding protective conditions, the vendor has not unfrequently to allow a deduction from the purchase-money to induce the purchaser not to press requisitions which the law allows him to make. All this shews that contracts for purchase of lands should contain something more than can be found in the short and meagre form of an ordinary letter . . . It comes, therefore, to this, that where you have a proposal or agreement made in writing expressed to be subject to a formal contract being prepared, it means what it says; it is subject to and is dependent upon a formal contract being prepared. When it is not expressly stated to be subject to a formal contract it becomes a question of construction, whether the parties intended that the terms agreed on should merely be put into form, or whether they should be subject to a new agreement the terms of which are not expressed in detail. The result is, that I must hold that there is no binding contract in this case, and there must therefore be judgment for the defendant.

The latter passage was cited by Moloney C.J. in the leading Irish case: *Thompson v The King* (Case 39). In that case, the words used were 'subject contract' and it was held that the agreement came within what might be called the 'subject to contract' line of authorities as distinct from the line of authorities applied in *Law v Robert Roberts & Co.* Accordingly, the agreement was held to be unenforceable. Gibson J. put the matter thus: '2. Did this expression 'subject contract' defer contractual obligation till a formal contract was settled, accepted, and executed; or does it mean that the purchase terms have been fully and finally settled, a further contract was only contemplated for the purpose of putting the bargain into legal shape, without substantial additions or alterations? I adopt the former construction.'

In *Lowis v Wilson* (1949) an attempt was made to distinguish *Winn v Bull* on the ground that the agreement signed by the plaintiff purchaser stated that it was 'subject to the preparation of a formal contract to be prepared by the solicitor for the vendor . . .'. Dixon J. rejected the submissions that this rendered the case distinguishable from *Winn v Bull* (1877). Recently, in *In re Hibernian Transport Cos. Ltd* (1972) Mr Justice Walsh said: ' . . . in the ordinary course of events an agreement for the sale or purchase of land subject to contract means nothing more than an agreement to enter into a contract for the sale of land and, as such, it is not enforceable as if it were a contract.' It is right to say that this observation of the learned judge was probably *obiter*, but it is nonetheless noteworthy that no other member of the full Supreme Court who agreed with his judgment on the principal issue expressed any dissent from his view on this matter.

The same principle was applied in England in a number of cases subsequent to *Winn v Bull* . . . It was also the view of a particularly strong Court of Appeal (consisting of Lord Greene M.R., Cohen and Asquith L.JJ.) in *Eccles v Bryant & Pollock* (1948). In this latter case, indeed, it was made clear that, in England at all events, where parties enter into an agreement for the sale of real property 'subject to contract', the contract is not complete until the parties have exchanged their copies in accordance with ordinary conveyancing practice in that country. Accordingly, in that case, even though the vendor's solicitors had signed the contract, it was held that the fact that no exchange of contracts had taken place was sufficient to prevent an enforceable contract from coming into being. In this country, however, the practice of exchanging contracts is not so universally followed as in England, at all events outside Dublin, as is borne out by the evidence of . . . the very experienced solicitor for the plaintiff. Subject to this qualification, however, the law in both jurisdictions on this topic was the same and, until recent years, was settled, in my view, by this massive body of authority beyond any serious doubt.

But while the law on this topic had the advantages of reasonable certainty, it was also capable of producing results which appeared harsh and unjust. The extraordinary volatile market in land which developed in England and Ireland during the 1970s also led to a practice as unattractive as its name which is 'gazumping'. A vendor of land who had shaken hands on a deal frequently found himself with a substantially more attractive offer for the property within days, or even hours. There were many vendors who, whatever the temptations, refused to resile from bargains freely entered into, whether they were legally enforceable or not. But there were also some who either accepted the higher offer or went back to their original purchaser and attempted to squeeze more money out of him. Where no shadow of a memorandum in writing existed, even the most resourceful of lawyers or courts were powerless to redress such inequities unless, indeed, the doctrine of part performance could be successfully invoked. But where anything which could conceivably be regarded as a memorandum existed, considerable ingenuity was naturally expended upon bringing about the downfall of the 'gazumper'. It was perhaps to be expected that, in this context, some attempt would be made to dislodge the well-entrenched 'subject to contract' rule.

The first bridgehead was effected in *Griffiths v Young* (1970). The plaintiff in that case wished to buy a plot of land from the defendant, who was not anxious to complete the contract of sale immediately. In April 1963, the defendant asked the plaintiff to guarantee his bank overdraft and the plaintiff said that he was prepared to consider doing so if the defendant would agree to sell the land in question. The parties discussed all the terms of the contract of sale and subsequently visited their solicitors. On 2 May the plaintiff's solicitor wrote to the defendant's solicitor setting out all the terms of the agreement for the sale of the land, but the price was expressed to be 'subject to contract'. On 3 May the defendant began pressing the plaintiff to provide the bank guarantee. The plaintiff got in touch with his solicitor, who telephoned the defendant's solicitor and informed him that if the defendant was to have the plaintiff's guarantee at once there must be a binding contract of sale at once, and that the reference to the arrangements being treated as 'subject to contract' must be regarded as having been amended. Later on the same day, the defendant's solicitor replied to the letter of 2 May as follows: 'With reference to your letter of the 2nd instant, we confirm that we have received instructions from Mr. Young *(the defendant)* to sell the property mentioned in your letter . . . for £3,500 with completion at Michaelmas 12 months . . .' He signed the letter as agent for the defendant. On 7 May the plaintiff gave the guarantee. In an action for specific performance of the agreement, the trial judge held that the letter of 2 May amounted to an unconditional offer and the letter of 3 May was an acceptance of this offer, and he granted a decree of specific performance. The defendant appealed on the ground that there was no sufficient memorandum or note of the agreement to satisfy s. 40, sub-s. 1, of the Act of 1925.

It was argued on behalf of the defendant that, while the two letters taken together constituted a memorandum, they could not constitute a memorandum of the agreement mentioned in s. 40, since the first letter contained on its face an assertion (in the words 'subject to contract') that no agreement had been concluded. It was argued on behalf of the plaintiff that the phrase 'subject to contract' was not a term of the contract but merely referred to a 'suspensive condition' which had been subsequently waived and could, accordingly, be ignored for the purpose of determining whether there was a sufficient memorandum or note of the agreement actually concluded. Widgery L.J., as he then was, thought the point a difficult one; but he appears to have accepted the general principle that a memorandum which, on its face, asserted that agreement had not been reached, could not be a memorandum for the purpose of section 40. He accepted the submission made on behalf of the plaintiff that this principle had no application where the only defect in the memorandum was a reference to a 'suspensive provision' which had subsequently been waived. The other members of the Court (Russell and Cross L.JJ.) came to the same conclusion, but neither of them appear to have experienced the same difficulty which troubled Widgery L.J. They were both satisfied that the subsequent oral waiver of the 'suspensive condition' cured any defect in the memorandum.

The far-reaching implications of the decision in *Griffiths v Young* soon became apparent when *Law v Jones* came before the same court—this time composed of Russell, Buckley and Orr L.JJ. In that case there was an oral agreement on 17 February 1972, for the sale by the defendant to the plaintiff of a certain property for £6,500. On 18 February, the defendant's solicitors wrote to the plaintiff's solicitors referring to the plaintiff's 'proposed purchase of the above property for £6,500 subject to contract' and stating that they would obtain the title deeds and submit a draft contract as soon as possible. On 25 February, they wrote again referring to the earlier letter and enclosing the draft contract which contained all the essential terms of the agreement. On 7 March the plaintiff's solicitors acknowledged receipt of both letters and the draft contract. The defendant then sought a further £1,000 and on 13 March the parties agreed orally to increase the price to £7,000. The trial judge accepted the plaintiff's evidence that on that occasion the defendant said to the plaintiff: 'I shall not go back on my word. My word is my bond. It is yours now: carry on and make all your arrangements.' The defendant's solicitors wrote on 17 March confirming that an increase in the purchase price to £7,000 had been agreed. A completion date of 21 April 1972, was agreed. But on the 13 April the defendant wrote to the plaintiff informing him that, because of the upsurge in house prices, he had decided to put the property up for auction. It was as blatant and indefensible a piece of 'gazumping' as could be imagined.

On this occasion, Russell L.J., found himself in the minority. He said that the language of the writings prior to the letter dated the 17 March could not constitute a sufficient memorandum of the oral contract of the 17 February at the price of £6,500 because of the language of the first letter in the chain dated the 18 February, i.e., the reference to a 'proposed purchase . . . subject to contract'. The letter of 17 March was, accordingly, no more than a written record of an agreed variation of a term in a contract which was still in the course of negotiation. He thought it unnecessary to decide whether the written memorandum had to point positively to an existing contract; it was clear, in his view, that at the very least, the language used must not negative the existence of a contract. He distinguished *Griffiths v Young* on the basis that in that case 'subject to contract' was merely a suspensive condition which had been later orally agreed to be waived and was, therefore, to be treated as not incorporated in the letter of the 3 May.

Buckley L.J. considered that little turned on the use of the expression 'his proposed purchase' in the letter of 18 February 1972. Much of his judgment is devoted to considering the effect of the words 'subject to contract' in the same letter. He accepted that a writing which denied the existence of a contract could not constitute a written memorandum or note for the purposes of the section: but he did not consider it necessary that the writing should positively acknowledge the existence of a contract. There was only one qualification, in his view, to the latter proposition. The qualification was that, where the writing denied liability under the contract, it was essential that the writing should also acknowledge the existence of the contract since, otherwise, it could only reasonably be read as a denial of its existence. In the instant case, an entirely new contract had been entered into on 13 March, the terms of which had admittedly to be ascertained by reference to the earlier contract of 17 February and the correspondence arising out of it, but in his view this did not mean that the letter of 17 March acknowledging the new contract should be read as being qualified by the words 'subject to contract' contained in the letter of 18 February.

So far as the applicable law is concerned, the crucial passage from the judgment of Buckley L.J. is:

> But it is not, in my judgment, necessary that the note or memorandum should acknowledge the existence of a contract. It is not the fact of agreement but the terms agreed upon that must be found recorded in writing.

In support of this far-reaching proposition, Buckley L.J. cited a passage from the judgment of Lord Westbury L.C. in *Chinnock v Ely* (1865) which had also been cited with approval by Lord Cairns in *Rossiter v Miller* (1878). He also referred to what he described as the 'well established law' that an offer in writing, signed by or on behalf of the offerer, may serve as an effective memorandum or note in writing although accepted only orally; he said that in such a case the writing clearly could not record or acknowledge a contract existing at the time of writing. One other feature of Buckley L.J.'s judgment must be noted. He said, 'It is clear that where a principal has entered into a binding contract, neither he nor his solicitor can thereafter deprive it of its binding effect by unilaterally treating the transaction as "subject to contract" . . . ' He also appears to have taken the view that the solicitor in that case when using the phrase 'subject to contract' had acted without authority.

Orr L.J. agreed with Buckley L.J. and, accordingly, the appeal in *Law v Jones* was dismissed.

In the words of Lord Denning M.R. in *Tiverton Ltd v Wearwell Ltd* (1975), the decision in *Law v Jones* 'sounded an alarm bell' in the offices of every solicitor in England. I recall the decision being greeted with equal consternation in Ireland. In England, it prompted a leading article in the *Solicitor's Journal* (117 Sol. Jo. 293) and a lengthy correspondence from solicitors in the same periodical. The earliest possible opportunity was taken of questioning the correctness of the decision. The appeal from the order of Goulding J. in *Tiverton Ltd v Wearwell Ltd* was heard by the Court of Appeal (Lord Denning M.R., Stamp and Scarman L.JJ.) as a matter of urgency within a few months.

In the *Tiverton Case* the plaintiffs orally agreed on 4 July 1973, on a sale of a property in Stepney to the defendants for £190,000. All the terms of the contract were agreed. Each side agreed to instruct their solicitors to confirm the sale. The purchasers' solicitors wrote on the same day to the vendors' solicitors as follows:

Empire House

We understand that you act for the vendor in respect of the proposed sale of the above-mentioned property to our clients Wearwell Ltd. at £190,000 leasehold subject to contract. We look forward to receiving the draft contract for approval together with copy of the lease at an early date.

On the next day the vendors wrote to the purchasers as follows:
> This is to confirm my telephone conversation with you this morning
> when you agreed that the completion of the purchase of the property
> can take place as soon as possible.

On 9 July the vendors' solicitors wrote to the purchasers' solicitors:
> We refer to your letter dated July 4, upon which we have taken our
> client's instructions. We now send you draft contract for approval,
> together with a spare copy for your use, together with a copy of the
> lease dated October 30, 1934, and photocopy entries on our client's land
> certificate. We await hearing from you.

On 19 July the vendors' solicitors wrote to the purchasers' solicitors
saying that they understood that the matter was not proceeding any
further. The purchasers' solicitors thereupon registered a caution at the
Land Registry to prevent any dealings with the property by the vendors.
The vendors thereupon issued proceedings claiming a declaration that
there was no valid and enforceable contract, and asking for an order that
the registration of the caution be vacated. Goulding J. ordered that the
caution be cancelled and the purchasers appealed to the Court of Appeal.
The appeal was specially expedited because of the importance of the point.

Lord Denning, after a detailed review of the authorities, summed up his
view of the law as follows:
> I cannot myself see any difference between a writing which—(i) denies
> there was any contract; (ii) does not admit there was any contract; (iii)
> says that the parties are in negotiation; or (iv) says that there was an
> agreement 'subject to contract,' for that comes to the same thing. The
> reason why none of those writings satisfies the statute is because none of
> them contains any recognition or admission of the existence of a
> contract.

He thought that *Griffiths v Young* could be distinguished. In his view,
however, *Law v Jones* was not capable of being distinguished; it was
wrongly decided and should be overruled. In the course of his judgment,
Lord Denning expressed his disagreement with the view of Buckley L.J.
that authority for the proposition that the writing need not recognise the
existence of a contract was to be found in a series of decisions dealing with
offers in writing which were accepted by the other party by word of mouth
or by conduct. He pointed out that these were decisions of common-law
courts which did not recognise the doctrine of part performance and were,
accordingly, necessary to meet the justice of the individual cases. It was
accordingly held that a proposal made in writing but accepted verbally was
capable of constituting a sufficient memorandum or note: see *Reuss v
Picksley* (1866). But Denning M.R. also cited a passage from the judgment
of Bowen L.J. in *In re New Eberhardt Co.* (1889) in which he said that
Reuss v Picksley had pushed the literal construction of the *Statute of
Frauds* 'to a limit beyond which it would perhaps be not easy to go'.

[In the] *Tiverton Case* Stamp L.J. posed the question for decision as being ' . . . whether it is the law of England that a note or memorandum can satisfy the statute if, when read alone or with other documents which can properly be read with it, he who has signed it does not thereby recognise the existence of the contract upon which the other party seeks to make him liable'. He went on to say that the letter of 9 July 1973, whether read in isolation or together with the letter to which it was a reply, did not recognise the existence of a contract made orally on 4 July or any contract. While he does not say so in so many words, I think it is an inescapable inference that it was the use of the phrase 'proposed sale . . . subject to contract'·in the letter of the 4 July which rendered that letter incapable of being read as recognising the existence of a contract. Having gone on to consider the authorities in detail, he summarised his view as follows:

> I consider that prior to the year 1970 it had been recognised by authorities binding upon this court (viz. *Buxton v Rust* (1872) and *Thirkell v Cambi* (1919)) that to satisfy the requirements of the statute there must be in the note or memorandum of the contract upon which the action is brought something to indicate that the party signing it thereby acknowledges or recognises the existence of the contract.

He also dealt with the 'offer' cases and said that they did not assist the defendants since those cases proceeded on the basis that a proposal in writing, though prior in time, could be a memorandum or note of a contract brought into being by the oral acceptance. He said that in such cases the court, in so holding, was accepting that the memorandum must recognise the contract on which the party charged is sued.

[In] the *Tiverton Case* Stamp L.J. quoted the succinct observation of Bowen L.J. in *In re Hoyle; Hoyle v Hoyle* (1893) that the court, in determining whether a document is a sufficient memorandum, is not 'in . quest of the intention of the parties, but only of evidence under the hand of one of the parties to the contract that he has entered into it'. He also pointed out that in *Buxton v Rust* (which was not cited to the court in *Law v Jones*) Willes J. and Lush J. both clearly indicated that, in their view, it was necessary that the letters relied on should constitute a recognition of the contract sued upon. He closely analysed the passage from *Chinnock v Ely*, on which Buckley L.J. had placed reliance, and concluded that it did not support the inferences drawn from it by Buckley L.J. He went on to express his view that *Griffiths v Young*, in so far as it decide the contrary, was in conflict with the earlier decisions to which he had referred in his judgment. Although accepting that *Law v Jones* was plainly in conflict with the view of the law which he considered had been established by the earlier authorities, he did not consider that the court had jurisdiction to overrule it and simply preferred to follow the earlier authorities.

Scarman L.J. agreed with Stamp L.J. In the result, the appeal in the *Tiverton Case* was dismissed. Leave to appeal to the House of Lords was granted but the appeal, so far as I can ascertain, was never pursued.

There are two features of the *Tiverton Case* which are of cardinal importance. In the first place, it proceeded on the assumption that the evidence would establish, if the issue had to be resolved, that there was a concluded oral agreement for the sale of the property. In the second place, the letter containing the words 'subject to contract' was written by the solicitors for the purchasers, i.e. the party who was seeking to enforce the oral agreement. The letter which was relied on as a memorandum did not contain those words, but it formed part of the same chain of correspondence. In its major features, accordingly, that case is indistinguishable from the present case.

Since the other members of the court did not share the view of Lord Denning that the Court of Appeal in England had jurisdiction to overrule its earlier decisions, the position in theory in England is that there are at least two conflicting decisions of the Court of Appeal and that the law in that jurisdiction cannot be regarded as certain beyond doubt. However, I think that it is more sensible to regard the forceful judgments of Lord Dennning and Stamp L.J. as representing the view of the law generally now held in England.

Buckley L.J. in *Daulia Ltd v Four Millbank* (1978) had this to say about the two cases:

Law v Jones did not decide that a letter written 'subject to contract' or forming part of a correspondence conducted subject to a 'subject to contract' stipulation can constitute a note or memorandum of an oral agreement to which it relates sufficient to satisfy the *Statute of Frauds*, at any rate so long as the 'subject to contract' stipulation remains operative. What it did decide was that, if the parties subsequently enter into a new and distinct oral agreement, the facts may be such that the earlier letter may form part of a sufficient note or memorandum of the later oral agreement notwithstanding that it was 'subject to contract' in relation to the earlier bargain. It also, of course, decided the quite different point that a written note or memorandum to satisfy the statute need not acknowledge the existence of the contract, although it must record all its essential terms. In that respect *Law v Jones* and *Tiverton Estates Ltd v Wearwell Ltd* are undoubtedly in conflict.

The reconciliation by the court in the *Tiverton Case* of the offer cases was sharply criticised by Buckley L.J. in the *Daulia Case*. But it also seems clear that the authority of *Law v Jones* must be significantly weakened by the fact that *Buxton v Rust*, a decision strongly in favour of the defendant, was not cited to the court.

The *Tiverton Case* was referred to in two subsequent English decisions. In *Michael Richards Properties v St Saviour's Parish* (1973) Goff, J., (as he then was) treated the words 'subject to contract' as meaningless where they appeared in a tender document which set out all the conditions which would normally appear in a standard contract of sale. He made it clear that his decision was not intended to cast any doubt on the meaning, effect and protection of the words 'subject to contract' as used in the normal conveyancing practice of everyday life. In *Munton v Greater London Council* (1976) the Court of Appeal (Lord Denning, Scarman and Goff L.JJ.) treated the earlier case as distinguishable. Lord Denning, in particular, treated it as a very special case which had been decided on its own facts. I may finally note that the opinion of academic commentators upon *Law v Jones* and the *Tiverton Case* appears to favour strongly the view taken in the latter case: see (1974) 90 L.Q.R. 1 and (1974) 37 M.L.R. 695. I have come to the conclusion that I should follow the latter case unless, of course, it has been disapproved of in this country.

It appears to me that the wording of s. 2 of the Statute of 1695 plainly envisages a writing which is evidence of a contract entered into by the party sought to be charged, and that this is not met by a writing which uses language inconsistent with the existence of a concluded contract. It also appears to me that a long line of authorities has clearly established that the use of the words 'subject to contract' is inconsistent with the existence of a concluded agreement, save in the most exceptional cases.

The post-1970 Irish decisions commence with *Arnold v Veale* (1979). That, as I have already indicated, was not a 'subject to contract' case when it was heard and decided by Mr Justice Costello. However, prior to the hearing of the defendant's appeal, a letter came to light written by the plaintiff to the defendant's auctioneer; in the course of that letter it was stated that certain matters remained to be agreed and that the sale was 'subject to contract'. The Supreme Court (the Chief Justice, Mr Justice Kenny and Mr Justice Parke) allowed the appeal. The main judgment of the Supreme Court was delivered ex tempore by Mr Justice Kenny and there is no written judgment available. However, it is clear from the judgment of Mr Justice Costello in the High Court that he found that there was a concluded oral agreement for the sale of the property. I appeared as counsel on the hearing of the appeal in the Supreme Court and my recollection is that it was not sought to disturb any finding of fact made by Mr Justice Costello and that the argument advanced on behalf of the defendant was that, in view of the plaintiff's letter to which I have referred, the correspondence could not constitute a sufficient memorandum to satisfy the requirements of the Statute of 1695. Accordingly, I take that decision as accepting, at least by implication, the principle that the writing relied on must acknowledge the existence of a concluded contract.

The next decision to which reference must be made is *Kelly v Park Hall School Ltd* (Case 40). In that case the trial judge (Mr Justice Hamilton) found that there was a concluded oral contract for the sale of the land. Two documents were relied upon as constituting a sufficient memorandum. The first was a letter dated 19 December 1977, from the auctioneers acting on behalf of the defendant vendors to the vendors' property adviser in the following terms:

Hall School—Lands at Rere

Dear Michael,

Further to our telephone conversation this morning, I confirm that we have agreed terms, subject to contract, for the sale of these lands to Mr Paddy Kelly of Berkeley Homes Ltd who were purchasers of the front lands. The principal terms to be included in the contract for sale are as follows:

Proposed purchaser: Hickey, Beauchamp, Kirwan & O'Reilly (in trust). Proposed price: £175,000.

A non-refundable deposit of £35,000 to be paid on exchange of contracts, the balance to be paid not later than 6 months thereafter with interest at 12% from the contract date until the closing date. I am sending a copy of this letter to Mr. Haugh of A. & L. Goodbody and perhaps you could kindly confirm instructions to him on behalf of the Committee.

The second writing relied on was a letter from the defendants' solicitors to the plaintiffs' solicitors dated 13 January 1978, which enclosed a draft contract and concluded with the following sentence: 'On the instructions of our clients, this offer remains open for acceptance by your clients for a period of seven days only from the date of this letter and we are instructed that, if the contract is not back with us within the said period of time, duly executed, the offer is deemed to be withdrawn.' In the High Court Mr Justice Hamilton held that this latter document was a sufficient memorandum, since it enclosed a draft contract containing all the material terms. On appeal to the Supreme Court (Mr Justice Henchy, Mr Justice Kenny and Mr Justice Parke) it was held that the letter from the auctioneers dated 19 December 1977, was a sufficient memorandum, and the appeal was dismissed. Mr Justice Henchy said:

The case hangs on whether the letter of the 19th December, 1977, which I have quoted, constitutes a sufficient memorandum for the purpose of the Statute of Frauds. In my opinion it does. *It contains not only all the essential terms of the contract but also a recognition that a contract had been made*. It says: ' . . . we have agreed terms, subject to contract . . . ' Since the judge, having heard oral evidence, held that the oral agreement recorded in the letter was a completed agreement in the sense that nothing further was left to be negotiated, the words 'we have agreed terms, subject to contract' must be taken to mean that a contract had been made, subject to its being formalised in writing. Therefore, it constitutes a sufficient memorandum.

The words which I have reproduced in italics appear to indicate an acceptance by Mr Justice Henchy of the proposition that the memorandum must recognise the existence of a concluded contract. Moreover, if the situation were otherwise, I consider it inevitable that the Supreme Court in that case would have expressed their disapproval of the decision in the *Tiverton Case*. It is noteworthy that Mr Justice Henchy appears not to have shared the view of the High Court judge that the letter of 13 January 1978 was a sufficient memorandum—presumably because he did not consider that that letter recognised the existence of a concluded contract. I am fortified in arriving at this conclusion on the effect of the decision in the *Park Hall Case* by the fact that a similar view of its effect was taken by Mr Justice Hamilton in *McInerney Properties Ltd v Roper* (1979).

While the decision in the *Park Hall Case* seems to have proceeded on the basis that the memorandum must contain a recognition that a contract has been made, it might on first reading appear to lend support to the proposition that the words 'subject to contract' are not inconsistent with the existence of a concluded contract. If that were the effect of the decision, it would mean that the Supreme Court, by necessary implication, was disapproving of the decision in the *Tiverton Case* and, also by implication, was overruling or disapproving of the long line of authority on the 'subject to contract' topic to which I have already referred. I doubt very much whether the Supreme Court intended to disapprove of the decision in the *Tiverton Case* or to disturb the authorities in question. Had that been their intention, I think it would have been made clear in the judgment of Mr Justice Henchy. It may be significant that the plaintiff in the *Park Hall Case* had already purchased the adjoining lands of the defendant and that, therefore, the title to the property being sold had been fully investigated by the plaintiff, so that the necessity for a formal contract had been significantly reduced. The actual wording used ('we have agreed terms, subject to contract') was also treated as being of importance. I think that the *Park Hall Case* should properly be regarded as a special one decided on particular facts which do not arise in the present case and, as such, to be more akin to the *St Saviour's Case* to which I have already referred.

The next case is *Casey v Irish Intercontinental Bank Ltd* (1979). In that case also the High Court found that there had been a concluded oral contract for the sale of the lands and that, as in the *Tiverton Case*, the oral agreement had not been made expressly 'subject to contract'. However, the writing relied on as a memorandum, so far as material, was in the following terms: 'I, Patrick Casey, Gurrane House, Donoughmore, agree to purchase Park House and lands for £110,000 subject to contract and title. I agree to pay £25,250 as deposit.' Mr Justice Costello found in favour of the plaintiff. I believe that he did so in a written judgment but, as the text is not available in the Central Office, I cannot say what his reasons were for arriving at this conclusion. On appeal his decision was upheld by the Supreme Court (Mr Justice Henchy, Mr Justice Kenny and Mr Justice Parke). The main judgment in the Supreme Court (with which the other two judges agreed) was delivered by Mr Justice Kenny. The greater part of that judgment is taken up with a point which does not arise in the present case. The only reference to the fact that the writing relied on had used the phrase 'subject to contract and title' is in the following passage from the judgment of Mr Justice Kenny at p. 368 of the report:

The words 'subject to contract and title' were not introduced into the transaction until the 2nd February when an oral contract for sale had already been made. Even if the reference to the contract and title is regarded as being incorporated in the contract, it does not make the execution of a contract a term of the agreement or a condition precedent to any contractual liability arising. I have already discussed this matter in the judgment which I gave, when I was a judge of the High Court, in *Law v Robert Roberts & Co.* That decision was affirmed by the Supreme Court and I do not intend to repeat what I said there.'

Before preparing this judgment I read with the utmost care the judgment delivered by Mr Justice Kenny in *Law v Robert Roberts & Co.* In none of the letters to which reference is made in the statement of facts taken from that judgment (and appearing at pp. 293–6 of the report) does the phrase 'subject to contract' or 'subject to contract and title' appear. Not merely are the letters in that case perfectly consistent with the existence of a concluded contract, but they go further. In his letter of 7 November 1960, Mr Hamilton, who was the auctioneer acting on behalf of the defendant vendors, said: 'We confirm herewith that acting on the instructions of our clients, Messrs Robert Roberts, we have accepted your offer of £4,750 and fees at $2\frac{1}{2}$ per cent for the above property . . . ' *Law v Robert Roberts & Co.* is in no sense a decision on the meaning of the words 'subject to contract.' Nor is it an authority on the question as to whether a writing which does not acknowledge the existence of a concluded contract can be a sufficient memorandum. As the letter of 7 November 1960 (and the other letters referred to in the judgment) recognised in the plainest terms the existence of a concluded contract, that question did not arise. In these circumstances, I confess to finding some difficulty in understanding the reference to the *Roberts Case* in the above passage from the judgment of Mr Justice Kenny in *Casey's Case*.

In the course of argument counsel suggested that Mr Justice Kenny, in delivering judgment in *Casey's Case*, must have overlooked the fact that the *Roberts Case* was not an authority on the 'subject to contract' issue. Whether that be so or not, I must apply the law as stated by the Supreme Court. If this passage has the effect contended for by counsel for the plaintiff, then, however that conclusion may have been arrived at, I am bound to apply the principle of law laid down. But it is stretching credibility too far for me to suppose that in this brief passage Mr Justice Kenny intended to overrule *Winn v Bull* and the other pre-1921 decisions on the 'subject to contract' point, *Thompson v The King* (Case 39) and *Lowis v Wilson*; and to express his disapproval of the numerous English authorities since 1921 on the same topic, culminating in the *Tiverton Case*. Since *Casey's Case* has not yet been reported, I do not know what arguments may have been advanced or what concessions made in the course of argument on either side. In these circumstances, I have come to the conclusion that I should not treat the decision as laying down any general principle of the nature contended for by counsel for the plaintiffs.

The last Irish case is *McInerney Properties Ltd v Roper* (1979). In this case again the High Court (Mr Justice Hamilton) found as a fact that there was a concluded oral contract for the sale of the land. The writings relied on by the plaintiff as constituting a sufficient memorandum were two letters (each being headed 'subject to contract') dated 23 March and 17 April 1978, from the defendant's solicitors, and a draft contract which, it was claimed, was incorporated therewith. Mr Justice Hamilton, having considered the authorities and, in particular, *Law v Jones*, the *Tiverton Case* and the *Park Hall Case*, came to the conclusion that the letters were a sufficient memorandum. He summarised his conclusion as to the effect of the *Tiverton Case* as follows: 'Consequently, it appears to me that the decision in *Tiverton Estates Ltd v Wearwell Ltd* was based not on the fact that the words "subject to contract" were used but that the writings sought to be relied upon as a sufficient note or memorandum did not contain an admission or a recognition that a contract had in fact been entered into.' That is a view which, with respect, I do not share. On the contrary, it seems to me that Lord Denning was at pains to emphasise that it was precisely the use of the words 'subject to contract' which prevented the writings from constituting an acknowledgment of the existence of a contract.

From this analysis of the authorities, I think that the following conclusions emerge:

1. A memorandum or note cannot satisfy the *Statute of Frauds* if, when it is read alone or with other documents which can properly be read with it, it does not contain a recognition, express or implied, of the existence of the oral contract sought to be enforced.

2. A letter, which expressly states that a transaction is 'subject to contract' cannot be a sufficient note or memorandum, since the use of those words is normally inconsistent with the existence of a concluded contract. It is only in certain rare and exceptional circumstances such as arose in *Kelly v Park Hall School* and *Michael Richards Properties v St Saviour's Parish* that the words 'subject to contract' can be treated as being of no effect.

3. In applying the two foregoing principles, it is immaterial whether the writing relied on itself contains the words 'subject to contract' or is part of a chain of correspondence initiated by a letter which makes it clear that any oral agreement already arrived at is 'subject to contract'.

It seems to me that the application of those principles to the present case is sufficient to dispose of the contention that the letters referred to can be treated as a sufficient note or memorandum.

It was urged on behalf of the plaintiff that the words 'subject to contract' had been inserted by the plaintiff's solicitor when he was acting on his own initiative and without any authority from his client and that, accordingly, they should be disregarded. If words which are clearly destructive of any recognition of a concluded contract appear in the memorandum, then it appears to me not to be a material consideration that they may have been inserted without authority. But altogether apart from that consideration, I cannot agree with the suggestion that these words were inserted by the solicitor without his client's authority. There was no question of his client's having expressly authorised him to use that expression; but I have not the smallest doubt that it was within his implied authority to do so. Any other view of the law would lead to the absurd consequences mentioned by Russell L.J. in his dissenting judgment in *Law v Jones*. A solicitor who is instructed by a party who has entered into an oral agreement for the sale of land is perfectly entitled, in my view, to write a letter which expressly prevents his client from being committed to an open contract and ensures that his client will have the full protection of a formal contract of sale. I think that this view of the law is consistent with the leading Irish authorities, i.e. *Cloncurry v Laffan* (1924); *Kerns v Manning* (1935); *Godley v Power* (1957) and *Black v Kavanagh* (1973). All of these cases emphasise that it is no part of a solicitor's function to alter the terms of an oral contract already entered into by his client. They also make it clear that a letter written by a solicitor for the purpose of carrying into effect an oral agreement already made *may* constitute a sufficient memorandum to satisfy the *Statute of Frauds*. But it would seem strange and illogical that a solicitor, whose function it is not to alter the terms of the bargain or to indulge in further negotiations, but to embody the bargain already concluded in a formal contract which gives his client the maximum protection consistent with that bargain—as contrasted with an open contract—should be regarded as exceeding his authority when he seeks to ensure that his client has the protection of a formal contract.

I indicated at an earlier stage of this judgment that there may indeed be cases in which a solicitor may feel that it is positively advantageous to his client to commit him to an open contract. I am far from saying that in such cases the solicitor is in any sense acting in dereliction of his duty to his client. But in the everyday case of a sale of property, where the parties have shaken hands on price but trust their respective solicitors to do everything that is necessary to protect them against all the traps and pitfalls that still beset the completion of sales of real property, a solicitor, in my view, is acting fully within the scope of his authority by making it clear in his initial letter that any oral agreement already concluded must be treated as 'subject to contract.' In so doing, he protects his client from the consequences of entering into an open contract. In the words of Lord Denning in the *Tiverton Case* he does it 'in the confidence that it protects his client. It means that the client is not bound by what has taken place in conversation. The reason is that, for over a hundred years, the courts have held that the effect of the words 'subject to contract' is that the matter remains in negotiation until a formal contract is executed . . . '

That seems to me to be both good law and good sense. Its practical application is indeed well illustrated by the present case. I have already said that the oral agreement in this case was plainly unconditional. The parties did not expressly say that their oral agreement was 'subject to contract.' Nor did they say that it was subject to the plaintiff obtaining the loan finance that he needed in order to complete the transaction; but the plaintiff's solicitor refrained from sending the formal contract back to the defendant's solicitors signed by his client until such time as he was satisfied that they were in funds to complete the transaction. I have not the slightest doubt that the plaintiff would have been appalled if, as a result of an unguarded letter written by his solicitor in the early stages of the transaction, he found himself faced with serious financial consequences because, for some unforeseen reason, the offer of loan finance was suddenly withdrawn. If the plaintiff's case is well founded, it would mean that, in those circumstances, he would have had no answer to a decree for specific performance in circumstances where he would not have had the finance to complete the transaction. The reason why the plaintiff did not expressly say to the auctioneer, or the defendant, that he regarded his oral agreement as subject to the obtaining of the necessary finance is obvious; he relied, as generations of house purchasers have relied, on the good sense and experience of their solicitor to protect them. If the submission made on behalf of the plaintiff is well founded, it means that persons entering into property transactions of this nature have been deprived of a very important protection. For the reasons I have already given, I do not think that the *Park Hall Case* and *Casey's Case* would support so far-reaching a proposition. In so far as the proposition is supported by *Law v Jones* and *McInerney Properties Ltd v Roper*, I must respectfully decline to follow those decisions.

I should add that solicitors in search of guidance on this topic could not do better, in my view, than to follow the advice given in Wylie's *Irish Conveyancing Law*, the authority of which is, of course, substantially enhanced by the fact that the consultant editor for the Republic of Ireland is Mr Justice Kenny. At par. 9.047 on p. 364 Mr Wylie had this to say:

> Thirdly, if explicit instructions have not been obtained, the greatest care should be taken in dealing with all correspondence relating to the transaction. If it is intended that the matter should be regarded as still subject to negotiation, i.e. in the pre-contract stage, this should be stated expressly in the correspondence, perhaps, *all* correspondence, e.g. by entering a note that the matter is still 'subject to contract'.

And he adds in a footnote: 'This will probably be enough to prevent the correspondence from being regarded as a sufficient memorandum, i.e. by denying the existence of an agreement . . . ' In this case, I think that the solicitor achieved precisely that result by his prudence in making it clear in the initial letters that he wrote that the matter was still 'subject to contract'. I am satisfied that the use of those words was sufficient to prevent any subsequent letter in that correspondence from being a valid memorandum or note for the purpose of the *Statute of Frauds* . . .

Case 42. Carthy v O'Neill*
Supreme Court [1981] I.L.R.M. 443

The plaintiff offered a stated sum for the defendant's licensed premises. The defendant consulted his solicitor, who then discussed it with the auctioneer who was advising the defendant. The auctioneer made the offer 'subject to contract'. The defendant agreed to sell the premises to the plaintiff. When it was discovered subsequently that the defendant was proposing to dispose of the premises to another party for a higher price the plaintiff sought specific performance of the contract.

Held that there was no concluded agreement between the parties in that the sole matter agreed was the price, and that the words 'subject to contract' were an indication that essential elements of the contract remained to be negotiated. The relief sought was refused.

Henchy J.:

. . . it is clear from the oral evidence and the three letters relied on that the agreement to sell made by the auctioneer on the defendant's behalf was made 'subject to contract'. This was no empty formula, as was the case in *Kelly v Park House School Ltd* (Case 40) where the memorandum relied on recited, and the trial judge found that all the terms of a completed oral contract had been agreed on, where the parties were each familiar with the title, where the vendor was willing to give and the purchaser was willing to accept that title, where nothing further remained to be negotiated, so that in the exceptional and special circumstances of that case the court could not avoid holding that 'subject to contract' meant no more than a proviso that what had been comprehensively but orally agreed on should be given the form of a written contract. The law on this topic has been carefully examined recently by Keane J. in *Mulhall v Haren* (Case 41) but unfortunately that decision has not been opened to us in this appeal.

The position here is quite different from the special circumstances disclosed in *Kelly v Park House School Ltd.* The three letters here alleged to constitute conjunctively a valid memorandum, far from reciting or evidencing a concluded oral contract, make clear that essential parts of what was expected to become a contract remained to be negotiated. They show that the date of completion had yet to be fixed, that the title on offer had to be submitted to the plaintiff's solicitor for approval, that no agreement had been come to as to the price to be paid for the stock and that other provisions such as require to be negotiated in a contract for the sale of a licensed premises as a going concern had yet to be agreed.

*This case is misentitled as *McCarthy v O'Neill* in the law report.

The auctioneer had died before the hearing in the High Court took place, but the three letters he wrote are ample testimony that all he had agreed on behalf of his principal, the defendant, was the purchase price, and that virtually every other aspect of the deal remained to be negotiated. Consequently, the words 'subject to contract' mean what they normally mean: that what had been agreed was subject to a full contract being agreed. The three letters, therefore, cannot be treated as a note or memorandum for the purpose of the *Statute of Frauds* . . .

O'Higgins C.J. and Kenny J. concurred.

CHAPTER 9.

CONSTRUCTION OF A CONTRACT

To construe the express terms of a contract, whether written or verbal, the courts have formulated rules of construction. In instances where one party is obliged to accept the written terms of the other party the courts have developed the *contra proferentem* rule which provides that the court will construe a written contract against the party who drew it up and insisted on its inclusion: *Alexander v Irish National Stud Co. Ltd* (Case 56) and *Western Potato Co-Operative Ltd v Durnan* (Case 43). The rule *generalia specialibus non derogant* is applied to written contracts: *Welch v Bowmaker (Ireland) Ltd* (Case 44).

In general, verbal, or parol evidence cannot be admitted to add to, vary, explain or contradict the terms of a written agreement. But the rigid application of such a rule in all cases would lead to injustice. In such cases extrinsic evidence is admitted to assist the court in resolving the dispute between the parties. Such evidence must not be doubtful: *Fallon v Robins* (Case 45). Parol evidence may be admitted to explain the circumstances surrounding the making of the agreement: *Revenue Commissioners v Moroney* (Case 46). It may also be admitted to ascertain the subject matter of the transaction: *Chambers v Kelly* (Case 47). Parol evidence may be admitted to ascertain the consideration: *Nolan v Graves* (Case 48).

Case 43. Western Potato Co-Operative Ltd v Durnan
Circuit Court [1985] I.L.R.M. 5

The parties entered into a written contract, which was in standard form, and drawn up by the plaintiff.

Held that insofar as the terms of the contract were contradictory and ambiguous they were to be interpreted *contra proferentem*, against the plaintiff in this instance.

Judge Clarke:

. . . In so far as any part of the clause proves to be in effect in conflict with or contradictory of the obligations imposed on the defendant, or proves to be ambiguous in its application to the facts of the case, then, under the rules of construction, it is to be construed against the plaintiff, *contra proferentem*; the contract having been prepared on behalf of the plaintiff as a standard form in use by them with their growers and couched generally in terms protective of the plaintiff. The growers' position is left uncertain in several respects, and the plaintiff is made sole and final arbiter in certain cases. On reading the contract form, one grower, as already mentioned, refused to sign, and a perusal of the document makes his attitude easy to understand . . .

Case 44. Welch v Bowmaker (Ireland) Ltd
Supreme Court [1980] I.R. 251

The facts are immaterial.

Henchy J.:

. . . The relevant rule of interpretation is that encapsulated in the maxim *generalia specialibus non derogant*. In plain English, when you find a particular situation dealt with in special terms, and later in the same document you find general words used which could be said to encompass and deal differently with that particular situation, the general words will not, in the absence of an indication of a definite intention to do so, be held to undermine or abrogate the effect of the special words which were used to deal with the particular situation. This is but a commonsense way of giving effect to the true or primary intention of a draftsman, for the general words will usually have been used in inadvertence of the fact that the particular situation has already been specially dealt with . . .

Case 45. Fallon v Robins
Chancery (1865) 16 Ir.Ch.Rep. 422

The parties entered into a lease for a term of thirty-one years, with liberty to have it determined after three years. The lease was ambiguously worded and the defendant, the landlord, purported to take advantage of the termination clause. The defendant sought to introduce parol evidence.

Held that a parol variation of the contract must be clearly established.

Smith M.R.:

The affidavit of the plaintiff and that of the defendant are in direct conflict. I do not see what right I have to decide, on the conflicting testimony in the case, what the agreement was. That is to be decided by reference to the agreement itself. If I had a right to construe this agreement by the evidence, I should either direct an issue, or a *viva voce* examination before the court. By the general rules of the common law, if there be a contract which has been reduced into writing, verbal evidence is not allowed to be given of what passed between the parties, either before the written instrument was made, or during the time it was in a state of preparation, so as to add to or subtract from, or in any manner to vary or qualify, the written contract. A court of equity may, under particular circumstances, admit such evidence; but a court of equity should not act upon doubtful evidence; either in a suit to reform the deed, or in a defence to a suit for specific performance. I am of opinion therefore that the case is to be decided on the construction of the agreement itself, and without reference to the conflicting affidavits as to the intention . . .

Case 46. Revenue Commissioners v Moroney
The facts are given on page 45
   Held that extrinsic evidence was admissible to refuse the receipt clause.

Kenny J.:

. . . Counsel for the plaintiffs has objected to the admission of the affidavit and declaration because, he says, no evidence of extrinsic circumstances is admissible to add to, contradict, vary or alter the terms of a deed; he referred to the statement of this rule at p. 135 in Norton's Treatise on Deeds (2nd edn 1928). This rule however does not apply to the statement of the consideration in the deed (ibid. p. 140) because 'the statement of the consideration forms no part of the terms of the deed, but is only a statement contained in the deed of an antecedent fact.' Moreover, if no evidence was admissible to contradict, vary or alter the terms of the deed, the plaintiff's claim would fail because there is a receipt for the consideration in the deed. It is not necessary to give authority for the proposition that evidence may be given to show that, despite the receipt, the consideration was not paid. Similarly, evidence is admissible when it is relevant to explain the circumstances in which the deed was executed and to establish that the parties did not intend that the purchase price mentioned in the deed should ever be paid . . .

(See also Case 26, regarding equitable estoppel.)

Case 47. Chambers v Kelly
Court of Exchequer (1873) 7 I.R.C.L. 231

The parties entered into an agreement in writing for the purchase by the defendant of oaks growing on lands owned by the plaintiff, 'together with all other trees growing through the oak plantations, and mixed with the oak'. The question in dispute being what trees beside oaks were included in the agreement.

Held that evidence of conversations between the parties in reference to the sale, prior to the written agreement, was properly received in order to identify the subject matter of the contract.

Fitzgerald B.:

We think that the objection that there was a reception of illegal evidence cannot be sustained. It appears plain, at least I think, that the term 'oak plantations', in the agreement in question does not mean plantations in which there was nothing but oak, because, in the agreement itself, trees of another kind are described as being mixed up with oak, and as growing through these 'oak plantations'; and, on the other hand, that it does not mean plantations in which there was any oak at all, because otherwise there would have been no necessity whatever for the introduction of the description 'oak plantations'.

That being so, it was necessary to go outside the written agreement to ascertain the subject matter in this respect, that is to say, 'oak plantations'. I am of opinion that, for this purpose, evidence of what passed, leading, in the words of the learned judge who tried the case, 'up to' the agreement, could not be excluded . . .

Deasy and Dowse BB. concurred.

Case 48. Nolan v Graves
High Court [1946] I.R. 376

A dispute arose between the parties as regards the price of premises sold at an auction. The plaintiff claimed that the price inserted in the written contract was the correct price whereas the defendant alleged that it was higher. When the defendant refused to complete the contract at the lower price the plaintiff sued for rescission of the contract and the defendant counterclaimed for rectification and specific performance of the contract. The plaintiff objected to the introduction of parol evidence to vary the terms of the written contract.

Held that the court was entitled to hear parol evidence in order to

ascertain the true contract between the parties. The party alleging that
the written contract was not a true record of the events must satisfy the
court beyond reasonable doubt that the parol evidence, rather than
the written contract, was true.

Haugh J.:

. . . Logically and consistently, the plaintiff's counsel say that, for any
reason, it was not necessary for her to go into evidence of the sale with
any particularity at all, beyond stating that she was the purchaser at that
price and that there was an agreement apparently signed on behalf of both
parties. They do admit that if she had sought to enforce the lower price on
the defendant and that if she was a plaintiff for specific performance, by
reason of the pleadings (even with a plea of mutual mistake and no
allegation of conduct amounting to fraud against her), then, in such
circumstances, the court might hear such evidence on behalf of the
defendant resisting such a claim. But that was not this case. Counsel for
the defendant urged me to hear this evidence. I heard many cases on the
topic and, having listened to them, I look on this branch of the case
shortly as follows: The pleadings have raised, as I have said, one issue of
fact only, and a very simple one in the sense that it is capable of very easy
appreciation: what was the price. If the plaintiff is correct in what she says
as regards the price, she must, of course, win. Accordingly, if she (through
her counsel) is correct in saying that I cannot hear any evidence on the
matter to contradict her, my hands are naturally tied, inasmuch as I cannot
try the issues raised by the pleadings in this action, and again she must
win . . .

However, I have come to the conclusion—and I reached that conclusion
at an early stage—that, on the issues that have been raised for me to try in
this case, and because of the matters alleged against the plaintiff, in order
to know what the contract was between the parties, I am entitled to hear
parol evidence, in common with a great many other cases in which such
evidence was heard; that the evidence was properly admissible, and that it
was relevant, and solely relevant, to the one issue I have got to try, and
that I am bound in fact to listen to it.

But having said that, I would like to say this with emphasis: the fact that
the plaintiff has in her possession this written memorandum (which, on its
face, purports to be an agreed record of the transaction that took place at
the public auction, made within some minutes of the event, and properly
ratified by the vendor's agents and by herself), almost goes the whole way
with her in her case, and the defendant, having made the case they have
made, have undertaken a very onerous burden. What I want to emphasise
is this: after listening to the evidence, I do not think that on its conclusion
I am entitled in the ordinary way to go in for what I might call weighing
the probabilities, and saying, in the ordinary way, where the balance of

probabilities lies. If the defendant only succeeded in proving that the plaintiff was probably incorrect, mistaken, or lying in her evidence, in my view that would be far short of the onus upon them after she has produced this written and signed contract. I think the burden of proof on the defendant is so heavy that any such evidence must be oppressive in its weight against her—it must be utterly conclusive. I think the onus on the defendant is to prove that that written record is not a true record of what took place at the auction. They must satisfy me beyond all reasonable doubt that what they say is true on oral evidence, and until they have so satisfied me, on consideration of that evidence, I would reject such evidence and hold that they have not discharged the onus which they have elected to put upon themselves . . .

(See also Case 74 regarding mistake, and Case 160 regarding rectification.)

Chapter 10.

EXEMPTION CLAUSES

An exemption clause is an express contractual stipulation which excludes, or diminishes, the liability of one of the parties to the contract. A party wishing to rely on such a clause must show that it was incorporated into the contract. One method of incorporation is for a party to require the other party to sign a document which contains the exemption clause: *Duff v Great Northern Railway Co.* (Case 49) and *Knox v Great Northern Railway Co.* (Case 50).

Or, an exemption clause may be incorporated into the contract by being printed on a single document given by the party relying on it to the other party: *Early v Great Southern Railways Co.* (Case 51) and *Miley v R.& J. McKechnie Ltd* (Case 52).

Or, an exemption clause may be incorporated by the display of a notice at the place where the contract is made. In such cases the party relying on the contents of the notice need only take reasonable steps to bring it to the notice of the other party: *Shea v Great Southern Railways Co.* (Case 53) and *Henigan v Ballybunion Picture House Ltd* (Case 54).

Where parties have a series of contracts over a period of time one party may attempt to introduce an exemption clause into their dealings. Whether this is successful or not will depend on whether that party has taken reasonable steps to do so: *Western Meats Ltd v National Ice & Cold Storage Co. Ltd* (Case 55).

To be effective the exclusions in the exemption clause must cover the act from which damage has resulted. Exemption clauses are construed *contra proferentem: Alexander v Irish National Stud Co. Ltd* (Case 56).

An exemption clause cannot be effective where a fundamental breach of contract has been committed: *Clayton Love & Sons (Dublin) Ltd v British & Irish Steampacket Co. Ltd* (Case 57).

Case 49. Duff v Great Northern Railway Co.
Court of Exchequer (1878) 4 L.R.Ir. 178

The plaintiff intended to transport cattle by train and signed the defendant's invoice. There was no reference on the face of it to passengers except the words: 'Drover in charge free', and at the foot of it were the words: 'For conditions of carriage, see back.' Amongst other conditions was the clause: 'that, as a drover is allowed to attend the cattle during transit, the company will allow such drover to travel free of charge, upon condition that he so travels at his own risk'. The plaintiff as drover travelled free. As a consequence of a collision on the journey, he received personal injuries and sued for damages for negligence.

Held that the condition which allowed a drover in charge of cattle to travel free, provided he did so at his own risk, was part of the written contract signed by the plaintiff. As he had elected to travel free he was bound by these conditions and could not therefore recover damages for the injuries sustained.

Palles C.B.:

. . . It seems to me to be clear that the conditions on the invoice, including those which I have read, are the conditions referred to in the document signed by the plaintiff, and that that document must be read as if the conditions were in terms stated therein. The agreement is to carry the cattle on the terms (*inter alia*) that the owner's drover may not only attend them during transit, but (if he elect to travel at his own risk) need not pay the ordinary fare of a passenger.

The plaintiff was not bound to travel on these terms, but unless he did so he was bound to pay his fare, and an election to travel free under this contract was an election to travel at his own risk.

Now it is admitted upon the evidence that the plaintiff did elect to travel under the contract. He himself states he travelled free, and the free pass proved is identified by the figures on it with the contract for carriage of the cattle. This appears to me to conclude the case. It reduces the question from one of fact—what was the contract under which plaintiff travelled—to matter of law, what is the legal effect and validity of the particular contract under which he shows as matter of fact he did travel? This latter question admits of no doubt. Under the contract the plaintiff is without remedy against the defendant for negligence during the journey, and such a contract is valid.

I do not think it necessary to refer in detail to any of the cases relied upon for the plaintiff. In all of them the contracts were by parol, and the question was what was the contract.

In *Henderson v Stevenson* (1875) Lord Cairns distinguishes between those cases and one such as the present, in which the terms of the contract have been reduced to writing. He says:

> There were a considerable number of other cases in which, for the conveyance of animals or of foods, a ticket or paper had been *actually signed* by the owner of the animals, or by the owner of the goods. With regard again to those cases, there might indeed be a question what was the construction of the contract, or how far the contract was valid. But there could be no question whatever that the contract, such as it was, was assented to, and entered into by the person who read the ticket.

> For those reasons, I am of opinion that the defendant is entitled to have a verdict directed for them upon the claim for personal injuries. I desire, however, to observe that my judgment is based upon the fact that the person who actually travelled as drover was the person who signed the contract. Had he been a different person, the connection of the drover with the contract might have involved a question of fact . . .

Dowse and Fitzgerald BB. concurred.

Case 50. Knox v Great Northern Railway Co.
Court of Appeal [1896] 2 I.R. 632

A groom took the plaintiff's horse to the railway station for transit by train. The defendant's porter failed to box the horse which slipped and suffered serious injuries. Almost immediately the horse was successfully boxed. The groom then signed a contract in writing for the carriage of the horse, subject to conditions, one of which read: 'that at the reduced rate the company carry at owner's risk . . . '. The plaintiff sued for damages for negligence.

Held that boxing the horse was necessarily and immediately connected with the carriage of the horse as to form one single transaction. The risks attendant on the horse's boxing were encompassed within the risks of carriage of the horse. The fact that the contract was signed after the injuries were received was immaterial.

Walker C.:

. . . The plaintiff's horse arrived at the station in charge of a groom, to be booked to Dublin. He was a man accustomed to such work, and clothed with full authority to contract for the carriage of the horse. The horse was brought into the company's premises—on to the bank next the horse-box. An attempt was made to box him, with the assistance of a porter, and in the effort (I assume, as I am bound to do, by the company's negligence), the horse's leg was hurt. There was then a discussion between the groom and the porter, the horse being still on the bank, and the attempt was renewed and perfected.

It is plain there was no such break as would make the final act of boxing a separate transaction. The act of boxing was commenced, and it never was really discontinued, and it is wholly unlike the case of a horse brought away from the station and brought back again. The horse, then, being in the box, the groom went to the booking office and proceeded to book him . . . The groom proceeded to enter into a contract for carriage, and he chose the lower rate with the incidents attached to it. It is said that though in an ordinary case this contract would have protected the company from all negligence in relation to the carriage of the horse, it did not in the present, for various reasons, which I shall now state.

It was said the carriage had not commenced. Now, it is plain that 'carriage' is a word which includes 'receiving, forwarding, and delivering' . . . and *Hodgman v West Midland Railway Co.* is a distinct authority that the horse is received, for the purpose of being received, forwarded, and delivered, when it enters the company's premises with a view to carriage, and here it was in the act of being boxed—a stronger case than *Hodgman's Case* on the point. The notice at the head of the contract points to the same thing.

Then, it is said, the contract only operates to protect from the date of its being signed, and that at that time an accrued injury existed; that this was a cause of action, and the parties cannot be presumed to have contracted in reference to it, and, as we said, release the cause of action.

But if the cause of action was negligence in the receiving, forwarding, and delivering—which are the equivalent of carriage—then we have only to see whether the contract signed was one which covered, as a matter of contract, all negligence accruing during all the carriage. That is a matter of law on the construction of the document, and would be the same question whether the injury accrued during the act of boxing, or in the middle of the journey, if the contract in fact was signed after it.

The plaintiff has the option of taking a rate which would cover the accrued injury, and for what appeared to him good consideration, he chose to take the lower rate; we must assume he did this voluntarily, and that there was no fraud or compulsion on the company's part. Therefore, the accrued injury was a common factor in both. It only comes to this, that the plaintiff in the events that happened acted imprudently in taking the lower rate. Suppose he thought the horse really was not injured; or suppose that there had been negligence which was the cause of an injury but not then developed: I do not think we can alter the signed contract as to reasonableness by the facts that turned out. I by no means say that the existence of the alternative would make the terms of every signed contract just and reasonable. But I say that as this contract covers the actual carriage, including the boxing, during which the negligence occurred, the plaintiff, when he chose for consideration to abandon his right to a contract which would indemnify him from that negligence, and took one, for consideration apparently sufficient to him, which protected the company from that negligence, is bound by it . . .

Sir Peter O'Brien L.C.J. and FitzGibbon L.J. delivered concurring judgments and Barry L.J. delivered a dissenting judgment.

Case 51. Early v Great Southern Railways Co.
Supreme Court [1940] I.R. 409

The plaintiff purchased a special excursion ticket at a cheap rate issued by the defendant at a train station. The ticket contained a clause that it was issued subject to the conditions in the company's timetables, one of which provided that the holder of a reduced fare ticket had no right of action against the company in the event of injury. A timetable was not available for inspection at the station, and no inquiry was made regarding it by the plaintiff. The plaintiff was injured when alighting from a train and sued the defendant for damages for negligence.

Held that the defendant had taken reasonable steps to bring to the plaintiff's attention the conditions on which he was accepted as a passenger. The action was dismissed.

Sullivan C.J.:

. . . At Fenagh, where the plaintiff purchased his ticket, there was a poster advertising the excurison to Mohill, which stated that excursion tickets and tickets issued at less than ordinary fares are issued subject to the notices and conditions shown in the company's timetables. The ticket purchased by the plaintiff bore on its fact the words: 'Special train—available for day of issue only—not transferable. See back.' On the back was printed—'Issued subject to the conditions and regulations in the company's timetables, books, bills and notices.' One of those conditions was that the holder of a ticket issued at a fare less than the ordinary fare should not have any right of action against the company in respect of injury, fatal or otherwise. No copy of the timetable or of any document containing those conditions was available for inspection by intending passengers at Fenagh 'halt'. The plaintiff, however, made no inquiry about them . . .

If the accident to the plaintiff had happened during the journey for which his ticket was available this case would be governed by the principles stated in the cases to which the learned judge referred—*Grand Trunk Railway Co. of Canada v Robinson* (1915) and *Thompson v London, Midland & Scottish Railway Co.* (1930). In the former case Lord Haldane L.C. in delivering the opinion of the Privy Council said:

If a passenger has entered a train on a mere invitation or permission from a railway company without more, and he receives injury in an accident caused by the negligence of its servants, the company is liable for damages for breach of a general duty to exercise care. Such a breach can be regarded as one either of an implied contract, or of a duty imposed by the general law, and in the latter case as in form a tort. But in either view this general duty may, subject to such statutory restrictions as exist in Canada and in England in different ways, be superseded by a specific contract, which may either enlarge, diminish, or exclude it. If the law authorises it, such a contract cannot be pronounced to be unreasonable by a court of justice. The specific contract, with its incidents either expressed or attached by law, becomes in such a case the only measure of the duties between the parties, and the plaintiff cannot by any device or form get more than the contract allows him . . . The only right to be carried will be one which arises under the terms of the contract itself, and these terms must be accepted in their entirety. The company owes the passenger no duty which the contract is expressed on the face of it to exclude, and if he has approbated that contract by travelling under it he cannot afterwards reprobate it by claiming a right inconsistent with it. For the only footing on which he has been accepted as a passenger is simply that which the contract has defined.

In *Thompson v London, Midland & Scottish Railway Co.* (1930) the ticket held by the plaintiff bore on its face the words: 'Excursion, for conditions see back', and on the back: 'Issued subject to the conditions and regulations in the company's timetables and notices and excursion and other bills.' In the course of his judgment Lord Hanworth M.R. says:

It appears to me that the right way of considering such notices is put by Swift J. in *Nunan v Southern Railway Co.* (1923). After referring to a number of cases which have been dealt with in the courts he says: 'I am of opinion that the proper method of considering such a matter is to proceed upon the assumption that where a contract is made by the delivery, by one of the contracting parties to the other, of a document in common form stating the terms upon which the person delivering it will enter into the proposed contract, such a form constitutes the offer of the party who tenders it, and if the form is accepted without objection by the person to whom it is tendered this person is as a general rule bound by its contents and his act amounts to an acceptance of the offer to him whether he reads the document or otherwise informs himself of its content or not, and the conditions contained in the document are binding upon him. It is, however, argued that it is a question of fact for the jury, whether or not sufficient notice was given of these conditions, and whether or not, therefore, the plaintiff ought to be held bound by the conditions; for it is said that the conditions are, I will not say past finding out, but difficult to ascertain. The learned Commissioner who tried the case appreciated that the verdict of the jury was based probably on the fact that you have to make a considerable search before you find out the conditions. I think he is right in saying that in the line of cases, and there are many, under which this case falls, it has not ever been held that the mere circuity which has to be followed to find the actual condition prevents the passenger having notice that there was a condition.

In my opinion the High Court was right in holding that the defendant had taken all reasonable steps to bring to the notice of the plaintiff the conditions on which he would be carried as a passenger, and that the plaintiff was bound by those conditions at the time when he sustained the injury for which he claims damages.

Murnaghan and Geoghegan JJ. concurred.

Case 52. Miley v R. & J. McKechnie Ltd
Circuit Court (1949) 84 I.L.T.R. 89

The plaintiff deposited an item of clothing for cleaning with the defendant. She was given a receipt bearing on its face in capital letters the words: 'All orders accepted without guarantee', followed in smaller letters by 'please read conditions overleaf'. The conditions stated that the defendant did not accept liability for damage however caused. The plaintiff had frequently dealt with the defendant and had on each occasion been given such a receipt. Notices to a similar effect were hanging in the defendant's premises. When the clothing was damaged the plaintiff sued for compensation.

Held that the acceptance by the plaintiff of the receipt and of similar receipts previously relieved the defendant of liability.

Judge Shannon:

The plaintiff had left in a costume to be cleaned, and received the customary ticket which was in very clear terms. There were capital letters on the front referring to the printed conditions on the back, which stated that all orders were accepted without guarantee. On the front there were also the date and number of the reception.

The plaintiff said that she never read the ticket, that she knew there was writing on it, but did not know that conditions were there set out, although by reason of having dealt with the firm for a number of years she must have had several such tickets in her house. She said she thought the ticket unimportant and had burnt or torn it.

The plaintiff said also that she had never seen the notices in the defendants' shop, one at the back of the counter and one facing the customer as he or she would go out.

If these notices in the shop were the only documents the defendants relied on, I think they would not be sufficient. A document, however, was invariably handed to the customer. It is marked IMPORTANT and if a customer saw this and did not care to read it he could not complain of the loss ensuing to him . . .

Case 53. Shea v Great Southern Railways Co.
Circuit Court [1944] Ir.Jur.Rep. 26

Before the plaintiff boarded a bus the defendant's employee placed the plaintiff's bicycle on top of the bus, securing it with rope. The bus conductor gave the plaintiff two tickets. The bicycle ticket bore the words "Receipt for Cycle . . . accompanied by passenger—At Owner's Risk—Issued subject to the Company's Rules and Regulations.' Printed on the back were the words 'It must be understood that all Bicycles . . . are carried solely at the risk of the owner and under no circumstances will claims for damage to such Bicycle . . . while being carried on the Buses be entertained.' At the entrance to the bus a notice contained the following provision: 'Luggage and Parcels which are accompanied by Passengers will be carried at Owner's Risk and the Company will not accept Responsibility for Loss or Damage or Delay to any such Luggage or Parcel.' The door of the bus when opened folded across the notice. During the journey the bicycle was damaged and the plaintiff sued for compensation.

Held that the company had made reasonable efforts to bring to the plaintiff's attention the conditions under which it intended to carry him and his goods. The plaintiff was bound by these and that the claim must be dismissed.

Judge Davitt:

I must hold that the plaintiff is bound by the conditions as to owner's risk provided that he knew or ought to have known of these conditions. If it were legally necessary to ensure that every condition were specifically brought to the notice of each passenger, then a ridiculous state of affairs would result, involving many delays and tending seriously to hold up transport. The matter has, therefore, to be dealt with differently, and so the law provides, as has now been settled by several decisions in the reports of which *Early v Great Southern Railways Co.* (1940) (Case 51) is one, that if the company take reasonable steps to bring to the passenger's notice the existence of certain conditions under which they propose to carry him or his goods he is bound by them whether he reads them or not or even whether he can conveniently read them or not.

There may be some criticism of the position of the notice posted behind the door, but no reasonable criticism can be directed against the notice on the ticket itself, and certainly not against that contained on the face of the ticket. It is plain to be seen from that notice that the ticket is issued subject to certain conditions, and in normal circumstances any passenger can see that. If, for any reason, including the reason that he does not know what the conditions are and cannot immediately find out, the passenger is not prepared to accept the conditions he is at liberty to get off the bus or remove his bicycle. I cannot accept the suggestion that the plaintiff had not a reasonable opportunity of reading what was on the face of his ticket.

Case 54. Henigan v Ballybunion Picture House Ltd
Circuit Court [1944] Ir.Jur.Rep. 62

The plaintiff went to a dance at the defendant's premises and deposited his overcoat in a room attached to the hall marked 'cloakroom'. A charge was made for admission to the dance but no separate charge was made for the use of the cloakroom. There was no attendant in the cloakroom. Several notices were displayed in the dance hall and cloakroom which read, 'The management will not accept responsibility for loss or damage to property of patrons left in this hall' but the plaintiff did not see these notices. The plaintiff's coat was found to be missing from the cloakroom and was never recovered. He sued for damages.

Held that the notices, provided they were displayed in a reasonably conspicuous manner, were sufficient to exclude the defendant's liability notwithstanding that the plaintiff had not seen them. The action was dismissed.

Judge O Briain:

. . . The fact that the plaintiff did not see the notices is irrelevant if, in fact, the defendants displayed the notices in a reasonably conspicuous place, as I am satisfied they did in this case.

Case 55. Western Meats Ltd v National Ice & Cold Storage Co. Ltd
High Court [1982] I.L.R.M. 99

The plaintiff meat processors stored goods in the defendant's cold storage facilities. When the plaintiff sought to withdraw a quantity of the goods, the defendant was unable to locate them because of over storage. As a result the plaintiff suffered loss and in an action against the defendant was met with a denial of liability on the ground that, in accordance with the standard conditions of trade, all goods were stored at owner's risk.

Held that the defendant had not given the plaintiff reasonable notice of the contents of the standard conditions of trade. Where a business enterprise offers a specialist service and accepts no responsibility for it the onus rested on it to intimate clearly to the party dealing with it that liability would not be accepted for any damage or loss which occured. The plaintiff was awarded damages.

Barrington J.:

. . . To the plaintiff's claim the defendant has two principal defences. The first is based on their standard conditions of trade . . . The conditions of trade, if part of the contract between the parties, appear to me to be a complete answer to the plaintiff's claim.

Clause I of the conditions of storage provides that all goods are stored at the owner's risk. Clause II provides that the company will not be answerable for any delay, loss or damage arising (*inter alia*) from maintaining too high or too low a temperature in the stores, failure of machinery or plant, negligence, thefts, including theft by the company's servants, 'or any other cause whatsoever'.

There is no doubt that it was competent for the parties to include such clauses in their contract if they wished to do so. We are not here dealing with a monopoly providing a necessary service for an ignorant and unwary public. We are dealing with two commercial concerns one of which is providing a specialist service for the other and each of which is competent to protect its own interests . . .

But the primary question is whether the plaintiff was given reasonable notice of these conditions. The plaintiff's director [who negotiated with the defendant] says he was not aware of them and there is no evidence that they were ever expressly brought to his attention.

In later years these conditions appeared on the back of the defendant's note-paper and also on the back of many of their storage documents. We only have a photostat copy of the original letter passing between the parties dated 22 September 1969. The conditions do not appear on the back of this copy though they may have been on the back of the original.

However, in the text of the letter itself there is no reference to the conditions, though certain terms are set out in the letter. I am satisfied that the terms were never expressly brought to the plaintiff's director's attention and I accept his word that he was not aware of them. I am satisfied that he is a man who carries on business by personal contact and on the telephone and that he relies greatly on his assessment of the men he is dealing with. Indeed, in the present case, even the defendant's managers do not appear to have been particularly conscious of the standard conditions. When disputes arose between the parties over the years, prior to the present dispute, these were resolved as between businessmen and, even in the present case, there was no reference to the standard conditions until the matter reached the hands of the lawyers.

It appears to me to be important that this is a case in which the defendant initially solicited the plaintiff's business. Had the initial negotiators expressly drawn to the plaintiff's director's attention not only the excellence of their services but also the fact that they accepted no responsibility whatsoever for the manner in which they would handle his goods, the plaintiff's director's decision of whether to retain them might well have been different. In all the circumstances of this case it appears to me that the defendant did not give the plaintiff reasonable notice of the contents of the standard conditions. It appears to me also that a businessman, offering a specialist service, but accepting no responsibility for it, must bring home clearly to the party dealing with him that he accepts no such responsibility. In all the circumstances I think, that in the present case, the defendant was guilty of negligence and breach of contract . . .

Case 56. Alexander v Irish National Stud Co. Ltd

High Court, unreported, 10 June 1977

The plaintiff sent his mare to the defendant's stud farm. The horse was killed due to the negligence of the defendant's employees. When the plaintiff sued for damages the defendant argued that a clause which exempted liability in the event of accident or disease was applicable and that the action should be dismissed.

Held that in construing the clause the test to be applied was what an ordinary sensible customer would understand the words used in the clause to mean. Such customer would not understand the words to mean that should the horse be injured by the negligence of the defendant's employees, the customer could not hold the defendant responsible. The clause covered inevitable risks rather than negligent risks. Therefore the clause was inapplicable and damages were awarded.

McMahon J.:

. . . The second issue is whether the defendant's liability for damages resulting from its negligence is excluded by Condition No. 1 of the defendant's 'Conditions of Acceptance of Nominations' which are part of the contract between the plaintiff and the defendant. The Condition is in the following terms: 'The Irish National Stud will not be responsible to any owner of any mare or foal in the event of an accident occurring to that mare or foal or in the event of a mare or foal incurring disease'.

The court was not referred to any Irish authorities and the law in England was until the decision of the Court of Appeal in *Hollier v Rambler Motors Ltd* (1972) set out in a line of authorities represented by *Ruttle v Palmer* (1922); *Fagan v Green* (1926) and *Alderslade v Hendon Laundry* (1945).

The effect of those cases was that a party who wanted to exclude his liability for negligence was required to do so in clear words but if the only liability of the party pleading an exempted clause is a liability for negligence the clause will, to use the expression employed by Scrutton L.J. in *Ruttle v Palmer*, 'more readily operate to exempt him'.

In *Alderslade v Hendon Laundry*, Greene M.R. went further than the previous decisions when he said:

Where the head of damage in respect of which limitation of liability is sought to be imposed is one which rests on negligence and nothing else the clause must be construed as extending to that head of damage because if it were not so construed it would lack subject matter.

In the judgment of Greene M.R. there is substituted for Scrutton L.J.'s 'more readily operate' the view that the clause 'must be construed as extending' to negligence.

In *Hollier's case* Salmon L.J., with whom Stamp L.J. and Latey J. agreed, held that notwithstanding that negligence is the only ground upon which liability can attach, nevertheless an exemption clause in these terms may, but does not necessarily, provide exemption from liability for negligence. The exemption clause may be understood by the other party merely as a warning that damage may occur to his property in the course of the performance of the contract for which the party carrying out the contract will not be liable. The proper test is to consider what the ordinary sensible customer would understand by the words.

It appears to me that the decision of the Court of Appeal in *Hollier's case* corresponds with the reality of the situation where the terms of the contract are not negotiated between the parties but are presented by one party to the other as a contract of adhesion which may be accepted or rejected but not modified in its terms. The contract terms may therefore be regarded as a communication from the party offering them to the other party and they are to be construed in the sense which an ordinary sensible person in the relevant circumstances would understand them.

Every breeder knows that accidents may befall a mare at a stud without negligence on the part of anyone. I think a breeder would read these words as a warning that the stud will not be liable for such an accident but he would not understand the words to mean that if his mare were injured in an accident caused by the negligence of the employees of the stud he could not hold the stud responsible. The fact that the condition includes disease as well as accident reinforces this view because it suggests that the subject matter dealt with is inevitable risks.

I have considered counsel for the defendant's submission that the expression 'will not be responsible' suggests that this is something the parties are agreeing to rather than a statement of an existing position but while I appreciate the weight of the point it appears to be not sufficient to outweigh the other considerations.

When as in the case of *Ruttle v Palmer* a garage stipulates 'Cars driven by our staff at customers' risk', it appears to me that this conveys to the customer a different kind of risk from that which the condition in the present contract would convey. The customer knows that the accidents referred to are accidents involving the negligence of the garage drivers because he would not expect the garage to be responsible for an accident to his car caused by the negligence of some third party. The clause is dealing with risks of damage which in the normal course arise only where some party is negligent. The condition in the present contract is dealing with a state of affairs where injury to a mare may easily occur without negligence on the part of anyone. For these reasons I conclude that the defendant is not exempted from liability by the condition in question . . .

Case 57. Clayton Love & Sons (Dublin) Ltd v British & Irish Steampacket Co. Ltd
Supreme Court (1970) 104 I.L.T.R. 157

The parties contracted for the transport by sea of a consignment of frozen foods. Preliminary conversations took place by telephone between the parties. The terms of the contract were to be found in these conversations and in the defendant's standard conditions of carriage which were incorporated in a consignment note and which had been signed by the plaintiff's agent. These standard conditions provided that the defendant was exempt from liability for any damage howsoever caused and required that any claim in respect of damage to goods should be made within three days from the time of arrival at their destination. The plaintiff understood that the goods were to be carried at a refrigerated temperature whereas the defendant's stance was that had such a request been made it would have been explained that loading could only have been made at atmospheric temperature because cross-channel dockers would not work in a refrigerated hold.

The cargo, having been carried at atmospheric temperature, was destroyed and the plaintiff sued for damages.

The High Court held that while the parties were not *ad idem* there was a contractual relationship existing between the parties as to how the goods were to be carried. The damages to the goods was fairly attributable to the defendant's breach of contract. Since the service the plaintiff received was something radically different from the service it had contracted for, there had been a breach by the defendant of a fundamental term. Accordingly the defendant was not entitled to avail of the general exemption in its standard conditions of carriage to escape liability. The court held that the clause limiting the time in which a claim could be made applied to a claim arising from a breach of a fundamental term of the contract and the plaintiff's claim was dismissed. The plaintiff appealed.

Held that the defendant having been found to have breached a fundamental term of the contract should not have been allowed to rely on a time bar to defeat a claim for damages. Therefore the plaintiff was entitled to damages.

Ó Dálaigh C.J.:

. . . The parties therefore were not *ad idem*; but it would, Davitt P. [in the High Court] said, nevertheless be wrong to conclude that there was no contractual relationship between the parties as to how the consignments were to be carried. He then cited with approval and as setting out the law applicable in these circumstances the following passage from the judgment of Blackburn J. in *Smith v Hughes* (1871):

> I apprehend that if one of the parties intends to make a contract on one set of terms, and the other intends to make a contract on another set of terms, or, as it is sometimes expressed, if the parties are not *ad idem*, there is no contract, unless the circumstances are such as to preclude one of the parties from denying that he has agreed to the terms of the other. The rule of law is that stated in *Freeman v Cooke* (1848). If, whatever a man's real intention may be, he so conducts himself that a reasonable man would believe that he was assenting to the terms proposed by the other party, and that other party upon that belief enters into the contract with him, the man thus conducting himself would be equally bound as if he had intended to agree to the other party's terms.

The President then continued:

> I take the view that a reasonable man, who had no knowledge of the circumstances of the defendants in relation to their dockers' refusal to work in refrigerated holds, would infer that the goods would be loaded into a hold which was at the time in fact refrigerated and not at atmospheric temperature. After all if a person speaks of putting food

into a refrigerator he will be normally understood as meaning a refrigerator which is in fact refrigerating and not a receptacle at atmospheric temperature. I take the view, accordingly, that the oral portion of the contract between the parties was that the consignments were to be carried as a very delicate refrigerated cargo and loaded last into the refrigeration hold which would at the time and at all material times be at refrigeration temperature and not at atmospheric temperature.

. . . The defendants in military language have laid down a thunderous attack on *Smith's Case*, or, more accurately, on the words of Blackburn J. in *Smith's Case* upon which the President based himself in the first branch of his decision. *Smith's Case* was a contract case which had been tried by jury and the judgments are largely concerned with the correctness, or otherwise, in law, of the trial judge's directions. The facts and the grounds of the decision are summarised as follows in the headnote.

The plaintiff offered to sell to the defendant oats, and exhibited a sample; the defendant took the sample, and on the following day wrote to say that he would take the oats at the price of 34s. per quarter. The defendant afterwards refused to accept the oats on the ground that they were new, and he thought he was buying old oats; nothing, however, was said at the time the sample was shown as to their being old; but the price was very high for new oats. The judge left to the jury the question whether the plaintiff had believed the defendant to believe, or to be under the impression, that he was contracting for old oats, and, if they were of opinion that the plaintiff had so believed, he directed them to find for the defendant. The jury having found for the defendant:

Held, that there must be a new trial.

Per Cockburn C.J., on the ground that the passive acquiescence of the seller in the self-deception of the buyer did not entitle the latter to avoid the contract.

Per Blackburn J., on the ground that there is no legal obligation on a vendor to inform a purchaser that the latter is under a mistake not induced by the act of the vendor; and that the direction did not bring to the minds of the jury the distinction between agreeing to take the oats under the belief that they were old, and agreeing to take the oats under the belief that the plaintiff contracted that they were old.

Per Hannen J., on the ground that the direction did not sufficiently explain to the jury that, in order to relieve the defendant from liability, it was necessary that they should find, not merely that the plaintiff believed the defendant to believe that he was buying old oats, but that the plaintiff believed the defendant to believe that he, the plaintiff, was contracting to sell old oats.

. . . The criticism advanced by the defendant on this appeal that Blackburn J.'s proposition is not borne out by *Freeman v Cooke* is in my opinion shown not to be well founded. I read *Freeman v Cooke* as acknowledging that where the parties are not *ad idem* there can nevertheless be a contract by estoppel. Here the position in my judgment was that the stipulations of plaintiff's agent with regard to the carriage of the goods were such that no reasonable person could have misunderstood that she was asking for transfer of the goods on delivery at the port into a refrigerated hold and, consequently, that the defendant's agent had only himself to blame if, faced with such a clear intimation of the plaintiff's requirements, he did nothing to correct [that] impression that the goods would be loaded into a refrigerated hold.

Blackburn J.'s statement of the law has been followed, as plaintiff's counsel pointed out in *Sullivan v Constable* (1932). Luxmoore J. in the High Court acted on the rule; and in the Court of Appeal Scrutton L.J. expressly approved of the application of *Smith v Hughes*. The plaintiff's requirements on the purchase of a yacht were there held to be part of the contract, the defendant by his silence being held to have accepted them.

In between *Freeman v Cooke* and *Smith v Hughes*, Pollock C.B., in *Cornish v Abington* (1859) stated the law in these terms:

If any person, by a course of conduct or by actual expressions, so conducts himself that another may reasonably infer the existence of an agreement . . . whether the party intends that he should do so or not, it has the effect that the party using that language, or who has so conducted himself, cannot afterwards gainsay the reasonable inference to be drawn from his words or conduct.

Moreover, cases apart, Blackburn J.'s proposition commends itself on principle and in common sense.

It is in my opinion not a valid objection, as the defendant has said, that estoppel is a weapon of defence and therefore cannot afford the plaintiff here a cause of action. Estoppel enters in only in determining whether there is a contract and what are its terms. The rights the plaintiff seeks to enforce flow from that contract that has been established by the application of the doctrine of estoppel.

I would uphold the President's judgment on the first branch of this case.

On the second branch the only matter which arises is whether the President was right in his view that the time clause of the standard conditions could avail the defendant notwithstanding breach of a fundamental obligation of the contract. The terms of the contract, as the President found them, having been upheld, it was not questioned by the defendant that the doctrine of fundamental breach precluded from relying on the exemptions . . . The President was of opinion that notwithstanding the very wide terms of the exemption clause there remained some subject matter upon which the time clause could operate, and that he should give effect to the clause. In particular, the President pointed out that the time clause contemplated a sustainable claim being made where the goods never arrive at all at their destination, and this would be a fundamental breach of the contract. He therefore held that the time clause was intended to apply in case of a claim arising from a fundamental breach of the contract.

It was submitted on behalf of the plaintiff that the correct position in law is that a defendant in breach of a fundamental obligation cannot avail of any exempting clause whatever; and accordingly that the time clause equally with the exemption clause must fall.

As Cheshire and Fifoot in their *Law of Contract* (6th edn p. 17) point out, a primary source of the doctrine of fundamental obligation is to be found in cases of carriage of goods by sea where a ship has deviated from its appointed course; and they instance *Joseph Thorley Ltd v Orchis S.S. Co. Ltd* (1907). Collins M.R., there explained the effect of the doctrine by saying '. . . it displaces the contract'. Cozens-Hardy L.J. put it in these words: '. . . the shipowner . . . cannot claim the benefit of an exception contained in the special contract'; and the words of Fletcher Moulton L.J. were, '. . . he cannot claim the benefit of stipulations in his favour contained in the bill of lading . . . The most favourable position which he can claim to occupy is that he has carried the goods as a common carrier for the agreed freight.'

Lord Sumner in *Atlantic Shipping & Trading Co. v Louis Dreyfus & Co.* (1922) uses language similar to Fletcher Moulton L.J.: 'The shipowners gain no advantage against the charterer from their neglect to make the ship sea-worthy; they merely cannot pray the clause in aid in that case.' In this last case the matter in question was the time provision of an arbitration clause.

Devlin J. (as he then was) dealt quite explicitly with this matter in *Smeaton Hanscomb & Co. Ltd v Sassoon I. Setty Son & Co.* (1953). He said: 'It is, no doubt, a principle of construction that exceptions are to be construed as not being applicable for the protection of those for whose benefit they are inserted if the beneficiary had committed a breach of a fundamental term of the contract, and that a clause requiring the claim to be brought within a specified period is to be regarded as an exception for this purpose'—and he refers to the *Atlantic Shipping & Trading Co. Case* (*supra*).

In my opinion the basis on which this doctrine rests requires that a party, who like the defendant, has been held to be in breach of a fundamental obligation, cannot rely on a time bar in the contract to defeat a claim for damages. Equally with other exempting provisions such a time clause cannot be prayed in aid. In my opinion the President should not have allowed the defendant here to rely on the time bar clause.

Lavery and Haugh JJ. concurred

CHAPTER 11.

CONTRACTUAL CAPACITY

The general rule is that every person has full contractual capacity to enter into binding contracts. But there are a number of exceptions to this rule in that the law imposes some restriction on freedom to contract.

a. Minors

A person attains full age, by virtue of the *Age of Majority Act 1985*, when he or she attains the age of eighteen years or, in case he or she marries before attaining that age, upon his or her marriage. For the purposes of contract law a minor is thus an unmarried person under the age of eighteen. The law does not impose a total prohibition on the capacity of a minor to contract. Contracts for necessaries are enforced, whereas contracts for luxuries are not: *Skrine v Gordon* (Case 58) and *Griffiths v Delaney* (Case 59).

A minor is bound by a contract of service, or apprenticeship, or training, or education. But such a contract is only binding on the minor when, construed as a whole, it is not harsh and oppressive: *Keays v Great Southern Railway Co.* (Case 60) and *Harnedy v National Greyhound Racing Co. Ltd* (Case 61).

A minor may avoid contracts of continuing obligation. This means that the contract is valid and binding on both parties until the minor repudiates it. But to be effective the act of repudiation must be clear and definite: *Slator v Brady* (Case 62). A minor is bound to discharge any obligations which have accrued until the act of repudiation: *Blake v Concannon* (Case 63). A minor may repudiate either during minority or within a reasonable time after reaching majority: *Stapleton v Prudential Assurance Co. Ltd* (Case 64).

The *Infants Relief Act 1874* provides that all contracts entered into by a minor for the repayment of money lent, or to be lent, or for goods supplied other than necessaries, are absolutely void: *Bateman v Kingston* (Case 65).

Case 58. Skrine v Gordon
Common Pleas (1875) I.R. 9 C.L. 479

The defendant, a minor accustomed to hunt his step-father's horses, purchased a hunter from the plaintiff. On his failure to pay the plaintiff sued and was met with the defence of infancy. The question arose whether the horse was a necessary or a luxury.

Held that the horse was a luxury and the action was dismissed.

Lawson J.:

This was an action for the price of a hunter. The defendant, being an infant, appeared by guardian and pleaded infancy. To this the plaintiff filed a reply that the goods supplied were necessaries. It was tried before Baron Deasy, and at the close of the plaintiff's case the defendant's counsel called upon the learned Baron to direct a verdict for the defendant. The judge left the question of 'necessaries' to the jury, who found that the hunter was a necessary article for the defendant, and returned a verdict for £100. The question argued before us was whether the learned Baron was right in leaving the question to the jury; i.e. whether there was any evidence fit to be submitted to a jury that the hunter was a necessary article for an infant in the defendant's position. The subject-matter of the action, as I have said, was the price of a hunter sold and delivered. It appeared that the plaintiff sold this horse to the defendant, who was a young English gentleman on a visit with a country gentleman in the North of Ireland. At the time of the bargain, which took place at a ball, the defendant stated he would pay for the horse by his bill at six months, and that it should be endorsed by his friend, and he stated that in six months he would be of age. The price agreed on was £150. The evidence before the court as to the property and station of the defendant is very scanty. The plaintiff says that the defendant talked of having an allowance of £600 a year from his father, and said that he would be of age in June 1875, and that he belonged to the Surrey Hunt, and rode his step-father's hunters. Are we to hold that this is any evidence, having regard to the social position of the defendant such as would justify a question being left to a jury, whether a hunter was a necessary for him? We think not; and we consider that there was no evidence proper to be submitted to a jury to find that a hunter was a necessary for the defendant. And we think that the question of 'necessaries', or 'not necessaries', is one of fact for the jury; but, like all other questions of fact, it should not be left to the jury by the judge unless there is evidence on which they can reasonably find in the affirmative. In my opinion that rule, within proper limits, is very much calculated to keep the law in a certain and steady condition, and prevent juries rendering it uncertain by finding upon insufficient evidence in favour of a plaintiff, on the ground, as Willes J. says, that it is a shabby thing to plead infancy. Of course we all know that hunting is a good sport and a manly exercise, but still that only shows it is a sport, and luxuries or amusement are quite distinct from necessaries. We are, therefore, of opinion that the rule should be made absolute for entering up a verdict for the defendant.

Keogh and Morris JJ. concurred.

Case 59. Griffiths v Delaney

High Court [1938] Ir. Jur. Rep. 1

The plaintiff sued three brothers, one of whom was a minor, for a sum of money alleged to be due on a contract for the sale of goods. The goods in question could not be described as necessaries.

Held that the action should be dismissed against the minor defendant. There was no evidence which showed that the plaintiff had been misled as to the age of the minor.

O'Byrne J.

I will give judgement for the plaintiff against [the two adult defendants]. I will dismiss the action against the [minor defendant]. The plaintiff has sued a person against whom he is not entitled to obtain judgment. The plaintiff could have made a special case . . . that he had been misled; if he had done I would have considered the matter.

Case 60. Keays v Great Southern Railway Co.

High Court [1941] I.R. 534

The plaintiff, a child of twelve years of age, held from the defendant a season ticket which had been issued at a reduced rate on special conditions absolving the company from all liability for injuries caused by its negligence. The ticket had been purchased by the plaintiff's parents to enable her to travel to and from school. While on a journey covered by the ticket the plaintiff sustained injuries in respect of which she sued the defendant for negligence.

Held that the contract was not for the plaintiff's benefit inasmuch as it purported to deprive her of every common law right that she had against the defendant in respect of its negligent acts and that therefore the plaintiff was entitled to repudiate the contract.

Hanna J.:

An important point is raised in this case, namely, that by reason of the contract that was made by the railway company with the plaintiff, she is disentitled to maintain any action for injuries received through the negligence of the company's servants. This matter has been decided forty-six years ago in *Flower v London & North Western Railway Co.* (1894), and that decision has been accepted as the law, both in this country and in England, for that long period. It is a clear enunciation by eminent judges that, in considering a contract of this kind made with an infant, the court has to peruse and consider the entire contract to decide whether it is for the benefit of the infant.

An infant *prima facie* cannot make a contract, but an infant has certain rights in law, and a contract made by an infant is not in itself a void contract; it is only a voidable contract. That means that it is open to the infant at any time to repudiate the contract. In determining whether the contract is for the benefit of the infant, the court must consider the contract as a whole. It is not sufficient that the infant gets some benefit from the contract. The court has to take into consideration the obligations or limitations imposed by the company on the natural or legal rights of the infant.

In this case, the benefit to the infant is to be carried for six shillings and three pence per month, but her common law rights are entirely wrested from her by the clauses in the contract which prevent her from making a claim against the railway company for any injury she may sustain through any negligence on the part of the company, or the servants of the company. It goes even further: that, in the case of her death, her parents or representatives are prohibited by the terms of the contract from making a claim that might otherwise be sustainable. These conditions are contained in a large notice which is properly put up, both in Irish and English, somewhere in the booking office.

It is, to my mind, manifestly absurd to think that a school child, even of twelve years of age, and even of the intelligence of this young girl, should be expected to be aware of the limitation on her rights. This contract is not a contract made with her father or mother; it is a contract made with the child, and while it is a valid contract, and capable of being acted upon while in operation, it is the law that the child is entitled to repudiate it and to have determined by the court whether a contract of this kind is for her benefit or not.

At first I thought this might be a serious matter for the railway company, but, apparently, all the railway companies have been quite satisfied for the past forty-six years to have the case of *Flower v London & North Western Railway Co.*, stand as law, and it is probably for this reason that the railway companies and their servants undoubtedly take very great care of children going to school; it may be that the railway companies are quite satisfied to allow the law to stand as it is, and in view of the rare cases in which children may be injured through the negligence of their servants, not to have the matter tested.

I am of opinion that the contract in this case is very unfair to the infant because it deprives her of practically every common law right that she has against the railway company in respect of the negligence of themselves or their servants. For that reason, I think it is not for her benefit, and accordingly, her case must go to the jury on ordinary principles of law, namely whether the servants of the company were guilty of negligence, and whether there was any negligence on the part of the plaintiff.

Case 61. Harnedy v National Greyhound Racing Co. Ltd
High Court [1944] I.R. 160

The plaintiff, a minor, was the registered owner of a greyhound. The defendant held frequent sales of greyhounds by public auction preceded by trials in which a number of greyhounds competed with each other in a test of speed. The plaintiff's father entered the greyhound in a trial as a prelude to its sale. He completed and signed an entry form which on its front had the printed statement that the defendant 'accepted no responsibility for accident or disease during trials or sales'. For the purpose of the sale the defendant printed a catalogue which contained a similar printed statement. During the course of the trial the greyhound was injured due to the negligence of the defendant's employees. When the plaintiff sued for damages it was claimed by the defendant that the express terms of the contract exonerated it from any liability for injury to the greyhound.

Held that the court would disregard these terms excluding liability because they were substantially detrimental to the minor plaintiff without any sufficient advantage which might correspondingly accrue.

Geoghegan J.:

The entry form and the catalogue constitute the contract. The effect of the contract, if binding on the infant plaintiff, is to relieve the defendant of all liability for negligence by its servants in connection with trials or sales of dogs held in pursuance of the contract. The comprehensiveness of the stipulation in the catalogue need not be stressed.

It follows that a person contracting with the defendant on this basis is deprived of certain rights which otherwise would be afforded to him by common law. Some of these rights might be of such a nature as to arise only in rare and unusual circumstances, but others might arise frequently. No doubt, an owner of a dog who sells the animal through the medium of the sales held by the defendant may obtain an enhanced price as compared with a sale by private negotiation or otherwise, but, in my opinion, the possible disadvantages for a legal standpoint flowing from the express terms of the contract to which I have adverted oblige me to disregard them as against this plaintiff, and to treat the special contract (taken as a whole) as one substantially to the detriment of the plaintiff. I must regard the sale as having been held on an open contract of employment affording no protection to the defendants against their common law liability for negligence.

In arriving at this conclusion I have followed the decision in *Keays v Great Southern Railway Co.* (Case 60).

Case 62. Slator v Brady

Court of Exchequer (1863) 16 I.C.L.R. 61

The plaintiff, when a minor, executed a lease in favour of the defendant. On attaining his majority he executed another lease, on similar terms, in favour of the defendant. The plaintiff sought to eject the defendant from the lands.

Held that the first lease was voidable by the minor and that the mere execution of the second lease did not have the effect of avoiding the first lease. Some stronger and more direct action was needed to avoid the lease. The action was dismissed.

Fitzgerald B.:

It was, I think, agreed on both sides that its sufficiency must depend on one or other of these two propositions, viz., that the lease of 19 June 1860 was absolutely void, being the act of an infant; or that, being voidable, it was avoided by the mere execution of the deed of 29 April 1861, after the plaintiff had attained age, and before confirmation of the deed of 19 June 1860 . . .

The real questions in the case appear therefore to me to arise on the replication, and to be the two questions already mentioned; and as to them, first, I am of opinion that the lease of June 1860 was not absolutely void. Doubtless, some acts of an infant are absolutely void, while some are voidable only. According to some authorities, the criterion of the distinction is this: If the act *may* be for the benefit of the infant, it is voidable only; if it *cannot be* for his benefit, it is void. According to others, it is said to be this: All such gifts, grants, or deeds as do not take effect by the delivery of the infant's hand, are void; but those which do take such effect, are voidable only.

It is unnecessary to determine which of these is the more correct. By our adopting either, it seems to me the result will be that the act in question here was voidable only.

The deed of June 1860 was a deed taking effect by the delivery of the infant's hand; and it seems quite impossible to say that it *could* not be an act for the benefit of the infant. It is not enough to say that it *might* not. In truth, the only ground on which it was argued that it could not be for the infant's benefit was, that upon the making of it a fine appeared to have been paid, which showed that the rent reserved was not the best. I am not aware of even a shadow of authority for the proposition that the rent reserved, in an infant's lease, must be the best, in order to prevent its being void.

If there be one undisputed proposition as to the acts of an infant it is this, that his leases reserving rent are voidable only, and not void. Whether, if the lease reserve no rent, or a nominal rent merely, it be not void, because then, as it is said, there is *no semblance* of benefit to the infant, has been doubted. But it seems to me that it would be unsettling foundations to hold that the lease of an infant, reserving a rent not nominal, was void, and not voidable only.

Secondly, I am of opinion that the mere execution of the deed of April 1861, before confirmation of the lease of June 1860, did not avoid the lease: First, the two deeds are not necessarily inconsistent; the second deed may have effect concurrently with the first, and pass the reversion in the lease. The deed has been produced in the argument; it purports to convey the lands common to both instruments, as in the possession of the lessee of 1860; and though it contains a covenant on the part of the plaintiff, under which he might be called on by the defendant to do any future act necessary to avoid the lease, it contains no declaration expressly avoiding it.

An important distinction between a void and voidable deed of an infant is this, the void, in short, is binding on neither party to it; but the power of rescinding the voidable instrument is in the infant only; and unless the mere execution of the deed of April 1861 would have enabled the defendant to say that the lease of 1860 was avoided, the mere execution of that instrument cannot, in my opinion, have that effect.

Now it seems to me that to the defendant insisting that the lease of 1860 was avoided by the deed of 1861, it would be a clear answer that the deeds might well stand together, as a lease and grant of the reversion.

Secondly, it seems to me that, an estate having passed under the voidable conveyance, and the defendant being in possession thereunder when the infant attained age, the estate could not, on principle, be divested but by some act of notoriety, as ejectment, entry, demand of possession, or the like; or, at the least, notice.

Here an estate of freehold, though voidable, passed; and no authority has been cited for the proposition that such an estate can be defeated by a mere chamber instrument between the grantor and a stranger.

Case 63. Blake v Concannon
Queen's Bench (1870) I.R. 4 C.L. 323

The plaintiff let land to a minor who possessed and enjoyed the land for a period until, while still a minor, he left possession. On attaining majority, which occurred shortly afterwards, he repudiated the tenancy contract. The plaintiff sued for rent which became due during the time the defendant possessed and enjoyed the lands.

Held that the defendant was liable for that rent.

Pigot C.B.:

. . . It appears to me now, upon a consideration of the grounds on which an infant is held to be liable where, by the authorities to which I have referred, his liability is established, if he does not waive or repudiate the tenancy and the land, that he ought to be held bound by that liability when it has been once attached to the payment of the rent which accrued while he has occupied, and before he has repudiated. He is not, in an action of debt for the rent, held liable upon the contract of tenancy alone. His liability arises from his occupation and enjoyment of the land, under the tenancy so created. If his liability arose from the contract alone, the repudiation of the contract, by annulling it, would annul its obligations, which would then exist only by reason of the contract. But the infant, though he can repudiate the contract of demise, and the tenancy under it, and can so revest the land in the landlord, cannot repudiate an occupation and enjoyment which are past, or restore to the landlord what he has lost by that occupation and enjoyment of the infant. The reason given by Justice Newton . . . lies at the root of the infant's liability: 'he has had a *quid pro quo*.' Though quaintly expressed, it is a reason sanctioned by common sense, and in accordance with plain justice. The infant owes the rent, because he has an equivalent in the occupation and enjoyment of the lands. The authorities to which I have referred appear to me sufficiently to indicate that, if the infant does not avoid the tenancy under which he occupies before the rent becomes due, the mere fact of infancy constitutes no defence. If, therefore, he continues so to occupy without repudiation, the landlord, on the accruing of the rent, has a vested right of suit against the infant for the rent which has so accrued. I cannot, on consideration, hold that such vested right can be divested by the mere repudiation of the infant, without a direct decision, or some unequivocal and acknowledged authority, sustained by general acquiescence or clear analogy of law. I have found none . . .

Case 64. Stapleton v Prudential Assurance Co. Ltd
High Court (1928) 62 I.L.T.R. 56

The plaintiff, when a minor, entered into a contract of life assurance with the defendant. She continued to pay the premiums for nine years after reaching majority. She sued for the return of these years' premiums.

Held that the plaintiff failed as her repudiation of the contract had not occurred within a reasonable time of attaining majority. Even if such repudiation was possible it was doubtful whether the plaintiff could recover the premiums.

Sullivan P.:

. . . This was a continuing contract, and the plaintiff if she wished to repudiate it on attaining full age was bound to do so within a reasonable time. Even if she could now repudiate, it did not follow that the premiums should be returned to her. If she had died between 1916 and 1927, the company would have been bound to pay, so it could not be held that no consideration had passed during those years . . .

O'Byrne J. concurred.

Case 65. Bateman v Kingston
Court of Common Pleas (1880) 6 L.R.Ir. 328

The plaintiff loaned money to the defendant, a minor, for the purchase of necessaries. The defendant gave the plaintiff a promissory note which carried interest. When the promissory note was dishonoured and the plaintiff sued, the defendant pleaded infancy. The plaintiff replied that at the time the loan was given the defendant fraudulently represented himself to be of full age.

Held that while it might be possible to maintain an action against a minor on a negotiable instrument given in return for necessaries, that was not so where the negotiable instrument reserved the payment of interest. It was further held that the contract could not be enforced simply because the defendant's fraud induced the plaintiff to contract.

Lawson J.:

We think both the points raised in this case are perfectly clear. It is stated in Byles on Bills [of Exchange], p. 60 (12th edn), 'Whether a promissory note given by an infant for necessaries be valid either at the suit of the original payee or his indorsee has never been expressly decided; but it should seem it is not, for even if not transferable it carries interest.' Here the note is transferable, and it carries interest at the rate of £20 per cent. So it would appear, even according to that statement, an action could not be maintained upon it. When we are asked to decide, for the first time, that an infant is liable on a promissory note bearing interest, passed by him and his mother, because the money was applied subsequently in the purchase of necessaries, we would expect some principle or authority to be cited in support of such a contention. *Prima facie* it is bad. It is a contract in which a mother and her son, who is an infant, go to a man and borrow £80, for which they make promissory notes. That is attempted to be made a good contract binding on the son, because it is made out that the money was applied subsequently for necessaries. There is no authority in the books in favour of such a case, and it seems contrary to sound principle. If an infant goes into a shop and buys necessaries and gives a bill for them, not bearing interest, it may be that an action on that bill might be maintained, but this is quite a different case. We are asked to decide that under the Judicature Act there is an equitable ground for maintaining the action; we do not think so. With respect to the second point, it is too much to ask us to overrule *Bartlett v Wells* (1862), in which, though the infant represented himself to be of full age, it was held the action did not lie.

Harrison J. concurred.

b. Lunatics

Representatives of persons of unsound mind, or such a person during a subsequent lucid period, can avoid contractual liability provided that party can prove that the other party was aware of the disability when the contract was made: *Hassard v Smith* (Case 66).

Case 66. Hassard v Smith
Chancery (1872) I.R. 6 Eq. 429

The plaintiff leased property to the defendant. Later the plaintiff was found to be of unsound mind from a date anterior to the execution of the lease. The plaintiff sought to have the lease set aside due to his mental instability.

Held that provided the contract was fair, *bona fide* and completely executed it could only be set aside had the defendant known of the plaintiff's incapacity at the time the contract was made.

Chatterton V.C.:

The rule which now prevails, both at law and in equity, in reference to contracts entered into by a person apparently of sound mind, and not known by the other contracting party to be insane, is, that such contracts, if executed and completed, and if fair and *bona fide*, will not be held void or set aside. The principal case at law upon this subject is that of *Molton v Camroux* (1849), in the Court of Exchequer, and affirmed by the Court of Exchequer Chamber. That was followed by the case of *Beavan v McDonnell*, where the contract was one for the purchase of land, entered into by the plaintiff, who paid a deposit on account of the purchase-money. He afterwards brought an action to recover back the money so paid, and, although it was proved that he was a lunatic at the time of the contract, and incapable of understanding its meaning, yet, as the defendant had entered into the contract and received the money fairly and in good faith, and without knowledge of the lunacy, it was held that the plaintiff could not recover back the money. But in courts of equity this principle is carried farther, for, even in cases where the contract may possibly be void at law, they will not interfere to set it aside, except in the case of fraud. In Storey's *Eq. Jur.*, s. 227, the rule is laid down thus: 'The ground upon which courts of equity now interfere to set aside the contracts and other acts, however solemn, of persons who are idiots, lunatics, and otherwise *non compotes mentis*, is fraud.' The learned commentator, in the following section, says: 'And so, if a purchase is made in good faith, without any knowledge of the incapacity, and no advantage has been taken, courts of equity will not interfere to set aside the contract, if injustice will be thereby done to the other side, and the parties cannot be placed *in statu quo*, or in the state in which they were before the purchase.' This principle is fully borne out by the case of *Niell v Morley*, where Sir William Grant refused to interfere, and left the party seeking to invalidate an executed contract, entered into *bona fide* and without knowledge of the plaintiff's insanity, to his remedy, if any, at law. In *Price v Berrington*, Lord Truro acted upon the same principle, and dismissed a bill to set aside a conveyance although the jury, on an issue directed by Lord Langdale, had found that the grantor was not of sound mind when he executed it, he having been already found a lunatic, by inquisition, from a date anterior to the conveyance, and without lucid intervals. In the case of *Elliot v Ince*, Lord Cranworth considered the law upon this subject, and referred with approbation to the case of *Molton v Camroux*, stating the principle of that case to be very sound—namely, that an executed contract, where parties have been dealing fairly, and in ignorance of the lunacy, shall not afterwards be set aside. He adds, 'that was a doctrine of necessity and a contrary doctrine would render all ordinary dealings between man and man unsafe.' He states that the result of the authorities seems to be, that dealings of sale and purchase by a person apparently sane, though subsequently found to be insane, will not be set aside against those who have dealt with him on the faith of his being a person of competent understanding. He showed that that principle did not affect the case before him, as grounds which do not touch the present case. The same principle was applied to a mortgage by a lunatic, in *Campbell v Hooper*.

The knowledge of the lunacy or incapacity above mentioned must be understood to mean not merely actual knowledge, but that which must be presumed, for circumstances known to the other contracting party, sufficient to lead any reasonable person to conclude that, at the time the contract was made, the person with whom he was dealing was of unsound mind. The plaintiff has contended that the transaction itself could not be relied on by the defendant as affording any evidence of sanity. In this proposition I cannot agree, as I think the circumstances attending the contract, though not conclusive, are, perhaps, of the greatest importance on the one side or the other. I have not to investigate the different theories put forward in the cases on this subject as to the effect of delusions not actually leading to the doing of the act in question, or as to partial unsoundness of mind, though, if I had, I should feel more disposed to concur in the views expressed by Lord Chief Justice Cockburn, in *Banks v Goodfellow*, than in those of an opposite tendency. But here, on the hypothesis on which I am proceeding, it is unnecessary for me to enter upon these difficult matters, for I assume the finding to be correct.

On the evidence in the case, it cannot be contended that the mind of the plaintiff, when he made this lease, was wholly unsound. His insanity was, at the most, partial; and he was proved beyond doubt to have acted in other transactions, at or after the date of the lease, as a sane man, and as quite capable of managing his affairs, and to have been so treated by his family. This consideration is of great importance upon the question whether knowledge of the plaintiff's insanity is to be imputed to the defendant. There is not a particle of evidence to show that the defendant had any actual knowledge of this insanity, and the contrary has been positively deposed to by him. Were, then, the circumstances of which the defendant is shown to have been aware, such as might lead him, as a reasonable man, to conclude that the plaintiff was of unsound mind? So far from their being so, it appears to me that every act of the plaintiff in the transaction, laying aside for the present the nature of the lease itself, had a directly opposite tendency. The only witnesses produced to prove facts leading to the conclusion that he was insane depose to matter of which, with one exception which I shall afterwards mention, the defendant could not have had any knowledge. They speak of changes in habit and manner, which probably were sufficient to attract the attention of members of his family and persons in daily intercourse with the plaintiff, but not of a nature to be known to, or observed by, others . . .

All these matters were not, however, of a public nature, with the exception of the plaintiff's conduct at the fair, which is that which I before referred to, and were not such as could have been known to or observed by the defendant. His conduct at the fair might have been such as to attract observation, but it is not alleged that the defendant was at that fair. The case of *Greenslade v Dare* is an important authority in the present case, in more points than one; and it was there held by Lord Romilly, that even a general reputation of insanity in the neighbourhood where the party resided was not evidece of notice of insanity. This is all the evidence of the plaintiff, and it has, in my opinion, wholly failed to show that the defendant had knowledge or notice of the plaintiff being of unsound mind . . .

The lease in question is, of course, an executed contract; it wants no element of completeness. Rent was paid and accepted under it; possession of everything demised was given to the defendant; of the land, by an actual delivery of possession, and occupation by the defendant; of the house and garden, by the acceptance of re-demise by the plaintiff from the defendant. The defendant could not be replaced in the same position, if it were now set aside. He has engaged in farming the land; he has relinquished other arrangements, and has changed his position on the faith of it.

It is, however, contended that the letting is of a nature itself to indicate advantage taken, and it has been represented as made at a great undervalue. It was urged that, as the place is stated to have been occupied as, and to be suited for, a gentleman's residence, letting it to a working farmer, however well-to-do, was evidence of incapacity. I cannot agree in this, for it is not always that a gentleman wishing to let his place, with a considerable amount of land, can find a gentleman ready to take it, and everyone knows that very many such places are let to working farmers. The lease contains all the ordinary covenants, and was prepared solely by the plaintiff's own solicitor, without any communication from or with the defendant. The term is as for five years only—a matter of some importance—since, if the defendant were planning to procure a lease at such an undervalue as is alleged, and had the power to influence a man of deficient capacity, I think it unlikely that he should not have got him to grant a longer term. In my opinion the plaintiff has failed to prove that the lease was at an undervalue . . .

I have now gone through this case in detail, and have examined the facts proved, in reference to the rules of law by which it is governed. I have shown that, in my opinion, assuming the plaintiff to have been of unsound mind at the time of the treaty for and execution of the lease, this was not known to the defendant; that to him he appeared to be of sound mind; that the contract was complete and executed; that it was an honest and *bona fide* transaction, and that the rent reserved was the fair value of the place. Under these circumstances, I am of opinion that the plaintiff has failed to sustain his case.

c. Diplomatic Immunity

Properly accedited diplomatic and consular personnel can claim immunity with regard to their contractual liabilities. The government of a foreign state cannot be sued in Irish courts: *Saorstát & Continental Steamship Co. Ltd v De Las Morenas* (Case 67).

Case 67. Saorstát & Continental Steamship Co. Ltd v De Las Morenas
Supreme Court [1945] I.R. 291

The defendant, an officer in the Spanish Army, came to this country as head of a commission appointed by the Spanish Government to purchase horses for use by the Spanish Army. He entered into a shipping contract with the plaintiff which he breached. When the plaintiff sued for damages the defendant claimed that he was entitled to immunity from the process of the court on the ground that, as he had contracted as an act of sovereignty on behalf of the Spanish Government, the proceedings impleaded that Government, and the action should be dismissed.

Held that as the plaintiff's claim did not seek redress against any person other than the defendant, the Government of Spain was not impleaded, and there was no basis for the defendant's claim that the action should be dismissed.

O'Byrne J.:

. . . The immunity of soverign states and their rulers from the jurisdiction of the courts of other states has long been recognised as a principle of international law, and must now be accepted as a part of our municipal law by reason of Article 29.3 of our Constitution, which provides that Ireland accepts the generally recognised principles of international law as its rule of conduct in its relations with other states.

The various authorities dealing with the matter were fully reviewed and considered in the leading case of *The Parlement Belge*, and the principle established by these authorities was stated by Lord Esher (then Brett L.J.) in that case and subsequently reiterated by the same learned judge in *Mighell v Sultan of Johore* (1894) in the following terms:

The principle to be deduced from all these cases is that as a consequence of the absolute independence of every sovereign authority, and of the international comity which induces every sovereign state to respect the independence and dignity of every other sovereign state, each and every one declines to exercise, by means of its courts, any of its territorial jurisdiction over the person of any sovereign or ambassador of any other state, or over the public property of any state which is destined to public use, or over the property of any ambassador, though such sovereign, ambassador, or property be within its territory, and therefore, but for the common agreement, subject to its jurisdiction.

The principle, so stated, has never been whittled down, though it has been considered, amplified and re-stated in many subsequent cases.

The matter was very fully considered by the House of Lords a few years ago in the case of *Compania Naviera Vascongado v S.S. Cristina* (1938) in which a ship, called *The Cristina,* belonging to the plaintiff company and registered at the port of Bilbao, was requisitioned by the Spanish Government; and the Spanish consul at Cardiff, where the ship was lying, having gone on board and dismissed the master and put a new master in charge, the plaintiff company commenced proceedings *in rem* claiming possession of the ship as being their property. The Spanish Government entered a conditional appearance and thereupon applied, by motion on notice, for an order that the writ should be set aside on the ground that it impleaded a foreign sovereign state. This application having been granted by Bucknill J., the plaintiff company appealed, unsuccessfully, to the Court of Appeal and to the House of Lords.

We are not concerned with several of the points discussed in that case; but I desire to cite, from the speech of Lord Atkin, two principles of

international law which, in the opinion of the learned law lord, were well
established and beyond dispute:

(*a*) The first is that the courts of a country will not implead a foreign
sovereign, that is, they will not by their process make him against his
will a party to legal proceedings whether the proceedings involve process
against his person or seek to recover from him specific property or
damages.

(*b*) The second is that they will not by their process, whether the
sovereign is a party to the proceedings or not, seize or detain property
which is his or of which he is in possession or control.

Lord Atkin proceeds:

There has been some difference in the practice of nations as to possible
limitations of this second principle as to whether it extends to property
only used for the commercial purposes of the sovereign or to personal
private property. In this country it is in my opinion well settled that it
applies to both.

The rule deals with the impleading of a foreign sovereign, against his
will, in the courts of another state. Such sovereign may, of course,
voluntarily submit to the jurisdiction, either by instituting proceedings
himself, or by entering an unconditional appearance in proceedings
brought against him personally or in respect of property which he claims;
in any such case no question arises.

It is unnecessary, in this case, to consider the immunity accorded to
ambassadors and other political or diplomatic representatives. Counsel on
behalf of the defendant expressly stated in this court that the defendant
does not claim any such immunity. As I understand the argument of
counsel, the case made on behalf of the defendant is that he came to this
country as an agent for, and on behalf of, the Government of Spain, that
he contracted on behalf of that Government, and that the Spanish
Government is, in truth and effect, defendant in these proceedings.

It was established by the evidence and I shall assume, for the purpose of
this decision, that the defendant is an officer of the Spanish army on active
service, that he came here on an official mission for the purpose of
purchasing horses for the Spanish army, and that the expenses incurred in
connection with such purchases or otherwise in connection with the mission
are to be defrayed out of the funds of the Government of Spain. It
remains to be considered whether, on this basis, the defendant is entitled
to have these proceedings set aside as being, in effect, an impleading of
the sovereign state of Spain or its Government in the courts of this
country.

It is clear that, in the proceedings, as framed, no relief is sought against
any person save the defendant. He is sued in his personal capacity and the
judgment which has been, or any judgment which may hereafter be,
obtained against him, will bind merely the defendant personally, and any
such judgment cannot be enforced against any property save that of the
defendant.

It is contended that the true rule of international law, as recognised in the courts of this country, is that a foreign sovereign cannot be impleaded *directly* or *indirectly* in these courts, and we have been referred to such judgments as that of Greene M.R. in the case of *Haile Selassie v Cable & Wireless Ltd* (1938), in which the rule is so stated. I do not think that the rule, as so stated, differs materially from the rules as stated by Lord Esher and Lord Atkin.

There is only one way in which a sovereign or state may be directly impleaded, viz., by his being named as defendant in the proceedings, and it is conceded that this has not been done in this case. It is, however, argued that there are many ways in which a sovereign or state may be indirectly impleaded, and it is contended that the Spanish State is impleaded here, because the defendant is an official agent of the state and would be entitled to be indemnified out of state funds in respect of any expenses incurred by him in the carrying out of his mission, including any damages awarded against, and any costs incurred by, him in these proceedings.

It may well be that, by virtue of the terms of his appointment, the defendant is, as between himself and his Government, entitled to be so indemnified; but it seems to me that this is far short of saying that the Government is being impleaded.

The claim made on behalf of the plaintiff is that the defendant, while in this country, entered into a contract with them, that he failed to carry out the terms of the contract, and that they, thereby, suffered loss and damage, and they sue him for damages for breach of the contract. It claims that the defendant is personally responsible to them, and it does not seek redress against any other person or persons. In these circumstances, and having regard to the nature and scope of the action, I am of opinion that there is no ground for the suggestion that the Government of Spain is being impleaded, either directly or indirectly, and no basis for the claim that the proceedings should be set aside.

Murnaghan, Geoghegan and Black JJ. concurred.

d. Companies

The capacity of a registered company to contract is generally governed by the objects clause in its memorandum of association. Prior to 1963, a company acting outside its objects could escape contractual liability by claiming that the contract was outside its objects: *In re Bansha Woollen Mills Ltd* (1888); *In re Cummins: Barton v Bank of Ireland* (1939), and *Ashbury Railway Carriage Co. Ltd v Riche* (1875). The *Companies Act 1963*, s. 8, mitigated the harsh effect of this rule by providing that a party *bona fide* contracting with a company that is acting *ultra vires* is entitled to enforce the contract unless it can be shown that party was actually aware that the company was acting *ultra vires: Northern Bank Finance Corporation Ltd v Quinn and Achates Investment Co.* (1979). This topic is discussed, and extracts from these cases are given, in the author's *A Casebook on Irish Company Law*, Chapter 2, pp. 16–24.

CHAPTER 12.

PROPER LAW OF THE CONTRACT

It is a general principle that the parties to a contract are entitled to agree what is to be the proper law of their contract. If they do not make any such agreement then the courts must determine what is the law which is to govern the contract. Should the parties expressly state that Irish law is the proper law of the contract, Irish courts will entertain actions on the contract irrespective of where the contract was made and whether the parties have any real connection with this country: *Kutchera v Buckingham International Holdings Ltd* (Case 68).

Case 68. Kutchera v Buckingham International Holdings Ltd
Supreme Court [1988] I.L.R.M. 501

In a contract between the plaintiff, a non-Irish citizen, and the defendant, a Canadian public company, it was expressly provided that the proper law of the contract should be that of Ireland, and that the parties, in the event of dispute, would irrevocably submit to the jurisdiction of the Irish courts exclusively. The plaintiff issued proceedings and the defendant entered an appearance for the purpose of contesting jurisdiction only and obtained an order of the High Court setting aside the proceedings on the ground that Irish law was unconnected with the realities of the contract. The plaintiff appealed.

Held that the proper law of the contract is Irish law because the contract expressly made it so and it was unnecessary to enquire whether or to what extent the contract was connected with Ireland.

Walsh J.:
***

The grounds upon which the learned judge discharged the order were that the High Court should refuse to accept jurisdiction on the ground that Irish law 'is unconnected with the realities of the contract. It has no

function to determine the validity of this contract which must be
determined by reference to Canadian law.'

In my view the opinion of the learned High Court judge was incorrect.
It would appear from her judgment that because of the fact that it might
become necessary to consider some aspects of Canadian law in the course
of the case with reference to the capacity of the defendants to enter into
the contract she thought this was tantamount to saying that Canadian law
was the proper law of the contract, 'thus contradicting clause 10'.

There is no dispute between the parties as to what is the proper law of
the contract. It is quite clearly Irish law because that is the express
provision of the contract according to the agreement of the parties. The
proper law of the contract in this case is Irish law and the parties have
expressly agreed that their rights and obligations under the contract are to
be determined in accordance with Irish law, and to be determined by an
Irish court. So far as the proper law of the contract is concerned there is
therefore no question of having to try to discover whether the contract has,
or to what extent is has, a connection with this country. Irish law is
applicable because the parties have chosen it and, in the absence of strong
evidence to the contrary, of which there is none, the parties must be
deemed to have intended to refer to the domestic rules of Irish law, and
not to the conflict rules of Irish law . . . The contract therefore falls to be
construed and interpreted by no law save Irish law, and therefore there is
no question of the Irish courts being called upon to apply any foreign law
in so far as the construction or interpretation of the contract is concerned.
It may well be necessary at some stage to refer to the law of Alberta in so
far as any issue may arise concerning the constitution of the defendant
company, because under the conflict of law rules matters concerning the
constitution of a corporation are governed by the laws of the place of the
incorporation of the company. In so far as the case may be concerned with
the capacity of the corporation to enter into any legal transaction, this is a
question which would be governed by the constitution of the company
itself and by the law which governs the transaction, namely, Irish law.

If an Irish court is called upon to apply any part of a foreign law, the
procedures for doing so are already well settled. See the decisions of the
former Supreme Court of Justice in *O'Callaghan v O'Sullivan* (1925) and
MacNamara & Son v Owner of the Steamship 'Hatteras' (1933). These
cases quite clearly establish that in Irish law foreign law must generally be
proved by expert evidence. The burden of proving foreign law lies upon
the party who bases a claim or a defence upon the foreign law, and if that
party produces no evidence, or only insufficient evidence of the foreign
law, the court applies Irish law. These cases also establish that if there is
any conflicting evidence as to what is the foreign law, or what is the
correct interpretation of the foreign law, then it is a matter for the Irish
court to decide as between the conflicting expert testimonies. The
possibility that some foreign law may need to be applied in a case cannot

be a justification for exclusive jurisdiction, notwithstanding that the Irish courts constitute a foreign jurisdiction for all of the parties . . .

The fact that the parties in this case have submitted in their contract to the jurisdiction of an Irish court would be a most important factor in the enforcement of any judgment abroad. It is well established in a series of decisions, not merely in this jurisdiction but in the jurisdiction of other common law countries that agreement by contract to submit to the jurisdiction of a foreign court is an unequivocal acceptance of the jurisdiction of that court, irrespective of whether the defendant fails to appear or fails to contest the case. See the judgment of Kenny J. in *International Alltex Corporation v Lawler Creations Ltd* (1965). It would appear that this is also the law in Canada according to the decision of the *Overseas Food Importers & Distributors v Brandt* (1978). The United States Supreme Court in the case of *Hilton v Guyot* (1895) held that even when there has not been an express submission to jurisdiction of a foreign court, once the court was satisfied that the system of the jurisprudence in question was likely to secure an impartial administration of justice between the citizens of that country and those of other countries, and where there was nothing to show prejudice or fraud in procuring the judgment or any other special reason why the comity of the nation should not allow its full effect, recognition would not be withheld. Other and similar questions have arisen in several English and US cases concerning the effect of entering a conditional appearance in a foreign court. However, one does not have to consider the latter matter in the present case because the defendants clearly and expressly agreed to the Irish courts having sole and exclusive jurisdiction. It is however of interest to note that Art. 18 of the EEC Judgments Convention does permit of conditional appearances not amounting to a submission to jurisdiction.

At no stage have the defendants suggested that a judgment of the Irish court would not be obeyed by them, nor indeed, have they suggested that it would not be enforced abroad. Indeed the defendants could scarcely have expected to impress any Irish court by telling it in advance that it did not propose to obey any order made by that court, notwithstanding the fact that the defendants had agreed to its jurisdiction. In so far as the defendants may be thought to have been arguing that the Irish courts do not constitute a convenient forum, they have not indicated what foreign court, if any, would have jurisdiction. Indeed it is not at all improbable that if proceedings were undertaken in Alberta, Ontario, Hong Kong or anywhere else that the courts there might refuse jurisdiction in view of the express acceptance by the defendants of the Irish jurisdiction.

The notion that an order should not be made by an Irish court where it is unlikely to be obeyed is an erroneous one. It is obvious that in many cases where the court permits service abroad under 0. 11 of the Rules of the Superior courts, resulting in judgment in favour of the plaintiff, the judgment will not be capable of enforcement if the foreign defendant has decided that the better course for him is not to participate in the Irish proceedings at all where he had not made any submission to Irish jurisdiction. Such an event would certainly reduce the chances of a judgment being enforced abroad against the defendant. The idea that an Irish court should on this account decline jurisdiction is quite unacceptable. In the present case the defendant has accepted jurisdiction and for the reasons I have already given that enables a judgment to be enforced abroad. In the present case the plaintiff has invoked the Irish jurisdiction, pursuant to the contract, to seek a declaration from the Irish courts. It is really the plaintiff's business to decide whether this is the most practical step for him to take. I do not believe it is the function of the Irish courts to try to be wiser than he is and to frustrate his expectations. There is in fact no reason to believe that the plaintiff is probably not acting well in his own interest. Because of the clear choice of Irish jurisdiction there is no certainty that proceedings initiated in any other jurisdiction would not fail because of that choice. If he gets judgment in Ireland in any form then it is a matter for him to endeavour to have it enforced in any other jurisdiction. The nature of his remedy in that jurisdiction is determined by the law of that jurisdiction. Thus if he sought to enforce his Irish judgment in Alberta the nature of the remedy the Albertan courts might give him would be determined by Albertan law. Remedies are procedures and there is no vested right in a particular cause of action. The plaintiff must take the remedies available in the forum as he finds them. Furthermore there was no reason offered in this court as to why a court in Alberta or Ontario or anywhere else would not be willing to give effect to an Irish judgment. In this connection it is of value to recall the statement of FitzGibbon L.J. in *Lett v Lett* (1906) where he quoted as a correct statement of the law the following passage from *Fry on Specific Performance* 4th edn, p. 52, ss. 126 and 127:

A contract made abroad may be enforced against a defendant within the jurisdiction of this country, and, as the remedies for breach of a contract are clearly governed by the *lex fori*, it follows that it is no objection to the specific performance in England of a foreign contract that the foreign law might have given no such remedy.

While the Irish courts probably would not enforce a foreign decree for specific performance they would certainly enforce one in Ireland, if one was made by an Irish court, even though the contract was a foreign contract.

However in the present case the plaintiff is not seeking specific performance. The principal remedies which he seeks are declarations and the injunction relief which he seeks is more in the nature of a *quia timet* nature, and would not, even in conjunction with the declaration which he seeks as his primary remedy, amount to specific performance. Even if one were to assume that the courts of Alberta or any other foreign jurisdiction would not enforce that part of an Irish judgment prescribing an injunction, they should have no similar difficulty so far as declarations are concerned. It is up to the Alberta courts applying the *lex fori* to translate these declarations into actual relief. No reason has been shown for the plaintiff to apprehend that he will in fact get no relief in a foreign court on foot of his Irish judgments. In my opinion there is certainly no basis for this court for this reason to decline to permit his case to be considered here on the very threshold of the proceedings in this jurisdiction. Apart from that, it may also be of considerable importance to the plaintiff to have a record of what the Irish court determined were, in accordance with Irish law, his rights under the contract regardless of the question of enforcing the judgment. He might, for example, seek to avail himself of his contractual entitlements, on the basis of the Irish declarations, in a manner which does not involve direct enforcement of the Irish judgment, but which is consistent with them as a statement of his rights under Irish law as the proper law and declared by an Irish court.

I am not aware of any decision in Ireland or indeed in England in which the choice of an Irish, or an English jurisdiction as the case may be, has been set aside in favour of permitting litigation elsewhere. Even if the proper law of this contract was not Irish law I believe that a court in Ireland would have jurisdiction to deal with this matter because of the express choice of the Irish jurisdiction by the parties concerned. In the present case the parties have not merely chosen an Irish jurisdiction but have also agreed and chosen Irish law as the proper law of the contract. Where better can Irish law be interpreted and applied than in an Irish court?

There is quite a number of decisions in courts of various common law countries, including England, to the effect that a person who has agreed to a foreign jurisdiction, and then in breach of that agreement seeks to institute proceedings in England, has had his action stayed. There are also many decisions of English courts to show that English courts are most reluctant to permit service out of the jurisdiction in the face of an agreement by the parties to submit their dispute to the exlusive jurisdiction of a foreign court. This is particularly so when the foreign jurisdiction clauses are 'exclusive jurisdiction' clauses. It appears from the English case law that the principles underlying the English decisions are to the effect that where a plaintiff elects to sue in England in breach of an agreement which referred the dispute to a foreign court, there is a very heavy burden upon such plaintiff to prove that there is a strong cause for the court not to exercise its jurisdiction to stay the proceedings. Admittedly there are also English decisions which indicate that English courts are often quite ready to assume jurisdiction in such cases by refusing a stay where the matter is one which would otherwise fall into the English jurisdiction. Such was the decision in one of the cases cited in the arguments before this court, namely, the case of *The Fehmarn* (1958). In fact that case is the converse of the present case. In that case the agreed law was Soviet Union law, and the agreed jurisdiction was Soviet Union jurisdiction. In my opinion, there is nothing in that decision to indicate that the English court would have declined to exercise jurisdiction in the face of a choice of English jurisdiction clause, nor have I been able to discover any commentator ever to have so understood it or so interpreted that decision.

As was stated recently by this court in *Grehan v Medical Incorporated and Valley Pines Associated* (1986) the permission to issue notice of proceedings out of the jurisdiction is within the discretion of the court. There is nothing whatever in the present case to show that discretion was not properly exercised and the case appears to have fallen squarely within the cases permitted by Order 11. The application by the defendant to have that order set aside is in effect asking the court to act in aid of the defendants in their efforts to act in breach of their own contract by endeavouring to avoid the Irish jurisdiction which they had expressly chosen and agreed to. In general the court should act in a way calculated to make people honour their contracts save where there is shown to exist some very grave cause to do otherwise. No such cause has been shown in the present case. This case is still only at its beginning and it would be a matter for the trial judge when it comes to trial to decide what, if any relief, he deems to be the appropriate relief. It will be a matter for him in the light of the case made and of the submissions made to him to decide whether or not he should grant the declarations sought and whether or not he should grant any injunctions. What is clear beyond all doubt is that the law, and the only law, which he shall be guided by in these decisions is Irish law.

PART TWO

INVALID CONTRACTS

A contract which contains the three essentials and is entered into by persons having full contractual capacity may be invalidated. Here we take a look at the grounds on which a contract may be set aside.

CHAPTER 13.

MISTAKE

Where a party has entered into a contract under an operative mistake that party may be entitled to some remedy. Where there is a fundamental mistake as to the nature of the document signed, the contract may not be binding: *Bank of Ireland v McManamy* (Case 69). Where the document does not incorporate the true intentions of the parties, and one party attempts to take advantage of the mistake, the court may order rectification at the behest of the innocent party: *Nolan v Nolan* (Case 70). The court will not rectify the agreement where there is no mutual mistake: *Lucey v Laurel Construction Co. Ltd* (Case 71).

Where the court feels that some hardship may be caused to the party who attempted to take advantage of the mistake it may refuse to order rectification: *Gun v McCarthy* (Case 72). Instead, rescission may be the remedy granted on the basis that should the parties wish to continue their association they can contract anew. But where the contract has been completely performed, rectification may be the only real remedy available: *Monaghan County Council v Vaughan* (Case 73). While the court might order rectification of the contract it may not grant an order for specific performance of the rectified contract: *Nolan v Graves* (Case 74).

While it is a general rule that money paid under a mistake of law cannot be recovered there are exceptions to that rule: *Rogers v Louth County Council* (Case 75).

Case 69. Bank of Ireland v McManamy

King's Bench [1916] 2 I.R. 161

A co-operative society of which the defendant was a member gave a guarantee to the plaintiff. When the defendant signed the document he honestly believed it to be a receipt for goods received by him from the co-operative. The mistake was not due to any negligence on his part. Nor was there any evidence that his signature was obtained by fraud.

Held that the defendant's plea of *non est factum* must succeed and that he was not bound by the document.

Cherry L.C.J.:
___

The principle of law which the learned judge [in the High Court] evidently had in his mind when framing the questions for the jury, was that laid down by Byles J., in delivering the judgment of the court in the well-known case of *Foster v McKinnon* (1869) namely this: That where a party signs a document under a fundamental mistake as to its nature and character, and that mistake is not due to negligence on his part, he is not bound by his signature, upon the ground that there is, in reality, no contract at all binding him on his part. It is true that in *Foster v McKinnon*, and I think also in nearly all the cases which have followed it, the cause of the error has been fraud on the part of some person, but this is due to the fact that such error as to the nature of the document can scarcely ever exist without fraud on somebody's part. The principle of the cases is not, however, that fraud vitiates consent, but rather that there is an entire absence of consent. That the mind of the party who signs under a fundamental error does not go with the act of signing, and that there is consequently no contract at all in fact. The defendant, if he succeeds, does so upon the issue *non est factum*, not upon the issue of fraud, though fraud, as I have said, is usually present, and is generally found by the jury to have existed.

The following passage, frequently quoted with approval from the judgment of Byles J. in *Foster v McKinnon*, clearly lays down the principle in that way. He says:

It seems plain, on principle and on authority, that if a blind man, or a man who cannot read, or who for some reason (not implying negligence) forbears to read, has a written contract falsely read over to him, the reader misreading to such a degree that the written contract is of a nature altogether different from the contract pretended to be read from the paper which the blind or illiterate man afterwards signs; then, at least if there be no negligence, the signature so obtained is of no force. And it is invalid not merely on the ground of fraud, where fraud exists, but on the ground that the mind of the signer did not accompany the signature; in other words, that he never intended to sign, and, therefore, in contemplation of law never did sign, the contract to which his name is appended.

Boyd J. concurred.

Case 70. Nolan v Nolan
High Court (1958) 92 I.L.T.R. 94

A separation agreement provided that the plaintiff husband should pay to the defendant wife, 'such sum as will after the deduction of income tax at the standard rate amount to the sum of £15 per week'. The words 'at the standard rate' were inserted by the plaintiff after the deed's execution. Later both parties initialled these words. The question arose whether the defendant was entitled to retain refunds of income tax on the sums paid to her, or whether she should account for them to the plaintiff. The plaintiff alleged that the insertion of the words 'at the standard rate' did not correctly reflect the prior agreement which was that he should pay the defendant £15 per week and that any refunds of tax obtained by her should be his property. The plaintiff sought rectification of the deed by the exclusion of the words 'at the standard rate'.

Held that the deed should be rectified to express correctly the prior agreement which was that the defendant should receive £15 per week free of income tax and nothing more and that she was not entitled to retain the refunds of tax.

Dixon J.:

. . . The solicitor's position was that he came in at a late stage when matters had already been finally agreed between the parties, but he did not appreciate nor was he made aware that he was dealing with a document which had been executed on one side. Thinking he was dealing with a draft he said the alteration could be made with a two-fold purpose and effect, viz. (1) to make definite the exact rate of tax at which the deduction was to be made; (2) to ensure that not only would the wife obtain the refunds, but that she would be entitled, or at least be able to make the case that she was entitled to retain them for her own benefit. It was probable that the solicitor had thought this alteration was to be submitted to the husband and his advisers as a far-reaching proposal, requiring express agreement on his part. On the other hand he might have taken the view that the effect which he intended to secure by the alteration was what had been already agreed by the parties and that the alteration purported to make it clear. Either interpretation was open. In any event the words 'at the standard rate' were inserted and the deed was then executed and the alteration initialled by the defendant. The deed was then sent to the plaintiff and initialled by him on the basis that there was a minor interlineation involving the assumption that no material alteration had been made in the deed and that the terms intended by the parties had not been departed from in any material respect.

The position was that the agreement—and the only agreement—between the parties was that the defendant should receive £15 a week, free of tax. The plaintiff brought the proceedings for rectification on the basis that the deed as finally executed did not express that agreement, or that by reason of the state of the authorities it might not express it sufficiently clearly . . .

It had been submitted on behalf of the defendant that it was not a case of mutual mistake, susceptible of rectification, and that seemed to be so in a limited sense, in as much as no case of rectification could really be regarded as a case of mutual mistake; if it were there would be no contest, for the parties could rectify the instrument themselves. The whole question whether a mistake was mutual or unilateral was largely one of phraseology. The present position was analogous to that with which his Lordship had to deal in *Monaghan County Council v Vaughan* (Case 73) and it was expressed in a different and probably better way in a passage quoted by counsel from Kerr on the *Law of Fraud and Mistake*. The basis of the decision in *Monaghan County Council v Vaughan* was that if there were a mistake in a document, in that it did not express the agreement between the parties and one party was not aware of that circumstance while the other party was aware of it, then that was a case of mutual mistake. The party who knew that the expression of the agreement was incorrect could not allege that there was not a mutual mistake because the other party was not aware of that mistake. What happened here came close to misrepresentation or estoppel. The defendant knew what the agreement was between herself and her husband and what was intended to be recorded in the separation deed. She knew when the alteration was made that the deed might not then correctly express the agreement, nevertheless she decided that she would have the alteration made and, if she could, take advantage of the legal consequences. In those circumstances she could not now be heard to say that there was not a mutual mistake. To hold otherwise would come close to permitting fraud.

Accordingly, I am of opinion that the plaintiff is entitled to have the deed rectified to express what I am satisfied was the agreement between the parties, and which the husband was under the impression it did record, while the defendant knew or suspected that it did not . . .

Case 71. Lucey v Laurel Construction Co. Ltd
High Court, unreported, 18 December 1970

The plaintiff wanted to purchase a house and he went to a site which the defendant was developing. He selected a site which was on open ground where no foundations for the walls of the site or for the walls of the house had been cut. He was informed that to book a site he must go to the defendant's Dublin office, which he did. When there he signed his name to a development plan which provided that the house had a length of 170 feet. The parties signed a building contract. Prior to the signing of this contract the defendant decided that two more houses could be fitted into the building scheme if the length of the existing houses were shortened to 120 feet. The development plan of the scheme was not altered nor was any attempt made to alter any of the agreements which had been signed by those intending to purchase houses in the scheme. When the plaintiff sought an injunction to restrain the defendant from trespassing or interferring with the site as purchased the defendant sought rectification of the contract on the ground of mistake.

Held that in the absence of mutual mistake the contract could not be rectified.

Kenny J.:

. . . The next argument was that this is the type of case in which the court would rectify the agreement of the 5 November 1965 so that the plaintiff would get what he knew he was getting when he saw the length of the wall built by the defendant. Throughout, the plaintiff believed that he was entitled to get what was shown on the site map which he signed and he assumed that the 120 feet in length which the defendant originally gave him when it built the wall was what was on the map. The court has jurisdiction to rectify a written agreement made between parties only when either there is a mutual mistake made by the two parties in the drafting of a written agreement which is to give effect to a prior oral agreement or when one party sees a mistake in the written agreement and when he knows that the other party has not seen it and then signs the document knowing that it contains a mistake. See the remarks of Lord Justice Denning in *Rose v Pim* (1953):

> Rectification is concerned with contracts and documents, not with intentions. In order to get rectification it is necessary to show that the parties were in complete agreement on the terms of their contract but by an error wrote them down wrongly. And in this regard, in order to ascertain the terms of their contract you do not look into the inner minds of the parties—into their intentions—any more than you do in the formation of any other contract. You look at their outward acts, i.e. at

what they said or wrote to one another in coming to their agreement, and then compare it with the document which they have signed. If you can predicate with certainty what their contract was, and that it is, by a common mistake, wrongly expressed in the document, then you rectify the document. But nothing less will suffice.

There is a passage in *Crane v Hegeman Harris Co. Inc.* (1939) which suggests that a continuing common intention alone will suffice, but I am clearly of opinion that a continuing intention is not sufficient unless it has found expression in outward agreement. There could be no certainty at all in business transactions if a party who had entered into a firm contract could afterwards turn round and claim to have it rectified on the ground that the parties intended something different. He is allowed to prove, if he can, that they *agreed something different* . . . but not that they *intended* something different.

(See also *Monaghan Co. Co. v Vaughan* (Case 73)).

In this case, however, there was not a mutual mistake. The defendant intended to give a site 120 feet in length but did not tell the plaintiff this and did not think of the measurements shown on the site plan which the plaintiff subsequently signed. The plaintiff thought that he was getting what was shown on the site plan. He did not know that the . . . site plan contained a mistake and he is not making a claim which he knows to be fraudulent . . .

Case 72. Gun v McCarthy
Chancery (1884) 13 L.R.Ir. 304

The parties agreed on the lease of certain premises. The defendant accepted the figure for rent which was in the document. Later it transpired that this figure had been inserted by mistake, a mistake which the defendant must have realised before he executed the lease. The plaintiff sought to have the lease rectified which the defendant resisted.

Held that this was a case of unilateral mistake of which the defendant attempted to benefit. In the circumstances rescission rather than rectification was the appropriate remedy.

Flanagan J.:

I have always understood the law to be that when you seek to reform a conveyance you must first establish—whether by parol evidence or otherwise—that there was a definite concluded agreement between the parties, but which, by mistake common to both parties to the agreement, had not been carried out in the conveyance executed pursuant to the real agreement. But when the mistake is not common, what can you reform by? To reform implies a previous *agreement*; but when the evidence shows that there was no agreement to which both parties assented, but only a mistake on one side, and not a common mistake, in my opinion it is impossible to support a suit to *reform*, whatever equity the party who has made the mistake may have in certain cases to rescind the conveyance.

. . . Mr. Justice Fry, in his book on *Specific Performance* (2nd edn, p. 340, § 759), says: 'The mistake of one party can never be a ground for compulsory rectification. It may be a reason for setting the whole thing aside, but never for imposing on one party the erroneous conception of the other.' So, in *Mortimer v Shortall*, Lord St. Leonards lays it down that a mistake on one side may be a ground for rescinding a contract; but that, unless there was evidence of a mistake on both sides, the contract could not be rectified . . .

Whether, however, parol evidence be admissible or not where a written agreement exists, I am clearly of opinion that so far as the relief sought is to reform the lease, a mutual mistake must be proved; and this, in my opinion, the facts show did not exist. But, further, I am of opinion that so far as the relief sought is to rescind the contract, parol evidence is admissible, whether there was or was not a written agreement prior to the executed conveyance; and that, on such facts, it becomes a question whether they raise a sufficient equity to justify the court in making a decree for the rescission of the contract as executed . . .

In my opinion, where there being a clear undoubted mistake by one party in reference to a material term of the contract which he entered into with another, and the other party knowingly seeks to avail himself of that, and seeks to bind the other to the mistake, the law of this court is, that it will not allow such a contract to be binding on the parties, but will give relief against it. I do not think the contract could be reformed; there is nothing to reform it by. If the court comes to the conclusion that the parties have never entered into an agreement, it would be a contradiction in terms for it to say that it could reform the agreement. I say that with the greatest respect for the decisions in *Garrard v Frankel* (1862), and *Harris v Pepperell* (1867), I confess I think these decisions can only be supported in the way suggested by Mr Justice Fry: that the contracts were reformed on the ground that the party, against whom the decision was, elected to take the contracts reformed. But where the party insists generally on his right to retain the contract in the terms of the conveyance as executed, my opinion is, that the contract ought to be rescinded: and the decision I have come to is, I shall reverse the decision of the County Court judge, so far as he directs this lease and agreement to be reformed, but I shall direct the lease and agreement to be delivered up to be cancelled, as I think the contract cannot be retained by the defendant, as I think his seeking to do so is uncandid and dishonest, and that if he had come in here to enforce the contract his action would have been dismissed . . .

(See also Case 159, regarding rectification.)

Case 73. Monaghan County Council v Vaughan
High Court [1948] I.R. 306

The plaintiff owners of a derelict building advertised for tenders for its demolition and debris removal from the site. The plaintiffs accepted a written tender submitted by the defendant. When advertising and accepting the tender the plaintiffs' intention was that the defendant should pay for the concession of keeping the materials removed from the site. The terms of the advertisement and tender were ambiguous. After the work's completion the defendant contended that he should be paid by the plaintiffs for doing the work. The plaintiffs sought to have the written contract rectified on the ground of mistake.

Held that the intention of both parties throughout had been that the defendant should pay to the plaintiffs the sum in question, that the common or mutual intention was misrepresented by the record of that intention and that the defendant realised, and attempted to take advantage of, the error made by the plaintiffs when the contract was read over to him. There being mutual mistake the remedy of rectification was appropriate.

Dixon J.:
_____

. . . My view of the facts in the case is this. At the close of the plaintiffs' case, I had no doubt (and still have none), that a mistake was made by them in the written form of the contract. The terms of the advertisement and of the form of tender, together with the prior offers made by [another tender] show that the contract was regarded by the plaintiffs as a valuable concession. In addition, the circumstances themselves indicated that valuable material would be obtained from the demolition work—material for which there was a rising market price, as a result of which, no doubt, the offers already received had been refused as insufficient. These factors, of course, do not all necessarily affect the defendant.

The clear intention of the plaintiffs was that they should be paid for granting the right to carry out the work of demolition, and, while the defendant's offer was ambiguous in form, leaving it doubtful as to whether it contemplated that he was to pay or to be paid the sum of £1,200, I have no doubt that the plaintiffs construed it as meaning that they were to be paid that sum by the defendant, particularly as they had already received and refused an offer by [the other tender] to do the work and to pay a sum of £1,125 for the concession.

As to what the defendant's intention really was, I regard his evidence as being very unconvincing and, having regard to his demeanour in the witness box, I am unable to accept very much of what he said. Furthermore, most of his evidence conflicts sharply with the probabilities in the matter.

The plaintiffs have made a *prima facie* case on the language of the advertisement, that their offer was for a payment to them of whatever sum should be agreed upon in return for the right to carry out the demolition work. Clause 13 of the specification was called to the attention of the defendant, and both its terms and the fact that the material to be obtained by way of salvage on the demolition would have a substantial value, are consistent only with the intention of both parties having been that the plaintiffs should be paid and not that they should have to pay. This conclusion appears to me to be strengthened rather than rebutted by the evidence of the defendant himself.

Accordingly, I must hold that the intention of the defendant as well as that of the plaintiffs was that the defendant should pay to the plaintiffs a sum of £1,200 for the right to carry out the demolition work . . .

For these reasons I am satisfied that it was the intention of both parties that the defendant should pay the sum of £1,200 to the plaintiffs, and I am of opinion that the defendant saw the error into which the plaintiffs had fallen when the contract was read over to him and decided to take advantage of it. I regard this as a case of mutual mistake. I think that it is immaterial that one party knows the document to be inaccurate for the purposes of the principles of law applicable to mutual mistake. What is material is that both parties were agreed upon certain matters and that the completed contract did not correctly represent the substance of their agreement. A unilateral mistake arises where one of two or more parties is not *ad idem* with the other party or parties, and there is therefore, no real agreement between them. In such a case, rescission may be appropriate, but the present is a different case. It is not a case of unilateral mistake in that sense, but to speak of it as a case of mutual mistake may obscure its true character of a common or mutual intention misrepresented by the record of that intention.

If the defendant had really intended that he should be paid the sum of £1,200 the position would be entirely different, but on the evidence I reject that view and hold that he attempted to take advantage of the error made by the plaintiffs and that his conduct was dishonest and approximated to fraud . . .

Case 74. Nolan v Graves
High Court [1946] I.R. 376

Premises were knocked down at an auction to the plaintiff for £4,550 but the defendant contended the true price was £5,550. In the written contract the price was stated to be £4,550 and the deposit and auctioneer's fees were calculated accordingly. The plaintiff called on the defendant to complete the contract at the lower price, or to return the deposit and fees. This the defendant refused. The plaintiff sued for rescission of the contract and the defendant counterclaimed for rectification and specific performance of the contract at the higher price.

Held that the figure of £4,550 was inserted in the contract by mistake, and that the figure should have been £5,550. The plaintiff was aware of this mistake and endeavoured to take advantage of it. Therefore she was not entitled to any relief. The contract was rectified but specific performance was refused. The plaintiff could then elect whether she would, or would not, complete the sale at the true price.

Haugh J.:

. . . The jurisdiction of the court as regards both rectification and specific performance is a delicate jurisdiction, and it is clear, from the mass of decisions cited before me, that it must be exercised with discretion and care . . .

The question is, has the defendant any remedy in law? The substance of the submissions made by the plaintiff is, No. Her counsel submits that even at the worst view of her evidence he has no redress other than rescission, by means of which the court would undo the contract and leave all the parties in their former position. I cannot see that rescission in itself will afford the defendant any remedy or redress for the wrong done to him. It is clear that he could have had that, on the plaintiff's submission, without ever coming into court, or without ever making a counterclaim, by simply handing back her money and having another auction on some other day. I cannot and do not, from his point of view, regard rescission of the contract even at £4,550 without rectification, or by rectifying it to the higher figure and then rescinding it, as being a real remedy at all to the defendant, though plaintiff's counsel say that that is his only right.

A great number of cases have been cited, some of which conflict. The case of *Craddock Brothers v Hunt* (1923) decided by the Court of Appeal in England and the case of *United States of America v Motor Trucks Ltd* (1924) were cited by counsel for the defendant as establishing from their point of view, the principles upon which I should act. Now, these cases have been referred to over and over again; and counsel for the plaintiff points out that in *Craddock's Case* the contract was an executed contract. It was a case in which the parties had gone into possession of the respective premises, portion of one of which was in dispute, and in which the persons who later became plaintiffs, actually received the rent of the yard in dispute for some years; and it was only when they sent out an architect for some building purpose who measured the yard and compared it with the parcels shown on the plaintiffs' deeds and plans and found that the plaintiffs, Craddock Brothers, had never, in fact, under their conveyance got this yard, that the defendant on his part for the first time realised that it was in the conveyance to him, and immediately and for the first time sought to take advantage of what he knew he never got at the sale. He took advantage of the actual conveyance to him and refused any relief, by way of rectification or otherwise, to the plaintiffs who had paid for the yard in question. Counsel for the plaintiff, with some force, pointed out that that was a case in which, if the court did not rectify the transaction, the man who had bought and paid for the disputed plot could not get any other form of relief: and the defendant, who had got possession of the disputed plot, could have retained it, although he was dishonestly in possession of it, and dishonestly making claim to it, even though he knew at the auction that he never got it and only found he had got it when he examined his conveyance. The difference between that case and this case is that there is no similar conclusion between the parties. There has been no conveyance here; no parting by the defendant with his houses to the plaintiff. At most there is only a contract made pursuant to the *Statute of Frauds* and in anticipation of the actual conveyance. For all one knows, this present contract might have broken down through some answers to the requisitions on title, as they sometimes do.

I see the difference between the altered position of the parties in *Craddock's Case* against what I might call the unaltered position of the parties in this case. At p. 151 of the report, the Master of the Rolls said:

I think I am at liberty, at any rate since the *Judicature Act 1873*, to express my opinion that rectification can be granted of a written agreement on parol evidence of mutual mistake, although that agreement is complete in itself, and has been carried out by a more formal document based upon it.

Well, in this case I have a written agreement complete in itself, the parties' names are there; it recites the auction, and contains all that it should. There is no ambiguity about the words; it recites clearly the purchase-price and the other figures based upon that purchase-price. The parol evidence is there, and counsel for the plaintiff has pressed very strongly upon me to note that that case, and indeed most of the other cases, are decided on what is called mutual mistake or common mistake. It seems to me that, on his contention, the defendant would be in a better position as regards the counter-claim if the plaintiff was only guilty of some mistake in common with the auctioneer leading to this incorrect memorandum being drawn— for instance, instead of seeing the figure £4,550, that she never looked at the figure at all, but signed her name to the memorandum and then sent up a cheque which was based on the wrong amount and went home. There you have a clear mistake on her part in signing the memorandum without reading it. Or at a later stage, if she sought to take advantage of what was a mistake on her part, it would seem to me, on the strict reading of the words 'mutual mistake,' the defendant would be in a stronger position than in this case where I hold there was no mistake on her part, but a deliberate attempt to take advantage of a one-sided error. I cannot, in equity at least, see why he should be in any weaker position by reason of the fact that her conduct is worse than that of making a mere mistake.

Why should the principle stated by the Master of the Rolls in *Craddock's Case* which I have just quoted, not apply here? Lord Warrington, at p. 159 of the report in *Craddock's Case* says:

The jurisdiction of courts of equity in this respect is to bring the written document executed in pursuance of an antecedent agreement into conformity with that agreement.

Now, that is the jurisdiction—to bring a written document, executed in pursuance of an antecedent agreement into conformity with that agreement. Translate that passage in reference to this case: The jurisdiction of courts of equity in this respect is to bring 'the memorandum', executed in pursuance of 'the bidding', into conformity with 'the bidding'. Lord Warrington goes on: 'The conditions to its exercise are that there must be an antecedent contract.' Well, the condition to the exercise of that jurisdiction in this case is that there must have been an antecedent agreement—antecedent to the memorandum. There is an offer to pay £5,550 and the acceptance of that offer. That is the antecedent agreement here. 'And the common intention of embodying or giving effect to the whole of that contract by the writing.' I am satisfied, as I said before, that the plaintiff's bid was one of £5,550; I am satisfied that her conversation with the auctioneer was on the basis of such an offer. I am satisfied that it was the common intention of the auctioneer, representing the vendor, and of the plaintiff, 'to bring the document into conformity with that agreement' (in the words of the learned Lord Justice in *Craddock's Case*; they had 'the common intention of embodying or giving effect to the whole of that contract by the writing'. To put it shortly, these two parties came together with the common intention of reducing to writing a sale at £5,550, 'and', as Lord Warrington continued, 'there must be clear evidence that the document, by common mistake, failed to embody such contract and either contained provisions not agreed upon or omitted something that was agreed upon, or otherwise departed from its terms'. There is cogent, clear and preponderating evidence in this case that this document failed to embody the contract, because the price is different. It contains a provision that has a lower price which is not agreed upon and omits something agreed upon, that is the higher price, and in that respect it departs from its terms. I can only repeat that I do not see why this lady, who is in a worse position than that of making a mistake in common with the defendant, should not be at least in the same position as if common mistake and common mistake only, was the cause of this incorrect document being executed.

The case of the *United States of America v Motor Trucks Ltd* has been referred to already. That was a case brought by the United States Government against Motor Trucks Ltd., who were a firm who, during the last war, agreed to make munitions for the American Government, subject to hostilities ceasing, when the contract could be terminated. Some time after the armistice the United States Government did serve notice of

termination and certain accounts had to be taken as to what amount of
money the United States Government owed to the defendant company. A
sum of a million and a half dollars was agreed upon, which included the
sum of 376,000 dollars, being the amount which the company claimed in
respect of certain lands and buildings which had been erected by them
following their activities as munition makers. After deducting large sums
from the above total, which the Government had already advanced to the
appellants, it was agreed that the sum of 637,812 dollars was due. Now,
one has to bear in mind that the sum included the 376,000 dollars for the
premises, and it was agreed that a contract should be drawn up.

It was drawn up between the parties and the schedule to the contract
failed to include those buildings in the conveyance although the
Government of the United States paid for them; and, when they realised
this omission, they sued before the appropriate Court in Ontario for
specific performance of the agreement. This was decreed by the trial judge
and the Truck Company appealed to the Supreme Court of Ontario and
succeeded. The matter then came for decision before the Judicial
Committee of the Privy Council, where the judgment of the Supreme
Court of Ontario was reversed and the judgment of the trial judge
(decreeing specific performance), restored. Now, it is well to recollect the
facts in that case because there, in a sense, there was a concluded contract;
that is to say, the Truck Company had been paid for these buildings, and it
would appear that they were in possession of them. Counsel for the
plaintiff points out in regard to this case that it, too, deals with what is
termed a mutual mistake or a 'common mistake'. He also points out that
there was a concluded contract. Money had passed and he says that it was
not (as in this case) a contract of an executory nature. It struck me that, if
that were so, and if the court in that case had no power to rectify or to
order specific performance, all the court should have done was to rescind
(which plaintiff's counsel says is all that can be done in this case). In that
case why not rescind the contract and simply order the Truck Company to
send back the 376,000 dollars for the premises? Why not order them to
hand that money back to the United States Government and rescind
merely? The trial judge and the Privy Council later, in effect, ordered
rectification and specific performance of the agreement. The learned judge
who delivered the judgment of the Privy Council, with clarity, put his
views as to the position between the parties in passages which I do not
intend to read fully but some of which I shall quote. He says:

> And indeed the power of the court to rectify mutual mistake implies that
> this power may be exercised notwithstanding that the true agreement of
> the parties has not been expressed in writing. Nor does the rule make
> any inroad upon another principle, that the plaintiff must show first, that
> there was an actually concluded agreement antecedent to the instrument
> which is sought to be rectified. (In this case the antecedent agreement is
> the bidding.) And secondly, that such agreement has been inaccurately
> represented in the instrument. (I have found that it has been.) When

this is proved either party (be it vendor or purchaser, in the capacity of plaintiff or defendant), may claim, in spite of the *Statute of Frauds*, that the instrument on which the other insists does not represent the real agreement.

I am satisfied from my reading of these cases that I have jurisdiction to rectify, and ought to rectify, the memorandum in such a way that it will represent the actual contract, voluntarily entered into between the plaintiff and the defendant. The mistake was one which the plaintiff had full power to remedy, every opportunity and chance of remedying, and it in no way prejudiced her; but she knowingly sought to take advantage of it for the reasons I have stated. I shall therefore decree rectification of this memorandum, not on the terms upon which the defendant in his counterclaim asks, because I cannot do so. I shall decree rectification of the figure of £4,550 to the figure of £5,550 and I will leave it at that, because that will make it right. Then I shall declare that the plaintiff was the highest bidder and was declared the purchaser at the price of £5,550 and has paid to the auctioneer, a sum of £1,137 10s. by way of deposit and a sum of £277 10s. by way of auctioneer's fees. That is all she has paid; and if I altered these figures I would be simply making the document read and relate to something that has not in fact happened. The position is that all she has paid is a sum of £227 10s. being five per cent on £4,550 and the balance, £1,137 10s. by way of deposit on a similar sum. Now, that is what has happened, and it would be wrong of me to alter these figures when, in truth and in fact, she has paid no more. I shall decree rectification and order that the first figure be changed to the higher sum of £5,550 and any consequential figures that may follow in respect of the deposit and auctioneer's fees. I shall also decree that the balance at the bottom shall be changed from £3,412 to the correct figure that follows from the purchase-price being £5,550 . . .

After rectification, there arises the question of the specific performance of the agreement. I rather think that under the circumstances I cannot give specific performance of this agreement because it is my view that the document has been rectified as against the written memorandum. It is only now that it becomes effective as an instrument required by the *Statute of Frauds*. From now on, at least from the time my order is made up, it remains for the plaintiff to elect whether she will, or will not, perform the sale at the price that she has contracted to buy the premises for. However, I am satisfied on the document that I rectify that the vendor will have the ordinary rights that accrue to him under what I now call the contract that correctly represents the intention of the parties, and for the same reasons I will not decree forfeiture of the deposit. The only relief I give is rectification of the memorandum to the figure of £5,550 and rectification of the necessary balances now due by the plaintiff to the defendant.

(See also Case 48, regarding the construction of a contract and Case 160, regarding the remedy of rectification.)

Case 75. Rogers v Louth County Council
Supreme Court [1981] I.L.R.M. 144; [1981] I.R. 265

The plaintiff was entitled to a cottage subject to payment to the defendants of an annuity of a stated sum for 49 years from 1958. When asked to state the amount of the payment required for the redemption of the annuity, the defendants replied in 1969 that the price was £1163. The plaintiff paid that sum to the defendants. The Supreme Court in another case held that the method of calculating the redemption price in such instances to date was incorrect. By applying the correct method it appeared that the plaintiff should only have paid £227 as the redemption price of the annuity. The plaintiff sued the defendants for the amount overpaid. It was accepted by the parties that the amount so overpaid by the plaintiff had been paid by her under a mistake of law.

Held that the sum overpaid by the plaintiff, although paid under a mistake of law, was recoverable as the overpayment was not a voluntary payment since the parties had not been on equal terms and the defendants had been responsible for the mistake.

Griffin J.:

. . . The real question for determination is whether a payment made in mistake of law, in circumstances such as the present, is recoverable. The general rule is usually stated to be that, where money is paid under the influence of a mistake of fact, an action will lie to recover it; but that, to entitle a plaintiff to recover, the mistake upon which he has acted must be one of fact and not of law. Thus in Pollock on Contracts (13th ed.) it is stated at p. 378 that 'money paid under a mistake of law cannot in any case be recovered.' Similar statements are to be found in many text-books.

However, the Judicial Committee of the Privy Council held in *Kiriri Cotton Co. Ltd v Dewani* (1960) that a plaintiff may recover money which was paid on a mistake of law, provided that he was not *in pari delicto* with the defendant in mistaking the law. In delivering the advice of the Privy Council, Lord Denning said:

> Nor is it correct to say that money paid under a mistake of law can never be recovered back. The true proposition is that money paid under a mistake of law, by itself and without more, cannot be recovered back. James L.J. pointed that out in *Rogers v Ingham* (1876). If there is something more in addition to a mistake of law—if there is something in the defendant's conduct which shows that, of the two of them, he is the one primarily responsible for the mistake—then it may be recovered back. Thus, if as between the two of them the duty of observing the law is placed on the shoulders of the one rather than the other—it being imposed on him specially for the protection of the other—then they are not *in pari delicto* and the money can be recovered back . . . Likewise,

if the responsibility for the mistake lies more on the one than the other—because he has misled the other when he ought to know better—then again they are not *in pari delicto* and the money can be recovered back . . .

That passage was cited with approval by Mr Justice Kenny in *Dolan v Neligan* (1967). Even where there has been no mistake of fact, a plaintiff in an action for money had and received may still recover monies so paid upon proof that the monies were paid by him involuntarily, that is to say, as the result of some extortion, coercion or compulsion in the legal sense: *per* Windeyer J. in *Mason v New South Wales* (1959). He cannot recover if the payment was made voluntarily. In this context a payment may be said to be voluntary when the payer makes it deliberately with a knowledge of all the relevant facts, being either indifferent to whether or not he is liable in law or knowing, or having reason to think, himself not liable, yet intending finally to close the transaction: *per* Windeyer J. Whether the payment has been voluntary in this sense may also be deduced from the relationship of the parties. As Abbot C.J. said in *Morgan v Palmer* (1824):

> It has been well argued that the payment having been voluntary, it cannot be recovered back in an action for money had and received. I agree that such a consequence would have followed had the parties been on equal terms. But if one party has the power of saying to the other, 'that which you require shall not be done except upon the conditions which I choose to impose', no person can contend that they stand upon anything like an equal footing.

In such a case, the payment is by no means to be considered to be voluntary: *per* McTiernan J. in *Bell Bros. Pty Ltd v Shire of Serpentine-Jarrahdale* (1969).

Applying these principles to the present case, in my judgment the plaintiff is entitled to recover the overpayment of £935.53 made by her. The payment of £1,163 made by the plaintiff was not 'voluntary' in the context aforesaid. The parties were not on equal terms. The defendants had the power, if they thought fit, to withhold permission for the redemption of the annuity; they were prepared to allow the plaintiff to redeem it but only on the conditions imposed by them, which included exacting a payment in excess of that permitted by the statute. The plaintiff was not in possession of all the relevant facts and did not know, nor had she reason to think, that she was not liable to pay the sum demanded by the defendants for the redemption of the annuity. In my view, the defendants were primarily responsible for the mistake and, accordingly, the parties were not *in pari delicto*.

O'Higgins C.J. concurred and Kenny J. delivered a concurring judgment.

CHAPTER 14.

MISREPRESENTATION

A misrepresentation is a false statement of a material fact made by one party which induces the other party to enter into the contract. Before a statement can take effect as a misrepresentation it must be shown that it was relied upon by the aggrieved party: *Grafton Court Ltd v Wadson Sales Ltd* (Case 76). Misrepresentation may be of two kinds, innocent misrepresentation and fraudulent misrepresentation.

Case 76. Grafton Court Ltd v Wadson Sales Ltd
High Court, unreported, 17 February 1975

The defendant leased a shop in the plaintiff's shopping arcade. When the plaintiff sued for arrears of rent the defendant alleged that the lease had been entered into on the representation, which was false, that the tenants occupying other units in the complex would be of the high-class quality retail type.

   Held that the quality of tenants of the other units had been known to the defendant before the agreement was made and that the defendant had not relied on the plaintiff's representation.

Finlay P.:

. . . I am satisfied that at a very early stage before the lease of 14 April 1972 was executed it was represented to defendant's director by an employee of the plaintiff that the other tenants occupying stalls or units in Grafton Court would be of high-class quality retail type. The evidence before me however, established that as of 14 April 1972 by far the great majority of all the stalls originally occupied by various leaseholders had been taken up and that the director's position at the time his company entered into the lease was that he knew the identity, type of trade and quality of trade which was being carried on by almost all the other tenants in Grafton Court. If, therefore, and I do not so decide, that quality and nature of those tenants and the type of trade they carried on fell short of the representations which were made by the plaintiff's employee that failure must have been known to the defendant company in the person of its director before the lease was executed and he could not therefore, in my judgment, have still been relying on any representations that had been made to him. I accordingly do not consider that there was any breach or failure of this representation in respect of which any relief can be afforded to the defendant company . . .

a. Innocent Misrepresentation

Should one party to a contract make a misrepresentation believing it to be true but which in fact is false that party commits innocent misrepresentation. Where innocent misrepresentation is proved after the contract is complete, the law gives no remedy to the injured party: *Lecky v Walter* (Case 77). Where the contract is not complete, such as one relating to property transactions, the courts will refuse to grant specific performance against a party who has suffered innocent misrepresentation: *Smelter Corporation of Ireland Ltd v O'Driscoll* (Case 78) or may order rescission of the incomplete contract: *Gahan v Boland* (Case 79). Where the party suffering the innocent misrepresentation applies to the court for assistance, the court may order specific performance of a rectified contract: *Connor v Potts* (Case 80).

Case 77. Lecky v Walter
High Court [1914] I.R. 378

The plaintiff purchased bonds in a company from the defendant. The bonds were purchased on the faith of a representation that they were a charge on the company's property. They were not in fact, but the representation was made innocently. The plaintiff sought rescission of the contract.

Held that as the plaintiff got what he bargained for, the contract could not be rescinded on account of the defendant's innocent misrepresentation.

O'Connor M.R.:

. . . Does this state of affairs give the plaintiff the right to set aside a transaction which has been in fact completed, and is not merely in the process of completion? It must be borne in mind that there is no allegation of fraudulent misrepresentation, and therefore the case is to be treated as one in which a *bona fide* mistake was made by the defendant.

Counsel for the defendant contended that in such circumstances the plaintiff had no cause of action, and he relied upon the judgment of Lord Campbell in the House of Lords in *Wilde v Gibson* (1848) where he says:

My Lords, after the very attentive and anxious consideration which this case has received, I have come to the clear conclusion that the decree appealed against ought to be reversed; and I must say that in the court below, the distinction between a bill for carrying into execution an executory contract, and a bill to set aside a conveyance that has been executed, has not been very distinctly borne in mind. With regard to the first: if there be, in any way whatever, misrepresentation or concealment which is material to the purchaser, a court of equity will not compel him to complete the purchase; but where the conveyance has been executed, I apprehend, my Lords, that a court of equity will set aside the conveyance only on the ground of actual fraud. And there would be no safety for the transactions of mankind, if, upon a discovery being made, at any distance of time, of a material fact not disclosed to the purchaser, of which the vendor had merely constructive notice, a conveyance which had been executed could be set aside.

In *Brownlie v Campbell* (1880), Lord Selbourne affirms the same principle. He says there:

Passing from the stage of correspondence and negotiation to the stage of written agreement, the purchaser takes upon himself the risk of errors. I assume them to be errors unconnected with fraud in the particulars, and when the conveyance takes place it is not, so far as I know, in either country the principle of equity that relief should afterwards be given against that conveyance, unless there be a case of fraud, or a case of misrepresentation amounting to fraud, by which the purchaser may have been deceived.

There appears to be no doubt that the law established by these cases is just as applicable to the sale of a chattel or a chose in action as to the sale of real property which is carried out by conveyance: *Seddon v North Eastern Salt Co. Ltd* (1905).

How are these authorities met by the plaintiff's counsel? He in reply admitted, as of course he was obliged to admit that the authorities referred to were binding on this court, but argued that they only apply to cases in which the purchaser has got in substance what he contracted to buy, and have no application when he has got something substantially different; and he relies upon the judgment of Blackburn J. in *Kennedy v Panama, New Zealand, Australian Mail Co.* (1867). Blackburn J. says:

There is, however, a very important difference between cases where a contract may be rescinded on account of fraud, and those in which it may be rescinded on the ground that there is a difference in substance between the thing bargained for and that obtained. It is enough to show that there was fraudulent representation as to *any part* of that which induced the party to enter into the contract which he seeks to rescind; but where there has been an innocent misrepresentation or misapprehension, it does not authorise a rescission unless it is such as to show that there is a complete difference in substance between what was supposed to be and what was taken, so as to constitute a failure of consideration. For example, where a horse is bought under the belief that it is sound, if the purchaser was induced to buy by a fraudulent representation as to the horse's soundness, the contract may be rescinded. If he was induced by an honest misrepresentation as to its soundness, though it may be clear that both vendor and purchaser though they were dealing about a sound horse and were in error, yet the purchaser must pay the whole price, unless there was a warranty; and even if there was a warranty, he cannot return the horse and claim back the whole price, unless there was a condition to that effect in the contract.

Now, if I may so speak of such an eminent judge as Lord Blackburn, the proposition which he there lays down must commend itself, not only to all lawyers, but to all persons of sound judgment. If there is a complete difference in substance between the thing contracted for and the thing delivered, there is a complete failure of consideration, and the price may be recovered. But if the thing delivered is in substance what was contracted for, and the price is paid, the transaction stands, and the purchaser has no remedy unless there has been a warranty. I am speaking of course of cases in which there has been no fraud, and where any misrepresentation which has induced the contract was a wholly innocent misrepresentation. Lord Blackburn gives as an example the common case of a horse bought on the representation that it was sound. The purchaser has no remedy unless he has got a warranty; and why? Because he has got in substance what he contracted for, viz., a horse. The horse may be in fact unsound, but still it is a horse, even though a very inferior one; and there is not a complete failure of consideration.

There would, of course, be a complete difference in substance if some animal other than a horse had been delivered, if such a thing can be imagined. I will try to give an example nearer akin to the present case. If a man contracts to purchase mortgage debentures of a public company, and takes delivery of what he believes to be such, but what he afterwards discovers to be ordinary shares, he has not got in substance what he bargained for, but something quite different, one being a specifically secured liability of the company, the other being a share in the company's undertaking on which the liability is imposed. Here again there is a complete failure of consideration. In *Kennedy v Panama, New Zealand, Australian Mail Co.* the plaintiff sought to set aside the contract for taking shares in the company on the ground that it was induced by an untrue statement in the company's prospectus that the company had a contract with the Government of New Zealand for an important monthly mail service. The statement was made quite innocently, and as the result of mistake. It was held that the plaintiff was not entitled to any relief, there having been no fraud, and he having got what he contracted for, viz., shares, although not so valuable as they would have been if the company had had the mail contract mentioned. Lord Blackburn, in his judgment, referred to two reported cases: *Gompertz v Bartlett* (1853) and *Gurney v Wormersley* (1854) in which the plaintiffs got relief on the ground that they did not get what they bargained for. In each case there was a sale of a bill of exchange: in one case the bill was a forgery; in the other the bill was void under the stamp laws. In neither case did the plaintiff get what he contracted for—a valid bill of exchange.

I think that these decisions make it easy to determine whether in the present case the plaintiff got in substance what he agreed to buy . . .

The plaintiff has got what he bought. He agreed to buy bonds and he has got bonds. They may be of little or no value, but they are bonds. It is not alleged that they are forgeries. Their validity is not in any way impeached. In substance, then, the plaintiff has got what he bargained for . . .

Case 78. Smelter Corporation of Ireland Ltd v O'Driscoll
Supreme Court [1977] I.R. 305

The plaintiff approached the defendant to purchase her land. She was reluctant to sell. During efforts to persuade her the plaintiff's agent informed her that should she refuse, the local authority would compulsorily acquire the land, a statement the agent believed true but which was without foundation. The defendant believed the statement to be true. The defendant's mistaken belief was reinforced by a visit of senior officials of the local authority together with the plaintiff's agent during which another reference was made to compulsory purchase. Eventually the defendant agreed to sell. When she refused to complete the sale the plaintiff sought an order for specific performance of the contract.

Held that by reason of the plaintiff's innocent misrepresentation the defendant was under a fundamental misapprehension about the true facts and that it would be unjust to grant the relief sought.

O'Higgins C.J.:

On behalf of the plaintiff an auctioneer interviewed the defendant's husband and offered £800 per acre for the land which was subsequently the subject of the options. Believing that the Cork County Council as the planning authority had power under [statute] to acquire these lands compulsorily for the development contemplated by the plaintiff, and further believing that, as a matter of probability, this power would be exercised, the auctioneer so informed the defendant's husband. He did this in good faith, as the learned trial judge has found, believing his statement to represent the reality of the situation facing the defendant. The auctioneer followed up this verbal statement with a letter dated 11 August 1969, which was written to the solicitor acting for the defendant. In this letter he again made an offer of £800 per acre but added:
> We are suggesting that, since the probability of a compulsory purchase order being made is admitted, the necessity of having the order made be dispensed with and that the value of the land be submitted to an independent arbitrator acceptable to both parties, and that both parties be bound by his decision.

This letter was a clear indication of the auctioneer's view, as the negotiator on behalf of the plaintiff, that if the £800 per acre was not acceptable the defendant ought to agree to the price being determined by an independent arbitrator in order to avoid a compulsory purchase order.

It seems clear that the defendant's solicitor did not doubt for a moment the soundness of the view expressed by the auctioneer, and that subsequent negotiations were conducted on the basis that, if agreement was not possible, compulsory purchase would be the next step . . .

Despite the efforts of the auctioneer, the defendant, through her husband, could not be persuaded to sell although the offer made on behalf of the plaintiff was substantially increased.

By 9 October 1969, all negotiations had come to an end and the possibility of the plaintiff securing the defendant's lands by agreement seemed remote in the extreme. On that date a number of people, representing the plaintiff, called to the County Hall in Cork which is the headquarters of the Cork County Council . . . Following this meeting the county manager, the chairman, the vice-chairman, the auctioneer and the development officer went in a body to see the defendant's husband for the purpose of urging him to resume negotiations with the plaintiff for the sale of the land. There was again a conflict in the evidence at the trial as to what was said at this interview with the defendant's husband. The defendant's husband maintained that it was made clear to him by the gentlemen who called to see him that, if he was not willing to sell, the lands would be acquired compulsorily by the county council. This was disputed by the county council witnesses. However, the learned trial judge was satisfied that at this interview there had been a reference to the compulsory purchase of the lands and that this, coupled with what had previously been said and written by the auctioneer, operated on the mind of the defendant's husband. This, of course, is a finding of fact by the learned trial judge which is binding on this court . . .

The defendant's husband, who acted for her throughout the negotiations, believed that if there was not a voluntary sale there would be a compulsory acquisition of the lands. He so believed because he was told this by the plaintiff's agent. It is quite clear that this view was repeated to him by the defendant's solicitor, and on 9 October 1969, further corroboration was provided by those who came to see him and who represented Cork County Council. Believing this to be the situation, there was no real purpose in refusing to sell or to give an option once, as was suggested, the price was to be determined by an agreed arbitrator. To refuse in these circumstances meant acquisition anyway, and the determination of the price by an arbitrator in whose appointment the defendant might have no say. It now transpires that the situation was not as was intimated to the defendant's husband. It is now clear that, at the time that these negotiations were proceeding, the county council had no plans whatsoever to interfere by way of the compulsory acquisition of the defendant's lands.

It is well established that the discretion to grant specific performance should not be exercised if the contact is not equal and fair. In this instance the defendant was under a fundamental misapprehension as to the true facts. This misapprehension was brought about by the plaintiff's agent. While the auctioneer acted *bona fide*, this does not alter the situation which he created. He led the defendant's husband and her solicitor to believe that, if the defendant did not agree to sell, the lands would be acquired. It appears clear also that the plaintiff's managing director was aware of the true position so far as compulsory acquisition was concerned. It is to be noted that he had the auctioneer's file of correspondence and, therefore, should have been aware of the incorrect picture which the auctioneer had painted. Nevertheless, the plaintiff's managing director allowed the negotiations to proceed.

In these circumstances it appears to me that there was a fundamental unfairness in the transaction. The defendant agreed to sell believing that she had no real option, and the plaintiff accepted her agreement to sell knowing that this was not so. In my view it would create a hardship and would be unjust to decree specific performance in this case . . .

Kenny and Parke JJ. concurred.

Case 79. Gahan v Boland
Supreme Court, unreported, 20 January 1984

During an inspection of the defendant's property the plaintiff inquired as to whether a projected motorway would affect the property. The defendant assured him that it would not and this led the plaintiff to enter into a written contract to purchase the property. In fact the projected motorway was planned to pass through the property, a fact not discovered until after the contract was signed. When the plaintiff sought to rescind the contract the defendant argued that the plaintiff should be held to have had constructive notice of the true position as to the route of the projected motorway.

Held that the defendant's innocent misrepresentation entitled the plaintiff to rescission of the contract. This misrepresentation could not be excused as to deprive the plaintiff of this right on the ground that instead of acting on the misrepresentation he should have pursued his own inquiries to establish the true position.

Henchy J.:

The order of the High Court for rescission was made as a result of certain events which are said to have taken place on 13 February 1981. On that day the plaintiff visited the defendant at the property. The purpose of the visit was to inspect the property and to make certain inquiries about it. The plaintiff says that amongst the inquiries he made was one as to whether a projected motorway would affect the property. His evidence was that the defendant assured him that the property would not be affected by the proposed motorway and that this assurance led him to enter into a written contract . . . for the purchase of the property. It seems to be common case that the proposed motorway is in fact routed to pass through the property. That is something the plaintiff did not discover until after he had signed the contract.

There was a conflict of evidence as to what representation, if any, was made as to the motorway. The judge, however, having reviewed the evidence was of the clear opinion that an innocent but false representation was made by the defendant to the effect that the property would not be affected by the motorway, if and when it came to be constructed; that this representation was a material one made with the intention of inducing the plaintiff to act on it; and that it was one of the factors that induced the plaintiff to enter into the written contract . . . to purchase the property.

Having perused the transcript of the evidence, I am satisfied that there was ample evidence to support those findings as to the misrepresentation relied on by the plaintiff for rescission of the contract. Once there was evidence to support the judge's findings in that respect, the defendant's main ground of appeal, namely that the findings as to misrepresentation are unsustainable, must be held to fail. This court cannot set aside primary facts of that nature found by the judge and supported by evidence.

The alternative or secondary ground of appeal argued was that, even if the defendant's argument as to the misrepresentation fails, the claim for rescission should have been rejected because the plaintiff should be held to have had constructive notice of the true position as to the route of the proposed motorway. It was suggested that the plaintiff, a solicitor and an intending purchaser, having made inquiries of the vendors as to whether the property would be affected by the motorway, was required, by the application of the doctrine of constructive notice, to pursue those inquiries in quarters where he would have been reliably informed as to the true position. For that reason, it is submitted, he should be held disentitled, for the purposes of rescission, to rely on the misrepresentation made and should be deemed to have constructive notice of the true position as to the route of the motorway.

I was unable to accept this argument. I consider it to be well-settled law that the only knowledge that will debar a purchaser from repudiating a contract he has been induced into by the vendor's misrepresentation is actual and complete knowledge of the true situation. It does not lie with a vendor, who has by his misrepresentation induced the purchaser to enter into a contract to purchase, to have his misrepresentation excused or overlooked and to have the purchaser deprived of a right to rescind because he did not ignore the misrepresentation and pursue matters further so as to establish the truth of what was misrepresented. That would be unconscionable and unfair . . .

Walsh and Hederman JJ. concurred.

Case 80. Connor v Potts
Chancery [1897] 1 I.R. 534

The plaintiff agreed to purchase two farms which according to the defendant contained 442 acres. The price was calculated by multiplying this number by the price of a single acre. In fact the farms were sixty-seven acres less than first believed. When the defendant refused to complete the sale the plaintiff sought specific performance.

Held that the plaintiff was induced to enter into the contract by the defendant's innocent misrepresentation and was entitled to specific performance as to the real acreage with a deduction in respect of the deficiency.

Chatterton V.C.:

The defendant was the [owner] of several farms including the farms in question. He employed estate agents, to obtain purchasers and receive proposals for the farms. The plaintiff is a farmer residing in the locality, and he desired to purchase the farms in question. In the beginning of November 1895, he applied to the agents on the subject, and informed them that he wished to buy the farms and named a sum of £5000 as the price; but nothing material was done on that occasion. On 22 November plaintiff received from them a letter. This is a very important letter, as it shows that the defendant required an exact statement of the quantity plaintiff desired to buy, and that the quantity the defendant had to sell was 316 acres . . .

The plaintiff, on the following Tuesday, which was the 26th, went to the office of the agents, and had a conversation with them on the subject. He swears that he then offered £5000 for the two farms, and that one of the agents asked if he was aware there were more than 400 acres in the lands mentioned in the letter, and that plaintiff said he had their letter to that effect, and that he would give £12 an acre for the whole lands, which would amount to close on the £5000, and that they stated they would lay his offer before the defendant. On 11 December the agents wrote to the plaintiff, stating that they had had a further interview with the defendant, and asking him to call on them. He did call, and as one of the agents stated in his evidence, they had some conversation, in which that agent stated that the defendant had not named any price, but that plaintiff had better make an offer, and they would submit it to him; that after some further conversation, which he did not state, the plaintiff eventually offered £5500, which that agent said he would submit to the defendant. The plaintiff swears that on that occasion the agent told him that the defendant had called on them and that they had gone through the figures of the farms, and calculated what plaintiff could afford to give for them, and that plaintiff had better increase his offer of £5000, and that the agent produced a list of all the farms of the defendant which they had to sell, and which was given in evidence. It contains figures in pencil, made by the agent, which show that one farm contained 316 acres and the other farm 126 acres, making together 442 acres, and that the rents were £155 and £80 respectively. Plaintiff swore that the agent thereupon multiplied the acreage by £12 10*s*., and brought out £5500 and a few pounds over, and that they were both acting on the 442 acres, and thereupon plaintiff offered him £5500. Now the agent admitted, on cross-examination, that he was himself then under the impression that the acreage was 442 acres, and that there was a talk about selling by the acre, and that plaintiff asked him how much £12 10*s*. an acre would make, and that he, the agent, made a rough calculation that made it something a little under or over £5500, and that when he saw it came so close he said to the plaintiff that he should make an offer of £5500. The other agent, who was also examined, admitted on cross-examination that he also believed that there were 442 acres in the farms, and that the plaintiff was buying and the defendant was selling 442 acres. Both agents attributed their mistake to some incorrect memorandum they had obtained from the defendant's estate office. However that may be, it is plain that all these three persons, plaintiff and the two agents, entertained at the time the belief that the lands did contain 442 acres, and the negotiation was carried on and closed in this mistaken belief. But if there was a doubt on this it is wholly removed by the very important letter written by the agents to the defendant, dated 18 December 1895.

On this evidence I have no doubt that the plaintiff offered the sum of £5500 on the representation by the defendant through his agents that the lands contained 442 acres . . . There was no fraud on their part in this, for they swear, and I believe it, that they themselves believed the lands did contain 442 acres. Fraudulent misrepresentation is not necessary for the plaintiff to establish, for a mistaken representation by the defendant of a matter that it was his duty to state correctly, and on the faith of which he knew the plaintiff acted, is sufficient, though he may himself have believed it to be true . . .

The general principle applicable to this case is well established that where a misrepresentation is made by a vendor as to a matter within his knowledge even though it may be founded upon an honest belief in the truth of what he states, and the purchaser has been misled by such misrepresentation, the purchaser is entitled to have the contract specifically performed so far as the vendor is able to do so, and to have compensation for the deficiency . . .

It was also contended that so large a deficiency of the estimated acreage prevents this court from dealing with the case as one for specific performance so far as the defendant can perform the contract with compensation for the deficiency. But that is not the rule on which the court proceeds, and it is only necessary to refer to *McKenzie v Hesketh* to show that the court will grant partial performance with compensation in such cases. There is no difficulty here in ascertaining the amount of the compensation, as it is a mere calculation of 67 acres at £12 10s. an acre which is to be deducted from the amount of the purchase money . . .

<hr>

b. Fraudulent Misrepresentation

An untrue statement made knowingly, or without belief in its truth, or made recklessly or carelessly without regard to whether it is true or false, amounts to fraudulent misrepresentation. There are a number of remedies available for such misrepresentation. Damages is the central remedy: *Delany v Keogh* (Case 81), *Cody v Connolly* (Case 82), *Sargent v Irish Multiwheel Ltd* (Case 83) and *Fenton v Schofield* (Case 84) and *Northern Bank Finance Corporation Ltd v Charlton* (Case 85). The court may not assist a party guilty of fraudulent misrepresentation by refusing to grant that party's request for the specific performance of the contract: *Power v Barrett* (Case 86). Or, the court may order rescission of the contract: *Carbin v Somerville* (Case 87).

Case 81. Delany v Keogh
Court of Appeal [1905] 2 I.R. 267

The defendant auctioneer was employed to sell a public house by auction. He published an advertisement, on instructions received from his principal, in which he said that although the premises were held on a lease at £25 per annum the landlord had been accepting £18 per annum for a number of years. Some days before the auction the landlord wrote to the defendant stating that in future he would insist on the payment of the proper rent. At the auction the defendant read out the particulars contained in the advertisement. The plaintiff purchased the premises and the landlord subsequently sued for the full rent. The plaintiff sued the defendant for damages for fraudulent misrepresentation.

Held that the statement in the advertisement and in the particulars of sale implied a representation that the defendant had no reason to believe that the reduction in the rent would not be continued. This in fact was not so and the defendant was guilty of fraudulent misrepresentation and the plaintiff was entitled to damages.

Holmes L.J.:

<hr>

The difficulty in this case arises in applying old and well-settled principles of law to an unusual state of facts. There is no doubt that to sustain an action for misrepresentation, there must be proof of fraud on the part of the defendant. It is, I think, equally certain that fraud is proved when it is shown that the defendant made the misrepresentation, knowing it to be false. To use the words of Lord Herschell, in *Derry v Peek* (1889): 'To prevent a false statement being fraudulent, there must always be an honest belief in its truth.' To these propositions I add another, suggested by the peculiar facts of the present case. It is not necessary that the misrepresentation which will sustain an action of deceit should be made in actual terms. Words may be used in such circumstances, and in such a connection, as to convey to the person to whom they are addressed a meaning or inference beyond what is expressed; and if it appears that the person employing them knew this, and also knew that such meaning or inference was false, there is sufficient proof of fraud.

Of course whether the misstatement be express or implied, the plaintiff must show that he has suffered loss by acting on it; but in the foregoing observations, I have only dealt with the mode of proving the defendant's fraud, which is an essential element in the cause of action . . .

The question is whether, in the circumstances, the particulars of sale, taken in connection with the suppression of the contents of the landlord's letter, showed fraud of the kind that entitles the plaintiff to recover in an action of deceit such damages, if any, as he sustained therefrom?

Let me present the case in a way suggested by counsel for the plaintiff. Let me assume that the defendant, after he received the particulars from [his principal], but before he made them public, had ascertained from the landlord that he would insist on the full rent for the future, would it not have been manifestly dishonest to frame the advertisement as he did? His doing so would be an example of the trick described by Lord Blackburn in *Smith v Chadwick* (1884):

If, with intent to lead the plaintiff to act upon it, they [i.e. the defendants] put forth a statement which they know may bear two meanings, one of which is false to their knowledge, and thereby the plaintiff, putting that meaning on it, is misled, I do not think they can escape by saying he ought to have put the other. If they palter with him in a double sense, it may be that they lie *like* truth; but I think they lie, and it is a fraud. Indeed, as a question of casuistry, I am inclined to think the fraud is aggravated by a shabby attempt to get the benefit of a fraud without incurring the responsibility.

But the information, which would have made the statement fraudulent if it had been obtained before the advertisement was issued, reached the defendant in time to enable him to prevent persons attending the auction from being misled; and the fact that the landlord communicated with him as auctioneer ought to have impressed, and I am sure did impress, him with the importance of correcting the false inference which his language was calculated and intended to convey. All that was necessary for the defendant to do was, after reading the particulars at the auction, to have added, that since they had been prepared the landlord had expressed his intention to insist on the rent of £25, but that the vendor's solicitor was of opinion that he was legally estopped from obtaining more than £18. He did not do this. He allowed the sale to proceed on the basis that the reduced rent might be voluntarily received in the future as in the past, or, at least, that he knew nothing to the contrary.

I have observed, not for the first time, in the discussion of this case the prevalence of an idea that *Derry v Peek* has laid down a new rule in actions of deceit, and has given a latitude to falsehood that did not previously exist. This seems to me to be a great mistake. The directors of a tramway company that had authority to use steam power with the consent of the Board of Trade, believing that this consent would be given as a matter of course, issued a prospectus in which it was stated that they had the right to use steam power without reference to any condition. It was held that this was not actionable, inasmuch as the statement was made in the honest belief that it was true. This is, I think, old law; but if the directors had known, before they issued the prospectus, that the Board of Trade had refused to consent, or had announced its intention to refuse, the case would have been like this, and the directors would have had no defence; nor in such case would their position have been improved if their solicitor had assured them that there would be no difficulty in obtaining from Parliament an amending Act removing the condition.

I am satisfied that when the defendant read in his auction mart to the assembled bidders the particulars of sale, unaccompanied with a statement that there would be no longer a voluntary abatement of the rent, he was knowingly deceiving them, and that the natural effect of the deception was to obtain a higher price for the public house than it was worth.

I believe that the plaintiff's bid of £430 was considerably higher than what he would have offered if he had the knowledge which the auctioneer possessed; and than the real value of the premises . . .

Lord Ashbourne C., and FitzGibbon and Walker L.JJ. concurred.

Case 82. Cody v Connolly
High Court [1940] Ir. Jur. Rep. 49

In a contract for the sale of a horse, the seller represented that the mare was all right and would do all kinds of work. In fact the horse, because of a condition known to the defendant, was only able to do light work. The plaintiff sued for a partial return of the price.

Held that the representation that the horse was sound influenced the plaintiff into entering into the contract, that it was material and false, and the plaintiff was entitled to recover the amount sought.

O'Byrne J.:

. . . Both parties are in substantial agreement as to what took place on the occasion of the sale and the case comes before me in what is, in effect, an agreed statement of facts. The questions I have to consider, therefore, are whether, on these facts, there was a warranty, and, if so has there been a breach of that warranty. It is clear that no particular form of expression is necessary in order to constitute a warranty. I have to consider whether a statement of fact was made at the sale and before the completion thereof which was intended to be a warranty. If such statement were made and acted upon, it is in law a warranty. It has been suggested that the plaintiff went to the fair deliberately for the purpose of buying this particular mare. There is nothing in the evidence to establish this. It is true that he had heard of this mare, but says he had never seen her before the fair and that has not been contradicted. The plaintiff met the defendant's agent, at the fair and asked him the price and was told £35. He went away and they met later and he was then told that the price was £30. The words used then by the buyer were: 'I asked was the mare all right and would she do all kinds of work and he answered "yes". I asked him her age and he said she was nine years old.'

I do not attach very much importance to the question of age in this case, though it was an undoubted fact that the defendant's agent represented the mare as being nine years old though knowing that his uncle, the defendant, had bought the mare nine years previously when she was about one and a half years old. I do not attach much importance to that. The evidence of the defendant's agent, as to the conversation that took place at the time of the sale was in terms practically identical. The statement that the mare was all right and would do all kinds of work was made immediately prior to the contract and I cannot think otherwise than that it influenced the plaintiff in entering into the contract; nor can I think that it was not intended to influence him. Some light is thrown on this by what took place immediately afterwards. The mare was taken down the street to be examined by the veterinary surgeon. When this was suggested the agent said: 'What do you want to do that for? Didn't I tell you she was all right.' I do not think one could have stronger evidence than that. The seller represented that his word should be acted upon for the purpose of completing the contract . . .

Case 83. Sargent v Irish Multiwheel Ltd
Circuit Court [1955–56] Ir.Jur.Rep 42

The defendant advertised a motor van for sale describing it as English assembled which the defendant knew to be untrue. The van was Irish assembled. Relying on the advertisement the plaintiff purchased the van and resold it. When the third party discovered the error the plaintiff was successfully sued for breach of warranty. The plaintiff in turn sued the defendant to recoup those damages.

Held there had been a fraudulent misrepresentation by the defendant and that the plaintiff was entitled to damages.

Judge McCarthy:

I have no hesitation in finding for the plaintiff in this case. The plaintiff came to the defendant and purchased a van in full reliance on a representation as to that van given in the defendant's advertisement. That representation was false, to the knowledge of the defendant. The defendant has said that the representation was made in error. It may be so. But once the plaintiff came to the defendant in consequence of their advertisement and was shown the subject of it, there was a duty on the defendant to warn the plaintiff of the error. It failed in this duty, and is liable to the plaintiff for the loss he suffered.

Case 84. Fenton v Schofield

High Court (1966) 100 I.L.T.R. 69

The plaintiff purchased a house and lands together with a fishery from the defendant. The defendant had made representations as to the number of the fish taken from the fishery over the previous years. These representations were false. When the plaintiff ascertained the true position he sued for damages.

Held that the defendant had been guilty of fraudulent misrepresentation which had induced the plaintiff to pay more for the fishery than it was worth. The plaintiff was entitled to damages.

Davitt P.:

. . . Such in brief appears to be the relevant evidence as to the amount of salmon caught in the defendant's time. What conclusions are to be drawn from it? The first conclusion I draw is that there are no reliable records and no reliable evidence otherwise, of the *number* of fish caught. The second is that whatever the number was, the defendant was dissatisfied with it. Dissatisfaction with the fishing is a constantly recurring theme of his four years' correspondence with the clerk of the local fishery board. He may have been lying in his references in that correspondence to the number of fish caught; but I am satisfied that his dissatisfaction was genuine. If, however, as his records purport to show, he was catching on average 262 fish a year (much more than one for every day of the season and about five times as many as his predecessor) he could have had little grounds for such dissatisfaction. He said in evidence that he lied from the very beginning because he feared an increase in the valuation of the fishery. It is true that in an early letter to the clerk he does refer to a possible increase in fishery rates; but I find it impossible to believe that all his complaints about poor catches are lies told with an eye on the fishery rates. He is a wealthy man. The amount involved could not be considerable. There was no question of an increase in valuation until 1960;

and then the proposed increase was only £5 involving an extra annual charge of £7. Am I to believe that he committed himself to a series of lying statements under his own hand to the clerk, to the Valuation Office, and to the Department of Fisheries in order to avoid the possibility of having to pay this amount? If he was prepared so to act for the sake of such a sum what would he not be prepared to do in the way of misrepresentation to clinch a deal which would yield him a profit of over £15,000? My third conclusion is that he could not have got anything like an average of 250. On one side of his four-year period was the previous owner with an average of 54; with a maximum of 103 and a minimum of 26. On the other side we have the plaintiff with his figure of 17 for the 1961 season before the eel weir was constructed. I have had no evidence from the defendant as to how many he caught on his 18 visits during that season. He presumably caught some fish. These figures suggest a pattern which is quite inconsistent with the figures claimed by the defendant. I do not believe that he got anything like an average of 250. I am prepared to believe that he had a good season in 1957; that the river was fished more assiduously in his time than in the previous owner's, and that he very possibly got better results. I discount largely the evidence as to the superabundance of fish in his time and in particular the evidence as to the brimming deep freeze. It is, of course, on the evidence impossible to arrive at any figure for the average annual catch; but I do not believe that it could have exceeded 100, and in mentioning that figure I believe that I am leaning considerably in favour of the defendant . . .

On 25 July 1960, the plaintiff wrote to the defendant's auctioneer asking him for an acknowledgment of the broad basis of the purchase transaction; in relation to the fishery he said: 'The fishing, I understand, produces about 300 fish per annum. Can this be confirmed? An assurance from the defendant that this has happened since he has been in possession would be adequate.' In response to this request for a confirmatory assurance as to the number of fish caught annually the defendant on 2 August left at the office of the auctioneer's a document which throughout the hearing has been referred to as 'document K'. This was forwarded to the plaintiff. It purported to give particulars of the number of fish caught in each of the years 1957 to 1960 as well as some other information about the fishery. The second last paragraph was as follows: 'All this information is strictly confidential for reasons previously given and is for the plaintiff's observation only. I would like this summary back in due course.' The plaintiff did return the summary to the defendant within a few days; having first taken the precaution to make a copy, which is in evidence. The original is not forthcoming as the defendant denied having got it back. I have no difficulty in accepting the plaintiff's evidence, or in accepting the copy as accurate. Its accuracy was in fact admitted by the defendant. The summary represents the catches for the years 1957 to 1960 as being respectively 479, 392, 237 and 260. It ends with this paragraph: 'Previous owner showed me the catch book it recorded over 300 some years, 400 and 500 other years and when the nets were in Ballygallon 2,500–3,000 fish were taken.' It is hardly necessary to say that the summary was a tissue of untruths. It was both false and fraudulent . . .

I have no doubt whatever that all the representations in question were false to the knowledge of the defendant and therefore fraudulent. They could have no rational purpose except to induce the plaintiff to purchase; and I have no doubt that they were made with that intention. There can be no question as to their materiality; and I am satisfied that they did influence him in deciding to purchase; and that they were therefore an inducing cause of the purchase. The representations made in the summary of 2 August 1960, were, of course, made after the parties had come to a general agreement on 15 July. That agreement, was, however, subject to contract, and I have no doubt that if the plaintiff had failed to get the confirmatory assurance which he asked for in his letter of 25 July to the auctioneer he would have balked at signing any contract. The plaintiff is, *prima facie*, clearly entitled to damages for fraudulent misrepresentation . . .

The defendant appealed to the Supreme Court only on the issue of damages.

Case 85. Northern Bank Finance Corporation Ltd v Charlton
High Court [1979] I.R. 149

A number of persons, including the defendant, wished to gain control of a public company. These promoters consulted the plaintiff about the best method of doing so. The plaintiff advised the promoters on a scheme which included a proposal that it would lend the major portion of the sum required to purchase the shares in the public company. The plaintiff stipulated that each promoter was to deposit and maintain a stated sum with the plaintiff until the bid for the shares either succeeded or failed. After the scheme was put into operation one of the promoters withdrew three-quarters of the amount of his contribution and the plaintiff failed to disclose that fact to the other promoters. Both before and after that event the plaintiff misrepresented to the defendant, in response to direct questions, the state of the fourth promoter's contribution. During the course of the scheme it appeared to be desirable that the fourth promoter should cease to be associated with it and the defendant purchased his shares with the aid of a loan advanced by the plaintiff. Before that advance was made the plaintiff told the defendant, in response to a direct question and contrary to the fact, that the fourth promoter was not indebted to the plaintiff in any substantial amount. For reasons unconnected with this scheme the shares in the public company became worthless. The plaintiff sued for the repayment of the loan and the defendant pleaded that he had been induced to enter into, and continue with, the original transaction and the purchase of the shares of the fourth promoter by the fraudulent misrepresentations of the plaintiff and counterclaimed for damages.

Held that the defendant had been induced by the fraudulent misrepresentation of the plaintiff to enter into the original transaction and the purchase of the shares of the fourth promoter and that therefore the transactions between the parties were invalid and should be set aside. All guarantees, pledges and security given by the defendant to the plaintiff were void and the defendant was entitled to damages.

Finlay P.:
___

At the hearing of this case the defendant [the first promoter] has claimed that he was induced to enter into the original commitments in 1972 by a series of fraudulent misrepresentations made by the servants of the bank as to the existence, the amount, and the continued existence of cash deposits made by the fourth promoter towards the venture; the defendant says that he was induced to purchase the shares of the fourth promoter by a continuance of those fraudulent misrepresentations and by a new fraudulent misrepresentation that at that time the fourth promoter was not indebted to the bank to any extent. The bank has denied these allegations most strenuously. Against the background of agreed or inescapable facts which I have recited, and in the light of these claims and denials, certain leading or vital contested issues of fact have arisen; these, in my view, are as follows.

It is alleged . . . and asserted in evidence by the defendant, that the original agreement made between the bank and the promoters in September 1972, was that the fourth promoter and the second promoter would each contribute immediately £200,000 in cash which was to be deposited with the bank and used in the event of the take-over bid being successful, and that at a later stage the defendant and the fifth promoter would contribute and deposit the sum of £50,000 each on similar terms. The defendant further swore that it was indicated that no bid would be made until the first two deposits were made. On the other hand, it is contended by the bank that the only requirement then made was for the deposit of an unspecified substantial sum by each of them (the fourth and second promoters) as an earnest or token of their commitment to the enterprise and as a proof of their financial standing which would be available for presentation to the board of the bank and to the credit committee of the Midland Bank Finance Corporation. I am satisfied that there is a very strong probability, almost amounting to a certainty, that the defendant's version of this arrangement is true . . .

Against the background of these conclusions it is necessary to examine the first express misrepresentation alleged by the defendant. The defendant swore that either on the occasion of his depositing the cheque for £200,000 or around that time, he had a conversation with the plaintiff's manager in which the latter enquired about the sale by the fourth promoter of his supermarket shares and complained that this promoter's money had not yet come in. It was agreed, according to the defendant, that if it did not come in no one would get involved in the venture. Subsequently, the defendant alleges that the manager told him that the money was all in and that the letter to the Allied Irish Investment Bank, indicating the bid, was going out. I have had some difficulty in reaching a conclusion about these conversations. If the first conversation took place at the time of the bringing in of the cheque for £200,000, then it can be said either that it was early for any worry about delay on the part of the fourth promoter to bring in his money or that possibly he may have already brought in his cheque for £150,000. Secondly, it is strongly urged on me that an enquiry by the manager to the defendant about the financial standing of the fourth promoter was inherently improbable. However, I am satisfied that these conversations did occur. On my finding as to what was the arrangement between the bank and the promoters, the manager should have been concerned about the shortage in the cash deposited by the fourth promoter. Also, on that finding, his sending the letter to the Allied Irish Investment Bank of itself constituted such a representation. The false representation then alleged to have been made by him to the defendant is identical in substance to the false representation which I am satisfied he had already communicated to the credit committee, though on this occasion it must have been knowingly false and could not have been made merely recklessly.

It has been suggested that the deposit of these monies by the fourth promoter was not a matter which was material to the other promoters but only to the bank and that, even if a misrepresentation were made concerning it, the defendant was not influenced by it. It is undoubtedly true that, for reasons not connected with these alleged misrepresentations, this take-over has gone wrong and that there are sound reasons why the defendant should seek to avoid the consequences of his participation in it. However, I am satisfied that representations made as to the contribution in cash by the fourth promotor were material not only to the bank but to the other promoters and that the defendant entered into and then continued with this venture partly, at least, in reliance upon them. Whilst it may well have been believed by the defendant that in 1972 the fourth promotor was a wealthy man, I am satisfied that they (particularly the second and third promotors) were interested in two matters. The first was the availability to the fourth promotor of liquid assets, not otherwise committed, which he was prepared to put into this venture. The second was his trustworthiness as a businessman upon whose word implicit reliance could be placed. This latter feature would have been particularly important if the bid had succeeded, since then all the promoters would have become close business associates in the running of the public company. If the defendant had been informed in September 1972, that the fourth promoter was £50,000 short in his required contribution and if he had been informed that by the end of November 1972, he had withdrawn the entire of the sum which he had deposited, it seems to me inevitable that this would have seriously affected his judgment on these two vital matters.

My decision that a representation was made to the defendant that the fourth promotor had deposited £200,000 in cash in September 1972, that such representation was false to the knowledge of the manager of the bank, and that it induced (in part at least) the entry and continuance by the defendants into this venture would decide the main issue of liability in this case—since there is no suggestion that the representation was ever corrected . . .

On my findings as to the original requirement for the deposit by the fourth promoter of £200,000 and its maintenance until the bid either failed or succeeded, the agreed facts relating to the meeting of 26 November 1972 assume particular importance. By that time, the fourth promotor's deposit account had been reduced to £25,000 approximately, although his undisputed stake was £100,000 and no loan had then been sought by him to add to that amount. The decisions made at that meeting constituted a watershed in that the promoters' contribution was to be used for the first time in unconditional purchases of shares. A controversy has arisen on the evidence before me as to how serious a risk that was, but that appears to me to be immaterial as, without doubt, some risk was involved. There is no doubt in my mind that at this meeting of 26 November both the manager and an official of the bank were aware of the state of the fourth promoter's deposit account. At the stage when the monies deposited by the second promoter were about to be expended and when, indeed, they requested, as I am satisfied they did, the immediate deposit . . . of a further £100,000, in my view there was the clearest duty on the manager and the official to disclose to the defendant interest the true position with regard to the fourth promoter's cash deposit. Not only did they not do so, but on the following day they permitted this promotor to withdraw the balance of his deposit.

I am satisfied that the silence of the manager and the official on the occasion of this meeting on 26 November would, standing on its own, constitute a fraudulent misrepresentation.

I am, however, satisfied that the manager, in or around 13 December, made to the defendant and the bank's solicitor a representation that all the money was in. The defendant gave evidence with considerable particularity of the circumstances of this telephone conversation which was amplified and which took place whilst he was in the solicitor's office. Either that occurred or it is a complete invention; there being no room for any inaccuracy of recollection. In my view, the solicitor was not only an entirely truthful but also a most careful witness; he has no recollection of any such conversation but could not deny that it could have occurred. He did say that, since the contribution of the promoters' monies was a pre-condition to the making of the loan, as the bank's solicitor he would have sought at some stage instructions from the bank as to whether that pre-condition was fulfilled or whether he, as solicitor, should concern himself with it. I am satisfied that he did make that enquiry on the occasion when the defendant was with him and that he received from the official an affirmative answer. It has been urged upon me that even if the offical had, at that stage, given an affirmative answer to such a question, it would not have been false having regard to the loan of £53,000 which then had been sanctioned to the fourth promotor and his purchase of £47,000 worth of shares in the public company. Having regard to my view of the arrangement between the promoters and the bank of which, I am satisfied, the official was aware, to answer by a simple affirmative a question on or about 13 December as to whether the money was in was to make a knowingly false representation . . .

On appeal by the plaintiff, the Supreme Court—O'Higgins C.J., Henchy, Griffin, Parke and Butler JJ.—held that there was sufficient evidence to support the findings of the High Court and the appeal was dismissed.

Case 86. Power v Barrett
Chancery (1887) 19 L.R.Ir. 450

The plaintiff held premises under a lease which contained a covenant not to use them in the course of any dangerous, noxious, or offensive trade or business. He agreed to sell his interest in the lease to the defendant. The plaintiff claimed he was unaware of this restrictive convenant. Prior to the contract he became aware that the defendant required the premises for the purposes of his trade and would require to store large quantities of oil in them. The defendant on discovering the covenant refused to complete the contract and the plaintiff sued for specific performance.

Held that the plaintiff should have known of the restrictive covenant and that he was bound to inform the defendant of it. Silence on the subject was equivalent to a representation that there was no such covenant. The storing of oil was a dangerous trade or business within the covenant. The plaintiff was not entitled to specific performance of the contract.

Chatterton V.C.:

In the view I take of the facts of this case, it is unnecessary for me to enter upon a consideration of the law of constructive notice, or to decide whether, under the circumstances disclosed by the evidence, the defendant must be taken to have had constructive notice of the restrictive covenant in the lease, under the general rule which says that notice of the existence of a lease amounts in law to notice of its contents. The question, in my opinion, turns upon misrepresentation, and in approaching the consideration of the facts of the case, I will assume that the defendant had constructive notice of the contents of the lease within the rule I have referred to. There is no proof of actual notice.

The plaintiff was aware at the time of the negotiations, of the object and purpose of the defendant in agreeing to take the premises. He was perfectly aware of the nature of the business intended to be carried on there, namely, that of chandler and oil merchant, which implies the sale of all goods ordinarily sold and stored by a person engaged in such a trade. The defendant, accompanied by two friends, visited the premises in question, when a conversation arose involving knowledge by the plaintiff of the purpose of the defendant; and the parties then discussed the quantity of oil with which the vaults and stores could be filled. It is idle to contend that the sale and storing of petroleum or paraffin is not within the business of the defendant as an oil merchant. It was, therefore, well known to the plaintiff that the defendant required the premises for the purpose of storing quantities of this substance—whether 1000 barrels or 100 barrels is unimportant—and it is clear that on the occasion of the defendant's visit there was mention of the quantity of oil the premises could contain.

This being so, it was the duty of the plaintiff to inform the defendant of the existence of the restrictive clause in the lease—to inform him of the existence of every covenant which could reasonably be a prohibition against carrying on the trade for which the defendant desired to take the premises.

It is immaterial whether the plaintiff was himself actually aware of the extent, or even of the existence, of this covenant. It was his duty to be aware and to know of it. Lord St. Leonards, in his work on Vendors and Purchasers (14th edn), p. 214, quoting the case of *Flight v Barton*, states the law on the subject. I take the law to be as there laid down, and that there is now no question that it is so—that if the purchaser state the object which he has in purchasing, and the seller is silent as to a covenant in the lease prohibiting or interfering with that object, his silence would be equivalent to a representation that there was no such prohibitory covenant, although he was not aware of the extent or operation of the covenant. I am of opinion that a vendor in the position of the plaintiff here is bound to know what covenants are in his lease, and that he is bound, moreover, to communicate such knowledge to an intending purchaser—provided such covenant can be reasonably interpreted as affecting the object which he is aware the purchaser has in view in purchasing the premises, and I think that the plaintiff has not fulfilled that obligation.

The plaintiff states he was not aware of the existence of this covenant. On this point, however, I entertain great doubt. I cannot understand why he should have paid a visit to the defendant, and inquired whether he was a manufacturer, unless he was aware of some restriction. The defendant says the plaintiff added a statement that the lease under which he held the premises contained a clause prohibiting the manufacture of certain articles. This is denied by the plaintiff, but I rather incline to believe the defendant's testimony on this point. Why should the plaintiff ask the defendant if he was a manufacturer, unless to avoid the consequences of not informing him of something which would interfere with his manufacture? I must assume the plaintiff to have been aware that the restriction in the lease was not confined to manufacture. It would be an extraordinary conclusion of law that the defendant is affected with constructive notice solely because he was informed that there was a lease, while the plaintiff should not be deemed to know the contents of that lease, under which he held, and which he was about to sell.

The plaintiff went farther than this; for the very fact that he made the inquiry as to whether the defendant was a manufacturer—even if there was no mention on that occasion by the plaintiff of a prohibition in the lease— was sufficient to induce the defendant to suppose that any such prohibition did not prevent anything but manufacturing. The plaintiff goes beyond mere silence, because his observations constituted an implied misrepresentation that there was no restriction except as to manufacturing . . .

It was further contended that there is no evidence that the storing of large quantities of petroleum or paraffin oil would be dangerous or offensive, and that affirmative evidence on this point should have been given by the defendant. I am of opinion that, on grounds of common sense and experience, the storing of quantities of such inflammable materials would in all probability be held a dangerous and noxious trade. It is enough to refer to the legislation on the subject to show that the legislature was of opinion that it is dangerous, as they felt called upon to interfere in reference to the quantity and quality which should be allowed to be stored in certain places; and, as I understand, a licence is necessary for the purpose. It is a matter of ordinary knowledge, that if a fire were to break out, even in any of the adjoining premises, not only might the injury to the lessors, who are owners of a place of worship close by, be most serious, but the result might also be that the lives of an entire congregation would be put in peril. I must dismiss this action, with costs.

Case 87. Carbin v Somerville
Supreme Court [1933] I.R. 276

In the course of inspecting the defendant's house for sale the plaintiff asked whether the house was dry and free from damp and whether the roof was in good condition. The defendant answered affirmatively to both questions though he knew his replies to be false. The house suffered from damp and the roof was faulty. The plaintiff purchased the house and on discovering the true facts sought to rescind the contract on the ground of fraudulent misrepresentation.

Held that the contract had been induced by the defendant's fraudulent misrepresentation as to the condition of the house. The plaintiff was entitled to rescission of the contract and the return of the purchase price.

FitzGibbon J.:

. . . The learned judge [in the High Court] has found expressly that the defendant was asked by the plaintiff's mother if the house which he was trying to sell to the plaintiff was dry and free from damp and that he was asked 'if the roof was all right'. He has also found that the defendant stated in reply to each of these questions that it was. He has further found that each of these statements 'was not in fact justified', in other words, that it was 'in point of fact not true', and he has found that the plaintiff entered into the contract, which she now seeks to rescind, in reliance upon the truth of the defendant's statements. He has, however, refused her the relief claimed, upon the ground that she has failed to prove actual fraud on the part of the defendant, because 'having regard to all that was known to the defendant, I cannot say that it is clear that he told a deliberate lie, when he said that the house was dry and free from damp'.

Now, that the house was neither dry nor free from damp, and that the roof was not perfect, as stated by the defendant, has been abundantly proved, but the question which we have to decide is whether it is so clear that the defendant knew his statement to be untrue (as the judge has found it was), or that he made it so recklessly without regard to its truth or falsehood, that the judge's findings that he was no more than 'unduly optimistic', that he was 'inclined to believe that he wanted to believe', and that 'his reticence on the question' which he was not asked, 'will not convict him of fraud', cannot stand.

At the trial, the plaintiff's case was overladen with a mass of evidence, fortified by photographs, regarding the condition of the house in May and June 1931, whereas the material question is what was the general state of the house, *as known to the defendant* on and prior to 13 May 1930, the date upon which he sold it to the plaintiff upon a representation—false in fact—that it was 'dry and free from damp' and that the roof was in 'perfect order'. That the house was neither dry nor free from damp, and that the roof was not in perfect order, are facts beyond the possibility of dispute, and I refrain from referring at length to the evidence of the plaintiff and her mother, the two architects who were examined on their behalf, or even the history of the defendant's three years occupation of the house, which is admitted to have been an almost unceasing struggle against the incursion of damp and the consequent discoloration of the paper on the walls.

. . . It is perfectly clear that when the defendant answered the question in the affirmative, as the judge has found he did, he intended his answer to be taken in the sense in which the question was asked, and in the sense in which the judge has found the plaintiff did take it and act upon it, and so given, the misrepresentation was false and fraudulent.

If there be no other ground for denying the plaintiff's claim to the relief by way of rescission, the conclusions I have stated establish it, in accordance with the statement of the law by Blackburn J. in *Kennedy v Panama, New Zealand, Australian Mail Co*:

> It is enough to show that there was a *fraudulent* representation as to any part of that which induced the party to enter into the contract which he seeks to rescind; but where there has been an *innocent* mis-representation or misapprehension, it does not authorise a rescission unless it is such as to show that there is a complete difference in substance between what was supposed to be, and what was, taken, so as to constitute a failure of consideration. (This case is also discussed on p. 154, 155).

The plaintiff has contended that there was such 'a complete difference' in the present case, and that even if the defendant's representation that the house was dry and free from damp was innocent or inadvertent, she is still entitled to rescind her bargain upon the ground of 'a failure of consideration'. I do not agree with this contention. To sell a leaky house or a leaky ship on a *fraudulent* misrepresentation that it is sound entitles the party defrauded to rescind the contract, but if the misrepresentation be innocent there is not that difference in the subject matter of the sale which would entitle the party to be relieved of his bargain on the ground of defect of substance when there is really only an inferiority of quality. Any remedy the purchaser may have in such a case would sound in damages only . . .

Kennedy C.J. and Murnaghan J. concurred.
(See also Case 158, regarding rescission as a remedy.)

CHAPTER 15.

UNDUE INFLUENCE

The equitable doctrine of undue influence gives relief to a party where agreement has been gained by improper pressure which falls short of duress. A contract induced by undue influence is voidable at the behest of the influenced party.

The law presumes that undue influence has been exerted in contracts where the parties stand in a fiduciary relationship to each other. A fiduciary relationship exists where there is trust between the parties. Where there is trust and confidence the law insists that no undue influence is used by the stronger party over the weaker party. A fiduciary relationship exists between a religious superior and a novice: *White v Meade* (Case 88), between a principal and agent: *King v Anderson* (Case 89), between a parent and a child: *McMackin v Hibernian Bank* (Case 90) and between a trustee and beneficiary: *Provincial Bank of Ireland v McKeever* (Case 91) and *Smyth v Smyth* (Case 92).

Where the presumption of undue influence exists the onus of proving that no impropriety took place is on the party wishing to uphold the transaction. To escape condemnation the party wishing to uphold the transaction must show that the other party exercised an independent will when entering the transaction. This can be done by proving that there had been a full disclosure of all material facts, that the consideration was adequate and that the weaker party was independently advised: *Provincial Bank of Ireland v McKeever* (Case 91) and *Smyth v Smyth* (Case 92). Or, the transaction may be upheld where it is proved that the fiduciary relationship had ended when the transaction was executed: *Kirwan v Cullen* (Case 93).

Case 88. White v Meade
Chancery (1840) 2 Ir.Eq.R. 420

When the plaintiff was eighteen years of age and possessed of considerable property she entered a convent. It was agreed at that time on behalf of the nuns that she should not be professed under the then age of majority, or without the knowledge of her friends prior to such event. The plaintiff was professed while a minor and without the knowledge of her friends. When she came of age she assigned most of her property to the nuns for the benefit of the convent without advice from relatives, friends or professional adviser. The deed for this purpose was prepared by the legal adviser to the convent. When the plaintiff left the convent she sought to have the deed set aside.

Held that the transaction should be set aside on the ground that it had been executed by the plaintiff under undue influence.

Pennefather B.:

In the year 1825, this young woman, the plaintiff in this cause, entered into the establishment of the defendants as a lodger, and unquestionably not as a person who had irrevocably bound herself to take the veil. That this was so is quite manifest, independent of the express evidence of what was stipulated at the time she entered the convent. And what is that which was so stipulated, and which ought not to be done without express arrangement? namely, that she was not to be professed until she attained the age of twenty-one; nor even then without communicating with her friends; that is the evidence of one of the witnesses; it is not denied, nor can there be a doubt thrown upon it. Under that stipulation she entered the convent, and it was further agreed that she was to pay £40 a-year until she took the veil, and £600 afterwards; the defendants have no pretence to claim the £600 until she took the veil. When the case, therefore, is put upon contract, there is no foundation for it: the contract was violated in every material point by the defendants; because the plaintiff took the veil, and we must suppose by the influence of the defendants, while she was under age—contrary to the duty of the defendants—even without any agreement upon the subject—but also in direct violation of the express agreement they entered into with the plaintiff and her friends. In February 1827 she remains under the same influence, it must be supposed; which, give me leave to say, is incontestably proved by her having taken the veil; and so she continues until 1829, when she becomes unwell. Her brother-in-law is denied access to her; her sister is allowed to see her, but never without a member of the convent being present; and in such circumstances as these she transfers £1100 to the defendants, and the whole of her real estate, with the exception of some small portion of it, which she gave to her relations. Can it be seriously said that a transaction like this ought to stand? that a deed executed by a person placed at a convent like this person—placed in a situation where that undue influence is more likely to be exercised than in any other, which courts of equity should interfere to prevent; and shall it not be presumed, beyond almost a doubt so strong as not to be rebutted, that the documents in question were executed by the plaintiff under undue influence. But that is not all; the deed was got up by the professional friend of the convent, without the presence of any professional friend, or of any friend at all, of the infant; and this gentleman takes upon himself to swear that these ladies are so incapable of erring, that all this young woman has done, was done without the slightest influence having been exercised over her—the spontaneous effusion of her own mind! When we find him thus volunteering to swear what the

Searcher of Hearts alone could tell, is it not plain that he gave his heart and mind, not to the unfortunate victim upon whom he was about to practise as far as he was able, but to the defendants in this cause? He is not called upon to say whether the deed was technical or not, or whether counsel saw it; we do not want to know what the plaintiff said to him; what we seek to know is this, if she had an intention to make this disposition of her property, how it was produced? And no man can doubt that it was produced by the influence of these ladies over a young person, secluded from every friend; her nearest relatives excluded from her. Can we hesitiate for one moment to believe that the intention was produced by an exercise of influence on the part of those who ought not to be engaged in secular pursuits, but ought to have been devoted to the instruction of the plaintiff's mind? Upon the whole we think, without any doubt, that we ought to decree a re-conveyance of these premises . . .

In this cause the court did not intend to lay down any general rule; but that the particular circumstances of this case brought it within that class of cases which decide that transactions like those disclosed in this case ought not to stand. There are cases in which dealings between guardian and ward are upheld, but it lies upon the party seeking to uphold them to prove that such transactions have been *bona fide*.

Richards B. concurred.

Case 89. King v Anderson
Chancery Appeal (1874) I.R. 8 Eq. 625

In an arrangement which was common to the time a family settled property on its various members. One of the family members appointed the defendant her agent in the management of the property, a post he held for seven years. The family member on whom the property eventually devolved sold it to the agent. Some fifteen years later she sought to have the transaction set aside.

Held that there was a fiduciary relationship between the parties and that the onus on the defendant of having acted fairly and honestly had not been discharged. When an agent deals with his principal in a transaction which will confer a benefit on the agent, the agent is under a duty to ensure that the principal has the benefit of competent and independent advice. Delay in bringing the proceedings did not defeat the action.

Sir J. Napier C.S.:

Before and at the time of the transaction that is sought to be set aside, the defendant was the agent of the plaintiff for the purpose of collecting the rents, and for the general management of the property, and that in this position an influence had been acquired by him, and a confidence obtained, that was sufficient to bring the case within the rule of a court of equity that applied to a purchase or other dealing for his own benefit by a trustee. Lord Kingsdown says in *Smith v Kay* (1859):

> The principle of this rule applies to every case where influence is acquired and abused, where confidence is reposed and betrayed. The relations with which the court of equity most ordinarily deals are those of trustee and *cestui que trust*, and such like. It applies specially to those cases, for this reason—and this reason only—that from those relations the court presumes confidence put and influence exerted. Whereas in all other cases, where those relations do not subsist, the confidence and the influence must be proved extrinsically; but where they are proved extrinsically, the rules of reason and of common sense, and the technical rules of a court of equity, are just as applicable in the one case as in the other.

Taking this to be clearly established, and that it governs the case of the defendant in relation to the purchase in question, the onus was thrown on him to prove to the satisfaction of the court that he acted according to what the rule of the court requires to be shown beyond question in such transactions, when they are impeached by a suit in equity. In his instructive judgment in the case of *Gibson v Jeyes*, Lord Eldon says:

> It is asked where is that rule to be found? I answer in that great rule of the court, that he who bargains in matter of advantage with a person placing confidence in him is bound to show that a reasonable use has been made of that confidence—a rule applying to trustees, attorneys, or any one else.

The confidence that was placed in the defendant is very distinctly shown by several letters of the plaintiff . . .

The circumstances of the case were therefore such that the defendant was specially bound to show that in dealing with his principal for this benefit to himself, he had taken care to provide that, as against such a combination of interested and adverse influences, she had the full protection of some competent and disinterested adviser in the transaction. The plaintiff, moreover, was not absolute owner, but merely tenant for life, with a power of sale, limited and guarded in its terms; she was a trustee for her infant son, and therefore in a peculiar degree required the protection of adequate independent advice, which a court of equity inexorably requires in all this class of transactions between parties in a relation of confidence, and when one of them is exposed to influence capable of being exerted by the other . . . No adviser intervened for her guidance and protection . . .

In the case of *Rhodes v Bate*, which was cited by counsel for the plaintiff in his very able and convincing argument, Lord Justice Turner states in emphatic and authoritative terms the great established principle of a court of equity, that:

> Persons standing in a confidential relation towards others cannot entitle themselves to hold benefits, which those others may have conferred

upon them, unless they can show to the satisfaction of the court, that the persons by whom the benefits have been conferred had competent and independent advice in conferring them. This, in my opinion, is a settled general principle of the court, and I do not think that either the age or capacity of the person conferring the benefit, or the nature of the benefit conferred, affects this principle.

. . . The evidence is decisive to show that, in negotiating and concluding the agreement, the plaintiff had not the independent advice required by the law of the court, and it was for the defendant to prove satisfactorily, as an essential part of his case, that she had the protection of a competent and independent adviser . . .

. . . Some reliance was placed, in argument, upon alleged laches [delays in asserting a legal right]; and on the circumstance of an outlay upon the property by the defendant, and other dealings with it since the date of the deed of sale to him. I do not find the defence of laches expressly relied on in the pleadings, and I cannot admit that it is of any weight in the case. In the case of *Murphy v O'Shea*, Sir Edward Sugden decided that, although eleven years had elapsed before the filing of the bill to set aside a deed between principal and agent in that case, the plaintiff's were not barred of relief by laches if otherwise entitled to it. Where there is no statutory enactment to govern by its authority, or to guide by analogy, the court must consider the nature and circumstances of the case. In *Napier v Staples*, Sir Anthony Hart says:

Lapse of time and neglect do not form of themselves a rule, but give to the judge a power and discretion to be used according to circumstances, and whenever a case arises where the inconvenience to the public administration of justice, or the prejudice to the individual overbalances the allowance of a just claim irregularly brought forward, it must be dealt with accordingly.

The peculiar circumstances of the present case explain and (reasonably) excuse the forbearance of the plaintiff during the minority of her son; she had never suspected the defendant, in whom she had full confidence; but he must be taken to have known that no acquiescence on her part could bind the rights of her son; and that the property which he (the defendant) had acquired under the deed was bound by a trust, which made his expenditure a matter of risk and speculation. The court has to consider the equities on both sides, and in upholding and enforcing the beneficial protective law by which the transaction must be dealt with, care will be taken to avoid injustice.

In the decree provision will be made for repayment of so much of the advances and outlay *bona fide* made in beneficial expenditure on the property as shall be found to be fairly and justly claimable by the defendant, and also for preventing the disturbance of sub-tenancies created since the purchase . . .

Lawson C.S. and Christian L.J. concurred.

Case 90. McMackin v Hibernian Bank
High Court [1905] 1 I.R. 296

A widow and her minor daughter, the plaintiff, were joint tenants of some property. The title documents were deposited with the defendant as security for an overdraft. The defendant had full knowledge of the insolvent condition of the widow's affairs and of the plaintiff's age and circumstances. Shortly before the daughter came of age, the defendant, deeming the security insufficient, applied to the widow for payment. After the plaintiff came of age the widow offered to secure payment of the overdraft by a joint promissory note of herself and the plaintiff. Two promissory notes were signed by the widow and daughter. The daughter had not the benefit of independent professional advice. The widow and the plaintiff defaulted on payment when the promissory notes became due and the bank recovered judgment against the plaintiff and registered it as a judgment mortgage on the property. The plaintiff sought to have the promissory notes set aside on the ground of the undue influence of her mother.

Held that the law recognised that a young person living with or under the influence of a parent is likely to remain for some time under parental dominion after reaching majority. While a young person may give security for a parent's debt it must be done after emancipation from parental control and influence. The presumption of undue influence, which arose in such cases, might be rebutted by proving that the young person had independent professional advice. That had not been done in this case and the plaintiff was entitled to succeed.

Barton J.:

. . . I am willing to believe that [the employees of the defendant] were ignorant of the rules of equity which guide this court in regard to taking securities from young persons just come of age and under parental influence. Those rules, which represent nothing more than the recognition by the courts of certain principles of right conduct, have been frequently stated by judges in clear and unmistakable terms [in] cases like the present one, of securities taken by bankers from young persons just come of age, in respect of debts of near relatives—in one case of an uncle, in another case of an elder brother. These rules have not been directly applied to a banking case in Ireland for some years; and this case may, perhaps, serve as a useful reminder to persons, part of whose duty or business it may be to adequately secure the debts of their employers. I gather from their cross-examination that these bank officials were under the impression that, in the case of a young person under parental influence and just come of age, a creditor, who has full knowledge and notice of the girl's age and rights and circumstances and of the parental influence, is at liberty to obtain by pressure upon the parent and by means of the parent's influence a security from that young girl for the parent's debt, and that a transaction of that kind can be supported without any proof that the young girl had independent professional advice, or was otherwise emancipated from control, so as to be in a position to exercise a free and unfettered judgment. If that was their view of their legal rights and obligations in such a matter, it is my duty to say that it was, in my opinion, a mistaken view.

It is quite true that young persons (male or female) upon coming of age obtain capacity to sign notes and to execute mortgages, and that they may render themselves liable by so doing. But it is not correct to suppose that, as soon as the clock has struck the hour of technical legal emancipation, the young person is discharged from all protection of the law. The law recognises that a young person, living with or under the influence of a parent, is likely to remain for some time under parental dominion, and is at an impressionable age, when gratitude, affection, and respect for a parent are fresh and strong, while knowledge and experience of the stress and struggle and varied obligations of human life have yet to be acquired. The law protects young persons under such circumstances and at such an age, not by curtailing their capacity to deal with others, but by binding the consciences of those who deal with them. A young person may pay or give security for a parent's or guardian's debt; and such a transaction will not be set aside if it can be shown to be a spontaneous act, carried out after real emancipation from control and influence, and with full knowledge of all material circumstances. Counsel for the defendant cited a case of that kind. But such cases are rare, and the court is jealous in its investigation of cases of the kind. When the child is living with or under the control of the parent or guardian, such influence is presumed—and the burden of proof is thrown upon the person who has obtained the gift or security through the parent's influence to displace that presumption, e.g. by showing that the young person acted under independent professional advice. Such independent advice must be a reality, not a sham; it must be a shield for the young person, not a mere cloak to cover up the transaction.

. . . With the full knowledge and notice which he possessed of the girl's age and position and rights, the insolvent position of the mother, and the impending attack upon the girl's small property by the 'legion' of the mother's creditors, the bank manager ought, in my opinion, to have insisted upon the girl having independent professional advice. She had a solicitor at that time acting for her in the suit in [another case] who never heard of this transaction until more than a year afterwards. Even the so-called 'family' solicitor, who had a few days previously given the confidential information to the local manager which immediately precipitated the action of the bank, was not informed and did not hear of this transaction of the signing of the notes until the following December, after a writ had been issued against the girl. He seems to have then looked after himself, and to have got a mortgage from the girl in January 1902, for £400. That mortgage is not now in issue before me, and I am not to be understood as expressing any opinion about it one way or the other. I only refer to the incident because it illustrates the helplessness of this young woman, both before and after this transaction, so far as any advice, independent or otherwise, was concerned.

A transaction of this kind cannot stand in a court of equity. This was a security obtained from a young girl just come of age by a creditor through the influence of her mother and guardian for the debt of that mother and guardian, without any real consideration moving to the girl. The girl had no independent advice or protection of any kind, while the creditor had full knowledge and full notice of all the circumstances that gave rise to the equity. From first to last her personality, her point of view, her rights, were never considered by anyone. It never occured to anybody to consult her wishes or take any serious notice of her in relation to these dealings. All the other parties to these transactions were fully informed and were looking keenly after their own interests; but she had no information or advice, and was a mere cypher; and her fortune and property were being parted with without any real knowledge of her rights or any adequate protection of her interests. I can best conclude by quoting certain apposite words of Lord Romilly's, in *Sercombe v Sanders*:

> It is important that creditors should understand that they cannot improve their security, taken from persons to whom they have given credit, by inducing them at the last moment to compel near relations or persons under their influence and not in a situation to resist their importunity to pay their debts.

For the reasons which I have given, there must be judgment for the plaintiff with costs.

Case 91. Provincial Bank of Ireland v McKeever
High Court [1941] I.R. 471

A father by will devised property in trust for the benefit of his wife and two sons. In the property's management the trustees became indebted, caused without mismanagement, dishonesty or negligence, to the plaintiff. On reaching their majority the sons, together with their mother, mortgaged the property in favour of the plaintiff to secure an overdraft incurred by the trustees. The mortgage was executed under the supervision of the trustees' solicitor, a close relative of the mother and sons. They had no other legal advice. When the plaintiff sought declarations as to its rights under the mortgage, the mother and sons claimed that they had been induced to mortgage by undue influence exercised by the trustees and by the plaintiff, since it was aware of the circumstances of the case.

Held that on the balance of probabilities the presumption of undue influence had been rebutted. The execution of the mortgage, irrespective of whether or not the mother and sons had independent advice, was the result of the free exercise of independent wills and that the nature and effect of the transaction had been explained and understood.

Black J.:

Broadly speaking, a person can make an irrevocable voluntary gift at his will and pleasure. It does not matter that it may be foolish. 'Courts of equity have never set aside gifts on the ground of the folly, imprudence, or want of foresight on the part of donors': *per* Lindley L.J. in *Allcard v Skinner*. So, in *Powell v Powell* (1900) Farwell J. says:

> A man of mature age and experience can make a gift to his father or mother because he stands free of all overriding influence except such as may spring from what I may call filial piety.

Yet, even in cases where the donor is a person of mature age and free from such overriding influence as Farwell J. referred to, and quite apart from anything in the nature of actual fraud, a gift may be set aside in certain circumstances on the ground of ignorance. The principle is thus expressed by Lord Hatherly L.C. in *Phillips v Mullings* (1871):

> Any one taking any advantage under a voluntary deed, and setting it up against the donor, must show that he thoroughly understood what he was doing, or, at all events, was protected by independent advice.

In such cases, however, it is sufficient to show that the deed is 'in all respects proper'. Moreover, 'any unusual clauses'—but only unusual clauses—must be shown to have been brought to the donor's notice.

Nor is the right to equitable relief confined to cases of voluntary gifts. It has often been upheld in cases of purchase transactions where the vendor was poor and ignorant and the purchase at an undervalue or otherwise unconscionable. Actual fraud need not be proved. In *Fry v Lane* (1888), for example, there was no moral fraud on the part of the purchasers, yet the sale was set aside. Fraud is presumed; but the fraud which is presumed, if I may employ the words of Lord Selborne L.C. in *Earl of Aylesford v Morris* (1873) 'does not here mean deceit or circumvention; it means an unconscientious use of the power arising out of these circumstances and conditions.' In such a case, the presumption may be repelled by proof that the transaction was, as Lord Selborne put it, 'in point of fact fair, just, and reasonable'.

In *Allcard v Skinner* (1887) Lindley L.J. says: 'As no court has ever attempted to define fraud, so no court has ever attempted to define undue influence, which includes one of its many varieties.' In that case the only influence that could be presumed to have impelled the plaintiff to make over all her property to a Protestant institution known as 'The Sisters of the Poor', was the influence necessarily incidental to her position in the sisterhood set in operation solely by the lady's own 'enthusiastic devotion to the life and work of the sisterhood'. There was no suggestion of fraud in the popular sense of the term. Yet, constructive fraud 'in one of its many varieties', as Lindley L.J. expressed it, was presumed, and would have enabled the lady to avoid the gift but for her own laches in taking action. Cotton L.J. points out, as judges had often done in other cases, that the presumption is drawn on grounds of public policy. That is why, as Lord Eldon said, 'the court will refuse to go into nice discussions as to whether the gift . . . was advantageous.'

It is enough for my purpose that the presumption is now recognised in all courts. This presumption does not arise in every case where any fiduciary relationship exists between donor and donee. But, it applies to 'all the variety of relations by which domination may be exercised by one person over another': *per* Lord Eldon in *Huguenin v Baseley* (1807) and, as I have stated, it certainly applies where the relationship is that of trustee and *cestui que trust* [a beneficiary].

So much generally for voluntary gifts and for certain other not entirely voluntary, but improvident, conveyances. Sometimes, however, the classes of cases above envisaged involve a special peculiarity, namely, that of a certain type of fiduciary relationship existing between the party who confers a benefit and the party who receives it. The principle then applicable is often referred to as the rule laid down in *Huguenin v Baseley*. It is thus expressed by Vaughan Williams L.J. in *Wright v Carter* (1903) interpreting the words of Lord Eldon in *Hatch v Hatch* (1904):

> Whenever you have these fiduciary relations . . . there arises a presumption of influence, which presumption will continue as long as the relation . . . continues, or at all events until it can be clearly inferred that the influence has come to an end . . . so long will it be very difficult to support the gift, and so long will the court refuse to go into nice distinctions as to whether the gift was advantageous to the client or whether it was not.

(He speaks of a 'client' because the relations in that case were those of solicitor and client). Lord Eldon in *Hatch v Hatch* places the relations of guardian and ward and of trustee and *cestui que trust* on the same footing as regards this doctrine, and it seems to be established by a series of cases since *Hatch v Hatch* that where a person in the postion of a trustee takes a voluntary benefit from his *cestui que trust*, there at once arises a presumption of undue influence in the sense in which that term was explained by Lord Selbourne in *Earl of Aylesford v Morris*, but not necessarily in any sense implying moral obliquity . . .

This and various other cases seem to me to establish that when a trustee induces his *cestui que trust* to execute a deed in favour of a third party, which deed directly or indirectly confers a voluntary benefit upon the trustee who is not himself a party to the deed, there arises a presumption of undue influence, not only as against the trustee, but also as against the third party, if that third party is aware of the circumstances which give rise to the equity against the trustee. I do not think it is necessary that the third party should 'claim under' the trustee . . .

In this connection I can see no logical distinction between actual proved undue influence and the undue influence which is presumed by courts of equity where certain fiduciary relations exist. I cannot see why a party who takes a benefit from another, knowing that the latter's trustee also takes a benefit under the same instrument indirectly, although not a party to it, and being supposed to know also that in such a case equity presumes that it was obtained by undue influence, should be in any better position than if such party knew that there had been undue influence in fact . . .

Those circumstances give rise to the equitable presumption that the defendants in executing it were acting under the undue influence of their trustees through their solicitor. The attitude taken up on behalf of the bank authorities appears to me to be that, whether there be any such presumption as against the trustees or not, such a presumption could not affect the bank's claim. They are not their brother's keepers. If that is their sheet anchor, then their case in my opinion breaks from its moorings. But I do not think it founders on that account. This equitable presumption of undue influence, where it exists, is always rebuttable, and I have to consider whether in this case it can be regarded as sufficiently rebutted . . .

It is now settled that proof of the giving of independent advice, although it may be, is not necessarily, the only way in which this presumption may be rebutted: nor is it necessary that such advice when given should have been acted upon. What it is necessary to show in order to rebut the presumption is that the transaction 'was the result of the free exercise of independent will'. The person entering into it must have had 'full appreciation of what he was doing'. The presumption is drawn upon grounds of public policy.

It is plain . . . that there might be a case in which it would be possible to show that the donor of a gift to his trustee had acted without undue influence even if he had no independent legal advice, or even if, having received such advice, he disregarded it. A donor might unwisely confer a benefit on his trustee contrary to the best independent advice duly given to him, yet he might do so with an independent will and with a full appreciation of what he was doing. In such a case, the transaction will stand; for, as Lindley L.J. said in *Allcard v Skinner*, equity does not seek 'to save persons from their own folly'. It only seeks 'to save them from being victimised by other people'. How is a court to know whether a *cestui que trust* who executed a deed conferring a benefit on his trustee was really free from undue influence? It possesses no X-ray contrivance that can lay bare the working of the human mind. Absolute proof there can hardly conceivably be.

Although independent advice is not a *sine qua non*, yet where it has been proved to have been given and rejected, there are indications in the decisions that proof of its having been given might alone be sufficient to rebut the presumption of undue influence. Nevertheless, the giving of such advice would not prove that the person to whom it was given fully understood it, and even if evidence were given (for instance of statements made by the advised person) showing that he did understand it, he might still have rejected it under the interested, or it might be, the well meant, perhaps even unconscious but none the less undue, influence of his trustee, parent, physician, solicitor, or religious superior. One cannot expect absolute disproof of undue influence. It is enough to establish a reasonable probability of the exercise of independent will founded upon adequate understanding . . .

The courts have, I think, contemplated that the proof of independent advice having been given may in certain cases alone suffice. It seems to me that a combination of surrounding circumstances might furnish as good evidence, imperfect though it be, of the probability of an independent will as any independent legal advice. After all, a main object of such advice is to ensure that the party knows what he is doing. If the transaction is of so plain a character that it may fairly be believed that he did know what he was doing, that object is achieved without advice. Even the best independent advice, if not fully understood, might not achieve it. I consider the whole nature of the transaction and its possible alternatives of much importance in determining whether there was a reasonable probability of the presence of a free and understanding mind. In nearly all the reported cases where transactions such as I am dealing with were avoided, there was an element of improvidence—often gross sacrifice. In these cases the presumption of undue influence would be very strong. The less improvident the transaction the less strong the presumption. If there is no improvidence at all, the presumption of undue influence may be very weak and the evidence required to rebut it proportionately slight for the simple reason that there is no natural improbability that a person would freely confer a benefit on another, if doing so was in every way prudent from his own point of view, merely because that other stood in a fiduciary relation towards him. In some cases the equitable presumption might dwindle almost to the insignificance of a technical scintilla.

Again, the selfish interest in the transaction of the person against whom undue influence is presumed may be much greater in some cases than in others, and the less that interest the less the incentive to exercise undue influence and the weaker the probability of its having been brought to bear. Then, the simplicity or complexity of the transaction has to be considered in its bearing on the likelihood of its author having understood what he was doing: and a full understanding may greatly weaken, although alone it may not rebut, the presumption of undue influence. So we find in case after case where this presumption was applied that great stress was laid by the courts on the fact that the complaining party did not understand what he or she was doing and upon the personal interest of the party whose undue influence was presumed.

Throughout the many relevant cases which I have studied with care, three things are repeatedly emphasised by the judges: 1. The probable inability of the complaining party to understand what he or she was doing. 2. The degree of personal interest in the transaction possessed by the party whose undue influence was presumed by reason of fiduciary relationship. 3. The existence of improvidence in the impugned transaction and the degree of such improvidence, if any. In my opinion, these matters would not have been so strongly and consistently emphasised in so many judgments if they were not matters of vital import in determining whether or not the presumption of undue influence could be regarded as rebutted.

I have considered all these matters in the present case. As to 1, I think upon the whole it is probable that the defendants when executing this mortgage understood quite well that they were purporting to assign their £9,000 legacy to the bank as security for the overdraft in fact intended to be secured. As to 2, and 3, which raise the same considerations, it seems to me that the interest of the trustees in obtaining this mortgage was very different from the interest of the persons against whom deeds have been set aside in most of the cases on the ground of a presumption of undue influence. In nearly all the cases the beneficiaries have taken a clear benefit which they would not have been able to get but for the impugned transaction. Here, the benefit the trustees got was that the mortgagors gave the bank security for a sum of between £3,800 and £3,900 which the trustees then personally owed to the bank. But that was vastly different from a sheer donation to the trustees.

A vital feature of this case is that there is no suggestion that the trustees mismanaged their trust, or did not honestly and without negligence incur this large debt to the bank, quite apart from giving their time and service, in the sole interest of their *cestui que trustent*. It was expressly admitted by counsel for the defendants that the trustees would have been entitled to be indemnified by the trust property in respect of every penny of this debt. If so, they would also have been entitled to any costs properly incurred in enforcing their indemnity. Therefore, in the net result, and as a sequel to the mortgage, all the trustees got was virtually their own money which, by pledging their personal credit, they had used for the beneift of their *cestui que trustent*, and which they would have been equally entitled and able to get back anyway, even if there never had been a mortgage. If the trustees had been obliged to take other means of getting back their own money instead of procuring this mortgage to be executed to the bank, the *cestui qui trustent* would have been no better off. No evidence has been offered, and I think it highly improbable, that the defendants had any better alternative open for the solution of their financial problem than the execution of this challenged mortgage. What the trustees got out of this transaction was fundamentally different from the voluntary benefits exemplified in the long range of cases decided upon the equitable doctrine of presumed undue influence based on fiduciary relationship, and it was equally different from the undervalue purchases and unconscionable dealings in the typical cases where deeds have been set aside. As Lindley L.J. said in *Allcard v Skinner*, the equitable doctrine of undue influence was devised to prevent victimisation. It was not even intended to save people from their own folly. It certainly never was developed to upset or avoid transactions where there was neither victimisation nor folly; and although those principles must be logically applied, even if in a particular case their application should happen to go beyond the intention with which they were evolved, I think a court of equity must be solicitous to see as far as it can, consistently with the decided cases, that an equitable doctrine is not used to work inequity . . .

Case 92. Smyth v Smyth
High Court, unreported, 22 November 1978

An uncle of the plaintiff devised some land by will to his brother, the defendant, for life and then absolutely to the plaintiff. The plaintiff sold his interest to his uncle, the defendant, when he was twenty-three years of age, and while he drank heavily he was not then an alcoholic. The parties lived in the same house for some time and were on good terms. The plaintiff first suggested the sale, initially through a third party and later on his own account. His uncle was then uninterested but later agreed. The parties had the advice of the same legal adviser and the transaction took five years to complete. The plaintiff sought to set aside the transaction on the grounds that it infringed the equitable principles which apply to dealings between trustees and beneficiaries, that it had been obtained by undue influence, and that it was an unconscionable bargain.

Held that since there was a fiduciary relationship between the parties the transaction had to be examined to ensure that the equitable principles which govern sales between trustees and beneficiaries had been observed, which on the evidence the court held that they had. The presumption of undue influence also arose which, on the evidence, had been rebutted. The defendant did not influence the plaintiff's decision to sell, the defendant had paid a fair price for the land, and the defendant was under no obligation to ensure that the plaintiff had independent professional advice before he entered into the transaction. It was probable that had the legal adviser considered there was a conflict of interest he would have advised the plaintiff to obtain independent legal advice. Nor was the transaction an unconscionable bargain.

Costello J.:

. . . I turn now from the facts of the case to the law. As I have already pointed out, various equitable principles have been relied on to defeat these [transactions]. For reasons which will become clear later, I will defer dealing with the undue influence claim until I have firstly considered the relevant principles applicable by reason of the fact that the transaction between the plaintiff and the defendant was a sale by a *cestui que trust* to a trustee.

I start by taking the following statement from Lewin on Trusts (16th edn pp. 697–8):

> While a purchase by a trustee conducting the sale, either personally or by his agent, cannot stand, a purchase by a trustee from a *cestui que trust* of the interest of the latter in the trust may stand, if the trustee can show that the fullest information, and every advantage were given to the *cestui que trust*. However, a purchase by a trustee from his *cestui que trust* is at all times a transaction of great nicety, and one which the courts will watch with the utmost jealousy and will set aside if the consideration was insufficient;

One of the authorities relied on to support the statement which I have just quoted is *Denton v Donner*.

This was a case in which the plaintiff sought to set aside a sale of his remainder interest to the defendant, to whom he owed money on foot of a mortgage. The court held that in the particular circumstances of the case the defendant was in the position of a trustee and the court had to consider what, as such trustee, his duties were. Romilly M.R. pointed out:

> No doubt where a person is a trustee for sale, and he sells the estate to himself, the transaction is absolutely and *ipso facto* void, but if a trustee purchases from his *cestui que trust* his reversionary interest which he is liable to pay, I do not assert it is absolutely void, but certainly the burden of proof lies on the trustee to show that every possible security and advantage were given to the *cestui que trust*, and that as much as possible was gained for him in the transaction, as he could have gained under any other circumstances. There is, in this respect, an absence of evidence which is strongly unfavourable to the defendant. It does not appear that any estimate was made of the value of this reversionary property for the purpose of the sale. If it was intended to be sold, the plaintiff ought to have been told what was the value, and the estimate that had been made of the value of the reversion of this property . . . I think the burden of proof necessary falls upon the defendant to show the *bona fides* of the transaction throughout, and that everything was done for the plaintiff which could have been done if the property had been sold to a stranger, and that the utmost that could possibly have been produced was obtained.

In addition to these authorities I should refer to a recent decision of the Court of Appeal in England on which counsel relied. *Lloyds Bank v*

Bundy (1975) concerned the validity of a guarantee and charge given by an elderly farmer in relation to a company owned by his son. The court held that in the particular circumstances of the case a fiduciary relationship existed between the bank and the defendant (against whom proceedings for possession had been taken on foot of the charge); that the defendant had reposed confidence in the bank and as a result the bank had a duty of care towards the defendant; that in the particular circumstances of the case that duty imposed an obligation on the bank to ensure that the defendant had the benefit of independent legal advice; that it had been guilty of breach of that duty. The charge and guarantee were set aside, the court holding that the absence of independent legal advice resulted in the transaction being voidable on the ground of undue influence. I am prepared to hold for the purposes of the present case that there may be circumstances in which a breach by a trustee-purchaser of a duty to ensure that the *cestui que trust* had obtained independent professional advice would justify the court in setting aside a sale by a *cestui que trust* apart from any question of undue influence that may arise in the case. I will now consider whether the present is such a case.

The authorities which I have quoted make it clear that the onus of proving the *bona fides* of the transaction I am considering is on the defendant, and that I am required to examine it with very great care for the purpose of ascertaining whether any unfair advantage was taken by the defendant in his dealings with the plaintiff. I am required to consider the particular duties which the defendant owed to the plaintiff in the circumstances of the fiduciary relationship which existed between the parties and to ascertain whether that duty was breached by the defendant. The findings of fact which I have made (arrived at by bearing in mind where the onus of proof lay in this case) enable me to reach the following conclusions on this part of the case. The defendant paid what he considered was a fair price for the land; and the price was in fact a fair one. The defendant had no special knowledge about its value of which the plaintiff was ignorant, and he made no effort either to take advantage of his special position as trustee of the plaintiff's property or to influence the plaintiff's decision to sell. What remains, however, to be considered (and this is perhaps the second most difficult aspect of the case) is whether the defendant owed a duty to the plaintiff to ensure that he obtained professional advice of some sort before he entered into the purchase agreement with him. The plaintiff was a young man of only twenty-three; the bargain was struck in a very casual and informal way. But it is clear that the parties envisaged that a formal contract would be required and the defendant was aware that the plaintiff would have available to him the advice of a solicitor before the formal contract was executed. This case is, therefore, different from those cases (including *Bundy*) in which the impugned transaction was completed before any professional advice was available to the grantor of the advantage contained in it. In this case the plaintiff had available to him the benefit of a solicitor's advice before he signed the contract. Is the defendant's duty affected by the fact that the one solicitor acted for both the defendant and the plaintiff? In other words, should the defendant have ensured that the plaintiff had independent legal advice? I do not think he was so obliged. It is of course clear that the defendant gave no thought to the notion that he should advise his nephew to get separate advice, but if he had, I think he would have been entitled to conclude not only that [the solicitor engaged] was an experienced solicitor but that if the solicitor considered that separate advice was necessary he would have so advised the plaintiff. That brings me to the solicitor's duties and responsibilities. There is no doubt that the solicitor's double role would have imposed on him a duty to inform the plaintiff of the necessity to get independent advice if he thought that a conflict of interest existed. If he failed in this duty the defendant would be liable for it. Naturally, the solicitor cannot recall what precisely was in his mind ten years ago, but I think I am entitled to conclude that if he considered that a conflict had existed he would have advised the plaintiff accordingly. The solicitor had acted in the administration of the estate of which the lands formed part. He says that he would have been aware of its value sworn for probate purposes (£2,400) and that if he had considered the transaction an improvident one from the plaintiff's point of view he believes he would have said so. I accept this evidence, and I conclude that in the particular circumstances of this case there was in fact no duty on the defendant or his agent (the solicitor) to advise the plaintiff to obtain the advice of an independent solicitor. Nor were either under a duty to advise an independent valuation prior to execution of the formal contract. The defendant and the solicitor thought the price a fair one and in my view they were right.

The deed of transfer was not executed until August 1973 at which time, of course, the value of the land had greatly increased. This fact would have been known to the defendant but I do not think it affects in any way his duty to the plaintiff. If a valid contract had been entered into in 1968 the plaintiff was legally bound by it, and the delay in completion did not impose any new obligations on the defendant.

I will now deal with the plaintiff's claim that the transaction is vitiated by the undue influence exercised by the defendant over him. This I can do shortly. The findings of fact which I made, make it clear that the defendant did not in fact attempt to influence the plaintiff's decision to sell, and that his decision was arrived at freely by the plaintiff. But it has been urged in this case that the relationship of trustee and *cestui que trust* is one of those fiduciary relationships which give rise to a presumption of undue influence and that this presumption operates to defeat the sale I am considering. I am quite satisfied that the presumption of undue influence does arise in the present case. I am equally satisfied that it is one which *can* be rebutted (see, for example, the decision of Black J. *Provincial Bank v McKeever* (Case 91): and Gavan Duffy J. *Grealish v Murphy* (Case 96)) and that it *has* been rebutted in this case. The test applied by Budd J. (in *Gregg v*

Kidd) was to ascertain whether the gift he was considering had resulted from the free exercise of the donor's will. Applying that test to the present case the evidence satisfies me that the plaintiff freely and with an independent will entered into the bargain with the defendant. It is, however, argued that even if this were so, his judgment was not an 'informed judgment', because of the failure of the defendant to ensure that the plaintiff had independent professional advice. It is submitted that I should apply the principles enunciated by the Court of Appeal in England in *Bundy* and hold that this failure rendered the transaction voidable by reason of the doctrine of undue influence. I have already decided that the defendant was not required to ensure that the plaintiff obtained independent professional advice. It is unnecessary then for me to consider whether, if he was so required, this would render the transaction invalid for undue influence as well as by virtue of the equitable principles relating to purchases by trustees from *cestui que trusts*. I should add that when the presumption of undue influence arises, the absence of independent professional advice does not necessarily render the transaction invalid, and I draw attention to a recent example of the application of this principle in England (see *In re Brocklehurst's Estate* (1977)). The claim of undue influence therefore fails.

Finally, I should refer to the submissions that the transaction in this case attracts the equitable principles relating to unconscionable bargains. This submission can be considered under two separate headings. As pointed out by Gavan Duffy J. in *Grealish v Murphy* (Case 96) equity comes to the rescue whenever the parties to a contract have not met on equal terms and if it is shown that an infirm grantor could not adequately protect himself the court will inquire whether he was given the protection which was his due by reason of his infirmity. I have, however, already recorded my conclusion that the plaintiff was not suffering from any physical or mental infirmity when the agreement was entered into in 1968 such as would attract the equitable doctrine to which I have referred. It is true that in 1973 when the transfer was executed the plaintiff's health had seriously deteriorated—he was by then an alcoholic. But if the agreement he had earlier entered into was a legally valid one, the subsequent deterioration in his health would not invalidate it, or entitle him to set aside the deed of transfer which it was his legal obligation to execute. Secondly, under the heading of unconscionable bargains, equity will set aside sales by reversioners in certain circumstances. But the sale in this case was not at an undervalue, nor in the light of the findings of fact I have already made could it otherwise be regarded as unconscionable . . .

Case 93. Kirwan v Cullen
Chancery (1856) 4 Ir.Ch.Rep. 322

An elderly lady transferred half of her property in trust for a convent. She appointed the Archbishop of Dublin, the defendant, and the superior of the Jesuits to be the trustees. The latter had been the lady's confessor two years before the date of the gift. Her confessor at the time was under the religious control of that trustee. Her personal representative sought to have the transfer set aside.

Held that when the gift was made the deceased was of competent understanding and of a charitable and religious disposition. She was not under the influence of the trustee, who did not receive any personal benefit from the transaction, at the material date, in that his role as confessor had ended two years before the making of the gift. The action was dismissed.

Brady L.C.:

. . . Here was a lady of full age and competent understanding, moving in the world, living with her family, who possessed a sum of money; this she transferred through the medium of a duly authorised agent, to the names of these gentlemen of high position in the church to which she belonged. We find the respondents not claiming any personal interest, admitting that they are mere trustees for the objects of the deceased's bounty, and that they are bound to carry out purposes not connected with themselves individually. We find the donation effected by the deceased through the intervention of a third person, whose name has been mentioned here, who was admittedly without interest in the subject of the gift, and who never has received the smallest portion of it. I do not think it possible to contend that this can be classed with the cases in which donations and gifts have been held by this court to have been tainted by the fact that they were made to a person who was placed in a situation giving him power to exercise undue influence over the donor . . . none of them seem to me to interfere with the decision of this case, which is, I think, to be resolved into this question, whether, in fact, there is evidence to show that when this lady made this gift, any influence was exercised to induce her to do so? On that subject the plaintiff's case is wholly without evidence. I do not say that we can at all wonder at this, for it is conceded by the respondents that the knowledge of the transaction was wholly confined to this lady herself, and the gentleman to whom she confided the arrangement of the business; but unquestionably there is no evidence to impeach the gift, beyond the broad circumstances of the case. Then, as I said, here is a lady of mature age and undoubted understanding, living with her sisters, making this gift more than a year before her death. She never complained of it to any one, not even to her sisters with whom she resided. It appears that some dividends on the sum were received by the trustees, and that she made no objection to the fact of their receiving them, but that some discussion arose as to the application: all these circumstances showing that she perfectly well knew of and approved of the transaction; and I must therefore say that I consider the case made by the petition entirely destitute of foundation. No doubt, the court would not have been satisfied unless some explanation had been given of this transfer, which in itself seems a little remarkable; but that has been fully given. We have here affidavits of the trustee and Archbishop Cullen, which show that so far as they are concerned they were wholly without influence. Dr Cullen swears 'that he never saw the said deceased, or had the slightest intimacy or acquaintance with her, or with any of her family, and did not know there was such a person until he was asked to become a trustee of the fund.'

The trustee seems to have had a more intimate acquaintance with this lady, he had filled the position of her spiritual adviser; but the relation between them had ceased two years before the transaction occurred, and she had been before this perfectly independent of him. The trustee and Dr Cullen both swear that they had no knowledge of the transaction; the trustee until he was informed by another person; Dr Cullen until he was told by the trustee. The trustee says that he declined to accept the burden of this trust alone, and that he suggested that Dr Cullen, the spiritual superior of himself and of all other members of his Church in Ireland, should be associated with him in the trust. He also states that they had an interview with this lady after the transfer, in which it did not appear that she had any wish to retract from the arrangement . . . .There is then the affidavit of a gentleman who intervened in the transaction, at least so far as procuring the assent of the trustees. He also was in the position of a person not taking any personal benefit from the transaction, and seems to have declined to be in any way concerned in it, beyond procuring these persons to act as trustees. His statement is not in any way controverted, and his evidence is full, clear and creditable to him. I will not say that the case might not assume a very different aspect if this claim were made by the deceased in her lifetime, and if she were to make affidavits contradicting these; but here we have the uncontroverted evidence of persons who appear only to have intervened between this lady and the objects of her bounty, without taking any personal benefit . . . It is said that such a gift is most extraordinary in its amount as well as in its circumstances; but this lady appears to have been of an unusually charitable and pious disposition. She does seem to have denuded herself of much property, but she still retained a considerable amount, which may have been enough for her desires. She frequently visited this institution which she benefited, and she seems to have esteemed it highly. She saw the purposes to which her bounty was to be devoted, and being of a charitable and religious disposition, she may have come to the conclusion that those were purposes which she ought to sustain, and to which her property ought to be devoted. I do not mean in saying this to call in aid of this gift the opinion that the object was charitable in a legal point of view; I do not mean to decide that these were what are legally denominated charitable purposes; I merely mean to show the motive, acting as it did seem to act on the mind of a person who was perhaps, if that be possible, religious and charitable even to excess—who approved of the purposes of this community, and, who in consequence devoted a large portion of her property to its support. It may be that, in the opinion of some persons, she pursued her purposes not wisely, but too well; but, sitting in this court, I cannot venture to set a limit to her bounty . . .

CHAPTER 16.

UNCONSCIONABLE BARGAIN

The law will grant relief in instances of unconscionable bargain, that is where one party to the transaction is in a position to exploit a particular weakness of the other party. *Slator v Nolan* (Case 94) established the principle that the court would set aside every conceivable transaction where one party, by fraud or chicanery, succeeds in gaining an advantage over another party not standing in an equal position of negotiation. The burden of proving that the bargain is not unconscionable rests on the party wishing to uphold the transaction.

The courts have come to the rescue of parties advanced in years: *Lydon v Coyne* (Case 95), and of those aged and mentally infirm: *Grealish v Murphy* (Case 96).

Should the party wishing to uphold the transaction prove that the other party had adequate protection—for example, by being independently advised and receiving the market value of the property—the court will uphold the transaction: *Kelly v Morrisroe* (Case 97) and *Haverty v Brooks* (Case 98). The essential feature is whether the weaker party exercised an independent will when entering the transaction: *McCormack v Bennett* (Case 99).

Case 94. Slator v Nolan
Chancery (1876) I.R. 11 Eq. 367

When the plaintiff was in destitute circumstances he sold his inheritance for an utterly inadequate consideration to the defendant, his brother-in-law, who was well versed in business. After the terms of the contract had been arranged, the plaintiff had legal assistance in the preparation and execution of the deed. The plaintiff sought to have the transaction set aside.

Held that the defendant had knowingly taken advantage of the plaintiff's recklessness and that since the plaintiff's professional advice had not been adequate the transaction should be set aside.

Sullivan M.R.:

. . . Now, before I review the precise circumstances under which the deed was taken from the plaintiff, it is right that I should clearly indicate what is my view of the law applicable to such matters as that before me. It is an idle thing to suppose that the relation of trustee and *cestui que trust*, or guardian and ward, or attorney and client, or some other confidential relation, must exist to entitle a man to get aid in this court in setting aside an unconscionable transaction. I take the law of the court to be that if two persons—no matter whether a confidential relation exists between them or not—stand in such a relation to each other that one can take an undue advantage of the other, whether by reason of distress or recklessness or wildness or want of care, and where the facts show that one party has taken undue advantage of the other, by reason of the circumstances I have mentioned—a transaction resting upon such unconscionable dealing will not be allowed to stand: and there are several cases which show, even where no confidential relation exists, that, where parties are not on equal terms, the party who gets a benefit cannot hold it without proving that everything has been right and fair and reasonable on his part.

It will be sufficient to refer to two cases of that sort, which, as Lord Justice Knight Bruce observes in *Baker v Monk*, have an interest outside the interests of the parties to them. In that case, an elderly lady sold a property to a person who was in a superior position in life. There was no confidential relation between them. He had a solicitor; she had not. The Court of Appeal, confirming Lord Romilly's decision, set aside the deed on the inadequacy of the consideration. Lord Justice Knight Bruce says:

> This is a case in which society is as much interested as are individuals. It is the case of a purchase of real estate belonging to an elderly woman in humble life, consisting of ground in a town in Kent, and rather a prosperous town than otherwise, occupied at present by some old buildings considerably out of repair and frequently wanting reparation. The respondent appears to have had some wish to be rid of the trouble and expense of the repairs, and to have instead a certain annuity for her life. Thereupon she mentioned the subject, and it came to the knowledge of the minister of the congregation to which she belongs, and he—probably with every good intention—spoke upon the subject to a substantial tradesman in the town, who was in such a good station in life that he had been once or twice mayor; and he, in consequence of the communication made to him, went to the respondent about it. There was a little chaffering between them, but it was ultimately arranged that he should have the property in fee-simple, subject to a right to the respondent, during the period of her father-in-law's life, to occupy a cottage, and the appellant was to have the property in fee-simple for a certain payment per week. The question is not merely or alone whether this lady was or was not acquainted with the value of the property. That circumstance alone might amount to next to nothing. But the question is

whether—to repeat an expression used in several cases—the parties to the transaction were on equal terms. The purchaser was a substantial tradesman in the town; in the station of life which I have mentioned. The vendor was a single woman in humble life, of slender education, between sixty and seventy years of age, unprotected and unaided. After some little chaffering, as I have said, she consented to accept the weekly payments during her life as the purchase-money of the fee-simple, subject to another qualification which is so slight that it is not necessary to mention it further. That transaction took place between this man and this poor woman without the interference on her part of any other person. She was, as I have said, wholly unassisted, unadvised and unaided. He placed the matter in the hands of his lawyer; the lawyer drew the instrument—I dare say with good intentions—without consulting any other person, and brought the document to the respondent for execution, and she executed it under his advice alone. The deed is, in one respect at least, framed without sufficient attention to the interests of the vendor, although, as I have said, probably with no wrong intention. The transaction was thus begun and ended, without any advice on her behalf. The purchase was wholly completed by the purchaser; who was in the station of life which I have mentioned, and his lawyer. The purchaser and vendor were in such a relative position as that, according to the known established doctrine of this court, it lies on the purchaser to show affirmatively that the price is the value. In my judgment, he has failed to do so . . . In my judgment, therefore, this is a case of undervalue affirmatively established, the circumstances of which, according to the established doctrines of this court, make it incumbent on the purchaser, contrary to the ordinary rule, to show that he has given the full value to the unadvised and unassisted vendor. I think that the purchaser fails in doing that; that the transaction ought not to have taken place under the circumstances in which it did take place, and the decree of the Master of the Rolls is right.

. . . In *Smith v Kay*, Lord Cranworth says:

There is, I take it, no branch of the jurisdiction of the Court of Chancery which it is more ready to exercise than that which protects infants and persons in a situation of dependence, as it were, upon others from being imposed upon by those upon whom they are so dependent. The familiar cases of the influence of a parent over his child, of a guardian over his ward, of an attorney over his client, are but instances. The principle is not confined to those cases, as was well stated by Lord Eldon in the case of *Gibson v Jeyes*, in which he says it is 'the great rule applying to trustees, attorneys or anyone else'. Now, what does 'anyone else' mean? It is contended that it applies only to persons who stand in what is called fiduciary relation. I believe if the principle is examined it will be found most frequently applied in such cases, for this simple reason, that the fiduciary relation gives a power of influence: but I could suggest fifty cases of fiduciary relation where the principle will not apply at all.

Lord Kingsdown says:

> I quite agree with my noble and learned friend on my right, that it is not the relation of solicitor and client, or of trustee and *cestui que trust*, which constitutes the sole title to relief in these cases, and which imposes upon those who obtain such securities as these the duty, before they obtain their confirmation, of making a free disclosure of every circumstance which it is important that the individual who is called upon for the confirmation should be apprised of. The principle applies to every case where confidence is reposed and betrayed.

Case 95. Lydon v Coyne

High Court [1946] Ir.Jur.Rep. 64

An elderly uncle conveyed his small farm to his nephew. He reserved a life interest for himself and his wife. The consideration provided by the nephew was to be periodic payments to his uncle, a benefit his uncle was unlikely to enjoy for long because of his advanced age. When the uncle died three months later, his widow sought to have the deed set aside as improvident.

Held that in view of the improvidence of the transaction, and the difficulty of construction presented by the deed, and having regard to the circumstances surrounding its execution, and the absence of a revocation clause, and the fact that the deceased had not had independent advice, and the evidence that the deceased had not properly understood the transaction, the deed must be set aside as improvident.

O'Byrne J.:

. . . This is an action to set aside a deed dated 25 January 1943, and made between the deceased of the one part and the defendant, his nephew of the other part . . . The transferor died within a few months, namely, on 10 April 1943, and the present proceedings have been brought by his widow who sues personally and as his personal representative.

The deceased owned a very small farm of land . . . Early on the morning of 25 January 1943, the defendant came to the offices of [a solicitor] and asked the solicitor to come out to the farm. The solicitor arrived at the farm between 11 and 12 o'clock that morning. He had been told beforehand that the old man was making over his land; but when he got to the house it appeared that the matter was not so simple, and a very long discussion took place between the parties. I can appreciate the very great difficulty in which the solicitor was placed, wishing to draw up the deed and finding that the parties had not come to any firm agreement. But solicitors must often protect parties against themselves.

The deed is technically not a voluntary deed by reason of two provisions therein. Firstly, there is the covenant to support the old couple, which is in the following terms: 'That he will support, clothe and maintain the said assignor and his said wife during their lives out of the rents and profits of the said lands.' It is to be noted that the wife, who takes a benefit under the deed, is not a party to it. Secondly, there is a covenant by the assignee for payment of £100 in the following terms: 'The assignee hereby covenants with the assignor for the payment of the sum of £100 to the assignor by instalments on demand in writing by the assignor, such instalments not to exceed the sum of £10 in any year.' That covenant, while technically sufficient, is in all the circumstances of this case quite illusory. I do not deal with the deed as a voluntary deed, but as one of a highly improvident character. In one respect it is quite unique; the habendum is worded as follows:

To hold the same unto the assignee to the use of the assignor for his life and should the wife of the assignor survive the assignor then and in such event to the use of said [wife] for her life and from and after the death of the assignor or the said [wife] or the death of the survivor of them then unto and to the use of the assignee his heirs executors administrators and assigns for all the estate right title term and interest of the assignor therein.

It is clear to me that the deceased never intended parting with the dominion over his property during his lifetime, for he kept insisting that his name should be in the rent receipt, showing in this way his intention that he should remain the owner while he lived. The limitation in the habendum purports to be controlled and governed by a subsequent covenant by the assignee in the following terms:

And the assignee hereby covenants with the assignor that he will reside in the dwellinghouse on the said lands and that he will manage and work the said lands in a good and husbandlike manner during the lifetime of the assignor and his said wife or the survivor of them . . . and the assignor hereby covenants with the assignee that he will allow the assignee to manage and to work the said lands during the lifetime of the assignor and during the lifetime of the said [wife] and the survivor of them and to retain the rents and profits of the said lands for his own use and benefit.

If (as I think is the fact) it was intended to reserve a life estate to the assignor, the terms of the deed with reference to the application of the rents and profits during the lifetime of the assignor are extremely peculiar. Apart from the peculiarity of form, it throws some light upon the value of the covenant to support, for this is enforceable only out of the rents and profits.

There is one question—the main question to which I must address myself—and it is whether the assignor understood the transaction into which he was entering. If this were a voluntary deed there would be an absolute onus upon the assignee to show that the transaction was the free and voluntary act of the assignor and that he understood the transaction. Owing to the circumstances of this case, the onus here is not so great. It seems to me that the solicitor, though undoubtedly doing his best for all parties, must be looked upon as the defendant's solicitor. He had acted for him before; the defendant brought him out and paid his fees for drawing the deed. But, approaching the transaction in that way and having regard to the improvidence of the transaction and the difficulty of interpreting some of the clauses in the deed, can I be satisfied that the deceased understood the transaction? I am quite satisfied he did not understand it. I do not understand it myself nor can I see how effect can be given to some of its provisions. That being so, and having regard to the fact that the deed contained no power of revocation and that no independent advice was given, this assignment cannot be allowed to stand . . .

Case 96. Grealish v Murphy
High Court [1946] I.R. 35

The plaintiff was over sixty years of age, mentally deficient, and lived alone on his farm in an isolated rural area. The defendant, aged thirty-two years of age and a road worker and haulier, was introduced to the plaintiff through the plaintiff's family. At their first meeting the plaintiff promised to leave the defendant his farm should he in the meantime work the land. Before the deed was signed the plaintiff consulted a solicitor, who took his instructions. The deed purported to assign the farm absolutely to the defendant on the plaintiff's death subject only to a life interest held by the plaintiff. The farm was charged with a right of residence in favour of the defendant and the defendant was to be supported and maintained out of the farm during the plaintiff's lifetime. In return the defendant agreed to reside in the house during the plaintiff's lifetime and work and manage the farm without reward and to account to the plaintiff for all monies expended and received. The plaintiff brought an action to have the deed set aside on the grounds on undue influence and improvident bargain.

Held that the deed could not be set aside on the ground of undue influence because some transaction had been expressly envisaged by the parties from the outset before the defendant could have acquired any influence over the plaintiff. But the deed was improvident. While the plaintiff had received legal advice, his solicitor was unaware of all the material facts, and had not given the plaintiff a complete explanation of the nature and effect of the deed, and was unaware of the full extent of the plaintiff's mental deficiency. By reason of the plaintiff's weakness of mind, coupled with the deficiencies in the legal advice under which he acted, and his own unawareness, the plaintiff was entitled to have the deed set aside.

Gavan Duffy J.:

Thus the plaintiff executed an improvident settlement, surrendering irrevocably his own absolute title for a life interest in consideration of personal covenants, backed by no adequate sanctions; the farm itself was hypothecated to secure the newcomer, beside whom the plaintiff was a Croesus; and the plaintiff was to be left for the remainder of his life very much at the mercy of a rather impecunious young man, who had no ties of blood and was still unproved as a friend. I think effective safeguards for the plaintiff could have been devised, if there was to be a settlement, or alternatively the plaintiff might have contracted to settle the property on the defendant by will . . . whatever plan was adopted, I think that suitable conditions could and should have been determined in negotiation between the solicitors for the parties, each of whom ought to have been separately represented. But these reflections are otiose, if the conclusive answer to the plaintiff's present claim is that he was separately advised by an independent solicitor.

That contention deserves careful examination and I have examined it with great care. I am satisfied that the plaintiff received from an experienced solicitor advice that was absolutely independent and I am satisfied that the draft deed was settled by very able counsel, upon instructions reflecting, of course, the state of mind and knowledge of the solicitor. Nevertheless, the question of the plaintiff's actual understanding of the solemn document that he executed on 24 October 1942, is a question of first importance. The solicitor, who avows that he looked upon the settlement as a transaction similar to the three attempts which, as the plaintiff told him, had broken down, says that he was absolutely satisfied that the plaintiff understood the instructions he gave for the deed. I have no doubt that the plaintiff did know that the deed would secure the land to the defendant at the plaintiff's death and that he knew generally the undertakings that the defendant was giving in return; the plaintiff showed his own understanding of the young man's obligations, when he formulated his grievance in his own words: 'He [the defendant] did not do anything about the agreement; he failed. . . . He was bound to look after me and buy and sell and give up the money—what he did not do.' But the trouble is that the solicitor, whose advice was essential to the plaintiff, did not advise *en connaissance de cause* and that the plaintiff's actual knowledge of what he was doing fell very short of the knowledge that the settlor ought to have had. That is the result in my mind of candid evidence from the solicitor himself and of inferences thereform. Consequently the principle . . . that a competent assignor, who knows what he is doing, must be held to his deed, does not apply here.

The evidence proves that the solicitor did not know all the material facts, that he did not give the plaintiff a complete explanation of the nature and effect of the deed, and that the duty of illuminating the plaintiff's benighted mind was more imperative and more formidable, if the task was possible, than the solicitor supposed . . .

Now, how is the defendant affected by any criticism reflecting upon the advice under which the plaintiff acted? I have shown that the defendant's own conduct in the matter was not beyond reproach, but any impartial person will see that it is quite impossible to say that the deed was procured through the defendant's undue influence, even if he did his part during nearly nine months, as he naturally would, to keep the old man's ardour alive. Nor is this the familiar case in which the court, from the relation of the parties, must presume undue influence until disproved positively by the recipient of the bounty; the defendant had constituted himself the plaintiff's interim confidential agent in January 1942, and had thus placed himself in a very delicate position, an exceptionally delicate position in view of the plaintiff's mentality; but the undoubted fact is that some such transaction as that eventuating in the actual settlement had been expressly envisaged by the parties from the outset, before the defendant can have acquired any influence whatsoever; therefore I cannot fairly impute to him the plaintiff's decision to put the business on a legal basis as soon as the way was made clear by the final elimination of [a previous attempt at a similar settlement with other parties], the only obstacle. And the defendant in no way interfered with the drafting of the deed in the particular form which it took.

The plaintiff had intended all through to leave the property to the defendant and to bind himself to that effect, in return for the precious services to be rendered by the vigorous young man to the rather helpless old one. As from January 1942, the defendant had only to be kind to the plaintiff, as he was, and to retain his goodwill, as he certainly did, in order to secure his reward from that eager benefactor.

Besides, the plan was not originated by the defendant but by the plaintiff and by him alone. The defendant on his side had faced appreciable risks in accepting the plaintiff's advances; and any picture of him as an adventurer, inveigling his witless victim into a trap in the October settlement, would be a caricature. Much as I blame the defendant for his reticence (partly perhaps through ignorance) as to the existence of his own solicitor and for his want of candour in suppressing the eccentric and disquieting £2,000 deposit in the joint names, I could not in common sense treat these faults as any evidence of undue influence in relation to the settlement on the facts; and, if the defendant throws doubt on the veracity of his own evidence concerning the plaintiff's alleged original offer to settle money on him, by his failure to mention that important promise to his solicitor and his failure to call upon the solicitor to make good that promise in the deed, here again my criticism of the defendant as a witness is foreign to the issue of undue influence in fact and remote from any evidence that would raise a legal presumption of undue influence against the defendant, so far as the settlement is concerned.

The result is that the plaintiff's attempt to set aside the deed on the ground of undue influence, whether actual or presumptive, by the defendant cannot succeed, and, if the deed had to stand or fall upon that issue, there would be nothing more to say. But the position in law as I see it, upon the pleadings, is not so simple as that; there is another crucial matter to be determined.

The plaintiff cannot avoid the deed for undue influence; but his claim is further based on the improvidence of the transaction and also he directly alleges (though in connection with the charge of undue influence) his own mental incapacity; I think I can reasonably read these averments together without calling for an amendment of his pleadings.

The issue thus raised brings into play Lord Hatherley's cardinal principle (from which the exceptions are rare) that equity comes to the rescue whenever the parties to a contract have not met upon equal terms, see Lord Hatherley's judgment (dissenting on facts) in *O'Rorke v Bolingbroke*; the corollary is that the court must inquire whether a grantor, shown to be unequal in protecting himself, has had the protection which was his due by reason of his infirmity, and the infirmity may take various forms. The deed here was in law a transaction for value, however tenuous the value may have proved to be in fact, and, of course, a court must be very much slower to undo a transaction for value; but the fundamental principle to justify radical interference by the court is the identical principle, whether value be shown or not, and the recorded examples run from gifts and voluntary settlements (including an abortive marriage settlement) to assignments for a money consideration. The principle has been applied to improvident grants, whether the particular disadvantage entailing the need for protection to the grantor were merely low station and surprise (though the grantor's rights were fully explained), or youth and inexperience, or age and weak intellect, short of total incapacity, with no fiduciary relation and no 'arts of inducement' to condemn the grantee. Even the exuberant or ill-considered dispositions of feckless middle-aged women have had to yield to the same principle. The principle prevailed, when the deed was 'the most honest thing in the world' so far as the settlor and her solicitor were concerned, and though the evidence of the solicitor acting for the grantor was fully accepted, and again where the deed had been prepared by the grantor's own solicitor, a man of honour, but the grantor, while fully understanding the benefit to accrue to the grantee, had not fully understood the effect of her deed as it affected her own interests. In several other instances the inadequacy of the explanations given to the grantor has been a conspicuous, indeed a decisive, factor in the court's action against an improvident deed, the court either assuming, or having direct evidence, to prove a serious lack of understanding. The least the court can demand is that an infirm grantor shall have known what he was doing. In the much more frequent, but analogous, instances of deeds attacked for undue influence the courts have insisted that the donor must have had a complete explanation of the nature and effect of the transaction, from an advisor who himself knew all the relevant circumstances, even where the advisor was selected by the donor, and the same imperative requirement was stressed in a transaction for value . . . upon a deed closely resembling the deed in this action in some aspects, but obtained by undue influence.

In my judgment, without any regard to any question of undue influence, upon Lord Hatherley's principle and the concurrent authorities the plaintiff by reason of his own weakness of mind, coupled with the deficiencies in the legal advice under which he acted and his unawareness, is entitled to have the improvident indenture of settlement, dated 24 October 1942, set aside . . .

Case 97. Kelly v Morrisroe
Court of Appeal (1919) 53 I.L.T.R. 145

An elderly woman in humble circumstances and of eccentric habits lived alone in a dilapidated cottage on a small plot of land. The property was situated between two business premises, both of which would benefit substantially by its acquisition. Apart from its value to either business it would not have been worth much. The defendant, owner of one of the adjacent businesses, offered to purchase the premises for slightly less than its value and to allow the woman the use of the cottage, rent-free, during her lifetime. The woman consulted her former employer who was a merchant in the same town and he advised her to ask for the full value of the property, which she did, and to which the defendant agreed. The woman was accompanied to the defendant's solicitor by her former employer, and the solicitor read and explained the deed to her. After her death her personal representative sought to have the deed set aside as improvident. The other businessman gave evidence that he would have purchased the property for a much higher sum.

Held that the woman had all the advice and protection necessary. Her age and circumstances threw the onus on the defendant of showing that the transaction was fair and honest. The discharge of this onus left the court with no evidence on which it could reasonably find that the transaction should be set aside.

Sir James Campbell L.C.:

How is it possible, then, to say that this old lady was without advice, or the best possible advice? The learned judge [in the High Court] does not say that this old lady was not capable of transacting business, but that she was eccentric in habits and mentally abnormal. It would have been a dangerous contention for the plaintiff to have put forward—that the old lady was not capable of transacting business, seeing that he claims as executor under a subsequent will. The judge merely says that she was eccentric and not normal, but we have all had experience of eccentric old ladies—eccentric in habits and eccentric in dress, but as cute as possible in money matters, and quite well able to understand the value of money and transact business, yet not mentally normal. The defendant's offer having been accepted, he went to his solicitor and instructed him to prepare a conveyance, and on the next day the old lady, accompanied by her former employer, called at the solicitor's office, and the solicitor—whose evidence the judge accepts—read out and explained the deed to her, and swears she understood it. The judge finds that she understood that she was getting £25, but he says the place had a sort of fancy value owing to the competition for it between the two merchants . . . But, apart from the other merchant's offer of £100 in court, its fancy value up to that time was something between £20 or £30, and there is no evidence that it was of any value except to these two gentlemen, and even for its adventitious value at that date neither went above £25. It is said that because the other merchant stated in court that he would have given £100, that there was something in the defendant's mind about the other merchant's anxiety to get the place, which should have been communicated to this old lady, but the price of £100 was apparently never suggested until after her death. There is no evidence upon which the judge could reasonably find that this deed could be set aside. This old lady had all the protection necessary; her former employer, whom she trusted, advised her in the matter, and was present when the deed was completed. It was a fair and honest transaction, and although the age of the old lady threw the onus on the defendant of showing that he took no advantage, that onus has been discharged by him. There is no ground whatever for any imputation either against him or the solicitor, and the validity of the deed cannot be impeached . . .

Ronan and O'Connor L.JJ. concurred.

Case 98. Haverty v Brooks
High Court [1970] I.R. 214

Two years before his death the deceased, a 76-year-old bachelor who had suffered from mental illness and lived alone on a small farm, sold it to the defendant, who farmed adjacent lands. The bulk of the purchase price was to be paid forthwith with the balance to be paid at a stated sum per annum without interest. The balance of the purchase price was secured by a mortgage of the farm. The deceased was to retain a right of residence in the house and the defendant agreed to put the house into repair and to be responsible for the deceased's funeral expenses. The same solicitor acted for both parties. The administrator of the deceased's estate sought to have the transaction set aside as improvident.

Held that the evidence established that there was nothing which indicated that the deceased was unequal in protecting his own interest at the time of the transaction in that he had recovered from his mental illness, there had been substantial monetary consideration, he understood the nature of the transaction and he trusted the defendant. The sale was not improvident and the action was dismissed.

McLoughlin J.:

There are two aspects of this case that require to be dealt with by me in some detail. First, the circumstances as to the mental condition of the deceased at the time of the disputed transaction and, secondly, the circumstances surrounding the actual carrying out of the transaction which was performed by a solicitor who acted for both parties to the transaction.

In the months of August and September 1963, the deceased was a voluntary patient in [a] mental hospital where he was treated . . . for symptoms of depression and confusion and some indication of suicidal ruminations without conviction. After his discharge, he continued to attend as an outpatient for a couple of months and afterwards he was supplied with doses of maintenance drugs. His last attendance . . . was on 31 March 1964. The doctor did see him casually afterwards, and gave it as his opinion that he was fully recovered and rational. However, the plaintiff gave evidence that, after the deceased had left hospital, the plaintiff found him depressed and irrational and 'not so sprightly as before'. The plaintiff also said that the deceased told him about a year before the deceased died that he would leave his farm to a niece . . . who lived in Scotland. Another niece . . . who also lived a short distance away from the deceased and who used to send food over to him, also gave evidence that after he left hospital the deceased was a little confused, being rather childish and very biddable. This evidence raises great suspicion as to the mental capacity of the deceased at the time of entering into this transaction, and it caused me to suspend giving any judgment until I had considered with extreme care and caution the evidence given by the defendant and by the solicitor . . . who acted for both parties.

The defendant said that he knew the deceased since he returned to this country in 1935 and went to live beside him. He rented the lands from him for 10 to 11 years before the transfer . . . and he did some repairs to the deceased's house. In January 1965, the deceased told him that he was going to sell his lands, that if he would buy he would give him preference and that he would expect to get £1,200. The defendant said that £1,000 would be a good price, and he declined to buy. Again in February, in a public house, the matter came up again and he again declined to buy at £1,200. In March he got a message to go to the deceased's house and the deceased told him that if he did not take the lands he would sell them to [another neighbour], who was interested, and the defendant then agreed to give the £1,200. The deceased asked would the sale cause him to lose his old-age pension and the defendant said that he did not know but that they should first go to a solicitor. The deceased said that he did not want to go to a Mr X, solicitor, who knew too much about him and might talk with people who would get to know his business; and the deceased mentioned [another solicitor]. Following this conversation the defendant went in to see [this solicitor] first on his own and again with the deceased on 29 March 1965. The subsequent evidence of the carrying out of the transaction is best obtained from the evidence given by the solicitor, except for the circumstance that the defendant told the deceased that he [the defendant] wanted the transfer to be made over to his son . . .

The solicitor . . . stated in evidence that the defendant called on his office on 27 March and told him that the deceased, aged 76 years, had agreed to sell his holding for £1,200 but retaining exclusive use of house and garden for his life; the sum of £400 to be paid at once and the balance to be paid by instalments of £100 yearly, free of interest. By arrangement, the deceased and the defendant called again on 29 March and the deceased gave instructions to him on these terms: 'Purchase price £1,200; £400 down, balance £100 yearly; reserving right of his use of house and garden and the defendant to put the house into repair.' When asked about interest on the balance of the purchase money, the deceased said that he did not want interest. The deceased also indicated that he wished the defendant to retain £50 of the purchase money to pay for his (the deceased's) funeral and burial expenses, and a contract was drawn up and signed on these terms—the defendant handing over £75 in cash to the solicitor as a deposit. Having regard to the deceased's age, the solicitor observed that £800 was too much to be left outstanding and the deceased asked him what was the largest amount he could get which would not disqualify him from receiving the old-age pension and he was told that it was £740. The solicitor, having obtained the Folio from the Land Office, got the note as to equities discharged, engrossed the usual form of transfer and arranged for the parties to attend his office on 10 May, which they did. The transfer was made in the name of the defendant's son, the down payment being increased to £700 which was duly paid over to the deceased, otherwise the transaction was effected in accordance with the terms of the contract—the balance being secured by a charge on the lands. Before signing, the deceased read over the document to himself and then had it read over and explained to him by the solicitor.

The solicitor has sworn that he had not doubts as to the deceased's capacity to understand the transaction which he was entering into, and I have no hesitation about accepting the solicitor's evidence. However, he did not know either of the parties before; he did not know of the deceased's family circumstances or of his having been in a mental institution; nor did he have any information as to the value of the property transferred other than what could be inferred from the acreage, rateable valuation and annuity. Although I do not attach any blame to the solicitor, I do emphasise that this is another example of the undesirability of one solicitor acting for both parties in a transaction of this kind.

There is one other feature which I should mention and it is this: none of the deceased's relations, although living in the same neighbourhood, became aware of his having sold his farm until after his death. The plaintiff did have some suspicion by reason of seeing the defendant carrying out substantial reclamation work on the farm with machinery, such as work connected with drainage, clearing and fertilising; and the plaintiff saw the defendant doing repairs to the house.

All the circumstances which I have mentioned undoubtedly justify recourse to a court of equity to determine whether, as Gavan Duffy J. said in *Grealish v Murphy* (Case 96): 'the issue thus raised brings into play Lord Hatherley's cardinal principle (from which the exceptions are rare) that equity comes to the rescue whenever the parties to a contract have not met upon equal terms . . .' The transaction here, as in *Grealish v Murphy*, was a transaction for value and, as pointed out by Gavan Duffy J., a court is very much slower to undo a transaction for value. In *Grealish v Murphy* it was held, nevertheless, that the transaction was an improvident one. But the circumstances of this case are very different from those of *Grealish v Murphy*. The plaintiff in that case was a farmer who assigned his farm to the defendant, a stranger, subject to a life interest in consideration of convenants by the latter to work and manage the farm and to account for the profits; there was no monetary consideration. In this case there is a substantial monetary consideration, but it is contended for the plaintiff that it amounted to such an undervalue as to render the transaction improvident . . .

Considering all these matters I have come to the conclusion that the transaction was not an improvident transaction and, although I do not rely on it conclusively, there was the evidence of one valuer that £1,200 was a fair value in 1965 to justify me in coming to this conclusion.

If the deceased had put his farm up for sale by auction in 1965, he might have got more than £1,200; but I believe that he did not want to do that, he wanted the defendant to buy it at the deceased's price and on his conditions because he knew the defendant and trusted him to repair the house, to pay the instalments of the purchase price without jeopardising his old-age pension and to keep secret the transaction from his relatives so that they might continue to supply him with meals . . .

Case 99. McCormack v Bennett

High Court (1973) 107 I.L.T.R. 127

A father aged 79 years, in consideration of the affection he bore his daughter, transferred all his property by deed to her, reserving only a life interest for himself and making no provision for his infirm wife, who lived with him. The daughter had agreed prior to the deed to take care of her parents for the duration of their lives. The deed was drawn up by a solicitor who advised the father independently of his daughter. After the father's death other members of the family sought to have the deed set aside on the ground that it was improvident.

Held that the daughter had not exerted undue influence over her father to procure the deed, that he had been free of any mental or physical infirmity, and that he had the benefit of independent legal advice. While the deed was *prima facie* improvident in that it made no provision for the parents, it was evident that the deed was made in consequence of the free exercise of the father's will. The action was dismissed.

Finlay J.:

. . . I find that this deed was not executed as a result of any undue influence on the part of the defendant. I find that the deceased had no mental or physical infirmity which prevented him from fully understanding the nature and consequences of this deed. I find that the deceased had the benefit of independent advice from the solicitor of his choice and that that was fully and carefully available to him. I find that the possibility of a clause of revocation was explained to the deceased and that the desirability of making a revocable disposition of his property was urged upon him. I find that the deed is on the face of it improvident in that the deceased disposed of the remainder interest in his only piece of property without any valuable consideration moving to him in respect of that disposition. I find that by reason of the failure of the deceased and of the defendant to inform the solicitor of the promises made by the defendant in respect of the care and maintenance of her father and mother that he was not aware of all the circumstances of the case when he was advising the deceased.

On these findings of fact I am satisfied that the legal position is as follows:

I accept and adopt as applicable to this case the reasoning of Mr Justice Budd in the case of *Gregg v Kitt* (1956). In particular I would adopt and repeat the portion of his judgment where he says:

Where the relations between the donor and another person raise a presumption that that other person had influence over the donor and the evidence shows that the third party is both closely related to the donee and was closely associated in action and interest with the donee at the time of events leading to the transaction, it would seem to be on principle that the onus in such circumstances must be likewise thrown on the donee to establish that the gift resulted from the free exercise of the donor's will. The presumption may of course be rebutted either by showing that the donor has had competent independent advice and acted of his own free will or in some other way. As Lord Hailsham says in *Inche Noriah v Shaik Allie Bin Omar*: 'The most obvious way to prove that the gift was the result of the free exercise of independent will is to establish that the gift was made after the nature and effect of the transaction had been fully explained to the donor by some independent and qualified person so completely as to satisfy the court that the donor was acting independently of any influence from the donee and with full appreciation of what he was doing.' If that method of rebutting the presumption is adopted and it is not the only method open the advice relied on must, in the words of Lord Hailsham, be given with a knowledge of all relevant circumstances and must be such as a competent and honest adviser would give if acting solely in the interests of the donor.

The ignorance by the solicitor at the time when he was advising the deceased of the promises made by the defendant in respect of a transfer of the land meant that he was not a person with knowledge of all relevant circumstances. If to defend this deed and to discharge the onus which is in my view upon her the defendant must rely only on the independent advice of the solicitor she must therefore fail. However, from the passage which I have quoted, that Mr Justice Budd was of the view, and in this I am in full agreement with his judgment, that the presence of full and satisfactory independent advice is not the only way of proving that a voluntary deed, even though it may be on the face of it improvident, resulted from the free exercise of the donor's will. I am satisfied that the deceased in October 1967 himself was particularly concerned to make an out and out transfer of these lands by deed to his daughter. I am satisfied that that idea for practical purposes originated with him and certainly did not originate with the defendant. His reason for making such a transfer instead of a will which would have been revocable was, I am satisfied, that he wanted a permanency and finality with regard to the disposition of his affairs. I think it is a reasonable inference from the evidence which I have heard that he was a sufficiently astute man to know that no form of bargain or commercial transaction concerned with his land was likely to secure for himself and his wife what they really needed and that was personal care and attention granted largely through affection and kindness by a member of their family. I believe therefore that the deceased when he executed this deed did so as an act entirely of his own free will and did so in the expectation and belief which was his own and not induced [by] them that by so doing he would secure or reinforce what he believed to be the affectionate attendance of his daughter for both himself and his wife. In these circumstances I conclude that there is evidence before me which I accept other than and in addition to the evidence of the independent advice which the deceased received before executing the deed which satisfies me that the deed was his own act and resulted from an exercise of his own free will. In these circumstances as I understand the legal principles applicable I must uphold this deed even though it may on the face of it appear improvident and even though events which occurred after its execution may have made the deceased in his lifetime dissatisfied with it. Having already concluded that there was no trespass on the life interest of the deceased in these lands I therefore dismiss this action.

CHAPTER 17.

ILLEGAL CONTRACTS

A contract to breach the provisions of the Constitution, such as an agreement to obtain a divorce, will not be enforced in the courts on the ground of public policy: *Dalton v Dalton* (Case 100).

Likewise a contract for an illegal or an immoral purpose, or a contract to breach a statute or the common law, will not be enforced for the same reason. The court hearing the case will itself take cognisance of the illegality in instances where it is not pleaded by the defendant: *McIlvenna v Ferris* (Case 101). The onus of proving illegality lies on the party asserting it: *Whitecross Potatoes (International) Ltd v Coyle* (Case 113).

A contract which infringes any provision of a statute is illegal. In *Daly v Daly* (Case 102) the bankruptcy laws were breached. *Gray v Cathcart* (Case 103) saw the refusal to enforce a contract which infringed the public hygiene laws. In *O'Shaughnessy v Lyons* (Case 104) the transportation statute was infringed. The court refused to enforce a letting which infringed the Land Acts: *Dempsey v O'Reilly* (Case 105).

A contract which infringes the common law is illegal on the ground of public policy. A contract which tends to promote corruption in public officials is illegal: *Dublin Corporation v Hayes* (Case 106). A contract which interferes with the prosecution of offences is void though to constitute such illegality there must be reasonable grounds for believing that an offence has actually been committed: *Rourke v Mealy* (Case 107). Once those reasonable grounds are present such a contract is void: *Nolan v Shiels* (Case 108).

A contract which is prejudicial to the due administration of justice is void. In *Rand v Flynn* (Case 109) the court refused to enforce a contract in which an accused person indemnified his bailsman, though expenses incurred in endeavouring to secure the accused's attendance in court was recoverable. But where a party advanced money and secured prior debts, the money to be used to flee from justice, the transaction was lawful provided the party acted *bona fide*: *Bagot v Arnott* (Case 110).

Gaming contracts cannot be enforced and money lent knowingly for that purpose cannot be recovered by action: *Anthony v Shea* (Case 111).

Contracts to defraud the revenue cannot be enforced: *Starling Securities Ltd v Woods Ltd* (Case 112) and *Whitecross Potatoes (International) Ltd v Coyle* (Case 113).

The court will not enforce a contract which involves the performance of an illegal act in a foreign country: *Stanhope v Hospitals Trust Ltd* (Case 114).

The courts will not grant relief which has the effect of compelling a party to perform an act prohibited by law: *Namlooze Venootschap De Faam v Dorset Manufacturing Co. Ltd* (Case 115).

Case 100. Dalton v Dalton
High Court [1982] I.L.R.M. 418

The parties entered into a separation agreement, which contained a clause that the parties agreed to obtain a decree of divorce *a vinculo matrimonii*, and applied to the High Court to have the agreement made a rule of court.

Held that since the Constitution did not favour divorce the court would be lending support to a course of conduct which was contrary to public policy should it grant the application.

O'Hanlon J.:

It appears to me that considerations of public policy require that the court shall not lend its support to an agreement providing for the obtaining of a divorce *a vinculo* by a husband and wife, and this may well be the position even if the parties are domiciled elsewhere than in Ireland when the application is made or proposed to take up such foreign domicile in the future.

I reach this conclusion principally by reference to passages in the judgments delivered in the case of *Mayo-Perrott v Mayo-Perrott* (1958). In the Supreme Court Kingsmill Moore J. states:

But to hold that our law accepts the cardinal principle that questions as to married or unmarried status depends on the law of the domicile of the parties at the time when such status is created or dissolved is not to say that our law will give active assistance to facilitate in any way the effecting of a dissolution of marriage in another country where the parties are domiciled. It cannot be doubted that the public policy of this country as reflected in the Constitution does not favour divorce *a vinculo* and though the law may recognise the change of status effected by it as an accomplished fact, it would fail to carry out public policy if, by a decree of its own courts, it gave assistance to the process of divorce by entertaining a suit for the costs of such proceedings. The debt which it is sought to enforce is one created by proceedings of a nature which could not be instituted in this country, proceedings the institution of which our public policy disapproves. For these reasons I hold that the appeal fails and the suit cannot be entertained in our courts.

. . . I am of opinion that to ask the court to make the agreement which has been concluded between the parties in the present case a rule of court is to ask the court to lend its support to a course of conduct which is contrary to public policy within this jurisdiction. For this reason I have decided that I should refuse the application.

Case 101. McIlvenna v Ferris
High Court [1955] I.R. 318

The parties entered into a building contract. When the defendant refused to pay for the work done the plaintiff sued. At the trial, the defendant argued that when the building contract was made it contravened statutory orders and was illegal. Additional work was agreed after the statutory orders had been revoked. The plaintiff argued that this defence could not be relied on because it had not been pleaded prior to the trial.

Held that where the plaintiff's claim at a trial discloses that a transaction which is the basis of the claim is illegal the court cannot properly ignore the illegality of that part of the claim or give effect to it, even where the illegality is not pleaded. The court declined to enforce the building contract but was prepared to consider the plaintiff's claim in respect of the contracts for extra work entered into subsequent to the revocation of the statutory orders.

Ó Dálaigh J.:

. . . At the close of the plaintiff's case, counsel applied on behalf of the defendant for a non-suit in respect of both parts of the plaintiff's claim. He puts his application on two grounds. His first ground is that the making of the several contracts without a licence contravened [a statutory instrument] and constituted a criminal offence, and the contracts are further declared by sub-para. (*b*) of art. 5 (1) to be unenforceable. Moreover, he says that the execution of the work was also a criminal offence, being a contravention of art. 4 (1) of the Order. The illegality of the contracts having come to light, the court will not, counsel argues, assist the plaintiff to enforce his claim notwithstanding that the illegality is not pleaded . . .

Counsel for the plaintiff opposes counsel for the defendant's application . . . on a number of grounds. He argues that the court is not bound to raise the illegality in the absence of a plea; that the evidence does not establish that a licence was not issued; that the [statutory instrument] recognises the existence of the contract and that the unenforceability must be pleaded . . .

In my opinion it is well settled that the court will not assist a plaintiff in the circumstances of this case—I refer only to the contract of September, 1951. The law is stated by Lindley L.J. with characteristic forthrightness in *Scott v Brown, Doering, McNab & Co.* (1892):

> *Ex turpi causa non oritur actio.* This old and well-known legal maxim is founded in good sense, and expresses a clear and well-recognised legal principle, which is not confined to indictable offences. No court ought to enforce an illegal contract or allow itself to be made the instrument of enforcing obligations alleged to arise out of a contract or transaction which is illegal, if the illegality is duly brought to the notice of the court, and if the person invoking the aid of the court is himself implicated in the illegality. It matters not whether the defendant has pleaded the illegality or whether he has not. If the evidence adduced by the plaintiff proves the illegality the court ought not to assist him.

The decision in *Scott v Brown, Doering, McNab & Co.* was followed by Kennedy J., in *Gedge's Case* (1900) where, as appears, the defendants did not wish the point of illegality to be taken by the court. 'But I hold', Kennedy J. said, 'that my judgment ought not to be affected by this consideration.' I might also refer to *Harry Parker Ltd v Mason* (1940) where McKinnon L.J. says: 'The rule *ex turpi causa non oritur actio* is, of course, not a matter by way of defence,' and Luxmoore L.J. says that 'this court will not assist either party once the illegality of the transaction has been brought to its notice.'

I cannot accept counsel for the plaintiff's view as to the effect of evidence as to the existence of a licence. Nor do I think that the provision in [the statutory instrument] that the illegal contract shall not be enforceable in any way assists his argument. It may indeed be that this is a recognition of the existence of the contract, but I rather think that that paragraph was added *ex abundante cautela.** In any event it does nothing to make the contract anything the less illegal. It follows that I must rule

---

**ex abundante cautela*, from excess of caution.

out so much of the plaintiff's claim as is based on the contract of September 1951 . . .

Case 102. Daly v Daly
Court of Exchequer (1870) I.R. 5 C.L. 108

The defendant was adjudicated a bankrupt and the plaintiff, one of his creditors, sought to have the bankruptcy set aside because it had been obtained by fraud. The parties then agreed, unknown to the other creditors, that the plaintiff would abandon these proceedings in return for the full discharge of his debt. When the cheque was dishonoured the plaintiff sued the defendant.

Held that the defendant's cheque was given in return for the plaintiff's undertaking to discontinue the proceedings to have the bankruptcy set aside. This consideration was contrary to public policy and was illegal. The claim was dismissed.

Fitzgerald B.:

. . . The defendant further pleaded a petition filed by him as an insolvent debtor to the Court of Bankruptcy and Insolvency; and a subsequent filing by him of a schedule setting forth, with all necessary particulars, according to the practice of the court, amongst other debts, a certain debt of £80 due by him to the plaintiff; that such proceedings were thereupon had, that the defendant was, in fact, discharged by an order of adjudication. The defendant then admits that the order of adjudication was obtained by fraud, but avers that the order was in full force and effect unless and until the same was set aside, of all which premises the plaintiff had notice. The defendant then avers that the plaintiff took proceedings in the Court of Bankruptcy and Insolvency to set aside the order of adjudication, on the ground that it had been obtained by fraud, and that a conditional order was made by the court, upon the plaintiff's application, to set aside the order of adjudication, unless cause was shown by the defendant, within a time limited for that purpose; and that thereupon it was privately agreed between the plaintiff and defendant, without the knowledge of the other creditors of the defendant, that the plaintiff should not proceed to make the said order absolute, and should not prosecute the said proceedings for that purpose, which the plaintiff could and might have done; in consideration of which the defendant was to execute the [cheque] in question. The defendant avers that he did execute the [cheque] in pursuance of that agreement, and for the said consideration alone; that the plaintiff did not prosecute the proceedings to set aside the order of adjudication; and insists that by reason of the premises the bond is illegal, and against the policy of the law.

To each defence a reply, the same in substance, has been pleaded. Each states, in detail, facts which show that the adjudication of discharge was fraudulently obtained; and, as there can be no doubt that the facts pleaded do show this, it is unnecessary to state them particularly. The fraud alleged is the fraud of the defendant . . .

As to the reply to the second defence, it is clear that the Court of Bankruptcy and Insolvency had jurisdiction to annul its adjudication on the ground of the fraud alleged in that reply and upon the application of the plaintiff; this is plain from the 233rd section of the *Irish Bankrupt and Insolvent Act 1857*; but the reply admits that the sole consideration for the bond was an agreement by the plaintiff to stifle, as far as in him lay, an inquiry by the court, set on foot by himself, into that fraud. I am disposed to think that such an agreement, for benefit to the party abandoning the proceeding, is against public policy.

I cannot but consider that the proceeding instituted by the plaintiff in the Court of Bankruptcy and Insolvency was one in which the public and the administration of justice in that court were deeply interested. The validity of the adjudication was not by any means a mere question between the defendant and the plaintiff. I do not think he can, consistently with public policy, be allowed to use such a proceeding as a means of procuring a money security for himself.

I think this view of the case affords an answer to what certainly created some difficulty in my mind, viz.—the consideration that the defendant is relying on his own fraud. To a certain extent this is true, but the gist of the defence is not fraud, but illegality and violation of other rules of public policy . . .

Hughes and Deasy BB. concurred.

Case 103. Gray v Cathcart
High Court (1899) 33 I.L.T.R. 35

The plaintiff let a house to the defendant which the plaintiff had been previously ordered to leave by the sanitary authority. Under statute it was an offence to occupy such accommodation. The plaintiff sued the defendant for arrears of rent.

Held that the agreement was illegal and contrary to public policy and the claim was dismissed.

Johnson J.:

Everyone commits a misdemeanor who does any act forbidden by a statute; accordingly when these parties entered into the agreement to occupy a house which had been condemned it was a contract to do that which the statute says that you could not do. It was a contract to do an illegal thing, and, though the parties might go through the form, yet such a contract is not binding, and cannot be sued upon.

Case 104. O'Shaughnessy v Lyons
Circuit Court [1957] Ir.Jur.Rep. 90

The plaintiff agreed to maintain and train the defendant's greyhound for an agreed weekly amount. The plaintiff sued for the greyhound's maintenance and claimed the expense of transporting the dog to meetings. The defendant argued that transporting the dog for reward was illegal and that portion of the claim should be dismissed.

Held that the transportation of goods for reward without a licence was illegal, being contrary to statute law. Accordingly that portion of the claim was dismissed.

Judge O Briain:

The point is taken here by the defendant that this is in effect a contract whereby the plaintiff, who did not hold one of the licences prescribed by the Act, was to get reward for the carriage of the dog owned by the defendant. Section 36 (1) of the *Road Transport Act 1933* is as follows:

> On and after the appointed day it shall not be lawful for any person to enter into an agreement for the carriage for reward of merchandise by any other person unless such other person is a licensee under a merchandise licence or such merchandise is to be carried exclusively within an exempted area.

Counsel for the plaintiff has agreed that a purported contract, made in contravention of that section, cannot be enforced.

The only answer would appear to me to be s. 112 (3) of the *Transport Act 1944*, which provides that:

> Where (*a*) a mechanically propelled vehicle owned by a person or a vehicle drawn by a mechanically propelled vehicle owned by a person is used for the carriage of merchandise the property of that person . . . .

then, subject to subsections (4) and (5) of this section, the merchandise shall be deemed, for the purposes of the Act of 1933, not to be carried for reward.

Counsel for the plaintiff says that the plaintiff, being, as he undoubtedly was, a bailee of this animal, was carrying his own property and therefore avoided the prohibition contained in the Act.

Subsection (5) of section 112 of the *Transport Act 1944*, allows the court to assume, under certain circumstances, that the property in the merchandise never passed to the person carrying the merchandise, and that therefore it was carried for reward.

It seems to me that the better construction of the relevant provisions is that this dog was the property of the defendant and not of the plaintiff. That being so, this was an illegal contract and, therefore, it cannot be enforced . . .

Case 105. Dempsey v O'Reilly
High Court [1958] Ir.Jur.Rep. 75

Without the Land Commission's permission the sub-letting of land on which a land purchase annuity was payable was contrary to statute. The parties, both of whom knew of the prohibition, entered into a sub-letting agreement. The plaintiff sued for arrears of rent.

Held that the contract was illegal as the violation of a statute and therefore the plaintiff's claim was dismissed.

Lavery J.:

The facts of the case are short and raise no difficulty. The premises the subject of the letting were purchased under [statute] and there is a land purchase annuity payable in respect of them. By [the statute] there can be no letting of a holding purchased under the [statute] and in respect of which a land purchase annuity is payable, without the consent of the Land Commission, and any such letting made without that consent is, by the sections, void as against all parties. In this case the required consent was not obtained. Both parties knew from the outset that the letting was contrary to the provisions of the *Land Acts*. The question now is whether the plaintiff can recover arrears of rent having regard to the fact that the consent of the Land Commission was not obtained, thus making this an illegal contract as being contrary to a statutory prohibition.

I regard the law on this question as being well settled. I do not think that the cases referred to by counsel for the plaintiff apply in a case like the present. Different circumstances are present. The type of prohibition against sub-letting with which we are dealing in this case is a matter of public policy. There was a similar prohibition under the older statutes. Such a prohibition continued to be provided for when the Land Commission made advances of purchase money to enable the purchase of their holdings by the tenants. The Land Commission advanced the money and this money had to be repaid by means of an annuity charged upon the land. The prohibition arose from the necessity of securing the money advanced—a matter of public policy.

The case presented by counsel for the plaintiff would clearly controvert that policy. The words in the section of prohibition are clear. *O'Kane v Burns* (1897) governs this case. The decision there was that an action did not lie for use and occupation in the case of a sub-letting which was void by reason of being contrary to a statutory prohibition . . . The defendant's position in this case is unmeritorious, but that is of no consequence in the circumstances. I therfore hold that the plaintiff's claim should be dismissed with costs.

Case 106. Dublin Corporation v Hayes
Court of Common Pleas (1876) I.R. 10 C.L. 226

In consideration of the plaintiffs' appointing the defendant to a particular office, from which he was entitled to receive considerable fees, he agreed to accept by way of fixed salary a sum less than the fees and to pay over these to the plaintiffs. When the defendant failed to pay over the fees the plaintiffs sued to recover them.

Held that the agreement was illegal as contrary to public policy.

Morris C.J.:

The defendant was City Marshal, and as such was Marshal of the Borough Court, and also Marshal of the Court of Conscience, and by the provisions of [a statute], as Marshal, he became Registrar of pawnbrokers, and received considerable fees much exceeding the salary he was appointed at by the plaintiffs. The arrangement the plaintiffs entered into with the defendant on his appointment and the bond entered into by him in compliance with the arrangement provides that he is to pay over all the fees and emoluments of his office to the treasurer of the plaintiffs. Does not such an agreement clearly contravene public policy? The plaintiffs could fix the salary of the City Marshal as an officer appointed to discharge duties which the Corporation required to be done . . . but, as the Registrar of pawnbrokers, the defendant had no privity with the plaintiffs. True his appointment as Marshal made him Registrar of pawnbrokers and entitled him as such to certain fees; but it would be to the last degree against public policy to allow the plaintiffs to bargain for fees with which they had no connection and to which they had no shadow of claim . . .

Keogh and Lawson JJ. concurred.

Case 107. Rourke v Mealy
Court of Exchequer (1879) 4 L.R. Ir. 166

A bill of exchange was passed to the plaintiff by the wife of the alleged drawer of the bill in satisfaction for a debt owed to the plaintiff by the wife. It was alleged that the bill was a forgery and the plaintiff threatened to institute criminal proceedings against the wife. In consideration of the plaintiff abandoning that action, which would have prevented scandal and disgrace to the wife, the defendant accepted the bill from the plaintiff. When the bill was dishonoured the plaintiff sued the defendant as acceptor of the bill.

Held that an agreement to abstain from instituting a threatened prosecution for a criminal offence is not illegal unless there are reasonable grounds for believing that the alleged offence has actually been committed or unless each party entered into the agreement on that assumption.

Palles C.B.:

. . . The public have an interest in every guilty person being brought to justice, and therefore, in every case in which an offence of a public nature has been in fact committed, an agreement to abstain from instituting a prosecution in respect of it, or to forbear proceeding with a prosecution already instituted, is illegal. When I say, 'every case in which a crime has been in fact committed,' I do not mean that in every case strict proof, such as would justify a jury in finding the accused person guilty, must be given. In many cases the acts and conduct of the parties to the agreement may be such as to induce the jury to believe that each of them acted upon the assumption that a crime had been in fact committed; and in such a case, upon a question of the nature of the agreement, I should be prepared to hold that both parties were estopped from alleging the contrary of that which was its basis.

When, although it is uncertain whether an offence of a public nature has or has not been committed, there are reasonable grounds for believing that it has been, the question is more difficult. It is unnecessary for the purposes of the present case to decide it, but for myself I may say that I see no reason to doubt the soundness of the opinion of Mr Justice Coltman in *Ward v Lloyd*, that an agreement to abstain from a prosecution under such circumstances would be illegal. But in such a case also I conceive that the public have an interest that the truth should be ascertained, and that the accused party, if guilty, should be brought to justice. It is this interest which in the case put (*i.e.*, where there is reasonable and probable cause) affords a defence to an action for the prosecution, irrespectively of the motives of the prosecutor.

There is another class of cases in which the public have obtained an interest in the inquiry, and this irrespectively of the actual commission of a crime—I mean where a prosecution in fact has been instituted. In such a case, when the criminal law has been set in motion, a duty is due to the state that nothing shall be done to interfere with the due course of such prosecution, and the public have an interest that it shall be brought to a conclusion in due course of law. Where, therefore, a prosecution has been commenced, a contract to terminate it, or, in the language of the old cases, to stifle it, is illegal, and this irrespectively of a crime having been committed, or of the existence of reasonable and probable cause of the guilt of the person charged.

But, passing from these cases, none of which apply here, and to which I have referred merely for the purpose of explaining the grounds of my decision, let us come to the question immediately before us.

No prosecution has in fact been instituted; therefore there is no question of stopping or stifling a prosecution. No crime has been committed. No one believed that a crime had been committed. No reasonable grounds were present to the mind of anyone, or in fact existed, which could form a foundation for such a belief. There is nothing more than an allegation of forgery made, I will assume, to the holder of the bill, but made by whom—whether a stranger, or by one interested, by a person with knowledge, or without knowledge—supported or unsupported by facts, is uncertain. In such a case the public has no interest in the truth of the allegation being ascertained. It is because the public have no such interest, that a prosecution without reasonable or probable cause may be made the subject of an action, if the motive of the prosecutor be an indirect one. Neither can the threat by the plaintiff *per se* create a public interest in the matter.

This is, in my opinion, demonstrated by the rule that where the debt arises out of a criminal act of the debtor, the civil remedy is suspended only, and that till public justice has been satisfied. The foundation of this rule is that the creditor owes a duty to the public to prosecute, and when that duty has been performed he may proceed for his debt. But where a debt arises out of an act which there is no reasonable or probable cause for believing to be criminal, to hold that, upon an allegation of criminality the remedy of the creditor was suspended, would be to force upon the creditor the institution of a prosecution which would in itself be a wrongful act, and might render him responsible in damages. Upon the whole, I am of opinion that, although there is a public interest that a prosecution already instituted shall be brought to a conclusion in due course of law, there is no such interest in a prosecution being commenced unless there is reasonable and probable cause for its institution . . .

Dowse and Fitzgerald BB. concurred.

Case 108. Nolan v Shiels
Circuit Court (1926) 60 I.L.T.R. 143

The plaintiff was given a cheque from the defendant in consideration of the plaintiff not prosecuting a third person for indecent assault. When the cheque was dishonoured the plaintiff sued the defendant.

Held that the contract was void in that the cheque had been given for an illegal consideration and that the action must be dismissed.

Judge Pigot:

. . . The defence was that this cheque was given in consideration of an abandonment of an intended prosecution against a third party for an indecent assault, and that the consideration for it was an illegal one, and that the cheque was properly withdrawn by the defendant. Plaintiff and a friend of hers met defendant and a male friend of his in Dublin and went to Dún Laoghaire, where plaintiff resided as a lodger with her friend. At the residence of the latter the male friend of the defendant attempted to commit an assault of an indecent nature on the plaintiff. A policeman was called in and the matter was stated to him. A conversation took place between the defendant and the plaintiff, and the latter declined to charge the third party with the alleged assault. As a result of that conversation between the plaintiff and the defendant the latter passed a cheque of £50 to the plaintiff in consideration of her forbearing to charge the third party with the assault. This, then, is not a case of felony but one of misdemeanour if the charge had been preferred. Indecent assault is a statutory offence punishable with two years' imprisonment. Common assault is punishable with one year's imprisonment and was indictable at common law. There is a clear distinction between compromising an indictable misdemeanour and 'stifling' a prosecution in respect of such an offence. By the latter phrase is to be understood an agreement not to take or refusing to take any part in a prosecution of a criminal nature. Before the time of Blackstone it had become a common practice, in the course of a criminal trial for a misdemeanour, for the defendant after conviction 'to speak with the prosecutor', and as a result, in consideration of compensation agreed to be given to the latter, the penalty was frequently made a nominal one. In one case reported the imprisonment was reduced from six to three months. Notwithstanding the adverse comments of that learned writer against such a custom, I have no doubt that it had become (and still is) a recognised part of the procedure in criminal trials for misdemeanour, if rarely practised. And it is in that sense that the compromising of prosecutions is to be read as being allowable in criminal cases. From the earliest times we read that to agree not to prosecute in a criminal case was illegal; that a promise to pay money for such a promise is an illegal consideration, and that such a contract is void. To constitute such illegality there must be reasonable grounds for believing that the offence had been actually committed and that each party must have entered on the agreement on that assumption: *Rourke v Mealy* (Case 107). Is there any exception to this general rule? The words used by Wilmot C.J. in *Collins v Blantern* giving the grounds and reason for this rule, are of general application, and would appear to cover the 'stifling' of any indictable prosecution. But as was admitted in argument in the Exchequer Chamber in the hearing on writ of error in *Keir v Leeman* exceptions to this general rule are to be found. And in the course of his judgment Tyndall C.J. says:

It is said, indeed, that in the case of an assault he (that is, the injured party) may also undertake not to prosecute on behalf of the public. It may be so. But we are not disposed to extend this any further.

That was a case of riot, a crime of a more public nature than assault. The grounds upon which it was supposed that an agreement might be made not to prosecute in such a case was, that compensation to the prosecutor might be commensurate with the possible penalty. And no doubt the elements of common assault regarded as an offence at common law were essentially the same as those giving rise to the right for assault in a civil action. If such an exception to a well known and general principle is to be recognised as still in existence (and I doubt whether it is), I am of opinion that any distinction should be laid hold of to prevent an interference with the right of the public to have protection through the criminal law. Inasmuch as no civil action could be brought for an indecent assault as distinguished from an ordinary assault, as the penalty to be possibly awarded to the court is a higher one for one offence than for the other, therein differing again from actionable assault; as I consider that the exception (if any) is probably founded on an historical development of our law rather than on principle; and finally because I am of opinion that the old and sound rule of the law should be restricted in the interests of the public welfare, I decide that this agreement was founded on an illegal consideration, that the contract was void and that the action fails.

Case 109. Rand v Flynn
High Court [1948] Ir.Jur.Rep. 30

The plaintiff went bail for the defendant and when he failed to appear in court the bail was forfeited. Subsequently the defendant was convicted. After the conviction the defendant undertook in writing to pay the plaintiff the sum estreated plus travelling expenses incurred in endeavouring to procure the defendant's attendance in court. The plaintiff sued when the defendant failed to pay.

Held that it was contrary to public policy that a person bailed should indemnify his bailsman though the court allowed the recovery of reasonable expenses incurred in endeavouring to secure the attendance in court of the person bailed.

O'Byrne J.:

Independently of the case cited and of the contract put in evidence I am satisfied that an action may lie for the recovery of expenses reasonably incurred in trying to secure the attendance in court of the person bailed. The plaintiff's claim should succeed for hotel expenses incurred before the case was heard in Belfast on 3 April 1945, when the defendant was convicted, also for solicitors' costs in endeavouring to locate the defendant to secure his attendance in court . . .

Case 110. Bagot v Arnott
Common Pleas (1867) I.R. 2 C.L. 1

The plaintiff had lent large sums of money to a party, who, in return for a further advance, gave bills of sale of some of his property to the plaintiff as security, instructing the plaintiff to sell the property covered by the bills to realise the security. The plaintiff knew that that party had committed forgery and would use the advance to flee abroad and avoid prosecution. When the goods were seized by other creditors the plaintiff sued for their return and was met with the argument that the transaction was tainted with illegality.

Held that where the possession of goods have been taken under a bill of sale, part of the consideration for which is money advanced for the *bona fide* purpose of obtaining security for a pre-existing debt, the transaction is not invalid, though the creditor is aware, at the time of the advance, that the debtor has committed a crime and intends to leave the country and to apply a portion of the money advanced for that purpose. The plaintiff succeeded.

Keogh J.:

. . . The short question is this—the jury found that the plaintiff was cognisant that these forgeries had been committed, and that he knew that a portion of the money advanced by him would be applied in taking Mr S. out of the country; but there is also an express finding, that the plaintiff advanced the money *bona fide* in order to obtain security for his *bona fide* debt previously due, and *not for the purpose of* enabling Mr S. to leave the country. It only amounts to an advance of money with knowledge that the person to whom it was advanced had committed felony, and was about leaving the country, and would use a portion of it for that purpose. It does not even appear as a matter of fact, that the departure was necessarily for an illegal purpose; but not resting my judgment upon that, and assuming that the object to which he intended to apply the money was illegal—did the knowledge of the plaintiff that the money advanced would be so applied, though there was a transfer of possession, and a regular bill of sale, so invalidate the whole transaction, that an execution creditor of the grantor can treat the property granted as still the property of his debtor?

This case is quite distinguishable from *Pearce v Brooks*. In that case a brougham was let by the plaintiff to a woman of immoral character, and it was found by the jury that it was so let by the plaintiff, they knowing that it was hired by the woman for the purpose of following her immoral traffic. Every part and parcel of the transaction between the parties was tainted with the immoral purpose. Here the jury negative this advance being for an immoral purpose on the part of the plaintiff, and expressly find that it was for the *bona fide* purpose of getting security for a part *bona fide* debt. The Chief Baron in *Pearce v Brooks*, referring to *Cannan v Bryce*, says: 'If this article was furnished to the defendant for the purpose of enabling her to make display favourable to her immoral purpose, the plaintiff cannot recover.' And Martin B. observes,

As to that case (*Cannan v Bryce*), I have a strong impression that that case has been questioned to this extent, that if money is lent, the lender, merely handing it over into the absolute control of the borrower, although he may have reason to believe that it will be employed illegally, he will not be disentitled to recover.

That observation of Baron Martin's is very much in point in this case. Baron Bramwell lays down the rule, quoting from Lord Abinger, in *Cannan v Bryce*, 'The principle is, that the repayment of money lent for the express purpose of affecting an illegal object cannot be enforced.' The distinction between *Pearce v Brooks* and the present case is, that there both parties united in the immoral purpose, which, according to the finding of the jury is not the case here, and that that was a letting on hire, while this is an absolute handing over of money, to the application of which the plaintiff was not bound to see.

Monahan C.J. and O'Hagan J. concurred.

Case 111. Anthony v Shea
Circuit Court (1951) 86 I.L.T.R. 29

The plaintiff loaned money to be used by the borrower for gaming. When the borrower died in a car accident, without having repaid the loan, the plaintiff sued the borrower's executor for the return of the money.

Held that the money could not be recovered because it had been loaned, with the plaintiff's knowledge, for the purposes of gaming.

Judge McCarthy:

. . . It is with regret that I must find for the defendant . . . I am satisfied that the money was knowingly lent for the purpose of gaming, and I must dismiss this claim.

Case 112. Starling Securities Ltd v Woods
High Court, unreported, 24 May 1977

The plaintiff agreed to sell the defendant a hotel for the true price of £215,000. The contract for sale stated the purchase price to be £190,000. The purpose of the different prices was an attempt to reduce the burden of stamp duty payable by the defendant. To safeguard their positions, the parties entered into a series of complicated transactions which resulted in the defendant agreeing to pay the plaintiff a further £25,000. When the defendant failed to complete the sale the plaintiff sought an order for specific performance and was met with the defence that the contract was illegal on the ground that it was an attempt to defraud the revenue.

Held that it would be contrary to public policy to enforce an agreement which attempted to defraud the revenue and the action should be dismissed.

McWilliam J.:

> . . . With regard to the defence of illegality it is argued that, *prima facie*, there is nothing to show any illegality and that full stamp duty could have been paid on a transaction completed in this manner and that, in any event, the defendant cannot rely on illegality without pleading it . . . The only interpretation I can put on the very peculiar method adopted to conduct these transactions is that both parties were trying to conceal from the Revenue authorities the true nature of the transactions. Certainly no other possible explanation has been suggested to me. Accordingly . . . it appears to me that I am not entitled to countenance such attempted frauds on the Revenue by enforcing the performance of the contracts at the instance of either party. The issue of illegality should certainly have been pleaded but, once the evidence of it has been properly introduced in respect to one issue in the case . . . I am not entitled to ignore it . . .

Case 113. Whitecross Potatoes (International) Ltd v Coyle
High Court, unreported, 23 February 1978

The plaintiff carried on the business of purchasing potatoes for resale to food processors in the United Kingdom. The defendant was a grower of potatoes. After preliminary negotiations the parties entered into a written contract for the purchase by the plaintiff of a quantity of potatoes, at specified intervals. The price was fixed by the contract, which also provided that the potatoes were to be collected by the plaintiff from the defendant's premises. At the making of the contract the agent of the plaintiff company believed that potatoes would be in short supply both in Ireland and the United Kingdom, that the price would rise, and the Irish authorities would introduce restrictions on the export of potatoes. The defendant believed there would be a glut of potatoes, that the price would fall, and that the United Kingdom authorities would prohibit the importation of potatoes. Following this exchange of views an addition clause was inserted into the agreement by consent which provided that in the event of import/export controls being imposed, the potatoes were to be supplied from Northern Ireland. The plaintiff alleged that the defendant asserted that he had contacts in Northern Ireland, and that in the event of restrictions, it was possible for him to purchase potatotes from these contacts in order to fulfil his obligations. The defendant alleged that it was explained to the plaintiff's agent that in the event of restrictions the potatoes would be smuggled into Northern Ireland. When the defendant failed to fulfil the terms of the contract completely, the plaintiff sued, and the defendant alleged that the breach was justified on the ground that the consideration was illegal.

Held that the onus of proving illegality was on the party asserting it, and that on the balance of probabilities the evidence failed to disclose that the plaintiff's agent had agreed to a smuggling contract. The contract was therefore valid, untainted by illegality, and the plaintiff was entitled to damages for breach of contract.

Finlay J.:

. . . I am satisfied that the legal principles applicable to this conflict of evidence are relatively straightforward. If this was a contract which, on the apparent intention of the parties at the time of its formation, could be and would be carried out in a legal fashion then even though one of the parties, namely the defendant, in reality intended to carry it out in an illegal fashion it is enforceable. If, on the other hand, the acknowledged and accepted intention of both the parties at the time of the formation of the contract was that, in the event of this export or import control being imposed, the contract would be carried out by a smuggling operation, it is unenforceable and is contrary to public policy and cannot be upheld by the court.

I have had the greatest possible difficulty in reaching a conclusion as to which of the two accounts of this transaction I should accept. I have ultimately come to the conclusion that the onus being on the defendant he has failed to discharge it and to establish to my satisfaction as a matter of probability that the agreed understanding between him and the plaintiff was that this contract should, in the event of a restriction on export, be carried out by a smuggling operation . . .

Case 114. Stanhope v Hospitals Trust Ltd
Supreme Court [1936] Ir.Jur.Rep 25

The plaintiff purchased tickets in South Africa, which was a criminal offence according to the law of that country, for a sweepstake promoted and carried out in this country by the defendant. The plaintiff claimed that due to the negligence and breach of contract of the defendant the tickets were not included in the draw for which the tickets were purchased. The plaintiff sued for breach of contract, including losses incurred in South Africa where he was a professional seller of sweepstake tickets.

Held that the plaintiff was entitled to sue for the alleged breach of contract capable of being performed lawfully in this country but that losses incurred in the foreign country, where the sale of tickets had been unlawfully effected, were not enforceable in that it was contrary to public policy and the comity of nations to enforce contracts which involved the performance of an illegal act in a foreign country.

FitzGibbon J.:

In my opinion, the judgment for the defendant cannot stand. The learned trial judge [in the High Court] based his direction upon the view taken by him that the whole cause of action was so tainted with illegality that the plaintiff cannot apply to the courts in this country to enforce any claim he may have for damages for breach of contract, or for negligence in the performance by the defendants of their contract with him. In the first place, one must see what the contract was before considering the question as to its illegality. In my opinion, the contract between the plaintiff and the defendants was contained in the offer by the latter, made upon the tickets issued by them and accepted by the plaintiff when he returned the counterfoils and the appropriate money, that they would put into the draw the counterfoils transmitted to them by him with the appropriate fee, and that such counterfoils would have their chance in a draw that was to take place on the result of the 'Grand National'. The contract seems to be created by the offer held out on the tickets, to be accepted by anyone who returns a counterfoil with the sum of ten shillings.

The plaintiff gave evidence from which the jury might have come to the conclusion—if that evidence should not be displaced by evidence to the contrary presented on the part of the defendants—that he returned a number of counterfoils with the appropriate sum of money, and that, through the negligence of the defendants, these counterfoils did not find their way into the drum, but of course the case was not heard to the end. It is quite possible that there might have been evidence produced by the defendants which would have negatived the receipt of the counterfoils by them, but all I can say is that on the plaintiff's evidence there was a case upon which it was open to the jury to find that the defendants received a number of counterfoils, and that, through their negligence, they did not find their way into the drum.

The contract was one which, to my mind, was to be performed in Dublin, and to be governed by the law of the place of performance, that is, the law of the Irish Free State, and I can find no evidence that the contract was illegal either by the law of this country or by the law of Natal. It was a contract entirely to be performed in Dublin—completed, possibly, by the posting, by the plaintiff in Natal, of the counterfoils and the appropriate money—but to be carried out in the Irish Free State where it was perfectly legal. In my opinion, therefore, the learned judge was not entitled to withdraw from the jury the issue whether there had been a breach of that contract, and to what damages, if any, the plaintiff had established his right in respect of that breach.

But the plaintiff has also claimed damages for a totally different thing, that is to say, damages occasioned to him by the loss of his trade as a professional seller of sweepstake tickets in Durban, a trade which the learned judge has decided was illegal by the law of the country in which it was carried on. I agree with the learned judge that the courts in this country will not allow themselves to be used for the purpose of establishing a claim for damages for the loss of an illegal business, and I think also that the judge has a duty, where the illegality appears either on the face of the pleadings or from the evidence, to take notice of it himself. I do not think that the parties, even by agreement, could call upon the court, on an apparent illegality, to assist them to carry out an illegal transaction between themselves . . .

Kennedy C.J. and Murnaghan J. concurred.

Case 115. Namlooze Venootschap De Faam v Dorset Manufacturing Co. Ltd
High Court [1949] I.R. 203

The plaintiff, a foreign firm, supplied goods to the defendant in Dublin. Statutory instruments prohibited the export of foreign currency and the making of payment to a person outside the State except with permission of the Minister for Finance. The defendant received permission to purchase goods to a stated value and part paid for the goods. When a dispute as to the quality of the goods was resolved the time limit on the permission had expired. The plaintiff sued for the balance of the price.

Held that the existence of the statutory instruments did not make the contract illegal because the prohibition related to the possible sequel to the contract rather that its essential nature. While the contract was legal it would be improper and contrary to public policy for the court to grant the relief sought because it would compel the defendant to perform an act prohibited by law.*

*This decision was approved and applied by the Supreme Court in *Fibretex (Société Personnes Responsibilité Limité) v Beleir Ltd*

Dixon J.:

. . . Since the contract and since the commencement of this action, a further [statutory instrument] has come into force, which contains somewhat similar prohibitions to those in the order of 1941. In particular, it prohibits any payment to or by the order of any person resident outside the scheduled territories or the placing of any sum to the credit of any person resident within the scheduled territories by the order of, or on behalf of, any person resident outside the scheduled territories. It is admitted that the plaintiff is a person resident outside the scheduled territories; and it is contended by the defendant that any attempt by it now to satisfy the claim of the plaintiff would contravene the terms of this last-mentioned order and would render the defendant liable to a penalty.

I think this contention is clearly right and, on the basis (which I understand to be conceded) that this is the only matter that could now defeat the plaintiff's claim, the sole question is whether the court should give judgment for the plaintiff notwithstanding the existence and terms of this order.

Whatever the terms of the court's order, the legal effect of it would be to put the plaintiff in a position to secure payment of the amount in question and it would thus, even if indirectly, compel the defendant to do an act prohibited by the law for the time being in force. Put thus, I feel that on general principles it would be improper and contrary to public policy for the court to give judgment for the plaintiff on its claim as now framed . . .

CHAPTER 18.

RESTRAINT OF TRADE

A contract in restraint of trade is one which restricts a party from freely exercising his trade, profession or calling. At common law such clauses in a contract are *prima facie* void and the onus of upholding the restriction as reasonable and necessary lies on the party seeking its enforcement. The courts have considered this doctrine under a number of separate headings.

a. Restraints in Employment Contracts

The freedom of a person to carry on an activity which adversely affects his or her former employer may be circumscribed by agreement. The employer has an interest which may need protection and the courts will enforce such restriction provided it is reasonable. The restriction on the range of activity which may be performed in the future must be reasonable: *Oates v Romano* (Case 116) and *Arclex Optical Corporation Ltd v McMurray* (Case 117). The restriction on the period of time within which the prohibited activity cannot be performed must be reasonable: *Cussen v O'Connor* (Case 118) and *ECI European Industries Ltd v Bell* (Case 119). And the geographical area to be protected must be reasonable: *Skerry v Moles* (Case 120) and *Mulligan v Corr* (Case 121).

A clause in restraint of trade may not be invoked where an employee has been dismissed unfairly or without just cause: *Coleborne v Kearns* (Case 122).

Case 116. Oates v Romano
Circuit Court (1950) 84 I.L.T.R. 161

The plaintiff, a ladies' hairdresser, engaged the defendant as an assistant. By an agreement which, after describing the parties as 'hairdressers' simpliciter, restrained the defendant from carrying on or taking employment in a 'like business' to the plaintiff's within one mile of the plaintiff's premises during the employment and for three years thereafter. On the termination of the defendant's employment he was employed in a 'like business' to the plaintiff's which was situated within a mile of the plaintiff's premises. The plaintiff sought to restrain the defendant by injunction from breaching his contract.

Held that the defendant was precluded from the hairdressing business and that this was unnecessarily wide for the proper protection of the plaintiff's interest and was according void.

Judge Shannon:

The facts in this case are not in dispute—at least, at this stage—the defendant not having yet gone into evidence. In April of this year the plaintiff was carrying on a ladies' hairdressing business of a very high class at his premises at 49 Grafton Street in the City of Dublin, indeed, the standard of his business was such that there are only two other firms in the City of the same standard. As a part of his business he sold to customers hair preparations and cosmetics to a limited extent. In 1948, he was anxious to get skilled assistance and he brought the defendant from London to serve on the terms of the agreement which has been read to the court. The defendant was very satisfactory in his service and agreeable and attractive to customers—so much so that his salary was very high and the plaintiff's business made satisfactory progress. Some months after the termination of the two years specified in the agreement, the defendant decided to leave the service of the plaintiff (not by reason of any disagreement or the like between the parties) and to seek employment elsewhere. He entered the employment of one of the firms which are in competition with the plaintiff in the high-class ladies' hairdressing business and the plaintiff brought these proceedings to restrain him from continuing in such employment.

Looking at the restrictive covenant entered into by the defendant it is abundantly clear that the plaintiff contemplated a protection for certain reasons and in a certain way and that the defendant understood the same—the plaintiff desired to protect his high-class business only, and the defendant understood that such was the intention. If the covenant were so framed as to allow only that interpretation, I would gladly hold with the plaintiff as the case stands at the moment (the defendant's case not having yet been heard, of course) . . .

The principles which I should apply in the construction of this document are clear. If the words have a clear meaning, I cannot look at extrinsic matters to give them a different meaning. If in their plain and clear meaning the words constitute a covenant not reasonably required for the protection of the plaintiff then in so far as it is not divisible the whole must be rejected. If the words have not a clear and definite meaning in themselves, then I can look at the surrounding circumstances in which the agreement was made and give them a meaning from those circumstances provided I do not stretch the language of the words used . . .

The defendant contends that he is precluded from carrying on a 'like business' to that of the plaintiff, and that either the phrase 'like business' is too indefinite and uncertain to be construed and enforced or that if capable of definite construction, then that no extrinsic circumstances or matters can be used to elucidate it. I have some doubt on the first point—whether it is vague or not—but the plaintiff is described in the agreement as a hairdresser and my conclusion is that, as he has been so described, the clause should be construed as follows:

> the employee shall not enter the service of any other person carrying on
> the business of hairdresser.

I am satisfied that the document can be given a definite meaning on its face and I do not think that I am free to do what the plaintiff suggests I should do, namely, look to the extrinsic circumstances to determine what 'like business' means. The plaintiff is described as carrying on the business of hairdresser but he says that I should disregard that and look to the business actually intended; the court, however, looks at the document and is bound by what the document definitely says. On that reading of the document the protection sought is too wide, for the law is that the onus of upholding the covenant lies on the plaintiff. In fact the covenant prohibits the defendant from carrying on the business of hairdresser at all, not merely ladies' hairdressing, and that part of the covenant cannot be severed . . .

Case 117. Arclex Optical Corporation Ltd v McMurray

High Court [1958] Ir.Jur.Rep. 65

The plaintiff, a dealer in optical goods, did business thoughout the country, and had customers in every county. It employed the defendant as salesman and traveller and over a two-year period he had contact with all of the plaintiff's customers. The defendant agreed in writing to devote his whole time to the plaintiff's service and not to engage in any other business. He further agreed that he would not, for a period of five years after the termination of his employment, engage in any of the businesses carried on by the plaintiff. The defendant terminated his employment. For some time prior to such termination it appeared that the defendant had been trading in optical goods on his own account, had invested considerable finances in the venture, and had received orders from some of the plaintiff's customers. Pending the hearing of an action for an injunction and damages, the plaintiff sought an interlocutory injunction to restrain the defendant from engaging in such activity.

Held that an interlocutory injunction would be granted to restrain the defendant from canvassing or soliciting orders from the plaintiff's existing customers.

Dixon J.:
___

It would not be unreasonable to grant an interlocutory injunction. As I see it, the plaintiff has a double-barrelled claim. The first claim is on clause 6—to prevent the defendant from carrying on a competing business for the residue of the five years commencing 16 February 1957. The other claim is under clause 10 [which prevents the defendant from carrying on, or assisting in, a similar business for a period of five years after the termination of employment]. The plaintiff here is trying to preserve the *status quo* until it sees what damage it suffers. The plaintiff is only concerned with clause 6. It is not unreasonable to restrain the defendant from competing actively with the plaintiff while he is employed by it, and it does not seem unreasonable that he now be likewise restrained until the matter is clarified, unless as was put in *Warner Brothers Pictures Incorporated v Nelson* (1937), that would involve specific performance or compel the defendant to idleness, so that the injunction would, in effect, enforce a contract to perform personal services . . .

On the merits and demerits of the case, there are good grounds for granting an injunction for the limited period pending hearing. The form the injunction will take is one against the canvassing and soliciting of orders by the defendant or his being associated with or connected with the canvassing and soliciting of orders from existing customers of the plaintiff.

Case 118. Cussen v O'Connor
Exchequer Division (1893) 32 L.R. Ir. 330

The plaintiff agreed to employ the defendant as a commercial traveller for ten years. The defendant agreed in writing not to engage in a similar business nor act as commercial traveller to a similar business to that of the plaintiff within twelve years from the date of the agreement or for two years after its termination should it continue beyond ten years. This restriction only extended to the counties the defendant travelled in at any time during his employment. The plaintiff dismissed the defendant for negligence in the discharge of his duties after three years and sought an injunction to compel the defendant to abide by the agreement.

Held that this restriction was reasonable for the protection of the plaintiff's interests and trade but that to enforce the agreement in full against the defendant would be unjust. Since the court had no power to vary the terms of the contract it would, in granting the injunction which was a discretionary remedy, limit its duration to two years from the date of the termination of the defendant's employment.

Andrews J.:
***

. . . The main question in the case is whether this restriction is one which the law will support as valid, or treat as unsustainable or void. In considering this question we must have regard to the position the parties stood in when the agreement was entered into. The defendant had for a number of years previous to the agreement been in the employment of persons now represented by the plaintiff, and to whose rights under the agreement he is admittedly entitled. By means of the defendant's employment under the agreement he was entitled to acquire further acquaintance with his employers' business, and their customers; and although the employers' right to dismiss the defendant, and his right to leave their employment for sufficient cause were not excluded by the agreement, still both parties may well be taken to have contemplated that the employment would last for ten years, which was the stipulated term, and might have been longer. Under these circumstances, can the restriction in question be regarded as going beyond what was fairly and reasonably necessary for the protection of the trade and interest of the employers? The defendant's yearly salary was a substantial and an increasing one, and the consideration for it is to be found in all the stipulations of the agreement, including the above restriction. It cannot be denied that some restriction of this kind would be reasonable, for why should not the defendant be restrained when leaving his employment from using against his employers the knowledge of their trade, and the acquaintance with their customers, which the employment he had been engaged in and paid for by them had enabled him to obtain? Is the restriction then as it stands so unreasonable as regards space or time, or both, as to be void? In my opinion, we cannot, in considering this, limit our view to the particular event which has happened. We should look at the agreement as a whole, and in all its aspects; and if in so regarding it we cannot pronounce it unreasonable, I do not think that we ought to hold it unreasonable because in the particular event which has happened its effect may press, and, if you wish to say so, press strongly, against the interests of the defendant. If such pressure is entitled to consideration, it cannot be left out of the consideration that it is occasioned by the defendant's own misconduct; and although, according to the findings of the jury, which I accept, his misconduct was not as grave as the plaintiff believed, still upon the evidence it was amply sufficient to destroy his employers' confidence in him and justify his dismissal. There is no ground for suggesting as regards space that the defendant did not travel for his employers in and through the six counties of Cork, Kerry, Limerick, Clare, Tipperary and Waterford, in the usual course of his business, as their commercial traveller, nor is there in my opinion any ground for holding that his employers' power, which I assume they possessed, to require him to travel in any other counties in Ireland, would have made it unreasonable for their fair protection to extend the restriction to such other counties. As regards time, taking the agreement as a whole, and in all its aspects, I cannot, upon the facts and arguments, regard the restriction as unreasonable; and in a case in which the restriction is reasonable in its nature, and is limited as regards both space and time, I am of opinion that it lies on the person who impeaches it to show that it is unreasonable. Many of the earlier cases rest the invalidity of contracts in restraint of trade upon 'public policy'. It has been quaintly, but not inaptly, said that public policy is a very unruly horse to get astride of. What it really is in any particular case may not be easy to define with precision; but if it be good public policy, as I hold it to be, to discourage, as a general rule, restrictions on trade, it ought not be forgotten, as has been justly observed, that it is also good public policy, as a general rule, to protect freedom of contract; and it may at least be gravely doubted whether we would advance public policy as a whole, if by that we mean the welfare of the community, by sacrificing the latter to the former. I prefer the principle which the recent authorities appear to me to adopt for determining whether a contract in restraint of trade is valid or void, viz. whether the restraint, having regard to all the circumstances of the case and the nature of the employment, is greater than is fairly and reasonably necessary for the protection of the person in whose favour it is imposed. This, in my opinion, is in substance the real question to be determined, although the terms in which it is put may vary . . .

The conclusion at which I have arrived on this question in the present case is that the restraint imposed upon the defendant by the agreement of

24 April 1889 was not under all the circumstances, and having regard to the position in which the parties then stood, and the events which might have happened, greater than was reasonable for the protection of the interests of the defendant's employers, and their trade, and was therefore valid; and, as I have already intimated, it ought not, in my opinion, to be held invalid because in the particular event which has happened it may press, and even strongly press, against the interests of the defendant. Holding the restraint therefore to be a legal one, it remains to be considered whether, in the particular event which has happened, the court is bound to enforce it by injunction to its utmost limit, or can exercise a discretion. I consider that the court has full jurisdiction to exercise a discretion in this respect when asked to apply the strong remedy of an injunction. We cannot vary the contract between the parties, so as to make an unreasonable and void contract a reasonable and valid one; but in dealing with a valid contract we may, as a court of equity, have regard to the effect upon the defendant, of the injunction we are asked to grant, and modify its severity, if injustice be not thereby done to the plaintiff. Had the employment continued for ten years or longer, as the parties when they entered into this agreement thought it might have done, a restraint of two years from the cessation of the employment was what they would have been satisfied with, and notwithstanding the defendant's misconduct, we think that a restraint of two years from his dismissal, though lenient towards him, will not be unjust towards the plaintiff; and we therefore give judgment for the plaintiff . . .

Murphy J. concurred.

Case 119. ECI European Chemical Industries Ltd v Bell
High Court [1981] I.L.R.M. 345

The parties entered into a contract of employment which contained a clause that the defendant would not take up employment with the plaintiff's competitors for a period of two years after termination of his employment with the plaintiff. The defendant was possessed of the plaintiff's manufacturing techniques, testing techniques, production processes and some trade secrets, gave notice of termination and proposed to take up employment with a competitor of the plaintiff. The plaintiff sought an injunction to restrain the defendant from taking this employment for a period of two years after the termination of his employment.

Held that *prima facie* there was a valid interest of the plaintiff to be protected and on the balance of convenience that damages would not be an adequate remedy for the plaintiff should the action be successful whereas the defendant could be adequately compensated by damages should the action fail. The court granted an interlocutory injunction.

McWilliam J.:

. . . The case presented on behalf of the defendant is that this is a contract in restraint of trade, that the plaintiff has not got a reasonable interest to be protected by the agreement, that the restraint is unreasonable with regard to the geographical area of the restraint and that it is unreasonable with regard to the length of the period of restraint. The argument necessitates the submission that, even on an interlocutory application, there is an onus on the plaintiff to establish the reasonableness of the restraint in each of these respects, that this has not been done and that the plaintiff is, therefore, not entitled to succeed on this application.

Having regard to this approach to the case and the arguments which have been addressed to me I feel I ought to consider the doctrine of restraints of trade and its application by the courts.

The relevant clauses in the agreement are clearly in restraint of trade and this has not been contested on behalf of the plaintiff. A long line of cases from *Nordenfelt v Maxim Nordenfelt Guns & Amunition Co. Ltd* (1894) to *Greig v Insoles* (1978) appears to establish that a contract in restraint of trade is contrary to public policy and void or unenforceable unless the restraint reasonably protects a valid interest of the person in whose favour it is imposed, is not unreasonable with regard to the person restrained and is not unreasonable as being injurious to the public interest.

On the affidavits before me, I am satisfied, notwithstanding the arguments to the contrary on behalf of the defendant, that there is *prima facie*, a valid interest of the plaintiff to be protected, that is to say, the protection of trade secrets, testing techniques and production processes which have come to the knowledge of the defendant. Certainly I cannot accept that there is not, at least, a serious issue to be tried in this respect.

A more substantial objection on behalf of the defendant is that the clause is unreasonable both because it is too wide in the area of its application geographically and as making the period of restraint too long. I was addressed at some length as to the power of the court to modify the agreement should it be considered to be unreasonable in its present form.

The most recent case to which I was referred is that of *Littlewoods Organisation v Harris* (1977). It has been discussed on behalf of both parties but I find some aspects difficult to follow. It seems to me that the majority of the court Appeal, Lord Denning M.R. and Megaw L.J. formed the opinion, contrary to the view expressed in the case of *Commercial Plastics v Vincent* (1964), that the court is entitled to ignore the literal meaning of such a covenant and construe it with regard to the surrounding circumstances existing at the time when the covenant was entered into. See Megaw L.J., or that the clause should be interpreted as limited to the reasonable objects which the parties to the agreement sought to achieve, see Lord Denning.

It seems to me that a point to be determined is whether a covenant which can be construed as being too wide in some respects and therefore unreasonable in those respects is wholly void in all respects or whether, although including unreasonable provisions which will not be enforced, reasonable provisions which are contained in it may be enforced. This is an aspect discussed by Lord Denning in a different form in the *Littlewoods Case*. He said:

> It has often been said that a covenant in restraint of trade is not to be rendered invalid simply by putting forward unlikely or improbable contingencies in which it might operate unreasonably . . . If such an unlikely or unusual event should happen, the court would not enforce it so as to work an injustice.

The conclusion of the Court of Appeal in the case of *Commercial Plastics v Vincent* was that the covenant, being too wide, had to be ruled out and declared void although the actual relief sought was held to be reasonable and proper to be granted; see Pearson L.J. The same view was taken by Browne L.J., in his dissenting judgment in the *Littlewoods Case*. He said: 'It seems to me that if the clause is read literally it is much too wide and is void or unenforceable.' This was also the view of the Court of Appeal in the case of *Gledhow Autoparts v Delaney* (1965) Sellers L.J. said:

> The injunction for which the plaintiffs asked and which they received is admittedly less than clause six in its terms would have permitted as regards area, that is, places where the defendant had operated. But when, as is the defendant's contention, the clause is said to be unenforceable because it is in restraint of trade, it must be construed as it stands and not to the extent that the employer seeks to enforce it. The modified request may reveal an apprehension as to the full effect of the clause. Whether this clause is, as the judge held, enforceable and not in restraint of trade, or whether it is too wide and not to be invoked, is a question of law and has to be decided on the authorities.

Diplock L.J. said:

> The defendant was in fact employed for over six years by the plaintiffs and no doubt became a valuable servant and acquired considerable knowledge of and personal relation with the plaintiff's customers. It is natural in these circumstances to tend to look at what in fact happened under the agreement. But the question of the validity of a covenant in restraint of trade has to be determined at the date at which the agreement was entered into and has to be determined in the light of what may happen under the agreement, although what may happen may cover many possibilities which in the event did not happen. A covenant of this kind is invalid *ab initio* or valid *ab initio*. There cannot be some moment at which it passes from the class of invalid to that of valid covenants.

These two statements are very clear and are difficult to reconcile with some of the views expressed in the *Littlewoods Case*.

At the same time, doubts have been cast on the correctness of this strict view and it might be considered that a court of equity is entitled to consider the effect of the contract as the circumstances come before it, so as to avoid working an injustice. The entire doctrine that contracts in restraint of trade are void or unenforceable is based on the proposition that such contracts are contrary to public policy or, as was said in a very old case, 'against the benefit of the commonwealth'. Can it be said that it is of any advantage to public policy to refuse relief which is held to be reasonable and proper to be granted, as in the *Commercial Plastics Case*?

In the case of *McEllistrim v Ballymacelligott Co-Operative Agricultural & Dairy Society* (1919) (Case 128), Viscount Finlay adopted a statement of James V.C. in the case of *Leather Cloth Co. v Lorsont* (1869). It is:

All the cases when they come to be examined seem to establish this principle—that all restraints upon trade are bad as being in violation of public policy unless they are natural, and not unreasonable for the protection of the parties dealing legally with some subject-matter of contract. The principle is this—public policy requires that every man shall be at liberty to work for himself, and shall not be at liberty to deprive himself or the State of his labour, skill or talent by any contract that he enters into. On the other hand, public policy requires that when a man has, by skill or other means, obtained something which he wants to sell, he should be at liberty to sell it in the most advantageous way in the market; and in order to enable him to sell it advantageously in the market, it is necessary that he should be able to preclude himself from entering into competition with the purchaser. In such a case the same public policy that enables him to do that does not restrain him from alienating that which he wants to alienate and, therefore, enables him to enter into any stipulation, however restrictive it is, provided that restriction, in the judgment of the court, is not unreasonable having regard to the subject-matter of the contract.

I have considered these matters at some length because the present application has been met to a large extent on the basis that it should be refused on the ground that the covenant is void and the plaintiff cannot succeed in its action. I am not satisfied about this as there seems to be a number of arguments open to the plaintiff and it would be improper for me on an interlocutory application to decide the main issue in the case without hearing the evidence which may be adduced and having a full argument on the various aspects to which I have referred. All I have to do on an interlocutory application is to decide whether the plaintiff has established a *prima facie* case in the sense that there is a serious question to be tried and, if so, what is the balance of convenience to the parties between granting and refusing an injunction.

From the facts which are before me and the review which I have made of the decisions, I am satisfied that there is a serious issue to be tried. On the question of the balance of convenience, it seems to me that the defendant can be adequately compensated in damages if he is successful in his defence and that an undertaking by the plaintiff to pay such damages will be met, whereas damages would not be an adequate remedy for the plaintiff and it is doubtful whether any damages could be recovered from the defendant if the plaintiff were to be successful. Accordingly, I am of the opinion that the *status quo* should be preserved and that I should grant the interlocutory injunction sought.

Case 120. Skerry v Moles

High Court (1908) 42 I.L.T.R. 46

The plaintiff carried on a business academy in one city and the defendant was employed as a shorthand teacher in that academy. The parties entered into a written contract whereby the defendant agreed not to carry on a similar business in three named cities during a period of three years from the date on which he should leave his employment. The plaintiff gave the defendant three months' notice and on the termination of the employment the defendant established a school of business training in the city in which he had been employed. The plaintiff sought an injunction to compel the defendant to abide by the agreement.

Held that the agreement was reasonable in relation to the city in which the defendant worked but was unreasonable in relation to the other two cities. Since the reasonable part of the agreement was severable from the unreasonable portions the injunction was granted.

Barton J.:

On 12 October 1904, the defendant signed an agreement with the plaintiff who was the proprietor of Civil Service Academics at Dublin, Belfast, and Cork, by which he was employed by them as teacher of shorthand, typewriting, and general business training at their Belfast Academy. It is upon the second clause of this agreement that this case turns. It was as follows: '2. In consideration of the said engagement, the said [defendant] shall not, during a period of three years, to be computed from the date on which the said [defendant] shall cease to be employed by the said [plaintiff] carry on or engage in the business of teacher of shorthand, typewriting, and general business training, or in any or either of the said businesses, either as principal or assistant, in Dublin, Belfast, or Cork, or within a radius of seven miles from the academy or place of business of the said [plaintiff] in any of the said cities. And if the said [defendant] shall so carry on or engage in such business, either as principal or assistant, he shall pay to the said [plaintiff], the sum of £20 for every month during which or any part of which he shall so carry on or engage in the said business as for liquidated damages.' The agreement provided for the engagement being terminable upon three months' notice by either party. On 22 February 1906, the plaintiff gave the defendant three months notice to terminate the engagement. Upon 21 May 1906, the defendant left his employment and set up a school for shorthand, typewriting, and general business training in Belfast . . . The present action to restrain the breach by the defendant of the restrictive clause in the agreement of October 1904 . . .

I approach the question whether this restrictive clause was void for unreasonableness, or in other words, whether the restraint was in excess of what was necessary for the covenantee's protection. The contract of employment was limited to Skerry's Academy in Belfast, but the restrictive clause extended also to Dublin and Cork. I have no difficulty in saying that the clause was unreasonable *qua* Dublin and Cork, but reasonable *qua* Belfast, and that it is a case in which the reasonable part is severable from the unreasonable part. It was suggested that because a course of instruction in these special subjects would only occupy from twelve to eighteen months three years would be an unreasonable limit of time. But the withdrawal of pupils is not the only mischief against which such a clause is directed. In the *Lowestoft College Case (Smith v Hawthorne)*, (1897) ten years was the period . . . But I think that the injunction can and ought to be granted so far as the City of Belfast is concerned.

Case 121. Mulligan v Corr
Supreme Court [1925] I.R. 169; 59 I.L.T.R. 157

The plaintiff solicitor opened an office in one town and a branch office in another town. He engaged the defendant, a solicitor's clerk of ten years experience, as his assistant for a year and at the end of that period was to grant him indentures of apprenticeship without fee. The defendant agreed, when qualified, not to practise as a solicitor within thirty miles of these two towns, and twenty miles of another. When qualified the defendant commenced to practise in partnership with another solicitor whose office was close to the plaintiff's office in one of the towns. The plaintiff sought an injunction to compel the defendant to abide by the terms of the agreement.

Held that the restriction against practising within thirty miles of two towns was unreasonable in that the geographical area which the plaintiff endeavoured to protect went far beyond anything which could reasonably be required for his protection. With regard to the restriction on practising within twenty miles of the other town, that was also unreasonable because it was imposed to protect a business which was not then in existence. Since the agreement could not entirely be upheld, the court examined the possibility of severing the reasonable portions from the unreasonable portions. On the evidence the court held this could not be done.

FitzGibbon J.:

... The agreement is dated 18 February 1919, and provides that the plaintiff should engage the defendant as his assistant for 12 months from its date, at a salary of £3 a week payable weekly; that on the expiration of the 12 months the plaintiff should grant the defendant indentures of apprenticeship without any fee, that his salary should not be reduced during the apprenticeship, but that no salary should be payable for any week during which the defendant was absent in attendance on lectures in connection with his apprenticeship, and the agreement then contains the following clause: '3.—The said [defendant] agrees not to practice within thirty miles from the towns of Ballina and Charlestown when qualified as such solicitor, nor within twenty miles from the town of Ballaghadereen.'

... The principles of law applicable to covenants of this description in restraint of trade may be regarded as now finally settled; the only difficulty is to ascertain the facts to which they are to be applied.

The restriction imposed must not be greater than is reasonably required for the protection of the covenantee. If it exceed in area or duration the limits which the court considers reasonable it is void. The question of reasonableness is one of law for the court to decide. A restriction though unlimited as to space may be reasonable if confined to a period of reasonable duration. All these points were settled by the *Nordenfelt Case* (1894) some thirty years ago, and the converse of the last proposition, viz.: that a restriction, though unlimited in point of time, was valid if limited to a reasonable area, was decided by the House of Lords in 1921 in the case of *Fitch v Dewes* (1921), which was, like this, an action brought by a solicitor to restrain a former clerk from practising as a solicitor within a radius of seven miles of the Town Hall of Tamworth, in breach of an agreement entered into by him, when taken into employment as managing clerk ten years previously. The area in that case was smaller than this, but it included a thickly populated district and portions of four English counties, Stafford, Warwick, Leicester, and Derby.

... Assuming the construction placed upon the agreement by the parties to be correct, does the restriction exceed that which was reasonably necessary for the protection of the plaintiff? He had not been long in practice, but he had good connections and might reasonably expect, before the defendant would be out of his indentures, to build up a fair business, which he was entitled to protect against the possibility that his managing clerk, with all the knowledge acquired in the plaintiff's service of the plaintiff's clients and their affairs, might set up, as he has done, in opposition to his former employer.

In my opinion, however, the area which the plaintiff endeavoured to protect was too large. It was certainly so if it included the two thirty-mile circles. They covered three county [circuit court] towns, practically the whole of Mayo, more than half of Sligo, a large part of Roscommon, and portions of Galway and Leitrim. That appears to us to go far beyond anything which the plaintiff could reasonably require for his protection. Even the more limited area which I believe to be covered by the clause is, in my opinion, excessive. The plaintiff does not appear to have done much business in Ballaghadereen or its vicinity, and it was suggested at the Bar by his counsel that the reason for including Ballaghadereen in the agreement was that if he did not make good in Ballina he might go to the other side of the county and work Ballaghadereen alone or in connection with Charlestown. If this were so, a restriction imposed to protect a business which was not in fact being worked and might never be set up at all was quite unreasonable.

Having come to the conclusion that the agreement cannot in any view of its construction be upheld in its entirety, questions arise whether it can be divided, and, if so, whether any fraction of it can be supported as reasonable.

As to the former, this restrictive covenant falls in our opinion within the principle of decisions such as *Mallan v May*, the case of a dentist's assistant; *Green v Price*, the case of the perfumery business; *Davies v Lowen*, the case of the carrier's clerk; and if, by eliminating part which appears to be void, we can leave a valid and effective contract remaining, such a course is lawful, though the court cannot make a new covenant or mould one which is already complete in itself so as to create a different restriction which would be reasonable in the opinion of the court. I confess that my own opinion has fluctuated during the argument (which was ably conducted on both sides), and since; but after very careful consideration, we have come to the unanimous conclusion that it is not reasonable for the plaintiff, though practising and having offices both in Ballina and Charlestown, to insist that his managing clerk should not practice or set up a business in any place which was within a distance so great as thirty miles from both or either of those towns. Even the more restricted area includes the town of Sligo, and although that part of County Sligo which is served by Ballina or Charlestown, each of which actually touches the county border, might fairly be the subject of a protective clause, we cannot hold that it is necessary for the fair protection of the plaintiff that the defendant should be precluded from practising in the capital of the adjoining county, a restriction which would in effect have debarred him from taking business at the [circuit court] from any part of the County Sligo, and would exclude him from all that portion of County Sligo which lies outside the thirty-mile circle, but whose inhabitants resort to Sligo for legal advice. There is no possible construction of this agreement which would not include the town of Sligo in the prohibited area, and the Ballina circle, which was adopted by Meredith J. [in the High Court], would include Westport, as well as Claremorris and Ballyhaunis, none of which is shown to be in any real competition with Ballina for legal affairs so far as the plaintiff is concerned. It is to be regretted that the plaintiff did not give fuller information as to his own business, and, in our opinion, having regard to the fact that, notwithstanding a dictum to the contrary of the Earl of Birkenhead [in *Fitch v Dawes*], the onus appears to be upon the plaintiff to establish the reasonableness of the restriction imposed, we have come to the conclusion that it is not reasonable or necessary for the protection of the plaintiff's business that the defendant should be restrained from practising as a solicitor at any place within thirty miles of Ballina and Charlestown or of either of those towns.

Kennedy C.J. and Murnaghan J. concurred.

Case 122. Coleborne v Kearns
Court of Appeal (1912) 46 I.L.T.R. 305

The plaintiff motor and cycle dealer employed the defendant mechanic. On entering the employment the defendant signed a contract which contained a clause that should the defendant leave the employment for any cause whatever he would not start business as cycle or motor agent on his own behalf or in partnership or enter the employment of any motor cycle agent, for a period of seven years from the time of ceasing the employment, at any place within fifteen miles from the town of Dunlavin, Co. Wicklow. A year later the defendant was dismissed for alleged gross irregularities. The defendant started business as a motor and cycle dealer in Dunlavin. The plaintiff sought an injunction to restrain him from carrying on that business.

Held that the word 'leave' in the document did not connote dismissal, and that therefore there was no breach of the agreement and the injunction was refused.

Barry L.C.:

. . . I do not think that in the ordinary acceptation of the term, 'leave' connotes dismissal from employment. I think the word connotes the voluntary act of leaving. If a servant said he had left his employment it would never occur to anybody that he had been dismissed. I sympathise with the view of the employer very much, but while we must take that into account, we must also take into account the view of the other contracting party; and here we are dealing with an agreement which imposes a great restraint upon his liberty, and we are all of opinion that it cannot be enforced against him unless it can be shown most clearly that he understood the character of the memorandum when he signed it. We have pointed out in the course of the argument that the result of the construction contended for by the plaintiff would be that those men who signed the agreement would be subject to dismissal the next week or month by the plaintiff without any redress whatever, and for a cause of which they may be perfectly innocent. Thereupon they would be obliged to quit their homes and abstain for seven years from entering into a similar business within fifteen miles of Dunlavin. If the agreement meant that, we should give effect to it . . . I feel certain, however, that none of these four men understood that he was submitting himself to such an obligation. I think they must have understood 'leave' to mean leaving voluntarily. The subsequent word 'ceasing' does not carry the plaintiff one step further. The important part is the earlier part, 'should we or any of us leave,' and the reference later to 'the time of ceasing' meant 'ceasing' to be in the employment by reason of having left the service. It is only common justice to employees that if such agreements are to be enforceable they ought to specify with a definiteness beyond all doubt all the conditions imposed upon the men undertaking these obligations. I do not think that the event which has happened throws any obligation upon the defendant, because he did not leave, but was dismissed, and dismissed because he closed the premises five minutes before eight o'clock on a particular evening.

Holmes and Cherry L.JJ. concurred.

b. Restraints in Rules of Voluntary Associations

The rules of a voluntary association to which a person belongs may attempt to restrict the employment, career or trade activities of its members. To be enforceable the restriction must be reasonable. The rules of a trade union which restricts the members' freedom to practise a trade or calling must be reasonable: *Langan v Cork Operative Bakers Trade Union* (Case 123). The rules of the governing association of a sport which interferes with the livelihood prospects of those participating in that sport must also be reasonable: *Macken v O'Reilly* (Case 124). And the rules governing price fixing by a trade association must be reasonable: *F. Cade & Sons v John Daly & Co. Ltd* (Case 125).

Case 123. Langan v Cork Operative Bakers Trade Union

High Court [1938] Ir.Jur.Rep. 65

The plaintiff baker was a member of the defendant trade union. He decided to emigrate and applied to the union for a grant to assist him. He was voted £25 on condition that he ceased union membership, that he would not seek readmission to the union, nor carry on the business of a baker, nor be employed in the bakery trade within the city in which he lived, or within twenty miles of it. The plaintiff received the £25 but did not emigrate and later sought readmission to the union which was refused. The plaintiff claimed that this agreement was an unreasonable restraint of trade.

Held that the agreement was void and contrary to public policy as an unreasonable restraint of trade. The court ordered that the £25 be refunded to the union.

Hanna J.:

The agreement must be set aside as a restraint of trade or power of work. The plaintiff has no means of living, except by exercising his trade as a baker; but by the agreement it is put out of his power reasonably to exercise his capacity as a baker in the place where he has always exercised it, or indeed in any other place where a baker's union exists, and that covers most of the country.

The union intended to act generously towards the plaintiff when they gave him £25 to emigrate. Unfortunately he was unable to get the necessary papers to enable him do so, and if he had got them the present trouble would not exist. When he could not emigrate he spent the £25 foolishly, but he is willing to make restitution to the union.

It is quite clear that under rule 21 the rights, and benefits of the plaintiff would end only when he would have booked his passage for the purpose of emigration, and in this case the man did not book. It is contrary to public policy that an agreement of this kind should be allowed to stand, and accordingly I uphold the view of the learned Circuit Court judge, and affirm, varying it only, that the sum of £25, and not £30 as awarded by the learned Circuit Court judge, be refunded to the union.

Case 124. Macken v O'Reilly
Supreme Court, unreported, 31 May 1979

The plaintiff was a professional horseman who represented Ireland in international competitions. The defendant was a member of the federation responsible for both national and international aspects of equestrian sports in this country. The federation passed a resolution that it would not select any horse to represent Ireland at certain events unless the horse was Irish bred. The plaintiff claimed, *inter alia*, that this resolution interfered with his freedom to earn his living and was an unreasonable restraint of trade.

Held that the federation's resolution was reasonable and in the public interest for the promotion of Irish bred horses. The policy could not be unfair merely because in its application to one individual, inconvenience or loss was suffered.

O'Higgins C.J.:

. . . The next question to be considered is whether the common law rule prohibiting restraints of trade applies in this case. All interference with an individual's freedom of action in trading is *per se* contrary to public policy and, therefore, void. This general prohibition is subject to the exception that certain restraints may be justified. Restraints, restrictions or interferences are permitted if they are, in the circumstances obtaining, fair and reasonable. Whether what is complained of can be justified on this basis involves a careful examination of all the circumstances—the need for the restraint, the object sought to be attained, the interests sought to be protected and the general interests of the public. What is done or sought to be done must be established as being reasonable and necessary and on balance to serve the public interest. The fact that the body or group imposing the restraint has the power to do so does not of itself justify its imposition. Any arbitrary or unreasonable use of power by those who have control or authority over a particular trade or profession would come within the prohibition. In this case the fact that its constitution and the international body's regulations appear to authorise the federation to act as it did, does not of itself authorise what was done. The question is whether in all the circumstances the action taken by the federation can be said to be fair and reasonable and in the public interest.

The learned trial judge [in the High Court], in holding that the federation acted within its powers in passing the resolution in question, said as follows:

> The federation is, under its constitution, the body responsible for both the national and international aspects of all equestrian sports in Ireland which are recognised by the federation and has sole jurisdiction in respect of international and ultimate authority in respect of national equestrian affairs. As such a body, is has, in my opinion, an interest in ensuring that the Irish half-bred breeding industry is in a healthy and thriving condition so as to ensure a reasonable supply of suitable horses available for all equestrian sports and is entitled to endeavour to take steps to protect that industry. Being so satisfied, I consider that the policy of the federation and the resolutions giving effect thereto are *intra vires* the power of the federation . . .

This view is amply supported by the evidence and as already indicated it is a view with which I entirely agree. The learned judge went on to say:

> There is nothing unreasonable and the interests of all parties including the public, probably require that the federation do everything possible to encourage Irish riders to ride Irish-bred horses in international competitions . . .

Having expressed this view he rather surprisingly went on to hold that by reason of the policy being inflexible he regarded it as an unreasonable restraint of trade in relation to the plaintiff. He gave his reasons as follows:

> None of the other national federations affiliated to the international body have such a policy or rule. I accept the plaintiff's evidence that there are not available to him at this point of time sufficient Irish-bred horses of the necessary quality to enable him to maintain his position as

one of the world's leading show jumpers. I consider that a policy which has the effect of inhibiting his efforts to maintain such a position to be unjust and unfair and that if he fails to maintain that position the public will be deprived of a great deal of pleasure. Having regard to the worldwide reputation of Irish half-bred horses I do not consider that the interests of the industry require that such a policy be maintained by the federation with regard to individual riders participating in international showjumping competitions as individuals and not representing their country officially.

It seems to me that in this part of his judgment the learned trial judge was in error. Having already held that the federation's policy was reasonable in the interests of all parties including the public, he nevertheless concluded that in its application to the plaintiff it was unjust and unfair. A policy of restraint which is held to be reasonable, having regard to all interests affected, including the public, cannot, in my view, properly be described as being unjust and unfair simply because in its particular application to one individual an inconvenience or loss is experienced. The trial judge was also influenced by the rule or policy being regarded as inflexible. This, it seems to me, is of the essence of any rule or policy until it is altered or changed. Any policy or ruling of this kind must be regarded in the light of all the circumstances to test whether it is reasonable or not. The mere fact that those who advocate it or enforce it are insistent as to their views cannot make what is otherwise reasonable suddenly unreasonable. In addition, it seems to me that the trial judge disregarded entirely the undisputed evidence as to the effect a change of policy would have on the horse-breeding industry and on equestrian sport in Ireland. This ought to have been considered as a balance to the harm or inconvenience caused to the plaintiff by adhering to the rule. Finally, in my view the trial judge misinterpreted the international body's regulations when he referred to individual riders in international showjumping competitions competing as individuals and not as representatives of their country. As I have already indicated, in my view, this is just not possible under the regulations which apply.

I take a different view on the evidence and facts established before the learned trial judge. I accept that the plaintiff has been, as the trial judge put it, 'inhibited in his efforts to maintain his position as one of the world's leading show jumpers' by reason of the federation's rule. He is engaged on the international showjumping circuit from March to December each year. He has not the time to school or bring on young horses. As he said in his evidence he is faced by the fact that 'the majority of quality young horses in Ireland are sold at a very early stage'. It would be easier for him while on the circuit to look around for what he described as 'a talented young horse with a lesser rider'. This would be a horse already trained for jumping that he could include in his string without too excessive a loss of time or undue effort being involved. If he were free to buy such a horse, irrespective of its breeding, his interests would be well served and he could continue on the international circuit without any cessation. This is quite understandable if only the plaintiff's position were to be considered. This, however, is not the case. Also to be considered are the interests of the public as represented by those concerned with the horsebreeding industry in Ireland, and also the interests of those already engaged in showjumping in this country who are looking for recognition and advancement in international events. The evidence established beyond question that if the plaintiff were permitted to ride foreign-bred horses as an accredited Irish competitor at international events then all others who wished to do so would have to get the same permission. This process once started would, through sponsorship and money, affect the standing of the Irish horsebreeding industry. It would also have the effect of depriving young riders at home, particularly those of limited means, of any reasonable opportunity of advancement. It seems to me that on balance the policy and ruling of the federation can be justified as being reasonable, necessary and fair, having regard to all the tests which should be applied. The need for the rule in the first instance and the object of maintaining it was and is to build up the Irish half-bred horse industry in the interests of equestrian sport generally in the country. It is my view of the federation, fairly and reasonably held, that in doing so it is serving the interests of the generality of young riders of limited means and thereby serving the general interests of the public. It is not a new rule. It is as old as the federation itself. It has been accepted and complied with by all Irish riders over the years and was of course so accepted by the plaintiff himself until recently. It can be said fairly that the plaintiff is where he is today because this policy was in operation over the years. The fact that his very success as a show jumper on the world circuit makes the application of the rule to him, now, inconvenient and expensive is no basis for condemning it as being unreasonable and unfair.

In my view, therefore, the resolution and ruling of the federation although in restraint of trade is, in the circumstances, reasonable and fair . . .

Griffin J. delivered a concurring judgment while Henchy J. delivered a dissenting judgment.

Case 125. F. Cade & Sons Ltd v John Daly & Co. Ltd
High Court [1910] 1 I.R. 306

A number of traders formed a trade association and some of the members, including the plaintiff and defendant, executed a deed whereby the association resolved to fix the price at which certain goods were to be sold by its members for a period of six months within a sixteen-mile radius of the city in which they traded. The defendant withdrew from the association and sold such goods at prices different to those agreed on. When the plaintiff sought an injunction to compel the defendant to abide by the agreement the defendant argued that the deed was in restraint of trade.

Held that a voluntary agreement between traders not to sell certain goods below specified prices which was bound by reasonable limits of space and time and made with the intention to protect local trade as far as it could legitimately be protected was not illegal as being in restraint of trade. The injunction was granted.

Meredith M.R.:

. . . The main argument centred round the plea that the deed was void as being in restraint of trade, or at least that it was a deed which a court of equity would not enforce. There is a mass of authority, not altogether homogeneous, on this question of what is a contract in restraint of trade and what is not; and also upon the question as to when, and under what circumstances, a court of equity will lend its aid to enforce a contact which appears to be in partial restraint of trade. The fact is that every case in which the question of restraint of trade, or partial restraint of trade, has arisen, or may arise, must be considered in the light of its own facts and circumstances, and if the case which appeared at one time so destructive to the case of the plaintiffs here, the case of *Urmston v Whitelegg Brothers*, is viewed in that light, it is no authority against the plaintiffs in the present case. In point of fact, when the facts of that case are closely examined, the judgment delivered in the Court of Appeal affirms what I have always thought was the law, namely, that a covenant between persons interested in a particular trade for the purpose of keeping the trade as far as possible among themselves, and perhaps incidentally of keeping up the prices, or, as I would prefer to put it, not cutting down the prices to a low level, is perfectly legitimate, provided that the parties to the covenant do no more than is necessary or reasonable to effect the object they have in view. And my comment on the decision in *Urmston v Whitelegg Brothers*, and on the authorities generally, is this—The test of validity is reasonableness—that is not my own observation, but I adopt it as my own—and I cannot imagine a more unreasonable contract or agreement than that in *Urmston v Whitelegg Brothers*. There was no limit as to what we are in the habit of calling space, and the limit as to time, instead of being six months as here, was the very considerable period of ten years. There was no clause enabling a party to retire from the agreement. In my judgment the defendant cannot escape its obligations under this deed on the ground that the contract embodied in the deed is unlawful, because it imposes a restraint upon trade, which the court cannot sanction. Now, in connection with that remark, I have not overlooked the argument of counsel for the defendant, who pressed upon me the case of *Mogul Steamship Co. v Mc Gregor Gow & Co.* (1892), in which, undoubtedly, it was pointed out that the word 'unlawful' was capable of being used in two senses—(1) unlawful *per se*, a combination which was so unlawful that it would give rise to an action at the suit of a person injuriously affected, and (2) a combination which, though not unlawful in the sense that it gave rise to an action by a person affected, yet was of such a character as to receive no countenance from a legal tribunal. I recognise that eminent Lords who took part in that decision apparently considered that there might be cases in which courts would refuse to sanction or enforce a contract or combination which, though not directed against any particular person, or class of persons, and not giving rise to any cause of action by a person or persons incidentally injuriously affected, might yet be injurious to the community as operating in restraint of trade. This case does not appear to me to come within the suggested judicial ban. This is a covenant of co-operation for what may be a brief period between a few local bottlers, operating within a distance of sixteen miles from the General Post Office in the City of Cork, subject to this important exception, that the towns of Midleton and Queenstown are excluded from the ambit of the covenant. To my mind, when the sphere of operations is 'cabined, cribbed, confined' within such limits of time and space, when there is no prohibition, and can be no prohibition, against outsiders coming in and competing against any one or all of the persons named as parties to the covenant, the public, at all events, cannot suffer wrong. The public can suffer no injustice, and, in the ordinary sense of the word, cannot be detrimentally affected. The arrangement seems in reality to have been found necessary by a few local bottlers to prevent some of their number obtaining an undue advantage during a short period by selling at unduly low prices. No one was compelled to execute the deed. But, as between the firms or individual traders who executed it, the deed prevented 'cutting'. A reputation for low prices once gained by a firm or individual trader sometimes lingers for a long time after normal trade prices have been adopted. Having regard to all the facts and circumstances of this case, I am prepared to hold not merely that this contract is not *per se* unlawful, but that it is a legitimate and fair arrangement to which a court of equity can give effect without infringing upon the principles by which the court is fettered by authority. The prices, no doubt, are prices which impose the maximum prices as the minimum limit. That was stated in evidence, and not contradicted. In other words, the maximum prices which the signatories to the deed were in the habit of getting are the minimum prices set forth in the schedule to the deed. But the evidence in the case satisfies me that all parties concerned, bottlers and their customers, considered the scheduled prices reasonably fair. How does this circumstance affect or injure the public? Outsiders are absolutely free to compete, and if the scheduled prices are too high, the publicans can buy elsewhere. I do not think, then, that the prices can render this contract objectionable . . .

An injunction must go. The only question that remains is one of costs. The action has been forced upon the plaintiffs. The validity of the contract has been absolutely denied. They have succeeded in establishing their rights, and have obtained a decision which is far more valuable than the sum recoverable. It is a decision which declares the right of persons in the position of the plaintiffs to enter into an agreement limited as this agreement was, bounded by reasonable limits of space and time, with a view to protecting local trade as far as it might legitimately be protected.

c. Restraints in the Sale of a Business

The purchaser of a business can restrict the seller from engaging in similar enterprises in the future. The need to impose such a restriction is accepted by the courts because the proprietary interest in the goodwill of the business may be worthy of protection. But such restrictions will not be upheld should they be deemed to be wider than are reasonably necessary for that protection: *John Orr Ltd v Orr* (Case 126).

Case 126. John Orr Ltd v Orr
High Court [1987] I.L.R.M.

The defendant established the plaintiff company and was its principal shareholder. After some years' trading it was in financial difficulties. To revitalise the plaintiff another company agreed to purchase its share capital. As part of the takeover arrangement the defendant became an employee of the plaintiff. Both the share transfer agreement and a service agreement contained clauses against competition and solicitation for a one-year period after the termination of the service agreement. Eight years later the defendant resigned and established a company in England trading in similar goods. The plaintiff sought an injunction to compel the defendant to abide by the agreements.

Held that the restraint of trade clauses must be tested by reference to the commercial realities which existed when they were imposed and not when it was sought to enforce them. The non-solicitation clause was reasonable with regard to the plaintiff's customers but unreasonable with regard to customers of the parent company and its associates or subsidiaries because the plaintiff was not then manufacturing the same type of goods as the parent company. The unreasonable portions of those clauses would be severed. The non-competitive clauses were unreasonable because the range of goods subject to the restraint was too wide in that it prohibited the defendant from manufacturing the same type of goods manufactured by the parent company and not then manufactured by the plaintiff. The worldwide restraint was unreasonable because the plaintiff's market was principally Europe and North

America. These unreasonable restraints could not be severed so the complete clauses were unenforceable.

Costello J.:

. . . The principles of law to be applied in the issue are not in controversy and can be briefly stated. All restraints of trade in the absence of special justifying circumstances are contrary to public policy and are therefore void. A restraint may be justified if it is reasonable, in the interests of the contacting parties and in the interests of the public. The onus of showing that a restraint is reasonable between the parties rests on the person alleging that it is so. Greater freedom of contract is allowable in a covenant entered into between the seller and the buyer of a business than in the case of one entered into between an employer and employee. A covenant against competition entered into by the seller of a business which is reasonably necessary to protect the business sold is valid and enforceable. A covenant by an employee not to compete may also be valid and enforceable if it is reasonably necessary to protect some proprietary interest of the employer such as may exist in a trade connection or trade secrets. The courts may in certain circumstances enforce a covenant in restraint of trade even though, taken as a whole, the covenant exceeds what is reasonable, by the severance of the void parts from the valid parts . . .

The share transfer agreement also contained a clause, clause 6(c) which falls for consideration in these proceedings. It provided that until the expiry of one year from the determination of his service agreement the defendant should:

(i)   not have any interest in any other firm or company nor be employed by, or act as representative or agent for any other person firm or company which manufactures or trades or markets similar or competing goods to those manufactured or traded or marketed by the company or by the parent company; or

(ii) not solicit nor seek to obtain orders from nor interfere with nor endeavour to entice away any person firm or company which at any time within the period of twelve months ending with the termination of employment of [the defendant] is customer of or in the habit of dealing with the company or the parent company or any associated or subsidiary company.

The defendant took up his duties under the service agreement. The company prospered (sales expanding to £1.7m in 1984). But the defendant decided to resign in 1985 and his resignation, having been accepted, became effective from 31 October of that year, from which date the restraints began to run. Unknown to the plaintiff the defendant had established in England a company which began trading on 1 November 1985 in upholstery fabrics. Early this year the plaintiff ascertained that this company was doing business with one of the plaintiff's most important customers in England and furthermore that the defendant had been visiting some of its most valuable customers in the United States soliciting business for his new company. These proceedings followed shortly thereafter.

The reasonableness of the restraints imposed on the defendant is to be tested by reference to the commercial realities of the situation which existed when they were imposed, that is in the year 1977. So the question for determination is whether in that year it was reasonably necessary, for the protection of the parent company's investment in the plaintiff, to impose the restraints contained in the share-purchase agreement and whether it was reasonably necessary, for the protection of the plaintiff's trade connections, that it should impose the restraints contained in the service agreement. The business actually carried on by the plaintiff in that year is obviously of crucial importance. But what was in the reasonable contemplation of the parties for its future development is also relevant . . .

(1) THE NON-SOLICITATION CLAUSES

(a) I am quite satisfied that it was reasonably necessary for the protection of the parent company's investment in the plaintiff that it should require the defendant not to solicit the customers of the plaintiff for a period of twelve months after the termination of his service agreement with that company. But the protection of that investment did not require the defendant to agree not to solicit the customers of the parent company or its subsidiaries or associated companies because the plaintiff was not manufacturing or trading in wall coverings and had no intention of doing so. The plaintiff's counsel submitted, a submission with which the defendant's counsel agreed, that the severance rule could be applied to this clause. I will therefore hold that in respect of the share-purchase agreement of 11 March 1977 clause 6(c) (ii) is valid and enforceable with the deletion of the words 'or the parent company or any associated or subsidiary company' at the end of the paragraph.

(b) I am also quite satisfied that it was reasonably necessary for the protection of the proprietary interest of the plaintiff in its trade connection with its customers that it should require the defendant not to solicit its customers for twelve months after the termination of his service agreement with the company. But the protection of that interest did not require that he would not solicit the customers of the parent company or its associates and subsidiaries. As in the case of the share purchase agreement, counsel agree that the severance rule can be applied to the service agreement. Accordingly I will declare that paragraph 7 (ii) of that agreement is enforceable with the deletion of the words 'or the parent company or any associated or subsidiary company' at the end of the paragraph. In neither case will there be any adverse effect on the public interest.

(2) THE NON-COMPETITION CLAUSES

(a) It will be recalled that the share purchase agreement restrained the defendant for one year after the termination of his service agreement from manufacturing or selling (either personally or through a company) goods manufactured or sold by the parent company as well as goods manufactured or sold by the plaintiff. In 1977, the plaintiff manufactured and sold upholstery and garment fabrics and did not manufacture or trade in wall coverings, which were the goods manufactured by the parent company. It had no intention of entering the market in these goods. The range of goods subjected to the restraints in clause 6 (c) (i) of the share-purchase agreement was therefore unreasonably wide as it was not necessary for the protection of the parent company's investment in the plaintiff that the defendant should be restrained from manufacturing or trading in wall coverings. The clause therefore imposes an excessive restraint.

It is also excessively restrictive for another reason. It prohibited the defendant from manufacturing or trading in upholstery fabrics in any part of the world during the limitation period. In 1977 the vast bulk of the business of the plaintiff was done with a limited number of customers in a limited number of countries. A restriction on the defendant which would prohibit him for one year after termination of his service contract from manufacturing or selling in the countries to which the plaintiff had customers could well have been justified as necessary to protect the parent company's investment in this case. Indeed, it might even have been possible to justify a wider restriction if it could have been shown that in 1977 the plaintiff had definite proposals for expanding into markets outside North America and Europe. But a blanket worldwide restraint based merely on the possibility that markets in other parts of the world might be entered by the company is to my mind an unreasonable one as it was not reasonably required for the protection of the parent company's investment in the company.

(b) Exactly the same considerations apply to the restrictions contained in clause 7(I) of the service agreement. The protection of the trade connection of the plaintiff did not require that the defendant should be restrained from manufacturing or trading in goods manufactured or sold by the parent company. And the protection of its trade connections could be assured without prohibiting the defendant from manufacturing or selling upholstery fabrics in any part of the world.

The defendant's counsel had urged that if I found that the restraints imposed by clause 6(c) (i) of the share-purchase agreement and clause 7(I) of the service agreement were excessive and therefore unreasonable, that the clauses were unenforceable because I could not apply the severance rule to them as to do so would amount to re-writing the parties' contracts. The plaintiff's counsel forcibly submitted that the worldwide restraints in the two agreements were reasonable ones, but did not suggest that if I were to hold otherwise that the infirmities could be cured by severing the unenforceable parts. In these circumstances I must hold that these two clauses are unenforceable . . .

d. Restraint by Exclusive Dealing Contracts

An exclusive dealing contract is one which provides for sole agency, or exclusive agreement, or contracts to exclusively supply goods to one party, or to exclusively purchase and use goods supplied by one party. The rules relating to the restraint of trade have been applied to exclusive trading contracts. Before the terms of such agreement can be judged as to their reasonableness the more fundamental question of whether the solus agreement has been breached must be determined: *Esso Petroleum Co. (Ireland) Ltd v Fogarty* (Case 127). Such a contract which had no time limit on its duration was held to be unreasonable: *McEllistrim v Ballymacelligott Co-operative Agricultural & Dairy Society* (Case 128). A solus agreement which had a twenty-year duration was held to be unreasonable: *McMullan Bros. Ltd v Condell* (Case 129), whereas a five-year duration was held to be reasonable: *Continental Oil Co. of Ireland v Moynihan* (Case 130).

Case 127. Esso Petroleum Co. (Ireland) Ltd v Fogarty
Supreme Court [1965] I.R. 531

The defendant by a written contract agreed to exclusively purchase his total requirements of motor fuel for his garage from the plaintiff for a period of five years, and not to sell, or offer for sale, the garage during that period without first giving the plaintiff an opportunity of introducing a purchaser, and to use his best endeavours to ensure that any purchaser would enter into a similar agreement with the plaintiff. Over a year later the defendant began to purchase motor fuel from a different source. The plaintiff obtained a temporary injunction to restrain the defendant from breaching the contract pending a full hearing of the case. The defendant then sub-let that part of his garage which contained the petrol pumps and storage tanks. The plaintiff then sought an interlocutory injunction.

   Held that since the plaintiff had not shown, to any substantial degree, that the sub-letting of portion of the garage was a breach of the contract, the application for an injunction should be refused.

Walsh J.:

The solus agreement of 21 April 1964, contains an undertaking on the part of the defendant not to sell or offer to sell the service station during the period of five years from the date of the agreement without first giving the plaintiff an opportunity of introducing a purchaser. It also provides that in the event of the defendant ceasing to carry on the business of retailer of motor fuels he would repay the sum of £500 which had been advanced to him by the plaintiff at the making of the agreement or part of it, depending upon the time of the cessation of the said business.

It is clear that at this stage the real point in this case is not whether the defendant himself may or may not sell any motor fuel other than the plaintiff's. It appears to be abundantly clear that, so far as he is personally concerned, he is not going to do so in the immediate future although initially and prior to the making of the agreement for the sub-demise he had committed a breach of his agreement. The question now is whether the agreement for the sub-lease is itself a breach of the solus agreement and whether it is a genuine agreement or whether [the tenant] is in reality only the agent of the defendant.

The solus agreement makes no reference to the possibility of a sub-demise and *prima facie* a sub-demise does not appear to be a breach of the agreement not to sell or offer to sell the service station.

This is a matter which does not appear to have weighed sufficiently with the learned judge [in the High Court] who, for the purpose of the interlocutory proceedings, appears to have acted on the assumption that a sale of motor fuel by [the tenant] would be a sale by the defendant.

It appears to me that, having regard to the real nature of the present contest, the plaintiff has not shown that there is a substantial question to be tried; that is, it has not shown to any substantial degree that the sub-demise would be a breach of the solus agreement.

Ó Dálaigh C.J. and Lavery J. concurred.

Case 128. McEllistrim v Ballymacelligott Co-operative Agricultural & Dairy Society Ltd
House of Lords* [1919] A.C. 548

The defendant society carried on the business of manufacturing for sale cheese and butter from milk supplied by certain of its members. By one of its rules (6) the society bound itself to take all milk produced by members' cows produced within a certain defined geographical area, provided that no member with milk to sell should, without the previous consent of the society's governing committee, sell any milk to any creamery other that the defendant. Under another rule (16) a member whose shares had been transferred or cancelled ceased to be a member, but a member was otherwise not entitled to withdraw from the society. A further rule (21) required the consent of the committee to any transfer of shares, but the committee were not bound to assign any reason for their refusal. The plaintiff, a member of the society, challenged these rules as being in restraint of trade.

*On appeal from the Court of Appeal in Ireland.

Held that the rules read in conjunction imposed upon members a greater restraint than was reasonably required for the protection of the society and were illegal as in restraint of trade and *ultra vires* the society.

Birkenhead L.C.:

. . . A contract which is in restraint of trade cannot be enforced unless (a) it is reasonable as between the parties; (b) it is consistent with the interests of the public.

Your Lordships have recently laid down rules as to where the onus lies in these matters. Such considerations however do not arise in the present case.

Every contract therefore which is impeached as being in restraint of trade must submit itself to the two standards indicated. Both still survive. The observation made by the Judicial Committee in the *Attorney-General of Australia v Adelaide Steamship Co.* (1913): 'Their Lordships are not aware of any case in which a restraint, though reasonable in the interests of the parties, has been held unenforceable because it involved some injury to the public,' is not, in my view, to be construed as if both the tests indicated were not still in existence. It is indeed not difficult to conceive of a case in which a contract in restraint of trade might be adjusted to safeguard the reasonable interests of the contracting parties, and yet might be opposed to the public interest.

There is much to be said for the view that the restraint objected to in this case would be opposed to the public interest, but I do not think it necessary to decide this, having regard to the clear view which I have formed that the rules under consideration are not reasonable as between the parties.

My Lords, so much guidance has been given by this House in recent decisions to those whose duty it is to understand the criteria by which one tests the meaning of 'reasonableness between the parties', that little need be added upon this point. The real test is, as your Lordships have so often pointed out, does the restriction exceed what is reasonably necessary for the protection of the covenantee? To make the matter particular your Lordships have to reach a conclusion as to whether the combined effect of rule 6 (2.), rule 16, and rule 21 is or is not to impose upon the plaintiff a greater degree of restraint than the reasonable protection of the defendants requires.

It is evident that the first question which requires an answer in this action is: 'What was it against which the society were reasonably entitled to protect themselves?' Until this question is answered no answer is possible to the principal inquiry whether that which was stipulated for exceeded the reasonable needs of the case. My Lords, before attempting to discover a positive answer to the question I have proposed, it may be possible to clear the ground somewhat by answering it negatively. The society was not entitled to be protected against mere competition. No excellence of motive on their part, no record of efficient public service, can for this purpose place them in a different position from that occupied by any private contracting party who is called upon to justify his restraint. And it has been laid down by your Lordships over and over again that in this class of case the covenantee is not entitled to be protected against competition per se. The present case is entirely different from those in which he who has bound himself by the restriction has obtained inside knowledge or competitive resource by reason of the fact that special confidence under unusual circumstances has been reposed in him.

But a negative answer is not enough. I addressed a question upon this point to the learned counsel who appeared for the society, and I am not indisposed to accept his answer as reasonable. Counsel replied to my question: 'The defendants are entitled to such a degree of protection as will ensure stability in the lists of their customers.' Let me then, without subscribing entirely to the words of this answer, treat it as being generally acceptable. Were the rules complained of necessary in order to secure stability in the lists of the society's customers? By 'stability' must, of course, be understood such reasonable stability of relationship as a careful merchant is content with.

In order to answer the question indicated above, the scope of the three rules complained of must be examined. I have already set out their terms. The combined effect is this. A member, if he joins young enough and lives long enough, may be precluded under heavy penalty for sixty years or more, and over a considerable area, from selling his milk to any creamery other than the society's creamery, or to any person who sells milk or manufactures butter for sale. It is necessary to notice that the penalty provided is avoided in favour of the member who obtains the written consent of the committee before making the sale otherwise prohibited. It is not pretended that it was the policy of the committee to give such consent. I say for sixty years or more, because having regard to the age at which members become eligible for election, and to the possibilities of human life, the supposition is by no means extravagant. It is possible that rule 6 (2.) could have been supported as part of a code which provided, in further rules, reasonable conditions of withdrawal. But the conditions of withdrawal which are contained in 16 and 21 are such as to make it for ever impossible for a member to withdraw, unless the committee gives its consent. Under rule 16 no member may withdraw unless his shares have been transferred or cancelled. Under rule 21 no share may be transferred unless with the consent of the committee of management. And it is expressly provided that no share shall be withdrawn. The result is that an unwilling member is to find himself precluded for life from disposing of the raw materials of his trade to anyone but the society (with the exceptions already noted) within a radius which may easily include every neighbouring centre of population which affords him the slightest prospect of a valuable market. It is no answer to such a man to say: 'You can go elsewhere.' He may easily be owner in fee of a small holding which has been in his family for generations. The fact that his integrity is known amongst his neighbours may be no small element in his stock of trade. Further, the power of migrating to a part of Ireland in which he may never have lived, and where nobody may know him, cannot be considered to be any alleviation of the severity or unreasonableness of the rule.

The position therefore is that the society claims to impose a restraint, within the limits already indicated, upon any one of their members which will last for life unless the committee empowers him to transfer his shares. My Lords, I see no reason whatever for supposing that, unless in the most exceptional cases, the committee would give such consent. In fact, they could not so consent without abandoning the whole spirit of their contentions and submissions before your Lordships. Indeed, holding the views they do they would be lacking in their duty to their members if they consented upon a large, or even upon a moderate, scale to such transfers, for they have explained very candidly to your Lordships the reasons which oblige them to insist upon continued membership. It is even necessary, so it is explained, to depress the prices paid to their members for milk in order to increase the capital available for new building operations. The result evidently may be that a member in township A receives admittedly less than the local value of his milk in order that township B ten miles away may be indulged with a creamery of its own. It is by no means to be supposed that I am disputing either the wisdom or the commercial justification of such a policy. I am using the illustration in order to make it clear that it is impossible for a society, whose extension requires such methods, to allow a wholesale transference of shares by members who find themselves in the position of the member whom I have imagined to be carrying on his business in what I called township A. I assume therefore— and indeed the contrary was not seriously argued—that transfers would not be granted by the committee.

It is therefore necessary to ask plainly whether it can be reasonably necessary for the protection of the defendants to tie the plaintiff for life unless the committee thinks fit to grant him a dispensation. I am clearly of opinion that it is not and cannot be so necessary. I am further of opinion that these three rules read together are bad as being in restraint of trade and not reasonable as between the parties. It is not for your Lordships to frame rules which would be good. It is, however, obvious that the objects indicated and claimed by counsel on behalf of the society could be secured in a variety of ways by imposing restraints which would fall short of those attempted to be enforced in the present case.

Lords Finlay, Atkinson, Shaw and Parmoor concurred.

Case 129. McMullan Bros. Ltd v Condell
High Court, unreported, 30 January 1970

The plaintiff was a petrol distributor and the defendant was the owner of a garage. The parties entered into a loan agreement whereby the plaintiff provided an interest-free loan for the development of the defendant's premises. The loan was to be repaid by an annual instalment over a twenty-year period. As part of the contract the defendant agreed to exclusively purchase all his supplies of petrol and other related products from the plaintiff and not to sell or transfer the business or assign or sub-let the premises without the written consent of the plaintiff. It was further provided that, except with the consent in writing of the plaintiff, which would not be unreasonably withheld, the defendant was not entitled to repay the loan otherwise than by way of the yearly instalments. The parties also entered into a solus agreement which was to continue for twenty years. The defendant considered the sale of the business and when the plaintiff drew his attention to the clauses of the loan agreement the defendant replied that he wished to redeem the loan. The plaintiff's consent would only be forthcoming if the purchaser of the business was willing to enter into a similar agreement with the plaintiff. When the plaintiff sought an injunction to prohibit the defendant from breaching the agreement the defendant claimed the agreement was in restraint of trade.

Held that in the absence of evidence justifying the restrictions, the period of twenty years was excessive and invalid as being an unreasonable restraint of trade. As a consequence the restriction which prevented the defendant from disposing of the business or the premises without the plaintiff's consent was also invalid.

Kenny J.:

. . . The defendant contends that the tie for 20 years is a clause in restraint of trade which is not reasonably required by the plaintiff for the protection of its legitimate interests and that it is therefore invalid and that it is so closely connected with the clause in the loan agreement relating to the sale by him of his business that the latter clause is also invalid. The plaintiff has submitted that the defendant may free himself from the tie by paying off the amount secured by the loan agreement and that the period for which he is restricted from purchasing from anybody is reasonable because it is one of the smaller petrol distributing companies who must have secure outlets for its goods so that it can plan in advance.

Clause 6 (a) of the loan agreement provides that the defendant is not to be entitled to pay off the advance except by way of the yearly instalments (which will last for 20 years) but if the amount advanced is paid off, the tie created by the solus agreement will continue to exist. Moreover an offer by the defendant to redeem the loan agreement was refused and the letter of 17 August 1965, written by the plaintiff's solicitors, makes it clear that they will accept a payment in redemption of the loan only when they are satisfied that this garage will be a solus outlet for their clients' products for the period of 20 years. I therefore reject the argument that the loan agreement is reasonable in so far as this is based on the view that it makes it possible for the defendant to free himself from the tie created by it by paying off the loan. He can do so only if a purchaser from him is prepared to bind himself to the plaintiff.

The general principle in relation to agreements in restraint of trade was stated by Lord Macnaghten in *Nordenfelt v Maxim Nordenfelt Guns Ltd* (1894) when he said:

The true view at the present time, I think, is this. The public have an interest in every person carrying on his trade freely; so has the individual. All interference with individual liberty of action in trading, and all restraints of trade of themselves, if there is nothing more, are contrary to public policy and therefore void. This is the general rule. But there are exceptions. Restraints of trade and interference with individual liberty of action may be justified by the special circumstances of a particular case. It is a sufficient justification, and indeed, it is the only justification, if the restriction is reasonable . . . reasonable, that is, in reference to the interests of the parties concerned and reasonable in reference to the interests of the public, so framed and so guarded as to afford adequate protection to the party in whose favour it is imposed, while at the same time it is in no way injurious to the public.

The only ground in which it was said that the restriction for 20 years was reasonable in this case was that the plaintiff has a small share of the petrol distributing market but this by itself, in the absence of evidence of the degree of competition and marketing conditions, does not justify a tie for 20 years. I do not know whether a solus outlet in Portlaoise tied to the plaintiff's products for 20 years is necessary to enable the plaintiff to plan its imports of petrol into Ireland or to arrange its transport system. The burden of establishing that this very lengthy tie is reasonably required by the plaintiff for the protection and advancement of its business lies on it and no evidence to justify this has been given. An attempt to justify a tie for 20 years was made in *Esso Petroleum Co. Ltd v Harpers Garage* (1967) and some evidence on this topic was given in that case but the three judges of the Court of Appeal and the five judges in the House of Lords held that a tie for this length was not reasonable, either in the interests of the supplier or in the public interest.

Is the length of the tie created by the two agreements reasonable in reference to the interests of the public? It is not possible to treat the interests of the parties concerned and the interests of the public separately because the interests of the parties which justify or do not justify an agreement restrictive of trade rest on considerations of public policy: if they did not, the courts could not release parties from obligations which they had voluntarily accepted. Again, no effort has been made to justify the length of this restriction on the basis of the public interest, and the *Restrictive Trade Practices (Motor Spirit and Motor Vehicle Lubricating Order) 1961*, made after a lengthy investigation by the Fair Trade Commission, shows that a solus agreement for a term of more than five years is not in the interests of the public and indeed is contrary to that interest which benefits by competition.

In my opinion, in the absence of evidence, clause 3 (a) of the loan agreement and clause 4 (a) of the solus agreement contain agreements which are invalid because they are in restraint of trade and are not justified either by the interests of the parties to them or in the public interest.

But if these clauses are invalid, does it follow that clause 6 of the loan agreement which prevents the defendant from selling or transferring his business or conveying the premises to any third party without first obtaining the written consent of the plaintiff and clause 7 of the solus agreement which requires him to get the consent of the plaintiff to a transfer of the benefit of that agreement are invalid? I think it does. Clause 6 which requires the written consent of the plaintiff to a transfer of the business and to a conveyance of the property to a third party is a safeguard for the tie only, and is intended to strengthen it. If there were no tie for 20 years, the plaintiff would have no interest in requiring the defendant to get its written consent to a sale of his business, and the clause that the amount of a loan is to be repaid only by the instalments was intended to give another support to the tie. The loan agreement was intended to bolster up the solus agreement . . .

I wish to emphasise that this is not a decision that every solus agreement for 20 years concluded before 25 July 1962 is invalid: it is a decision that, in the absence of evidence justifying such a tie, it is invalid.

Case 130. Continental Oil Co. of Ireland Ltd v Moynihan
High Court (1977) 111 I.L.T.R. 5

The parties entered into a solus agreement for the supply of motor fuel for a five year period. The agreement contained a tying clause, a compulsory trading clause and a continuity clause. The defendant also entered into interest-free hire-purchase agreements for the acquisition of new petrol pumps from the plaintiff. When the price of petrol was raised by the plaintiff it threatened the defendant's slender profit margin and he sought supplies elsewhere. The plaintiff sought an injunction to compel the defendant to abide by the agreement.

Held that the agreement in restraint of trade was reasonable in that the period the contract was to run was not excessive and the defendant had the benefit of interest-free loans. The fact that the agreement had effects which were not contemplated does not make it unreasonable. The injunction was granted.

Kenny J.:

. . . The Arrow business [purchased by the plaintiff] had no solus or exclusivity agreements with any petrol dealers and they sold petrol on a day-to-day basis. The solus system by which a dealer binds himself to sell the products of one petrol company, had been introduced into the Republic of Ireland at the end of 1950 and, in 1966, about 90 per cent of the dealers had entered into solus agreements. The plaintiff tried to persuade those who had formerly sold Arrow petrol to enter into solus agreements for five years with them and, in cases where garage owners had entered into these with other suppliers, attempted to persuade them to enter into agreements with them when the existing ones expired. The plaintiff has spent £1.8 million in the Republic of Ireland of which about a half million has been spent on building terminals and depots and buying lorries.

The solus system was adopted by the petrol companies to secure certainty of outlets. They have to make their policy decisions on the amount to be produced in their refinery on the assumption that they will be able to sell a known amount of petrol and this can be achieved only by having solus agreements. When the plaintiff began business in the Republic of Ireland, it was essential for them to try to get solus agreements. This system has many advantages for the public. Before it was introduced most garages sold a number of brands of petrol and so, lorries from each of the companies had to stop at all the garages. By limiting the number of garages at which the lorries from each company had to stop, a considerable saving in the costs of distribution was effected and it is notorious that the price of petrol to the motorists (if one excludes the duties levied by the State) has not increased to the same extent as have the prices of most other commodities. As the plaintiff entered a market in 1966 where 90 per cent of the dealers were bound by solus agreements, their adoption of this policy was reasonable . . .

At the time when the defendant entered into the agreement of 1968 with the plaintiff his sales of petrol were about 800 gallons a week. He made the agreement of 1968 because he hoped to increase substantially his sales and thought that he would thereby earn bigger profits. He did not succeed in his hope of increasing his sales and as his margin, when the plaintiff's petrol is sold, is less than that which he would get from the major oil companies, he has no profit on his sales of petrol. In November 1972 the Minister for Industry and Commerce allowed the petrol companies to increase their wholesale price to dealers by a halfpenny. There is price control of the wholesale price at which petrol may be sold to dealers but there is none on the retail price. When the Minister gave this permission, the plaintiff offered its dealers a choice of either increasing their price to the public by a $\frac{1}{2}$p a gallon and then the plaintiff would charge them this extra amount on the wholesale price or keeping their price to the public at the amount it was before and, in that event, the plaintiff would pay them a publicity allowance of one-quarter of a penny per gallon which was to be deducted from the price of the petrol paid by the dealer. Though called a publicity allowance, the effect of this offer was that the dealers who did not increase their price to the public would be getting their petrol at $\frac{1}{4}$p per gallon less than those who did. The result for those who decided that they would not increase the price to the public was a further reduction in the profit margin. The defendant was determined that he would not accept this reduction and that he would continue to sell petrol at the former price and so, when he received his bills after 27 November, he deducted $\frac{1}{2}$p per gallon from the price. The defendant was then interviewed by the dealer representative of the plaintiff . . . [and was] told [by] him that as he had not increased his price to the public, the price to him of petrol supplied by the plaintiff would be increased by $\frac{1}{4}$p per gallon and that this would be carried out by giving him a credit note for the excess charged. The defendant was not prepared to accept this suggestion: he wanted petrol supplied to him at the price which was in force before 27 November and was not prepared to pay more. The plaintiff therefore discontinued supplies to the defendant who has now made arrangements with [another company] for the sale by them to him of his petrol requirements. The plaintiff has now brought these proceedings seeking an injunction to restrain the defendant from receiving or selling at his premises any motor fuels other than those which he shall have purchased from it. It has been agreed that the hearing of the motion is to be treated as the trial of the action.

Counsel for the defendant has said that the agreement of 19 August 1970, is in restraint of trade and is unreasonable and so should not be enforced . . .

The legal rules to be applied were discussed by Mr Justice Budd in *Irish Shell & B.P. Ltd v Ryan* (1966), by the House of Lords in *Esso Petroleum Co. v Harpers Garage* (1967), by me in the judgment in *McMullan Bros. Ltd v Condell* (Case 129) and by Mr Justice Ungoed-Thomas in *Texaco Ltd v Mulberry Filling Station* (1972). Mr Justice Budd's judgment in *Irish Shell & B.P. Ltd v Ryan* was based upon decisions of the Court of Appeal in England which were subsequently overruled in *Harpers case* and so cannot now be regarded as a correct statement of the law. The basic principle was stated by Lord Macnaghten in *Nordenfelt v Maxim Nordenfelt Guns & Ammunition Co Ltd* (1894):

Restraints of trade and interference with individual liberty of action, may be justified in the special circumstances of a particular case. It is a sufficient justification, and indeed it is the only justification, if the restriction is reasonable—reasonable, that is, in reference to the interests of the parties concerned and reasonable in reference to the interests of the public, so framed and so guarded as to afford adequate protection to the party in whose favour it is imposed while at the same time it is in no way injurious to the public.

The effect of this was summarised by Lord Reid in *Harpers Case* in this way:

So in every case it is necessary to consider, first whether the restraint went further than to afford adequate protection to the party in whose favour it was granted, secondly whether it can be justified as being in the interests of the party restrained, and thirdly whether it must be held contrary to the public interest. I find it difficult to agree with the way in which the court has in some cases treated the interests of the party restrained. Surely it can never be in the interest of a person to agree to suffer a restraint unless he gets some compensating advantage direct or indirect; and Lord Macnaghten said 'of course the quantum of consideration may enter into the question of the reasonableness of the contract'. Where two experienced traders are bargaining on equal terms and one has agreed to a restraint for reasons which seem good to him, the court is in grave danger of stultifying itself if it says that it knows that trader's interest better than he does himself. There may well be cases, however, where, although the party to be restrained has deliberately accepted the main terms of the contract, he has been at a disadvantage as regards other terms: for example, where a set of conditions has been incorporated which has not been the subject of negotiation—there the court may have greater freedom to hold them unreasonable.

I am satisfied that when the defendant made the agreement of 1968 he was a free agent bargaining on equal terms with the plaintiff. He could have made an agreement with any of the petrol companies all of whom were anxious to secure the maximum number of outlets. The defendant made the agreement of 1970 because he wanted new pumps and he was supplied with these on hire-purchase terms without any charge for interest. His expectations of larger profits have not been realised because he has not been able to sell the amount of petrol which he thought he would be able to at the lower price. The question, however, is whether the agreement of 1970 was reasonable at the time it was made. The fact that it had effects which were not contemplated does not make it unreasonable. The plaintiff acted reasonably in entering into the agreement because security of outlets for the petrol which they produce at the Humber refinery is essential if the refinery is to continue to operate and it found the system of solus trading in force when it came to the Republic of Ireland. The agreement was reasonable from the defendant's standpoint as he got new pumps on hire-purchase terms without having to pay the heavy interest charges which are usually connected with these transactions. The period of five years was reasonable both as between the parties and in the public interest. Four years and five months was held to be reasonable by the House of Lords in the *Harper case*, five years was approved in Canada (*British American Oil Co. v Hey* (1941) . . .

I do not accept the submission that clause 5 in relation to the sale is unreasonable. It is reasonable for the plaintiff to stipulate that if the defendant sells his premises during the five years the purchaser shall enter into a solus agreement with the plaintiff for otherwise the tie would be of no value, nor do I agree with the argument that the agreement could compel the defendant to trade at a loss. The words 'without the written consent of the supplier which shall not be unreasonably withheld' in clause 3 (a) relate both to the obligation to carry on the business of retailing motor fuels and not to reduce the number of petrol pumps and if the defendant could establish that he was selling petrol at a loss and wished to discontinue this business, the plaintiff could not reasonably withhold its consent if he decided not to sell it at all.

It was also argued that the plaintiff had to establish that the retention of the tie with the defendant was essential for the carrying on of its business and so that a garage with a small sale of petrol such as this could not be regarded as essential. The plaintiff does not in my opinion have to establish that the retention of the tie for each garage is essential for their business. If it had to do this, almost all the solus agreements in the country would be unenforceable: it has to prove that the system of solus agreements and the terms of the agreement in dispute are reasonable. In pursuit of that policy they acted reasonably in entering into the agreement of 1970. I think that the system is reasonable in the interests of the public. It has the result that the distribution costs of petrol are reduced and because of it and of the fierce competition between petrol companies, the cost of petrol to the motorist (if duty is excluded) has risen far less than the price of other commodities. The court is not concerned with the questions whether a better system could be introduced or whether it would be in the public interest that the business of distributing petrol should be conducted by the State.

The question which such unreasonableness raises would thus not be whether the restraint might be less in a different organisation of industry or society or whether the abolition of the restraint might lead to a different organisation of industry or society, and thus, on balance of many considerations, to the economic or social advantage of the country, but whether the restraint is in fact in our industry and society as at present organised, and with reference to which our law operates, unreasonable in the public interest as recognised and formulated in such principle or proposition of law. —Mr Justice Ungoed-Thomas in *Texaco Ltd v Mulberry Filling Station Ltd* (1972).

I am of opinion that the agreement of 1970 was reasonable between the parties and in the interests of each of them and was reasonable so far as the public interest was concerned.

PART THREE

DISCHARGE OF CONTRACT

Every valid contractual obligation gives rise to a corresponding contractual right. It follows that where all the obligations of one party have been fully honoured the corresponding rights of the other party are extinguished. When this occurs a contract is said to be discharged. A contract may be discharged in a number of ways.

CHAPTER 19.

DISCHARGE BY PERFORMANCE

A contractual obligation is discharged by a complete performance of the contract. The performance must be complete and be exactly in accordance with the terms of the contract: *Coughlan v Moloney* (Case 131). The courts have developed the doctrine of substantial performance. Whether it operates in any particular case depends on the circumstances: *Kincora Builders Ltd v Cronin* (Case 132).

Case 131. Coughlan v Moloney
King's Bench (1905) 39 I.L.T.R. 153

The plaintiff had agreed in July to build a house for the defendant. There was no provision with regard to payment by instalment though the defendant made two payments to the plaintiff. The work was not completed by Christmas. By the following October the work remained unfinished, and the defendant wrote to the plaintiff requesting him 'to furnish particulars of the work that he had done and an estimate of its value in order that the matter should be finally wound up between them'. In November the defendant took possession of the premises in their unfinished state and prevented the plaintiff having further access to them. The plaintiff sued for (a) the balance of the contract price, or (b) for the amount due for the labour and materials expended by him on the premises.

Held that since the contract had not been completed the plaintiff was not entitled to the balance of the contract price. The plaintiff could not succeed on a *quantum meruit** merely because the defendant had received the benefit of the plaintiff's part performance of the contract unless the defendant had done so under circumstances sufficient to raise an implied contract to pay for the work done.

Palles L.C.B.:

. . . Ultimately, the question comes to what were the plaintif's rights in reference, not to the mere taking over and entering upon this building by the defendants, but to the circumstances under which it was so entered. Evidence was given of two letters asking the plaintiff to furnish particulars of the work that he had done, and for an estimate of its value, in order that the matter should be finally wound up. I do not say that if the terms of these letters had been assented to by the plaintiff that there would not have been a complete contract to pay on a *quantum meruit*. But, then, there was no assent to those terms by the plaintiff, and, on the contrary, it is clear that from that time and always he has been insisting on his right to recover on the special contract. The plaintiff's right to recover upon this *quantum meruit* depended on a state of facts which it would have been impossible for the jury to have found. I am clear that the view of counsel was that they were entitled to recover on a *quantum meruit*, based not upon any contract found by the jury, but upon the fact that possession was taken up of the work by the defendant—that he retained the benefit of it— and that under the circumstances the plaintiff was entitled to recover the full value of his work. That proposition, stated nakedly, is simply that *Munro v Butt*, and cases of that description, are not law. It is going upon the principle applicable to chattels, that if a certain thing is done, not in performance of a contract, but under circumstances under which the defendant is able to obtain benefit from it, and if the defendant accepts and avails himself of it, then the plaintiff is able to recover on a *quantum meruit*. The decision in *Munro v Butt* is that this principle does not apply to a house on a man's land, because there is no possibility of rejecting the benefit of what has been done, unless he destroys the house built on it. Again, it was argued that if there was nothing more than the mere taking up of possession—that is, if the possession was availed of, and the house improved, that would render the defendant liable. I am of opinion that it cannot. I do not go into the question of hardship. *Cutter v Powell* (1795) is always apt to work hardship, but I think that this application should be refused with costs, and that the verdict for the defendant should stand.

quantum meruit, the reasonable amount to be paid for services rendered or work done, when the price had not been fixed by the contract.

Johnson and Gibson JJ. concurred. The Court of Appeal (Lord Ashbourne C., Walker and Holmes L.JJ.) dismissed the plaintiff's appeal.

Case 132. Kincora Builders Ltd v Cronin
High Court, unreported, 5 May 1973

The plaintiff agreed to build a house for the defendant. The plaintiff claimed to have completed the house, except for one deviation from the specifications which related to insulation. The parties held discussions on the issue and came to an agreement. The defendant understood that all the insulation was to be finished whereas the plaintiff understood that only the ceilings were to be finished and the defendant was to be compensated for the non-insulation of the walls. Despite the fact that the house had been completed for a year the defendant refused to take possession. The plaintiff sued for all outstanding moneys and interest claiming that under the doctrine of substantial performance it was entitled to insist on the completion of the contract subject to whatever deduction the defendant was entitled to for defective work, if any.

Held that there had been an abandonment of the contract which disentitled the plaintiff to the relief sought.

Pringle J.:

Counsel for the plaintiff submitted that, as the contract had been *substantially* completed, his client was entitled to insist on the completion of the contract, subject to whatever deductions the defendant was entitled to for defective work (if any). He referred to the case of *Bolton v Mahadeva* (1972) in which the Court of Appeal in England dealt with the question of the circumstances under which a building contractor, who has entered into a lump sum contract, can recover anything on foot thereof, if the contract has not been completely performed. The court reviewed the authorities, and in particular distinguished an earlier decision of the Court of Appeal in the case of *H. Dakin & Co. v Lee* (1916), which had been followed in the case of *Hoenig v Isaacs* (1952).

In *Dakin's Case* the plaintiffs had agreed to carry out certain repairs to the defendant's house for the sum of £264 and the plaintiffs claimed that sum and a sum for extras. The defendant, who had gone back into the house after the plaintiffs' workmen had left, disputed her liability to pay any part of the contract sum on the ground that the contract had not been fulfilled in three respects: (1) the concrete which was to be placed under a part of one of the side walls of the house which was to be underpinned was to be of the depth of four feet and it was in fact only done to a depth of two feet, (2) columns of hollow iron, 5 inches in diameter were to be used to support a certain bay window, whereas the columns supplied were of solid iron 4 inches in diameter, and (3) the joists over the bay window were to be cleated at the angles and bolted to caps and to each other and this was not done. The Official Referee found as a fact that the contract had not been fulfilled in the three instances mentioned, and he held that the plaintiffs were therefore not entitled to recover any part of the contract price, or to the amount claimed for extras, but he allowed £70 for the additional work. This decision was reversed by Ridley and Sankey JJ. in the King's Bench Division and their decision was upheld by the Court of Appeal. The Master of The Rolls, Lord Cozens-Hardy, said in his judgment, after dealing with the deviations from the contract:

In these circumstances it has been argued before us that, in a contract of this kind to do work for a lump sum, the defect in some of the items of the specification, or the failure to do every item in the specification, puts an end to the whole contract and prevents the builders from making any claim upon it: and therefore, where there is no ground for presuming any fresh contract, he cannot obtain any payment. The matter has been treated in the argument as though the omission to do every item perfectly was an abandonment of the contract. That seems to me, with great respect, to be absolutely and entirely wrong. An illustration of the abandonment of a contract which was given from one of the authorities was that of a builder who, when he had half finished the work, said to the employer 'I cannot finish it because I have no money' and left the job undone at that stage. That is an abandonment of the contract and prevents the builder, therefore, from making any claim, unless there be some circumstances leading to a different conclusion. But to say that a builder cannot recover from a building owner merely because some item of the work has been done negligently, or inefficiently, or improperly, is a proposition which I should not listen to, unless compelled by a decision of the House of Lords. Take a contract for a lump sum to decorate a house: the contract provides that there shall be three coats of oil paint, but in one of the rooms only two coats of paint are put on, can anybody seriously say that, under these circumstances, the building owner could go and occupy the house and take the benefit of all the decorations which had been done in the other rooms without paying a penny for all the work done by the builder, just because two coats of paint had been put on in one room where there ought to have been three? I regard the present case as one of negligence and bad workmanship and not as a case where there has been an omission of any one of the items in the specification. The builders thought apparently, as they have sworn, that they had done all that was intended to be done in reference to the contract: and I suppose that the defects are due to carelessness on the part of some of the workmen or of the foreman: but the existence of these defects does not amount to a refusal by them to perform part of the contract: it simply shows negligence in the way they have done the work.

Lord Justice Pickford in his judgment said:

> Certainly I have not the slightest wish to differ from the view that, if a man agrees to do a certain amount of work for a lump sum and only does part of it, he cannot sue for the lump sum, but I cannot accept the proposition that, if a man agrees to do a certain amount of work for a lump sum, every breach which he makes of that contract by doing his work badly, or by omitting some small portion of it, is an abandonment of the contract, or is only a performance of part of the contract so that he cannot be paid his lump sum.

Lord Justice Warrington agreed with these judgments.

In *Bolton's case* the plaintiff agreed to instal a combined heating and domestic hot water system in the defendant's house at a cost of £560. It was proved that there were certain defects in the work done by the plaintiff, the main one being that the heating system did not heat adequately and gave out fumes, and to cure these defects would cost £174. The Court of Appeal, reversing the decision of the County Court judge, held that the plaintiff had not substantially completed his contract and that he was therefore not entitled to recover the contract price. Lord Justice Cairns in his judgment said:

> The main question in the case is whether the defects in workmanship found by the judge to be such as to cost £174 to repair—that is between one third and one quarter of the contract price—were of such a character and amount that the plaintiff could not be said to have substantially performed his contract. That is in my view clearly the legal principle which has to be applied in this case. In considering whether there was substantial performance, I am of opinion that it is relevant to take into account both the nature of the defects and the proprotion between the cost of rectifying them and the contract price. It would be wrong to say that the contractor is only entitled to payment if the defects are so trifling as to be covered by the *de minimis* rule.

Lord Justice Sachs in his judgment said:

> So far as the law is concerned, I would merely add that it seems to me to be compactly and accurately stated in Cheshire and Fifoot's *Law of Contract* (7th edn 1969) at page 492 in the following terms: '. . . the present rule is that, so long as there is a substantial performance, the contractor is entitled to the stipulated price, subject only to a cross-action or counterclaim for the omissions of defects in execution', and to cross-action or counterclaim I would of course add 'set off'. The converse however is equally correct—if there is not a substantial compliance the contractor cannot recover. It is upon the application of that converse rule that the plaintiff's case here fails. This rule does not now work hardly on a contractor, if only he is prepared to remedy the defects before seeking to resort to litigation to recover the lump sum. It

is entirely the fault of the contractor in this instant case that he has placed himself in a difficulty by his refusal on 4 December 1969 to remedy the defects of which complaint was being made.

Applying the principles of law laid down in these cases, with which I agree, to the facts of this case, I am satisfied that, while the cost of installing the insulation in the ceiling of the attic would be a very small figure compared with the contract price, the position is materially different from that which existed in *Dakin's case* in that the plaintiff, owing no doubt to what I have held to be an erroneous interpretation of what had been agreed in regard to the payment of the £350, has up to the present time refused to do this work which was clearly part of its contract. There has therefore been a refusal by the plaintiff to carry out part of its contract, and this amounts in law to an abandonment of the contract, which would have disentitled them to payment of the balance of the contract price until it did this work. I should also say that no question arises here as to the defendant having entered into possession and obtained any benefit from the work which has been done, as was the case in *Dakin's case* . . .

CHAPTER 20.

DISCHARGE BY NOTICE

Many contracts are for a single transaction. Some contracts are of a continuing nature. Invariably such contracts expressly provide for their termination by a stated period of notice. Should the parties have failed to cover the matter the courts have decided that contracts can be terminated by reasonable notice: *Fluid Power Technology Co. Ltd v Sperry Ltd* (Case 133). The law does not countenance the idea that a contract is permanent.

Case 133. Fluid Power Technology Co. Ltd v Sperry Ltd
High Court, unreported, 22 February 1985

The plaintiff purchased the assets of a company which had been the sole distributors of certain products and entered into two distribution contracts with the defendant. The first, in relation to hydraulic goods, provided that the contract was subject to termination by either party giving six months' notice in writing setting out in full the reasons for such termination. The other contract, in relation to pneumatic goods, was to terminate one year after its commencement unless either party earlier renewed it in writing, which neither party did, but which in practice was renewed. In December the defendant gave written notice terminating the hydraulic contract from the following June, and stating the reason as the plaintiff's inability and failure to comply with the contractual payments term. In January, the defendant gave notice terminating the pneumatic contract as from July. In January it was announced in the public press that another company was to be appointed distributors of the hydraulic goods. The plaintiff sought an injunction restraining a breach of these contracts and the questions arose as to (a) the grounds on which termination could take place, and (b) the appropriate amount of notice to be given.

Held that in relation to the hydraulic contract there was an implied obligation to exercise the termination power in a *bona fide* manner, though there was no evidence that the defendant had acted *mala fide*. In relation to the pneumatic contract it was reasonable that the contract was terminable on six months' rather than nine months' notice, that once notice was given there was an implied obligation to state the reasons and that the power must be exercised in a *bona fide* manner.

Costello J.:

. . . The next issue that arises relates to the termination of the contract. As to the hydraulic agreement, an issue arises (a) whether the obligation to give reasons implies an obligation that the reasons given will be *bona fide* ones and (b) if so, whether there has been a breach of that obligation. The issues that arise in relation to the pneumatic agreement are, (a) whether it is to be implied in the pneumatic agreement that if it is renewed that on renewal it can be terminated by a nine months' notice or a six months' notice, it being agreed that it is terminable by reasonable notice; (b) whether there is an implied obligation to state reasons for termination as was provided for in the hydraulic agreement; (c) whether there is in addition an implied obligation that the reasons given will be *bona fide* ones; and (d) whether these obligations have been breached by [the defendant].

My views on these issues are as follows. As to the hydraulic agreement, in order to avoid any possible ambiguity in the formulation of the plaintiff's case on this point, it seems to me that the plaintiff had made out a fair case that there is an implied obligation to exercise the termination power in a *bona fide* manner. This means that when the [defendant] gives reasons for termination these reasons must not be spurious ones, but it also means that if it honestly believe them to be valid, then even if they are subsequently proved to have been wrong the notice is valid. So, if honestly dissatisfied with the plaintiff as distributors, this would mean that notice of termination could be given. Secondly, I do not think that a fair case has been made out that the reasons were not *bona fide* as stated previously, and it seems to me that on the material before me that the plaintiff has not been able to show any real prospect that at the trial of the action it will show that the defendant acted *mala fide*. Of course differences have arisen between the parties. It is not possible to say how the court will resolve the disputes which have arisen between the parties, but it seems to me that the affidavits have not disclosed any case that the plaintiff has any real prospect of success in establishing either that the reasons given were spurious ones, or that the defendant did not honestly believe that the reasons they gave were valid ones. For these reasons the plaintiff on this part of the case has failed to show it has a fair case that the notice of termination given of the hydraulic agreement was invalid.

As to the pneumatic agreement, I do not think the plaintiff has shown any fair case that the agreement is terminable on a nine month notice. I think it has shown it has a fair case that it it terminable on six months' notice. Even though the agreements were separate agreements, and even though obviously drafted by different legal advisers, the fact is that the businesses these two companies carried on were the same, i.e. the business of the same parent company, and a very close relationship existed between the two businesses at the time the contracts were entered into. So it seems to me reasonable to asume that the parties intended that notice of termination of both would be of the same length. It seems to me then that the plaintiff has no reasonable prospect of showing that a nine months' notice of termination was to be given in relation to the pneumatic agreement. Secondly, I think they have made out a fair case that there is an implied obligation to state reasons once the notice is given because such a requirement was contained in the hydraulic agreement. And for the reasons which I have already given, I think there was involved in this also an implied obligation that the power to terminate would be exercised in a *bona fide* manner. But for reasons which I have already given it does not seem to me that the plaintiff has been able to make out a fair case that there was any breach of these obligations and so it follows that the termination notice of the pneumatic agreement was a valid one . . .

(See also Case 156, regarding injunction as a remedy.)

CHAPTER 21.

DISCHARGE BY FRUSTRATION

Where a contract possible to perform when made, becomes impossible to complete because of some intervening act not caused by either party, the contract is said to be discharged by impossibility of performance: *O'Crowley v Minister for Finance* (Case 134) or discharged by frustration: *Kearney v Saorstát & Continental Shipping Co. Ltd* (Case 135) and *Flynn v Great Northern Railway Co. Ltd* (Case 136). The doctrine cannot be invoked where the event which makes performance of the contract impossible was caused by the negligence of one of the parties: *Herman v Owners of S.S.Vicia* (Case 137), or where permission to perform some act is refused and the party pleading frustration has not taken reasonable steps to have the refusal withdrawn: *Byrne v Limerick Steamship Co. Ltd* (Case 138), or where the event should have been anticipated: *McGuill v Aer Lingus Teo and United Airlines Incorporated* (Case 139). A contract cannot be discharged by frustration where a term expressly covers the event which is alleged to constitute frustration: *Browne v Mulligan* (Case 140).

Case 134. O'Crowley v Minister for Finance*
High Court [1935] I.R. 536; 68 I.L.T.R. 174

The plaintiff became a judge of the Dáil Éireann Supreme Court in 1920. After the Treaty between Great Britain and Ireland was signed in December 1921 the Dáil courts continued to function for a while. In July 1922 the Minister for Home Affairs rescinded the decree of the First Dáil which had established these courts. The *Dáil Éireann (Winding Up) Act 1923* gave statutory recognition to these courts and provided that their authority was withdrawn from 30 October 1922. The plaintiff was paid his salary up to that date. Subsequently, after the enactment of the Dáil Éireann Supreme Court (Pensions) Act 1925 the plaintiff was granted a pension for life, which he accepted and was paid. In later years he reopened the question of the payment of his salary claiming that since his original office had been for life he was entitled to the payment of his salary for life.

Held that as the plaintiff's office of judge had been abolished by statute and he could no longer act in it, he was no longer entitled to be paid any salary in respect of it, any existing contract having been discharged by impossibility of performance.

Johnson J.:

. . . First of all, I may say that there is evidence of the plaintiff's appointment to a judgeship at a salary of £750, but there is no evidence save his own bare statement that he was appointed for life. The document that he produces is entitled 'The Courts of Justice of the Irish Republic'

---

* This case is entitled *O Cruadhlaoich v Minister for Finance* in the *Irish Law Times Reports*.

and purports to be a 'Provisional Constitution'; but there is no suggestion that this Constitution ever was anything other than provisional, and I must assume that everything that was done under it was provisional in its turn. Whatever authority this Dáil Éireann Supreme Court possessed or had acquired all such authority ceased and the court became extinct as on 25 July 1922, by virtue of the Act of 1923, and the possibility of a person retaining rights, whether as to salary or otherwise, in respect of an office which has come to an end passes my powers of comprehension.

This principle was applied in a Canadian case—*Reilly v The King* (1934) which came quite recently before the Judicial Committee of the Privy Council, and the judgment of Maclean J. in the Exchequer Court of Canada and, on appeal, that of the Supreme Court of Canada, were upheld. Mr C.B. Reilly had been appointed by the Governor-in-Council, on the recommendation of the Minister of Justice, a member of 'the Federal Appeal Board', constituted under a Canadian Act of Parliament, Mr Reilly being at the time a practising member of the Bar of Quebec. His term of office was extended from time to time; but on 30 May 1930, the Canadian Legislature passed an Act establishing two new boards, a pension tribunal and a pension appeal court, and as a result of that Act the office which Mr Reilly held was abolished. He was not appointed a member of either the new tribunal or the new court, nor was any compensation paid to him. Mr Reilly filed a petition of right, claiming that there was a contract between him and the Crown, and that the contract had been broken and he claimed damages. Lord Atkin, who delivered the judgment of the Judicial Committee, said that 'their Lordships do not find it necessary to express a final opinion on the theory accepted in the Exchequer Court that the relations between the Crown and the holder of a public office are in no degree constituted by contract.' He contented himself with saying that in some offices at least it was difficult to negative some contractual relations. The conclusion at which their Lordships arrived was based on this reasoning:

> But the present case appears to their Lordships to be determined by the elementary proposition that if further performance of a contract becomes impossible by legislation having that effect the contract is discharged. In the present case the office held by the appellant was abolished by statute; thenceforward it was illegal for the executive to continue him in that office or pay him any salary; and impossible for him to exercise his office . . . So far as the rights and obligations rested on contract, further performance of the contract had been made by statute impossible, and the contract was discharged.

'It is perhaps unnecessary to add,' said Lord Atkin, 'that discharged means put an end to and does not mean broken. In the result, therefore, the appellant had failed to show a breach of contract on which to found damages.'

Now, in citing that case I am not to be taken as suggesting that the class

and volume of evidence that Mr Reilly was able to adduce as to his office
and its terms and his former contractual rights are present in this case.
That is far indeed from my intention. I am merely pointing out that even if
the plaintiff's proofs were as complete as those of Mr Reilly, his claim is
still unsustainable by virtue of the extinction of the office by statute law.

But even if all these difficulties were surmounted there still remains the
deadly fact that the Oireachtas passed in 1925 an Act enabling the Minister
for Justice, with the sanction of the Minister for Finance, to grant a
pension to any person 'who *held* office as a judge of the Dáil Supreme
Court'. That Act does not attempt to define or indicate the persons for
whose benefit it was passed. It leaves that matter to those whom 'the cap
fits'; and the plaintiff was granted a pension on the basis of that statute,
and it has been paid to him ever since. Counsel says that the plaintiff
never applied for a pension under the Act. Not only did he apply for a
pension, as his letter shows, but he clamoured for it. He applied to the
Minister as a person who 'held office,' and he was granted a pension which
in the terms of the Act did not exceed two-thirds of the annual salary of
which he was in receipt 'as a judge of the Dáil Supreme Court immediately
before he ceased to hold office as such judge.' . . .

Case 135. Kearney v Saorstát & Continental Shipping Co. Ltd
Circuit Court [1943] Ir.Jur.Rep. 8

The plaintiff's son was a seaman on the defendant's merchant ship. As
a result of a collision this ship sank and the seamen were picked up by
a British merchant ship which two days later was bombed and sank
because of hostilities in which Britain was engaged and in the course of
which the plaintiff's son was killed. The plaintiff sought compensation
for the death of his son.

Held that the contract of employment was terminated with the
sinking of the ship on which the plaintiff's son served, by reason of
frustration.

Judge Davitt:

It is clear from [the relevant statutes] that the legislature contemplated that
the sinking of a ship put an end to the contract of service existing between
the sailor in the ship and the owners of the ship, and that is consistent with
the ordinary law of contract and the doctrine of frustration. When two
parties contract on the basis that a certain object will be in existence, and
that object comes to an end, then the contract must come to an end. I
must come to the conclusion that the contract of service of the deceased
seaman in this case came to an end on the sinking of his ship, and
therefore I must dismiss the application. No costs.

Case 136. Flynn v Great Northern Railway Co. Ltd
High Court (1955) 89 I.L.T.R. 46

The plaintiff was seriously injured in the course of his employment with the defendant. Some months later, after medical examination, he was reported to be unfit for work. It was apparent that his condition was such as to permanently incapacitate him from performing the duties of his employment.

Held that the contract of employment was terminated on the ground that the plaintiff's permanent incapacity was such as to frustrate the business object of the contract.

Budd J.:

. . . The precise result of the illness of a servant on a contract of service is not always easy to determine. From a perusal of the cases it would seem that in law the illness or physical incapacity of the servant will determine the contract if it is of such a nature as to frustrate the business object of the engagement. In *Poussard v Spiers* (1876), an opera singer was engaged to sing in an opera for three months, provided the opera ran so long. The plaintiff was unable to sing on the first night through illness, which was serious and of uncertain duration. It was held that the failure on the plaintiff's part went to the root of the matter and discharged the contract. The result was different in *Storey v Fulham Steel Works*, where six months illness, after two years service in a five years engagement, was held not to determine the contract. Lord Alverstone, however, in that case adopted what was said in *Jenkinson v Union Marine Insurance Co.* by Baron Bramwell as a correct statement of the law, namely, that if the illness was such as to put an end in the business sense of their business engagement and would frustrate the object of that engagement, then the employer could dismiss its servant and no action would lie against him. What Lord Alverstone said seems to indicate the necessity of the master giving notice before the contract is terminated, but that point was not at issue in the case. Lord Campbell used words in *Cuckson v Stone* which would also seem to indicate that notice would be necessary where he says that, if the plaintiff in that case had by illness become permanently incapacitated to act in the capacity of a brewer, the defendant might in the view of the court have determined the contract. Again, Lord Atkinson in *Price v Guest Keen & Nettlefolds* (1918) said that illness might be of such a permanent character that it would justify dismissal, thereby implying that notice was necessary, but again in neither of these cases was that precise point in issue. On the other hand, Scrutton L.J., in *Warburton v Co-Operative Wholesale Society Ltd* (1917) said that under the decided cases a servant incapacitated by illness and in the absence of notice does not cease to be employed unless the illness is such as seriously to interfere with or frustrate the business purpose of the contract, thereby implying that in such case notice is unnecessary. From the words used by Blackburn J., delivering the judgment of the court in *Poussard v Spiers* 'that the failure on the plaintiff's part went to the root of the matter and discharged the defendant' and from the nature of the decision, it would appear that the court in that case did not regard notice as necessary, but it is right to bear in mind that the engagement was to commence on a specific date and was of particular nature. Of recent years as a result, no doubt, of cases arising from war conditions, the doctrine of frustration has received more detailed consideration. In *Denny Mott & Dickson Ltd v Fraser* (1944), Lord Wright points out that where there is frustration a dissolution of the contract occurs automatically. Overend J., in *Byrne v Limerick Steamship Co. Ltd* (1946) (Case 138) also accepted the view that frustration operates automatically to determine the entire contract and does not depend upon the volition of the parties or even on their knowledge. It is right to add that he decided that the contract in that case had not been determined by frustration. If frustration is the test, there does not in principle seem to be any reason why a master should have to give notice to terminate a contract, already frustrated, and my view, therefore, is that notice is unnecessary.

It would seem to be a question of fact to be determined in each case as to whether or not the illness is of such a kind and duration, or likely duration, as to frustrate the business object of the contract, and I must consider what the true position is in this case, having regard to the nature of the plaintiff's illness or incapacity, and the nature of his contract. I have determined that he was a weekly wage earner whose contract was subject to be determined by a week's notice. He is a manual worker but without him and men of his grade the engines of the company cannot be properly manned and the service maintained. His incapacity is, I am satisfied, now permanent for work as a fireman. His incapacity on 16 October 1947, was such that it was the doctor's view, communicated to the company, that it would be undesirable that he should ever again resume duty as a fireman on the foot-plate, a view that has been amply substantiated by subsequent events. I am satisfied that in all the circumstances his incapacity was such at that time as to frustrate the business object of the engagement . . .

Case 137. Herman v Owners of S.S.Vicia
High Court [1942] I.R. 305

The plaintiff seaman contracted to serve on board the *S.S. Vicia* on a voyage from the USA to a port in England or Africa, or to any other port that may be required by the master or owners for the safety of the vessel, cargo and crew, and back to a final port in the USA. The owners of this Finnish registered vessel had been granted a British ship's warrant, which protected the vessel from British seizure and granted it access to all available commercial shipping facilities under British control though this had expired by the time the vessel reached Dublin. Britain declared war on Finland in December 1941. The ship's master paid off the plaintiff who sued its owners for damages for wrongful dismissal. The owners pleaded that the contract had been discharged by frustration when they were unable to obtain the British shipping warrant to enable the vessel to sail to an English port and hence on to the USA.

Held that the contract was not discharged by frustration but by the negligence of the master in not renewing the British shipping warrant. The plaintiff was entitled to compensation.

Hanna J.:

. . . What is frustration? In the case of *Joseph Constantine S.S. Line Ltd v Imperial Smelting Corporation Ltd* (1942) various definitions are given of frustration—incidental to the main question involved in that case—namely, upon whom the burden of proof lies. In that case, the ship in question, the *Kingswood*, was chartered to agents of the respondents in a voyage with ores from Port Pirie in South Australia to Europe. Before she became an 'arrived ship' at Port Pirie, there was a severe explosion in the neighbourhood of her auxiliary boiler, causing such damage that she could not perform her charter party. As the headnote says, that was 'a destruction of the essential subject-matter of the contract so as to frustrate the commercial object of the adventure'. In that respect the case differs from the one under consideration. As there was no negligence or default found with either party, it was held to discharge all liability under the charter. Viscount Simon L.C. says that 'when "frustration" in the legal sense occurs, it does not merely provide one party with a defence in an action brought by the other. It kills the contract itself and discharges both parties automatically. The plaintiff sues for breach at a past date and the defendant pleads that at that date no contract existed.' He further says that frustration depends on the terms of the contract and the surrounding circumstances of each case, as some kinds of impossibility may not discharge the contract at all.

Lord Maughan says that 'frustration is based on the presumed common intention of the parties,' and he also states that the legal rights already accrued are unaffected.

Lord Wright, while recognising frustration by the destruction of the subject-matter, gives a wider conception of impossibility and says:

Another illustration is where the actual object still exists and is available, but the object of the contract as contemplated by both parties was its employment for a particular purpose, which has become impossible, as in the Coronation cases. In these and similar cases, where there is not in the strict sense impossibility by some casual happening, there has been so vital a change in the circumstances as to defeat the contract. . . . The common object of the parties is frustrated. The contract has perished, *quoad* any rights or liabilities subsequent to the change . . . the court is exercising its powers, when it decides that a contract is frustrated, in order to achieve a result which is just and reasonable.

The converse proposition is that it is not to be held to be frustrated unless it is just and reasonable.

Lord Porter, in the same case, seems to give a larger interpretation to frustration, where he says:

Frustration is the term now in common use in cases in which the performance of a contract becomes impossible because its subject-matter has ceased to be available for the purpose for which both parties intended it to be used. He points out that in that case no question arises as to the extension of the doctrine to a case where the subject-matter of the contract is not itself destroyed but the underlying purpose alone has been frustrated.

On these principles I am of opinion that the evidence on the part of the owners is not sufficient to justify a finding of frustration of the plaintiff's contracts. Adopting the words of Lord Wright, I decline to hold that it would be just and reasonable under the circumstances to decide that the plaintiff's contracts had been frustrated. The vessel had gone from Lisbon to Tampa without a convoy and was not interfered with. She sailed for thirteen days alone in the Atlantic without a convoy and without a proper warrant. I can find no case similar in facts to this, where it has been alleged, or held to be, a frustration for the owners of the vessel, apart from any hostile act of an enemy, to be unwilling to send her to sea on account of the risks and perils of war, with possible interception or seizure. It seems to me that the vessel could have reasonably reached Cardiff to obtain bunkers as she had the undertaking of the British Ministry of Shipping to give her facilities to a port in the United Kingdom. As Lord Sumner described the rule in *Hirji Mulji v Cheong Yue S.S. Co.* (1926):

The rule as to frustration is to reconcile justice with the absolute contract. The seamen's contract was in this case an absolute contract. If the contingency was known to the parties as something which might happen and they did not provide for it, the contract ought to stand.

Upon this point of the implied term in the contract, in the case of *Emanuel v La Compagnie Fermière* (1889) Lord Esher says:

A term which was not actually contained in a written contract could not be implied unless the court came to a clear conclusion that both parties must have intended that term to be implied. It was not enough that both parties should have contemplated that a certain state of circumstances would exist. The court must be satisfied that the party against whom the implied term was to be enforced intended to bind himself that that state of circumstances should exist.

A similar principle is stated . . . in *Jacob Marcus & Co. v Credit Lyonnais* Bowen L.J. said:

One of the incidents which the English law attaches to a contract is that . . . a person who expressly contracts absolutely to do a thing not naturally impossible, is not excused for non-performance because of being prevented by *vis major*.

And in the case of *Larrinaga & Co. v Société Franco-Americaine des Phosphates* Lord Sumner said:

If the appellants' own ships were under requisition, they could have fulfilled their contract with other ships, of which they might be able to obtain the disposition.

Applying that principle to this case the agents here might have made arrangements to take the seamen back to America in other vessels, but they did not do so and relied upon frustration.

This case is obviously different, on the facts, from any other, and the critical point is the British shipping warrant. I am not satisfied that the plaintiff had information as to the British shipping warrant having expired, or that the captain did not renew it. The captain knew, and it would have been his duty to anticipate, that if he did not get it renewed to the United Kingdom while in Charleston, or Halifax, or Sydney, there might be some difficulty in Dublin, and, therefore, he should have included in the conditions of the contract the rights of the crew on the kind of frustration which actually occurred as well as frustration by 'torpedo, mine or loss'. As he did not, I find as a fact that the alleged frustration in Dublin, if the British shipping warrant was necessary and the letter from the British Ministry of Shipping insufficient, was due to the neglect of the captain who was responsible to the owners. If the full British warrant was not absolutely necessary and the letter from the British Ministry of Shipping sufficient, then there was no frustration in the port of Dublin as it would have carried the vessel to Cardiff.

For these reasons I am of opinion, when the case is carefully analysed, that in the port of Dublin there was no ground for concluding that there was impossibility of performance. There is no evidence that the British Ministry of Shipping definitely refused a new warrant and, in my judgment, the owners' agent's concern was really to reduce expenses until arrangements had been made for the trading of the vessel. If the ship had gone to Cardiff she might have got, as previously, a cargo to Lisbon and a British warrant . . .

Case 138. Byrne v Limerick Steamship Co. Ltd
High Court [1946] I.R. 138

A crew was signed on for the defendant's ship which during the voyage was to call at a British port. In such circumstances the crew-list was required to be approved by the British authorities before the ship departed Dublin. The plaintiff was signed on as a late substitute, went on board and started work. When the crew-list was supplied to the British authorities the plaintiff's permit was refused. The ship was ready to sail and could not be delayed. The master discharged the plaintiff. The only reason for the plaintiff's discharge was the refusal of the permit. The plaintiff had sailed on nine previous voyages without objection from the British authorities. There was nothing to suggest that the British authorities would have persisted in their refusal of the permit had their attention been called to this fact and had they had time to investigate. The plaintiff sued for wrongful dismissal and the defendant pleaded frustration.

Held that where an essential licence or permission is refused the party pleading frustration must prove that all reasonable steps had been taken to have the refusal withdrawn. Since this had not been done in this case the contract had not been determined by frustration and the plaintiff was entitled to damages.

Overend J.:

. . . I am clearly of opinion that the defence of frustration fails. The articles were of the kind described in s. 115, sub-s. 5. of the *Merchant Shipping Act 1894*, as a 'running agreement'. Under such an agreement the seaman is employed, not for one voyage, but for a period of time, during which two or more voyages are contemplated, and the agreement terminateş on the next half-yearly date, or with the first arrival of the ship in a home port after that date, or the discharge of the cargo consequent on that arrival. In the present case it ran from 3 February 1943 to 30 June 1943, or the first arrival of the ship in a home port after that date (Abbott, *Shipping*, 14th edn p. 225). Normally the *Kyleclare* took some four to five weeks to accomplish the round trip to the Iberian Peninsula and back to Ireland, and could complete four or five such voyages within the term of these articles.

The plaintiff had sailed on nine previous voyages since March 1941, without objection, and I see no reason to suppose that the British Permit Office would have persisted in refusing him a permit had their attention been called to this fact, and had they had time for investigation. In fact he did go to England six weeks later, and sailed in the *Lanabrone* in the autumn when he next applied to the defendant for engagement. However, at the date in question the circumstances were somewhat special, the plaintiff had signed on as a substitute in the afternoon of 3 February. It was still later that evening when the 'crew-list' was prepared and submitted to the British Permit Office. As it was a matter of urgency, the Permit Office telephoned to the company that the plaintiff was refused, and intimated that the Office would be kept open to allow a new name to be substituted, as the *Kyleclare* was ready to sail and only awaiting papers required by the British Authorities.

The company, in the interests of the owners, could not delay the ship, even if they had thought it involved a breach of the plaintiff's agreement, and told the captain he would have to get a substitute and to discharge him. This was done, and the ship sailed shortly after midnight, in the early hours of Thursday 4 February 1943.

Now, assuming, as I do, that it was impossible, from a practical point of view to undertake this voyage save under the aegis and with the facilities afforded by the British, yet the defendant has proved nothing amounting to frustration on the 3 February, as of which date the rights of the parties must be determined. Where an essential licence or permission is refused, the defendant must prove that he has taken all reasonable steps to have such refusal withdrawn: *Bakubhai & Ambalal v South Australian Farmers' Co-operative Union of Adelaide.*

The plaintiff has been given an excellent character and there is no evidence that the refusal of a permit would have been continued had it been questioned, or that he would have been refused permission to sail on any of the subsequent voyages contemplated by the articles. As I have already indicated, I must decide what were the plaintiff's rights on 3 February and without regard to the fact that the *Kyleclare* was subsequently lost.

In *F.A. Tamplin Steamship Co. Ltd v Anglo-Mexican Petroleum Products Co. Ltd* (1916), the ship—a tanker—was chartered by the respondents on a time charter for sixty months from 4 December 1912 to 4 December 1917. The ship was requisitioned by the British Government early in December 1914, and before her release was again requisitioned in February 1915. She was still under requisition at the date of the hearing in July 1916, having meantime been structurally altered to carry troops. The owners claimed that the charter had been determined. The judge of first instance, the Court of Appeal, and the majority of the House of Lords all held there had been no frustration. Lord Parker in his speech emphasises the difficulty of applying this principle of frustration in the case of a time charter in which no definite commercial adventure is contemplated, and especially where the contract is already partly performed.

In *Barras v Aberdeen Steam Trawling Fishing Co.* (1933) a seaman was employed on a running agreement for six months fishing in the North Sea. On the trawler's first return she collided with another and had to be docked for some days for repairs, the seaman being paid off. Four members of the court (Viscount Buckmaster L.C. and Lords Warrington, Russell, and Macmillan) clearly expressed the view that there was no frustration of the contract. The reasoning mentioned seems to me to apply with equal force in the present case.

It has been frequently stressed that frustration operates automatically to determine the entire contract and does not depend on the volition, or even the knowledge, of the parties: *Joseph Constantine Steamship Line Ltd v Imperial Smelting Corporation Ltd* (1942); *Hirji Mulji v Cheong Yue Steamship Co. Ltd* (1926); *Cricklewood Property and Investment Trust Ltd v Leighton's Investment Trust Ltd* (1945); *Maritime National Fish Ltd v Ocean Trawlers Ltd* (1935).

In my opinion the plaintiff's contract with the defendant company was not determined by frustration, but by his discharge by the captain on 3 February. This brings me to the next question, was this dismissal in breach of his contract? . . .

Case 139. McGuill v Aer Lingus Teoranta and United Airlines Incorporated

High Court, unreported, 3 October 1983

The plaintiff tour promoter contracted with the first defendant to fly a group of passengers return to the USA, and with the second defendant to fly the group between various destinations within the USA. A strike by the second defendant's employees began before the group were due to leave Ireland. Alternative arrangements were made but at additional expense to the plaintiff. When sued to recoup these expenses the second defendant argued that the contract had been frustrated by the strike.

Held that the second defendant was aware of the threat or possibility of a strike but, anxious to obtain the business, undertook the risk of contracting without safeguarding its position. The contract was not discharged by frustration and the plaintiff was entitled to damages.

McWilliam J.:

. . . From various authorities, the following principles appear to apply when considering a claim that a contract has been frustrated:

1. A party may bind himself by an absolute contract to perform something which subsequently becomes impossible.
2. Frustration occurs when, without default of either party, a contractual obligation has become incapable of being performed.
3. The circumstances alleged to occasion frustration should be strictly scrutinised and the doctrine is not to be lightly applied.
4. Where the circumstances alleged to cause the frustration have arisen from the act or default of one of the parties, that party cannot rely on the doctrine.
5. All the circumstances of the contract should also be strictly scrutinised.
6. The event must be an unexpected event.

7. If one party anticipated or should have anticipated the possibility of the event which is alleged to cause the frustration and did not incorporate a clause in the contract to deal with it, he should not be permitted to rely on the happening of the event as causing frustration.

It does not appear, from the authorities to which I have been referred, what principle is to apply in considering frustration of a contract in circumstances such as the present so as to establish when a contract comes to an end. No evidence was tendered on behalf of the second defendant to indicate that it claimed at any particular time that the contract had come to an end and no submission was made as to the time of the termination of the contract. The suggestion on behalf of the second defendant seems to be that, once the parties became aware of the strike, a new agreement must be implied that the contract would continue until it was clear that the strike would not be settled in time to enable the second defendant to carry the group. Although the decision in one case appears to support this proposition to some extent I am not satisfied that such a proposition should be extended to the circumstances of the present case.

A significant circumstance in the present case is the fact stated by two witnesses for the second defendant, that there had been a 'cooling-off' period of sixty days in operation prior to the strike being declared and taking effect. This must have been within the knowledge of the second defendant at all times during that period, that is to say, from 30 January 1979. It can hardly be suggested that there had not been some threat of industrial action before the 'cooling-off' period started to run and that, whatever the dispute was about, there had not previously been negotiations in progress between the second defendant and their employees. At no time was any communication about these circumstances made to the plaintiff and I conclude that this was because the second defendant felt that, if the plaintiff were made aware of the possibility of a strike, he might try to get another airline to carry the group. In my opinion this means that the second defendant, being aware of the threat or possibility of a strike—and the evidence is that the second defendant had had a somewhat similar strike a few years previously—but being anxious to obtain the business, took the risk of entering into the contract without including a provision to safeguard its position in the event of a strike taking place.

Under these circumstances I am of opinion that the second defendant is not entitled to succeed on its defence that the contract was frustrated.

I do not accept the argument made on behalf of the plaintiff: that a strike by the employees of a party cannot cause frustration of a contract. In my opinion it depends entirely on the circumstances whether it does or not, but, on the view I have formed as to the position of the second defendant, it is not necessary for me to deal with this further . . .

Case 140. Brown v Mulligan

Supreme Court, unreported, 23 November 1977

A hospital was established with funds devised in trust by a benefactor. The hospital survived for many years on funds from the trust and a grant from public funds. The governors employed the plaintiff as a doctor in the hospital. His contract of employment provided that three months' notice of its termination would be given should there be insufficient funds to enable the hospital to continue in operation. Because of the declining revenue from the trust and the withdrawal of public funds the financial position of the hospital became so critical that the funds available were insufficient to enable it to carry out the charitable objects of the trust. The governors applied to the High Court to have the small amount of funds remaining applied *cy-pres** which was granted. The governors gave the plaintiff one week's notice and three months' salary. The plaintiff sued for wrongful dismissal on the ground that once the governors had any funds they should have kept the hospital open. The defendant pleaded, *inter alia*, that the contract of employment had been frustrated by the order of the High Court.

Held that for the doctrine of frustration to apply, the event on which reliance is placed must not have been anticipated by the parties. Since the contract of employment dealt with the possible termination of the contract in the event of insufficiency of funds the doctrine of frustration was inapplicable.

Kenny J.:

. . . The doctrine of frustration of a contract has been considered in one Irish case only (*Byrne v Limerick S.S. Co.* (Case 138)) where it was dealt with very briefly. During the past seventy years it has, however, been developed and refined by many decisions of the House of Lords and the Privy Council. The expression 'the contract is frustrated' so commonly used today is misleading: the doctrine relates, not to the contract but to the events or transactions which are the basis of the contract. It is these which make performance of the contracts impossible. This apsect of the doctrine was explained by Lord Wright in *Joseph Constantine Line v Imperial Smelting Corporation* (1942):

> In more recent days, the phrase more commonly used is 'frustration of the contract' or more shortly 'frustration'. 'Frustration of the contract' however is an elliptical expression. The fuller and more accurate phrase

cy-pres is applied where the intention of a donor or testator is incapable of being literally acted upon. The courts will allow the intention to be carried into effect as nearly as may be practicable.

is 'frustration of the adventure or of the commercial or practical purpose of the contract'. The change in language corresponds to a wider conception of impossibility, which has extended the rule beyond contracts which depend on the existence, at the relevant time of a specific object . . . to cases when the essential object does indeed exist, but its condition has by some casualty been so changed as to be not available for the purposes of the contract, either at the contract date or, if no date is fixed, within any time consistent with the commercial or practical adventure.

There has been considerable judicial controversy as to its foundation. At least three possible bases for it have been suggested each of which can claim eminent judicial support. The first is that it depends upon an implied term in the contract (Viscount Simon in *Constantine Line v Imperial Smelting Corporation* or upon 'the presumed common intention of the parties' (Viscount Maugham in the same case). The second rejects wholly the implied term theory and rests the doctrine on the true construction of the contract:

> It appears to me that frustration depends, at least in most cases, not on adding any implied term but on the true construction of the terms which are, in the contract, read in light of the nature of the contract and of the relevant surrounding circumstances when the contract was made,'—Lord Reid in *Davis Contractors v Farnham U.D.C.* (1956)

And:

> So perhaps, it would be simpler to say at the outset that frustration occurs whenever the law recognises that, without default of either party, a contractual obligation has become incapable of being performed because the circumstances in which performance is called for would render it a thing radically different from that which was undertaken by the contract,—Lord Radcliffe in the same case.

The third theory—associated with Lord Wright—is that where the dispute between the parties arises from an event which they never thought of, the court imposes the solution that in the circumstances is just and reasonable (Lord Wright's *Legal Essays and Addresses*, at p. 258, and *Denny Mott & Dickson Ltd v Fraser & Co. Ltd* (1944)).

I do not think it necessary to decide which theory we should adopt because, in my opinion, the doctrine does not apply to this case. The event on which reliance is placed as terminating the contract must be unanticipated by the parties and so not mentioned in the contract. If it is dealt with in the contract, then it was within the contemplation of the parties and the doctrine cannot apply. 'Equally, if the terms of the agreement show that the parties contemplated the possibility of such an intervening circumstance arising, frustration does not occur,' per Viscount Simon in *Cricklewood Property Trust Ltd v Leightons Investment Trust Ltd* (1945). The contract dealt with the closing down of the hospital when there were not sufficient funds available to allow it to continue in operation. This is the event which happened and the parties provided in the contract for its effect on the plaintiff's position. The order of the High Court of 11 February 1974 was a recognition of the impossibility of carrying on the hospital . . .

O'Higgins C.J. and Parke J. concurred.

CHAPTER 22.

DISCHARGE BY BREACH

This method of discharging a contract occurs where one party fails to perform contractual obligations, or where that party repudiates the contract, either expressly or impliedly, without justification. But the contract is not discharged unless the other party elects to treat the breach as a repudiation.

One party to a contract may, before the time fixed for performance, indicate that the terms of the contract will not be observed. Such conduct is known as anticipatory breach: *Leeson v North British Oil & Candle Co.* (Case 141).

Some breaches of contract are so serious that the injured party is entitled to repudiate the contract. The breach is of such a fundamental character as to terminate the contract: *Robb & Co. v James* (Case 142).

As a general rule the breach of a time clause will not amount to such a breach: *Laird Brothers v City of Dublin Steampacket Co.* (Case 143), though where time is made of the essence, the result might be different.

Case 141. Leeson v North British Oil & Candle Co.
Queen's Bench (1874) 8 Ir.C.L.R. 309

The defendants contracted to supply a quantity of paraffin over a winter season to customers nominated by the plaintiff. In January the plaintiff was informed by the defendants that due to a strike it was not possible to supply the paraffin for a period of two months, by which time the season would have ended. As a consequence the plaintiff refused to take further orders from customers apprehensive that should he be unable to fulfil such orders his customers might sue him for breach of contract. The plaintiff sued for damages for loss of the orders and the defendants argued that the plaintiff should have placed the orders with the defendants on the possibility that supplies might have been obtainable elsewhere.

Held that the statement by the defendants of their inability to perform the contract was a breach on which the plaintiff could successfully sue.

Whiteside C.J.:

. . . A contract is to be regarded in reference to its subject matter. In this instance it was for the sale of a certain quantity of oil which was to be delivered by the defendants to persons named by the plaintiff in the orders sent by him from time to time. For a while the contract was kept, and the orders of the plaintiff were duly executed by the defendants, but after a time the defendants became irregular in the delivery of the oil. The plaintiff thereupon complained to their agent, who advised him to write direct to the manager in Glasgow. He did so, and subsequently the agent to whom he showed the letter he had received in reply pointedly informed him that the defendants had no oil to give them. It has been contended that, notwithstanding this announcement by the agent of the defendants, the plaintiff should have continued as before to send his orders for oil pursuant to the contract, and that having failed to do so, he is not entitled to retain his verdict. We are of opinion that he was quite justified in accepting the statement made by the defendants' agent, and in acting upon it, and that he was not any longer bound by the contract.

It has been argued that although the defendants may have been at the time this statement was made incapable of supplying the oil, yet their inability might have been merely temporary, and it might have passed away altogether in a short time. Their contract was, however, to deliver whenever the plaintiff transmitted an order. It does not appear that there was any particular time fixed until the arrival of which they could not be required to deliver, so that the argument which has been suggested does not apply . . .

Case 142. Robb & Co. v James
Queen's Bench (1881) 15 I.L.T.R. 59

Goods were sold at an auction to the plaintiffs by the defendant. It was a term of the contract that the price be paid and the goods removed within twenty-four hours. Some dispute arose concerning the price. When the plaintiffs refused to pay the price demanded by the defendant and refused to remove the goods, the defendant resold the goods. The plaintiffs sued for damages.

Held that the plaintiffs' failure to fulfil one of the essential terms of the contract entitled the defendant to treat the contract as abandoned by the plaintiffs. The action was dismissed.

May C.J.:

On their pleadings it is admitted that the plaintiffs absolutely refused to perform the most essential term of the contract, viz., to pay for and remove the goods of which they had been declared the purchasers. It is well established that, under such circumstances, the seller may treat the contract as abandoned by the purchaser, and may detain and re-sell the goods. The law confers this right on the seller wholly independently of any consent of the purchaser.

O'Brien, Fitzgerald and Barry JJ. concurred.

Case 143. Laird Brothers v City of Dublin Steampacket Co.
High Court (1900) 34 I.L.T.R. 9

By a contract in writing the plaintiffs agreed to build and deliver a ship to the defendants on or before 1 August 1897. The ship was not delivered until 18 September 1897 but otherwise the contract was duly carried out and the defendants suffered no loss by reason of the delay. The contract provided that should the ship be handed over by the contract date the defendants should pay £5,000 to the plaintiffs, being the balance due on the price of the ship. The defendants refused to pay over the £5,000 and the plaintiffs sued for it.

Held that the delivery of the ship on the contract date was not of the essence of the contract so as to constitute a condition precedent to the plaintiffs' right to recover the £5,000.

Andrews J.:

. . . Now in the present case it is admitted that the defendants got from the plaintiffs a vessel in all respects in accordance with the contract between them, and the only particular in which the contract was not fully and completely performed on the plaintiffs' part was that the vessel was not delivered on 1 August, nor until 18 September. It is impossible to hold that this delay went to the root of the matter, so as to render the performance of the rest of the contract by the plaintiffs a thing different in substance from what the defendants stipulated for. Had the defendants sustained any loss by reason of the delay, it could have been compensated for in damages. Their loss, if any, might have been comparatively inconsiderable, but if the stipulation in question were held to be a condition precedent, no matter how small the defendants' loss might be, the plaintiffs' loss would be £5,000, and on the now admitted facts their loss would be £5,000, though the defendants have sustained no loss at all . . .

Are the words of the clause commencing 'and if this present contract shall be in all respects duly performed by the said contractors,' so 'precise, express, and strong' when taken in connection with the entire contract that the intention, *prima facie* so unreasonable, is the only one compatible with the terms employed? Taking the whole of the contract together, and applying the recognised rules of construction, and having regard to what has been decided in a variety of cases as regards words capable by themselves in their strict literal sense of constituting a condition precedent, and yet not receiving that construction, I do not think that the words I am now dealing with either necessarily or reasonably show that the parties intended that the delivery of the vessel on the precise 1 August should be a condition precedent to the payment of the balance of the contract price, amounting to £5,000 . . . Then arises the question, do the stipulations in the contract, respecting the payment of the £5,000, constitute that amount of liquidated damages for the breach of contract in relation to the delivery of the vessel on the 1 August or only a penalty to secure such delivery? This also is a question of construction to be determined upon the entire contract itself. Applying then what I think ought now to be regarded as the settled rule on this question, I am of opinion that the stipulations in the contract in question in the case respecting the payment by the defendants to the plaintiffs of the last instalment of £5,000 of the contract price of the *Connaught* amount, at the furthest, to make the withholding of it a penalty only, so far as the non-performance of the plaintiffs' agreement to deliver the vessel on the 1 August 1897, is concerned, and as it is admitted that there was no other breach or non-performance of the contract on the part of the plaintiffs, and that the defendants sustained no damage by the delay in the delivery of the vessel, I find for the plaintiffs that they are entitled to payment by the defendants of the £5,000 sued for, and I give judgment for the plaintiffs accordingly with costs.

PART FOUR

REMEDIES IN CONTRACT LAW

There are a variety of remedies available in contract law. The remedy sought will be the one considered most appropriate to the circumstances of the party seeking the assistance of the courts. In such proceedings the injured party may seek the general remedy of damages, or some form of specific relief such as specific performance, injunction, rescission or rectification.

CHAPTER 23.

DAMAGES

An award of damages following a breach of contract is designed to compensate the injured party. A party in breach of contract is not liable to compensate for all loss resulting from the breach of contract: *Hadley v Baxendale* (Case 144), *Wilson v Dunville* (Case 145) and *Waller v Great Western Railway (Ireland) Co.* (Case 146). It is a general rule that where there is a breach of contract to pay a sum of money nothing can be recovered in excess of that sum except interest: *Parker v Dickie* (Case 147). But where the money is to be used for a particular purpose known to the defaulting party damages in excess of the sum may be awarded: *Mackenzie v Corballis* (Case 148).

The courts may award damages for inconvenience or loss of enjoyment when these are within the presumed contemplation of the parties as likely to result from the breach of contract: *Johnson v Longleat Properties Ltd* (Case 149).

Damages to cover loss of profits will be awarded where it is appropriate: *Hickey & Co. Ltd v Roches Stores (Dublin) Ltd* (Case 150).

The injured party must mitigate his or her loss. Loss attributable to a deliberate decision of the injured party is not recoverable.

The inflationary decrease in the purchasing power of money

between the date or the breach and the date of the award may or may not be recoverable: *Hickey & Co. Ltd v Roches Stores (Dublin) Ltd* (Case 150).

As a general rule the damages awarded are not decreased to take account of the burden of taxation on those damages: *Hickey & Co. Ltd v Roches Stores (Dublin) Ltd* (Case 150).

Where the parties to the contract determine the amounts to be payable on a breach, this term is known as the liquidated damages clause. The courts will enforce such terms provided they are not considered to be in the nature of a penalty clause: *Schiesser International (Ireland) Ltd v Gallagher* (Case 151).

Case 144. Hadley v Baxendale
(1854) 9 Exch. Rep. 341

The plaintiff owner of a mill sent a broken shaft to the defendant carrier to be conveyed for repair with the instruction that it be transported immediately. The delivery was unreasonably delayed by the defendant in consequence of which the shaft was not returned to the plaintiff until some days after it should have been returned whereby the plaintiff suffered loss of profits and sued the defendant for damages.

Held that where two parties have made a contract, which one of them has broken, the damages which the other party ought to receive in respect of such breach should be such as may fairly be considered either arising naturally, i.e. according to the usual course of things, from such breach of contract itself, or such as may reasonably be supposed to have been in the contemplation of both parties at the time the contract was made, as the probable result of the breach of it. In this case the loss of profits cannot reasonably be considered such a consequence of the breach of contract as could have been fairly and reasonably contemplated by both the parties when they made the contract, and the action should be dismissed.

Alderson B.:

. . . Now we think the proper rule in such a case as the present is this: Where two parties have made a contract which one of them has broken, the damages which the other party ought to receive in respect of such breach of contract should be such as may fairly and reasonably be considered either arising naturally, i.e. according to the usual course of things, from such breach of contract itself, or such as may reasonably be supposed to have been in the contemplation of both parties, at the time they made the contract, as the probable result of the breach of it. Now, if the special circumstances under which the contract was actually made were communicated by the plaintiff to the defendant, and thus known to both parties, the damages resulting from the breach of such a contract, which they would reasonably contemplate, would be the amount of injury which would ordinarily follow from a breach of contract under these special circumstances so known and communicated. But, on the other hand, if these special circumstances were wholly unknown to the party breaking the contract, he, at the most, could only be supposed to have had in his contemplation the amount of injury which would arise generally, and in the great multitude of cases not affected by any special circumstances, from such a breach of contract. For, had the special circumstances been known, the parties might have specially provided for the breach of contract, by special terms as to the damages in that case; and of this advantage it would be very unjust to deprive them. Now the above principles are those by which we think the jury ought to be guided in estimating the damages arising out of any breach of contract. It is said that other cases, such as breaches of contract in the non-payment of money, or in the not making a good title to land, are to be treated as exceptions from this, and as governed by a conventional rule. But as, in such cases, both parties must be supposed to be cognisant of that well-known rule, these cases may, we think, be more properly classed under the rule above enunciated as to cases under known special circumstances, because there both parties may reasonably be presumed to contemplate the estimation of the amount of damages according to the conventional rule. Now, in the present case, if we are to apply the principles above laid down, we find that the only circumstances here communicated by the plaintiff to the defendants at the time the contract was made, were, that the article to be carried was the broken shaft of a mill, and that the plaintiff's were the millers of that mill. But how do these circumstances show reasonably that the profits of the mill must be stopped by an unreasonable delay in the delivery of the broken shaft by the carrier to the third person? Suppose the plaintiff had another shaft in his possession put up or putting up at the time, and that he only wished to send back the broken shaft to the engineer who made it; it is clear that this would be quite consistent with the above circumstances, and yet the unreasonable delay in the delivery would have no effect upon the intermediate profits of the mill. Or, again, suppose that, at the time of the delivery to the carrier, the machinery of the mill had been in other respects defective, then, also, the same results would follow. Here it is true that the shaft was actually sent back to serve as a model for a new one, and that the want of a new one was the only cause of the stoppage of the mill, and that the loss of profits really arose from not sending down the new shaft in proper time, and that this arose from the delay in delivering the broken one to serve as a model. But it is obvious that, in the great multitude of cases of millers sending off broken shafts to third persons by a carrier under ordinary circumstances, such consequences would not, in all probability, have occurred; and these special circumstances were here never communicated by the plaintiff to the the defendants. It follows, therefore, that the loss of profits here cannot reasonably be considered such a consequence of the breach of contract as could have been fairly and reasonably contemplated by both the parties when they made this contract. For such loss would neither have flowed naturally from the breach of this contract in the great multitude of such cases occurring under ordinary circumstances, nor were the special circumstances, which perhaps, would have made it a reasonable and natural consequence of such breach of contract, communicated to or known by the defendant. The judge ought, therefore, to have told the jury that, upon the facts then before them, they ought not to take the loss of profits into consideration at all in estimating the damages.

Case 145. Wilson v Dunville

Exchequer Division (1879) 6 L.R. Ir. 210

The plaintiff purchased from the defendant a quantity of grain, warranted by the defendant as being good, sound and merchantable. These grains were ordinarily used in feeding cattle, as the defendant knew, though the sale to the plaintiff was not expressly made for that purpose. The substance delivered to the plaintiff and which was used by him in feeding cattle contained particles of deleterious matter which had become accidently intermixed with the grain during a fire which had occurred at the defendant's premises. The cattle fed with the grain were poisoned and died. The plaintiff sued for the loss of the cattle.

Held that the defendant was liable for the ordinary consequence of his action and it was immaterial whether the actual breach was within the contemplation of the parties, or whether the breach was foreseen or unforeseen.

Palles C.B.:

. . . For the purpose of rendering a defendant responsible for damages which in the ordinary course of things flow from a particular breach, it is unnecessary that the actual breach of contract which ensued should have been within the contemplation of the parties. For anything which amounts to a breach of contract, whether foreseen or unforeseen, the party who breaks the contract is responsible. In the present case the delivery of poison as food did not cease to be the defendant's act because of any want of knowledge of the nature of the thing delivered. Nor was the plaintiff by reason of the absence of knowledge in them the less entitled to act upon their contract that the thing sold was grains, or the less damnified by its being in fact poison. It is because the consequences of the defendant's acts are not themselves necessarily the acts of the defendant, that the liability for consequences is limited. If those consequences result solely from the act in question, and a usual state of things, they are the ordinary and usual consequences of that act, and the defendant is liable.

Case 146. Waller v Great Western Railway (Ireland) Co.
Court of Appeal (1879) 4 L.R. Ir. 376

The defendants agreed to transport the plaintiff's horses to Dublin. When the defendants failed to perform the contract the plaintiff sent the horses by road. The horses, which were in soft condition, deteriorated further in condition because of the journey and while some remained unsold, those that were disposed of were sold below the expected price. Had the horses been in hard condition they would have borne the journey better. The plaintiff sued for all his loss.

Held that the defendants were not liable for all the loss occasioned by the breach of contract but only for the deterioration which the horses, if in ordinary condition and fit to make the journey, would have suffered together with the time and labour expended on the journey.

FitzGibbon L.J.:

It is impossible to hold those who break contracts answerable for all consequences, however remote, unexpected or serious; and hence, in each case it must be decided whether the damage which has arisen is so closely connected with the breach as to make it just and reasonable to hold the person in default liable to make compensation for it. This question of remoteness of damage should be decided by the court . . . and, though the general principle of decision may be easily stated, its application must depend upon the special circumstances of the particular case . . . The general principle is, that the person breaking his contract must answer for the necessary, natural, or probable consequences of his default, and for those which ought to have been within the reasonable contemplation of both parties when making their contract, as likely to arise from its breach. These are not separate definitions: it is presumed that every necessary, natural and probable result was contemplated by the parties. But if the injured party wishes to go beyond presumption, he may prove that any specified result was, in fact, contemplated as likely to arise from a breach of the particular contract.

To recover compensation, however, for extraordinary damage, he must show that the defendant ought to have contemplated, or did in fact contemplate it, as likely to arise, and undertook, expressly or by implication, in case of breach, to answer for it.

The Court of Queen's Bench held that the injury sustained in this case was a natural and probable consequence of the breach, and also was, or ought to have been, contemplated by the parties as likely to arise.

I am quite unable to agree with this decision; it seems to me to rest on a confusion of the enforced journey which the horses took, and which was a probable or perhaps a necessary consequence of the failure to send them by train, with the lameness and other serious injury, and the depreciation at a particular sale, which followed from that journey, and for which it is conceded that the jury have compensated the plaintiff . . .

Morris C.J. and Deasy L.J. concurred.

Case 147. Parker v Dickie

Common Pleas (1879) 4 L.R. Ir. 244

The defendant solicitor was employed to raise a sum on the mortgage of the plaintiff's property. The defendant allowed portion of the amount to remain in his hands for some time before remitting it to the plaintiff. When the plaintiff sued for damages the defendant paid into court a sum sufficient, with payments made before the action was brought, to cover the amount raised on the mortgage together with a sum for interest. No special damage was alleged or proved by the plaintiff.

Held that the plaintiff was not entitled to damages in excess of the sum so paid into court.

Lawson J.:

It is quite settled that where the action is brought to recover a money demand, the proper measure of damages is the interest of the money during the period it has remained in the hands of the debtor. The question is, does that rule apply to this case? and, in my opinion, it does. The action is for breach of contract or duty in not paying over the money. The defendant has lodged in court interest on the sum calculated at £10 per cent., as the plaintiff was, at the time the money should have been remitted to him, in New Zealand. No special damage is stated or proved. The question of damages was left at large to the jury, and they have given a verdict for £160, which exceeds the amount lodged. I cannot ascertain on what principle these damages were ascertained, and I think it would be very dangerous in actions against an agent or solicitor, or other accounting party, for not paying over his balance, to leave it open to the jury to mulct the defendant according to their notions of the amount of punishment he deserved. In *Fletcher v Tayleur* (1855), Mr Justice Willes says: 'No matter what the amount of inconvenience sustained by the plaintiff in the case of non-payment of money, the measure of damages is the interest of the money only.' In *Hamlin v Great Northern Railway Co.*, Pollock C.B. thus lays down the rule: 'In the case of wrongs not founded on contract, the damages are entirely a question for the jury, who may consider the injury to the feelings and many other matters which have no place in questions of contract. In actions for breaches of contract the damages must be such as are capable of being appreciated or estimated.'

Morris C.J. gave a concurring judgment.

Case 148. Mackenzie v Corballis
King's Bench (1905) 31 I.L.T.R. 28

The defendant, returning from South Africa with his family, engaged the plaintiff as a children's nurse on conditions which included the provision that should the plaintiff leave the defendant's employment her return fare to South Africa would be paid by the defendant. When the plaintiff left her employment the defendant refused to pay the fare and she sued for damages to cover lodgings and loss of income which she had incurred due to her inability, because of the lack of funds which resulted from the defendant's breach of contract, to return to South Africa.

   Held that the general rule of law that for a mere breach of a contract to pay a sum of money nothing can be recoverd beyond the actual sum due with interest does not apply to the case of a contract in which there are terms showing that injurious consequences of a particular character may result from the non-payment of the money as, for example, where the money is to be paid for a particular purpose known to the party in default.

Andrews J.:

. . . The argument proceeded on the question whether the plaintiff was entitled to nominal or substantial damages. In my opinion this case is not governed by the settled general rule of law—that in the case of non-payment of money the measure of damages is merely the amount of the debt with interest. The foundation of the rule, that nothing beyond this can be recovered, is that the uncertain consequences that may happen by reason of the non-payment of the sum of money cannot be regarded as flowing naturally from the breach of the contract or within the contemplation of the parties at the time they entered into the contract. But this rule of law does not apply to the case of a special contract in which there are terms showing that injurious consequences of a particular character may result from the non-payment of the money, and which consequences may, therefore, be taken to have been in the contemplation of the parties at the time. What was laid down by the court in *Fletcher v Tayleur* (1855) had reference only to a common money demand. In *Wallis v Smith*, Jessel J. in his judgment, was referring to the general rule as to non-payment of a simple money demand where there was no special contract. He says:

> It has always appeared to me that the doctrine of the English Law as to non-payment of money—the general rule being that you cannot recover damages because it is not paid by a certain day—is not quite consistent with reason.

If the money was to be paid with no reference to any particular purpose the damages sustained have been held to be too remote. Here, however, the defendant agreed to pay the plaintiff money for the specific purpose of meeting the expenses of her return to South Africa. This special agreement may reasonably be supposed to have brought it within the defendant's contemplation that the plaintiff might suffer damage through being detained by reason of not having any funds to return to South Africa. Consequently, I am of opinion that the damage here comes within the principle of *Hadley v Baxendale* (Case 144). The principle on which special damage has been held recoverable has also been laid down in cases dealing with the liability of carriers. The case of *Millen v Brash & Co.*, went very far in the direction of imposing liability. In *Prehn v Royal Bank of Liverpool* the court held that the general rule of law was not applicable, the plaintiffs having suffered special damage. I am, therefore, of opinion that the plaintiff in the present case was not limited to merely nominal damages.

Gibson and Boyd JJ. concurred.

Case 149. Johnson v Longleat Properties Ltd
High Court, unreported, 19 May 1976

The defendant agreed to build a house for the plaintiff. A dispute arose between the parties over its condition after the plaintiff had taken possession of it. On one occasion the plaintiff moved out of the house in order that the remedial work could be done. The plaintiff sued the defendant for damages for the cost of further remedial work and for inconvenience.

Held that the damages to be awarded for the cost of the remedial work were to be measured at the date of the breach and not at the later date of the court proceedings on the ground that the plaintiff had not mitigated his loss but he was entitled to damages for inconvenience.

McMahon J.:

. . . A further question arises as to the time at which the cost of necessary remedial works should be taken. It is clear on the evidence that by November 1973 the plaintiff knew that the defendant intended to do no further work on the house and the plaintiff would have to take the necessary steps to have any remaining defects put right. In England the law as settled by the decisions in *Mertens v Home Freeholds Co.* (1921) and the decision of the House of Lords in *Eastham Corporation v Bernard Sunley & Sons Ltd* (1966) is that the measure of damges is the amount it would actually cost the employer to complete a contract work as it was originally intended and in a reasonable manner and at the earliest reasonable opportunity. This measure is arrived at by applying the first limb of the rule in *Hadley v Baxendale* (Case 144) that the damages which the injured party ought to receive in respect of a breach of contract should be such as may fairly and reasonably be considered as arising naturally, i.e. according to the usual course of things, from such breach of contract itself. As the same principle applies in our law it appears to me that it should lead to the same result and this would exclude from the measure of damages loss which is attributable to a deliberate decision of the injured party. In the present case in my opinion the delay in carrying out remedial works and the consequent extra cost over and above what such works would have cost if carried out in November 1973 must be attributed to the plaintiff's decision in a period of rising costs to allow the defects to remain in existence until this litigation is concluded and that decision cannot in my view be regarded as either a reasonable or a necessary consequence of the defendant's breach of contract. Accordingly the proper cost of the necessary remedial works is their cost in November 1973 . . .

There remains the claim, [which] relates to inconvenience suffered by the plaintiff through having to vacate his house while remedial works were being carried out, that was dealt with by agreement between the parties when the plaintiff by arrangement with the defendant was accommodated free of charge in a hotel in April and May 1972, and no further claim can arise under that head. What the plaintiff has put forward is a claim for damages for inconvenience and loss of enjoyment. This head of damages in actions for breach of contract has only recently received recognition and that mainly because of defaults by travel agencies as in *Jarvis v Swan Tours Ltd* (1973).

It appears to me that in principle damages may be awarded for inconvenience or loss of enjoyment when these are within the presumed contemplation of the parties as likely to result from the breach of contract. That will usually be the case in contracts to provide entertainment or enjoyment but there is no reason why it should not also be the case in other types of contract where the parties can foresee that enjoyment or convenience is likely to be an important benefit to be obtained by one party from the due performance of the contract. In my view the present contract falls within the class for breach of which damages may be awarded for inconvenience or loss of enjoyment, but there is no evidence that, apart from the period when the plaintiff and his family removed to the hotel, his enjoyment or convenience in living in the house was affected by structural defects. So far as the plaintiff's sojourn in the hotel is concerned, that took place upon terms agreed between the plaintiff and the defendant and which are intended to and did satisfy all claims of the plaintiff arising out of that instant. The repairs necessary to make the central heating installation work properly will obviously lead to substantial inconvenience on the part of the plaintiff and his family because these will involve having workmen in the house and taking up carpets and tiles and excavating the concrete sub-floor in order to expose heating ducts. In my view damages should be recovered for this inconvenience and I measure the damages at £200 on this head.

Case 150. Hickey & Co. Ltd v Roches Stores (Dublin) Ltd
High Court [1980] I.L.R.M. 107

The plaintiff contracted to retail fashion fabrics in the defendant's premises on a profit-sharing basis. The agreement contained provisions relating to termination, the payment of compensation and an undertaking by the defendant not to sell fashion fabrics for 12 months after termination. The defendant terminated the agreement without notice, compensation or the giving of the undertaking. The plaintiff was awarded damages in the High Court (a) for loss of profit during the period of notice, (b) for the loss occasioned by the defendant continuing to trade for the 12 months after termination, and (c) for loss occasioned by the benefits obtained through the defendant trading with the goodwill built up from its association with the plaintiff, less an amount earned by the plaintiff in mitigation of damages through trading elsewhere. The parties were unable to agree these amounts to be awarded and they returned to the court four years later for this purpose. In addition the plaintiff claimed an upward adjustment in the sums to be awarded to take account of the inflationary decrease in the purchasing power of money and the defendant argued for a deduction in the award to take account of the burden of taxation on it.

Held that in applying the general principles the plaintiff had not established that such a factor as the inflationary decrease in the purchasing power of money was necessary to put it in the same position, as far as money could do so, as if its rights under the contract had been observed, since the sums would have become part of the plaintiff's general income and susceptible to loss and depreciation. Nor could it have reasonably been in the contemplation of the parties at the time of entering into the contract that an award would be made four years after the breach was declared. Since the damages to be awarded to the plaintiff would be taxable in its hands as the equivalent of income earned in the ordinary way, it would not be appropriate to make any deduction under this heading from the gross amount awarded to the plaintiff.

Finlay P.:

Counsel, on behalf of the plaintiff, stated this portion of the claim upon the simple proposition that the loss suffered by the plaintiff, having been incurred by them in the years 1972 to 1976 and having been calculated in accordance with the figures actually lost during those three years, bearing in mind the very significant decrease in the purchasing power of money since that period, if they are now paid by the defendant those figures only, they are not fully and adequately compensated and in particular cannot be said to have been put in the same position as if the breach of contract had not occurred.

He relied in the first instance on the well known decision of the House of Lords in *Livingstone v Rawyards Coal Co.* (1880) and in particular upon that portion of the opinion of Lord Blackburn in which he stated:

> The point may be reduced to a small compass when you come to look at it. I do not think there is any difference of opinion as to its being a general rule that, where any injury is to be compensated by damages, in settling the sum of money to be given for reparation of damages you should as nearly as possible get at that sum of money which will put the party who has been injured, or who has suffered, in the same position as he would have been in if he had not sustained the wrong for which he is now getting his compensation or reparation.

He relied in addition upon my own decision in *Quinn v Quality Homes Ltd* (1977) in which, in a case concerning a warranty with regard to the structural condition of a house, I assessed damages on the basis of the cost of obtaining alternative accommodation at the time of trial rather than at the time when the faults were first discovered. He also submitted that the same principle appeared to have been accepted, if not expressly, impliedly, by the Supreme Court in *Munnelly v Calcon Ltd* (1978) and pointed also to the decision of the Supreme Court under the Landlord and Tenant Act with regard to the calculation of rent upon renewal of leases in *Byrne v Loftus* (1978) which clearly involves an acceptance or an appreciation by the court of the consequences of inflation. Counsel, who on behalf of the defendant dealt with this portion of the argument, contended, firstly, that damages for breach of contract in a case such as the present are clearly confined on principle to damages within the contemplation of the parties and reasonably foreseeable by them having regard to their knowledge, and that the effects and extent of inflation could not come within that category.

He further submitted, in the alternative, that the claim to apply an inflationary factor on the losses assessed was nothing more than a substituted form of claim for interest and that the decisions and principles applicable clearly inhibited the court from granting interest in a case of this description. Neither counsel could refer me to any decision, nor am I aware of any, dealing directly with a claim for an increase in losses assessed consisting of a factor based on a decrease in the purchasing power of money between the date when the losses were incurred and the date when judgment came to be given.

I have considered the submissions made to me on this issue and the cases to which I have been referred and I have come to the following conclusions. I am not satisfied that either the decision in *Munnelly v Calcon Ltd* or the decision in *Quinn v Quality Homes Ltd* is of any direct or real assistance to the resolution of this issue. Both of those cases appear to me to have proceeded directly upon the question as to the steps which the injured party might have taken to mitigate his loss rather than on any question of a simple or direct increase of the loss suffered as ascertained by an inflationary factor.

For the resolution of this issue, therefore, it is in my view necessary to return to the fundamental principles upon which damages in cases of breach of contract should be assessed. For the purpose of this case I would accept those principles as stated in *Hadley v Baxendale* (Case 144) and re-stated in the judgment of Asquith L.J. in *Victoria Laundry (Windsor) Ltd v Newman Industries Ltd* (1949) subject to the comments made on that decision by the House of Lords in *C. Czarnikow Ltd v Koufos; The Heron II* (1969).

In particular, as relevant to the issue now being considered, I would adopt the propositions set out in the judgment of Asquith L.J. in the *Victoria Laundry case* namely:

(1). It is well settled that the governing purpose of damages is to put the party whose rights have been violated in the same position, so far as money can do so, as if his rights had been observed . . .

(2). In cases of breach of contract the aggrieved party is only entitled to recover such part of the loss actually resulting as was at the time of the contract reasonably foreseeable as liable to result from the breach.

(3). What was at that time reasonably so foreseeable depends on the knowledge then possessed by the parties or, at all events, by the party who later commits the breach.

The comments of these statements of principle arising from the decision of the House of Lords in *C. Czarnikow Ltd v Koufos: The Heron II* may be summarised as being restricted to the question as to what is reasonably foreseeable and as indicating that there should be considered as being reasonably foreseeable only such matters as were not unlikely to occur, excluding matters likely to occur only in a small minority of cases or being very unusual.

Adopting these principles, it is first necessary it seems to me for the resolution of this issue to consider whether the application of an inflationary factor to the figures assessed as loss incurred in years 1972 to 1976 is something which is necessary to put the plaintiff in the same position, so far as money can do, as if their rights under the contract had been observed.

On the facts of this case I am not satisfied that the plaintiff has established that this is so. What the plaintiff lost in the periods concerned were ordinary trading profits. Had they been earned as the contract provided, they would have become part of the general income of the plaintiff company and would presumably have either been applied in part or in whole as dividends to individual shareholders, towards defraying the company's debts, liabilities and running costs or towards the creation of some form of reserve. In the absence of proof, which did not occur in this case, of the manner in which the company's income was applied in the intervening period it would appear to me to be an unwarrantable assumption that such trading profits would now be held by this company in full, exempt from any intervening loss or depreciation, and so increased that their present value expressed in currency had the same purchasing power as would the profits have had when originally earned.

The second issue which arises, namely as to whether the defendant, at least having regard to its knowledge at the time of the formation of this contract, could reasonably have foreseen in the manner which I have outlined this particular consequence of its breach, depends upon the consideration of a number of different factors. The breach of this contract occurred in part at least upon the service of what was held to be the improper notice of termination in December 1971 and was concluded by the continued trading by the defendant in fashion fabrics after 2 February 1972. The plaintiff's cause of action for damages for breach of contract then clearly arose, and whilst it could only then be formulated upon the basis of estimates with regard to the amount of the loss as distinct from the way in which it has been formulated largely dependent upon actual experience, it was a cause of action which could immediately have been pursued. Under the terms of the agreement, the first step in pursuance of the plaintiff's claim was to submit the question as to whether the defendant had been justified in its method and timing of termination to arbitration, and the award of the arbitrator was not delivered until 12 July 1973. These proceedings were instituted in March 1975 by plenary summons and, an issue having been directed by the court in March 1976 by way of preliminary issue on the principles applicable to the assessment of damages, judgment was delivered in that in July 1976. From July 1976 to July 1979 a delay in bringing forward the further assessment of the damages in pursuance of the principles decided in that judgment originated from the very practical and commonsense attempt of the parties, by the exchange of figures and information, to reach agreement on all or part of the damages. From August 1979 until the present, the delay in determining this issue was due to an application in July 1979 by the defendant for an adjournment, which was granted by me only on terms that it pay interest on the amount eventually recovered by the plaintiffs from that date until the final determination in the High Court, and therefore that period is not part of the claim in relation to inflation and the decrease in the purchasing power of money.

On this short recital of the facts, in which I do not suggest that there has been established to me culpability on the part of either the plaintiff or the defendant, the question which seems to me to arise is as to whether, not only what might be described as the ravages of inflation but also what is in fact claimed, namely the effect of inflation over such a lengthy period could have been a heading of loss, within the principles which I have set out in this judgment, reasonably within the contemplation of the defendants. I have come to the decision that it could not. I think it reasonable to infer that any person engaged in trade as the defendants had been in the decade or so before 1969 would have been able to foresee as a not unlikely event that inflation and a consequential decrease in the purchasing power of money would probably continue. It is not, however, in my view on the evidence before me a reasonable inference to draw in this case that the defendants in 1969, at the time of the formation of this contract, could have reasonably foreseen even if they had directed their mind towards it that, in the event of a breach by them of the contract in 1971, the assessment of the damages recoverable by the plaintiff as a consequence of that breach would not be determined until 1980. On this basis I conlude that an increase on the loss assessed by me to compensate for the inflationary decrease in the purchasing power of money is not an allowable heading of loss in this case.

The defendant in making this submission relied in the main upon the decision of Kenny J. in *Glover v BLN Ltd (No. 2)* (1973). Kenny J. there held that, in assessing damages for wrongful dismissal consisting of loss of salary, commission and fees, so much of the sum being awarded as did not exceed £3,000 and was therefore not chargeable to income tax pursuant to the provisions of [the relevent statute] should be reduced by an appropriate amount for the income tax and surtax which the plaintiff would have paid upon such salary, commission or fees had he earned them in his employment. In reaching that decision the learned judge followed and applied the decision of the House of Lords in *British Transport Commission v Gourley* (1956) and since in that case it has been conceded that the damages recoverable were not chargeable to tax he independently examined the question as to whether, in an action for wrongful dismissal, damages for loss of earnings, fees or commission are . . . chargeable to tax. His decision was that they are not . . .

The defendant's submission in short is that, whereas the decision of Kenny J. in *Glover v BLN Ltd (No. 2)* and the cases therein referred to all refer expressly and exclusively to a breach of a contract for services and to a claim for damages for wrongful dismissal, the principles contained in them can and must be equally applied to a claim for damages consisting of loss of trading profits.

I accept and follow the decision of Kenny J. in *Glover v BLN Ltd (No.2)* and therefore proceed upon the basis that, if the damages recoverable by the plaintiff in this case are not chargeable to tax when recovered and coming to their hands, it is appropriate that a deduction from the gross amount of the loss suffered by them should be made and calculated in respect of corporation profit tax and income tax which they would have paid had the profits in respect of which the damages are assessed been earned by them.

The only issue remaining, therefore, with regard to this submission, is the issue as to whether damages assessed as I have already assessed them in this judgment as loss of net trading profits by the plaintiff due to a breach of the trading agreement contract by the defendant are or are not chargeable to tax. Having carefully considered the submissions made to me and the cases referred to I have come to the conclusion that such damages are chargeable to tax and that, therefore, it is not appropriate as the defendant claims to make any deduction from the gross amount of them when assessed in respect of liability for corporation profit tax or income tax . . .

Case 151. Schiesser International (Ireland) Ltd v Gallagher
Circuit Court (1971) 106 I.L.T.R. 22

By a contract in writing the plaintiff agreed to employ and train the defendant as a textile cutter. This training included a period in Germany. The agreement contained a clause to the effect that in the event of the defendant's leaving the employment of the plaintiff at any time within three years of his return to Ireland then he should pay to the plaintiff the travelling expenses of the journey to and from Germany and the cost of the training expenses incurred by the plaintiff for the training period. When the defendant left the employment two years after returning from Germany the plaintiff sued for these expenses.

Held that the clause was in the nature of a penalty in that the sum to be repaid was the same whether the defendant left the employment one day after his return from Germany, or if he had left just one day short of the three years. Exercising the equitable jurisdiction of the court the plaintiff would only be awarded the loss as proved.

Judge O Briain:

. . . The answer to the question whether the terms amount to a penalty clause or liquidated damages depends upon which interpretation is the true one in the view of the court . . .

The law relating to the distinction between a penalty and liquidated damages is stated in the *Law of Contracts* by Cheshire and Fifoot (7th edn 1969) at p. 561 as follows:

The parties to a contract may agree beforehand what sum shall be payable by way of damages in the event of breach . . . A sum fixed in this manner falls into one of two classes. First, it may be a genuine pre-estimate of the loss that will be caused to one party if the contract is broken by the other. In this case it is called liquidated damages and it constitutes the amount, no more and no less, that the plaintiff is entitled to recover in the event of breach without being required to prove actual damage. . . . Secondly, it may be in the nature of a threat held over the other party *in terrorem*—a security to the promisee that the contract will be performed. A sum of this nature is called a penalty, and it has long been subject to equitable jurisdiction. Courts of equity have taken the view that, since a penalty is designed as mere security for the performance of the contract, the promisee is sufficiently compensated by being indemnified for his actual loss, and that he acts unconscionably if he demands a sum which, though certainly fixed by agreement, may well be disproportionate to the injury.

I accept this as a correct statement of the law.

In this present case I have to consider the question as to what the position would be if the defendant had left the employment of the plaintiff one day after his return from Germany and alternatively, if he had left just one day short of the period of three years. Under the agreement as interpreted by the plaintiff the same sum of money was to be repaid in both instances. Counsel for the defendant has argued ably and forcibly that this points to its being a penalty clause and I have come to the conclusion that he is right and that clause 8 of the agreement is a penalty clause. It is thus subject to equitable jurisdiction, but is enforceable by the court to the extent that the plaintiff can recover the loss which has been proved to have been actually suffered by it, due to the breach on the defendant's part, but nothing more. It has proved to my satisfaction figures for travelling expenses and training expenses . . .

CHAPTER 24.

SPECIFIC PERFORMANCE

The law may, by an order of specific performance, enforce the due performance of the contract. But not every contract may be enforced by specific performance, as for example a contract to loan money: *Duggan v Allied Irish Building Society* (Case 152) or to enforce contracts for personal services: *Dublin Port & Docks Board v Brittania Dredging Co. Ltd* (Case 153). Specific performance will not be granted where damages are an adequate remedy. It is a discretionary remedy. It may not be granted against a party the victim of innocent misrepresentation: *Smelter Corporation of Ireland v O'Driscoll* (Case 78). Damages may be awarded where the court deems it inappropriate to grant specific performance: *Duggan v Allied Irish Building Society* (Case 152). Should an order of specific performance not be observed the party in whose favour it was made may apply to the court for enforcement of the order, or apply to dissolve the order and put an end to the contract. In such an event damages may be awarded: *Vandeluer v Dargan* (Case 154). Specific performance may not be awarded in cases of hardship: *Roberts v O'Neill* (Case 155).

Case 152. Duggan v Allied Irish Building Society
High Court, unreported, 4 March 1976

The facts are immaterial.

Finlay P.:

. . . With regard to the second ground of defence ultimately relied upon, namely that the plaintiff is not entitled as a matter of law to a decree for specific performance and that accordingly the court cannot award to him damages as an alternative I am satisfied on the authority of the decision in *Rogers v Challis* and of *Larios v Gurety* that the court cannot and should not grant specific performance of a contract to advance money even where the contract is in the form of a contract to enter by the defendants into a legal mortgage. The second part of the contention, however, which of course is the vital one from the defendants' point of view, namely, that there being no power to grant specific performance there is no power to grant damages in lieu thereof fails completely, having regard to the provisions of the *Judicature (Ireland) Act 1877*. It is quite clear that the necessity for a right to exist or to have existed at the time of the commencement of an action to an order for specific performance as a condition precedent to the granting of damages applied only at a time when the courts of equity were separated from and distinct in their powers and jurisdiction from the courts of common law. If in fact I am satisfied that the defendants had been in breach of this contract, then the plaintiff upon proof of loss is entitled to damages for that breach irrespective of whether he could at law have obtained an order for specific performance of it . . .

Case 153. Dublin Port & Docks Board v Brittania Dredging Co. Ltd

Supreme Court [1968] I.R. 136

The parties contracted to perform certain dredging works. The defendant had assessed its costs of the works on the basis of a survey of the site which the plaintiffs had delivered before it had tendered for the work. The defendant maintained that the plaintiffs had misrepresented the material to be dredged which differed fundamentally from the material described in the survey, and the defendant stated that, as a consequence, it was losing a considerable sum of money per week in executing the works and that it would be compelled soon to abandon performance of the contract. A clause in the contract stipulated that all equipment brought to the site by the defendant should be deemed to be the plaintiffs' property and that such equipment should not be removed by the defendant without the written consent of the plaintiffs which would not be withheld unreasonably. The plaintiffs sought an interlocutory injunction to restrain the defendant from removing the equipment from the site. It was argued by the defendant that the granting of the injunction would be tantamount to enforcing the specific performance of a contract for personal services.

Held that the clause relating to equipment was designed to enable the plaintiffs to have the works completed in the event of the defendant ceasing to perform its part of the contract and that, accordingly, the injunction sought by the plaintiffs was not equivalent to ordering the specific performance of the contract.

Ó Dálaigh C.J.:

Mr Justice Teevan [in the High Court] came to the conclusion that the plaintiffs, on the terms of the contract, were entitled to an interlocutory injunction, but he declined to make the order sought because his view was that, in the circumstances of this case, the granting of the injunction would amount to an order for specific performance of a contract for personal service . . . He therefore refused the application, and reserved the costs until the termination of the action. Counsel for the plaintiffs on this appeal has submitted that the judge has misconceived the position, and that the enforcement of the clause is not equivalent to specific performance. Counsel for the defendant has supported the judge's view. He submitted that the application is an attempt on the plaintiffs' part to keep the defendant working on the site.

An examination of the clause indicates that its purpose is to make the plant, temporary works and materials, provided by the defendant, available to the plaintiffs to proceed with the completion of the works in the absence and independent of the defendant. This is to say, it contemplates not the continuation of the work by the defendant but, on the contrary, its discontinuance of the work, arising either from voluntary withdrawal or compulsory exclusion from the site. Far from being designed to compel specific performance, the purpose of the clause is to assist the plaintiffs whose contractor, for whatever reason, has abandoned the work. It is appreciated that inability to remove plant and gear might deter a contractor from withdrawing from the work on a calculation of balance of monetary advantage or disadvantage. But this is an extraneous factor and, in any event, is wholly absent in this case. The court is, therefore, of opinion that the judge was wrong in holding that to grant the injunction sought would amount to ordering specific performance of the work . . .

Haugh and Budd JJ. concurred.

Case 154. Vandeluer v Dargan

High Court [1981] I.L.R.M. 75

The parties entered into a contract for the sale of land and the defendant, the purchaser, failed to complete the sale. The plaintiff obtained an order for specific performance with which the defendant failed to comply. The plaintiff then sought damages, in lieu of specific performance.

Held that a contract is not merged in the judgment for specific performance but remains in effect. Should the order not be complied with, the party not at fault may either apply to the court for enforcement of the order, or apply to the court to dissolve the order and put an end to the contract. Should the latter course of action be taken damages may be awarded.

McWilliam J.:

By an agreement in writing dated 5 June 1979, the defendant agreed to buy [some] land for the sum of £320,000. The defendant was depending on a sale of his own lands to enable him to complete the purchase. Unfortunately the market for land collapsed shortly afterwards and the defendant was unable to sell his land for a price which would enable him to complete the purchase from the plaintiff. The deposit paid by the defendant was only £20,000 and the plaintiffs issued proceedings for specific performance on 12 September 1979. On 7 October 1980, I made an order for specific performance of the contract. The date for completion named in the contract was 5 September 1979, and I ordered interest at 18% per annum, as was provided by the contract, to be paid from that date until completion. The defendant has not complied with the order and the plaintiffs now seek damages in lieu of specific performance.

I have been referred to the case of *Johnson v Agnew* (1980) in which the House of Lords considered the question of damages in lieu of specific performance where an order for specific performance made against him has not been carried out by a purchaser. A full review of the authorities was made by Lord Wilberforce who stated five propositions with regard to contracts for the sale of land which purchasers fail to complete. Of these, the fourth and fifth are relevant to the present case.

Lord Wilberforce said: 'Fourthly, if an order for specific performance is sought and is made, the contract remains in effect and is not merged in the judgment for specific performance.' He said further:

Fifthly, if the order for specific performance is not complied with by the purchaser, the vendor may *either* apply to the court for enforcement of the order, *or* may apply to the court to dissolve the order and ask the court to put an end to the contract. This proposition is as stated in *Austins of East Ham Ltd v Macey* (1941), and see *Singh (Sudagar) v Nazeer* (1978), and is in my opinion undoubted law, both on principle and authority. It follows, indeed, automatically from the facts that the contract remains in force after the order for specific performance and that the purchaser has committed a breach of it of a repudiatory character which he has not remedied, or as Megarry VC puts it that he is refusing to complete . . .

These propositions being, as I think they are, uncontrovertible, there only remains the question whether, if the vendor takes the latter course, i.e. of applying to the court to put an end to the contract, he is entitled to recover damages for breach of contract. On principle one may ask 'Why ever not?' If, as is clear, the vendor is entitled, after, and notwithstanding that an order for specific performance has been made, if the purchaser still does not complete the contract, to ask the court to permit him to accept the purchaser's repudiation and to declare the contract to be terminated, why, if the court accedes to this, should there not follow the ordinary consequences, undoubted under the general law of contract, that on such acceptance and termination the vendor may recover damages for breach of the contract?

Having then considered, in considerable detail, the arguments said to support a negative answer, Lord Wilberforce came to the conclusion . . . that

The vendors should have been entitled, upon discharge of the contract, on grounds of normal and accepted principle, to damages appropriate for a breach of contract.

And he decided that, as the vendors acted reasonably in pursuing the remedy of specific performance, the date at which that remedy became aborted (not by the vendor's fault) should logically be fixed as the date on which damages should be assessed. In the present case, this must be the date of the application to dissolve the order for specific performance on the ground of non-compliance with it by the defendant.

No argument has been advanced which persuades me that the plaintiff is not entitled to damages once the order for specific performance has been dissolved but the way in which damages should be measured has been keenly contested . . .

Case 155. Roberts v O'Neill
Supreme Court [1983] I.L.R.M. 206; [1983] I.R. 47

The parties entered into a written contract for the sale of licensed premises. Before completion of this contract another party commenced an action,* later dismissed, against the defendant claiming specific performance of another alleged contract for the sale of the same premises. Later the same year the plaintiff commenced proceedings for specific performance. Three years later a defence was filed which pleaded that the licensed premises had increased greatly in value, as had licensed premises generally, since the contract of sale and that it would be unjust, and cause great hardship, should the defendant be obliged to sell at the contract price and that the more appropriate remedy was damages.

Held that specific performance of the contract should be ordered. Hardship existing at the time of the contract may ground a refusal of specific performance. That general rule might be breached in a case of hardship arising after the contract, where in order to do justice the court would override this strict legal principle, but that this was not one of those occasions.

McCarthy J.:

. . . Counsel for the defendant has argued that the correct approach is to measure the hardship as of the date of the hearing; this argument is unsupported by authority and is indeed, contradicted by *Lavan v Walsh* (1964) in which Budd J. said:

> The defendant in this case also relies on the plea that enforcement of the contract in this case would cause great hardship on her. It is pointed out that the order is a discretionary one and it is strongly urged that the court in the exercise of a proper judicial discretion should not grant the relief of specific performance because of the special facts of the case which I will deal with later. Again, however, I must first refer to a matter of law. The court, it is well established, will not enforce the specific performance of a contract the result of which would be to impose great hardship on either of the parties to it. It is conceded,

---

* See Carthy v O'Neill, Case 42.

however, that the question of the hardship of a contract is generally to be judged at the time it is entered into. Change of circumstances taking place later, making the contract less beneficial to one party, are immaterial as a rule unless brought about by the action of the other party. It is stated, however, in *Fry on Specific Performance* (6th edn at p. 220): 'It cannot, however, be denied that there are cases in which the court has refused its interference by reason of events subsequent to the contract.' From an examination of the cases of *The City of London v Nash* and *Costigan v Hastler* it appears that this is so, but exceptions to the general rule appear very rare . . . I must, however, approach the consideration of these matters dispassionately and exercise what I conceive to be the proper judicial discretion. In the first place, as I have pointed out, it is undoubtedly the position in law that save in exceptional cases only a matter of hardship existing at the time of the contract can be taken into consideration. Hardship existing at the time of the contract is out of the case. It thus requires a strong case to be made out before one should accede to a plea for the exercise of judicial discretion in a quite unusual way, that is, by reason of hardship arising subsequently to the contract, and the onus being on the defendant to satisfy me of the existence and genuineness of the hardship on her, that proof of it should be strong and above suspicion.

. . . Counsel for the defendant has suggested that there is an illogicality in taking the date of the contract as the relevant one, since it was unlikely that there would be any contract if the hardship were then known. This very argument perhaps answers the problem—hardship is permitted to defeat specific performance where an existing hardship was not known at the relevant time—the date of the contract. While recognising that there may be cases in which hardship occurring later is such that to decree specific performance would result in great injury, such cases must be few and far between and, in my view, would not, ordinarily, include cases of hardship resulting from inflation alone. To permit, as an ordinary rule, a defence of subsequent hardship, would be adding a further hazard to the already trouble-strewn area of the law of contracts for the sale of land.

. . . It may be that there are other circumstances surrounding the alleged hardship but I think I have cited the salient ones. In my judgment, they fall far short of establishing the type of case in which the court should intervene to deny the ordinary remedy to one of the contracting parties in what was, at the time, a perfectly fair and proper transaction. There may be cases in which the court should intervene or, to put it more crudely, interfere with the express wording of a contract—the duty to do justice may override strictly legal principles and the well recognised procedures of the courts of equity. Such is not the case here—indeed, justice here demands that the contract be specifically performed.

O'Higgins C.J. and Hederman J. concurred.

CHAPTER 25.

INJUNCTION

An injunction is an order of the court directing a party to the proceedings to do, or to refrain from doing, a specified act. The courts may restrain a party by injunction from committing a breach of contract. It is granted in cases in which monetary compensation affords an inadequate remedy to an injured party: *Fluid Power Technology Co. Ltd v Sperry Ltd* (Case 156). This remedy is most appropriate where the contract is negative in nature, or contains a negative stipulation. This remedy is a common feature in disputes arising over contracts in restraint of trade and exclusive dealing contracts. The remedy is discretionary.

A perpetual injunction is granted only after the plaintiff has established his or her right and the actual or threatened infringement of that right by the defendant: *Continental Oil Co. of Ireland Ltd v Moynihan* (Case 130). An interlocutory, or interim, injunction, is granted before the trial of an action. Its object is to keep things *in statu quo* until the question at issue before the parties can be determined. In order for an interlocutory injunction to issue the plaintiff must establish that there is a fair issue to be tried and that the balance of convenience lies on the side of the granting of the injunction: *Esso Petroleum (Ireland) Ltd v Fogarty* (Case 157)* and *ECI European Chemicals Industries Ltd v Bell* (Case 119).

Case 156. Fluid Power Technology Co. Ltd v Sperry Ltd
High Court, unreported, 22 February 1985

The plaintiff purchased the assets of a company which had been the sole distributors of certain goods. The plaintiff entered into two distributive contracts with the defendant which could be terminated by giving appropriate notice. The defendant purported to terminate one of these agreements by giving the appropriate notice and appointed another party distributors of these goods to act forthwith. With regard to the other agreement the defendant purported to terminate it by giving the appropriate notice but did not appoint another distributor. The plaintiff sought an injunction to restrain these terminations alleging that they were in breach of contract.

Held that since damages would not be adequate remedy for the

---

* These principles were restated by the Supreme Court in *Campus Oil Ltd v Minister for Industry and Energy* (1983).

plaintiff, the balance of convenience demanded an injunction should be granted to restrain breach of the first agreement provided the plaintiff observed its remaining terms. Since there was no intention to appoint another distributor with regards to the second contract, the granting of an injunction would not be appropriate.

Costello J.:

. . . I can now summarise then my view in relation to the claim for interlocutory relief as follows. First of all, in relation to the hydraulic agreement, as the plaintiff had an exclusive distributorship, as the notice was properly given, then it would appear that the plaintiff is entitled to continue as exclusive distributor, but only until the termination notice expires, i.e. 30 June next. In addition it would appear that during that period it is entitled to the payment terms in . . . the agreement, i.e. 60 days net. I should make clear that this right is subject to the defendant's right to terminate the agreement during the balance of the six months' termination notice if [other] breaches [of the agreement] should arise.

Secondly, as to the pneumatic agreement, as the plaintiff had an exclusive distributorship, as the notice of termination was properly given, then the plaintiff was entitled to continue with the distributorship until 31 July next. But no threat to appoint another distributor of the pneumatic goods has been established, so no fair case for an injunction in relation to the pneumatic agreement has been made out. I should make clear that during this period the defendant is entitled to supply, as it has indicated it is prepared to supply, on a cash on order basis.

This view of the case does not determine the right of the plaintiff to an interlocutory injunction because I have to consider certain other matters. I have to consider in relation to the plaintiff's right to an injunction relating to the hydraulic agreement whether damages for breach of contract would be an adequate remedy. It seems to me that from the plaintiff's point of view damages would not be an adequate remedy, and that the plaintiff has made out a fair case in this point. Its business, which it has been carrying on with the defendant has been its only business. It is obviously going to have to look around for alternative sources of supply. During this period it would have to maintain the goodwill of its customers and also to maintain staff. It seems to me that it would be very difficult to measure the damages if in fact an injunction was refused today, because these factors might well be imponderable at the trial of this action. On the other hand as to the plaintiff's undertaking as to damages, it seems to me that the defendant will not suffer any real damage if the plaintiff carries out the contract for the remainder of the termination notice. It seems to me also that [the other company] will not suffer any considerable damage by not being appointed stockists until 30 June. They have other business interests, and even if some loss of profits can be established, it has not been shown that an undertaking in this connection would be of no value to them. So it seems to me that on the question of the adequacy of damages, the plaintiff has made out a case for injunctive relief. On the balance of convenience, the same reason I have given in relation to the inadequacy of damages point in the case. I conclude therefore as follows. The plaintiff has made out a case for an interlocutory injunction in relation to the hydraulic agreement and this should restrain the defendant until 30 June next from appointing [the other company] or any other person distributors or stockists of the goods referred to in the hydraulic agreement. The injunction would restrain them from supplying to the plaintiff the goods other than on 60 days net as per . . . the agreement, or otherwise as agreed between the parties.

I will require the plaintiff to give an undertaking as to the damages, and I will reserve costs as the matter in relation to costs cannot be properly determined until the full issues in the case have been clarified at an oral hearing.

Finally, I would like to make clear that in reaching the conclusions that I have just announced, I have sought to apply the principles established by the Supreme Court in *Campus Ireland Ltd v the Minister for Industry and Energy* (1985). This means I have not sought to see whether on the issues in this case the plaintiff has shown that on the balance of probability it will succeed. I have sought to see whether it has established a fair case or a serious case—the words are synonymous in the view of Griffin J., as agreed to by Hederman J. There are different issues in this case and it seems to me that the strength of the plaintiff's case has varied on these different issues. I have reached my decision bearing this fact in mind. I have in the course of this judgment referred to a fair question as being raised and I have quoted what Diplock L.J. said in *American Cyanamid v Ethicon Ltd* (1975) namely that if the plaintiff has failed to show any real prospect of success then a plaintiff has failed to show that a fair question has been raised.

(See also Case 133, regarding termination of contract.)

Case 157. Esso Petroleum (Ireland) Ltd v Fogarty
The facts are given on page 258.

Ó Dálaigh C.J.:

The principles of law to be applied by this court on the hearing of an appeal to set aside an order granting an interlocutory injunction are well summarised in the judgment of Mr Justice Lavery in the *Educational Company of Ireland Ltd v Fitzpatrick* (1961). I refer to two passages: firstly, Mr Justice Lavery there quoted with approval the following passages from the 6th edition of Kerr on *Injunctions*, at pp. 15-16:

The office of the court to interfere being founded on the existence of the legal right, a man who seeks the aid of the court must be able to show a fair *prima facie* case in support of the title which he asserts. He is not required to make out a clear legal title, but he must satisfy the court that he has a fair question to raise as to the existence of the legal right which he sets up, and that there are substantial grounds for doubting the existence of the alleged legal right, the exercise of which he seeks to prevent. The court must, before disturbing any man's legal right, or stripping him of any of the rights with which the law has clothed him, be satisfied that the probability is in favour of his case ultimately failing in the final issue of the suit. The mere existence of a doubt as to the plaintiff's right to the property, interference with which he seeks to restrain, does not of itself constitute a sufficient ground for refusing an injunction, though it is always a circumstance which calls for the attention of the court.

Secondly, as to the considerations which guide the court, Mr Justice Lavery quoted with approval the following passage from the article on injunctions in the Hailsham edition of the *Laws of England*, written by Mr Justice Eve:

. . . in the absence of very special circumstances [the court] will impose only such restraint as will suffice to stop the mischief and keep things as they are until the hearing. Where any doubt exists as to the plaintiff's right, or if his right is not disputed, but its violation is denied, the court, in determining whether an interlocutory injunction should be granted, takes into consideration the balance of convenience to the parties and the nature of the injury which the defendant, on the one hand, would suffer if the injunction was granted and he should ultimately turn out to be right and that which the plaintiff, on the other hand, might sustain if the injuction was refused and he should ultimately turn out to be right. The burden of proof that the inconvenience which the plaintiff will suffer by the refusal of the injunction is greater than that which the defendant will suffer, if it is granted, lies on the plaintiff.

Mr Justice Kenny [in the High Court] considers only the terms of the solus agreement. He does not examine the terms of the sub-demise by the defendant . . . except to advert to the circumstance that it was made after the making of the interim injunction and during the period when the defendant had been granted an adjournment of the plaintiff's motion for an interlocutory injunction.

Inter alia, the defendant says that he is, under the terms of the solus agreement, entitled to sub-demise the part of his premises used for the sale of petrol and that his agreement with [his tenant] is valid.

The plaintiff in the circumstances existing on the granting of the interlocutory injunction was required to show that, in the language of Kerr, there are substantial grounds for doubting the existence of the alleged legal right, the exercise of which it seeks to prevent. This in my judgment means in effect that the defendant had no power to make the sub-demise . . . This is the right which the defendant says the law has clothed him with. The court before stripping him of this right must be satisfied that the probability is in favour of the defendant's case ultimately failing in the final issue of this suit.

I am not so satisfied.

If I examine the matter from the reverse side—from the point of view of the right asserted by the plaintiff—again I consider there is a doubt existing as to that right. In such case one is to take into account the balance of convenience to the parties and the nature of the injury which the defendant on the one hand would suffer if the injunction was granted—in this instance maintained—and he should ultimately turn out to be right, and that which the plaintiff on the other hand might sustain if the injunction was refused—in this instance dissolved—and it should turn out to be right.

The burden of proof here lies on the plaintiff.

It seems to me that the defendant's garage business might well wither away if this injunction is maintained, whereas I cannot see that the plaintiff will suffer any marked inconvenience or hardship if this laneway garage does not continue to sell their petrol.

Lavery and Walsh JJ. concurred.

(See also Case 127, regarding contracts in restraint of trade).

CHAPTER 26.

RESCISSION

The right to rescind is a right which a party to a transaction sometimes had to set that transaction aside and be restored to his or her former position. The object of rescission is to release the parties from the contract. A party who rescinds a contract is entitled to be restored to the position he or she would have been in had the contract not been made. Therefore, property must be returned, possession given up, and accounts taken of profits or deterioration. But damages are not recoverable since the purpose of damages is to place the party recovering them in the same position, so far as money can do it, as he or she would have been, had the contract been carried out.

Rescission can be claimed in cases of mistake: *Gun v McCarthy* (Case 72), fraudulent misrepresentation: *Carbin v Somerville* (Case 158). Rescission is universally sought in cases of undue influence:

White v Meade (Case 88) and improvident contracts: *Grealish v Murphy* (Case 96).

Case 158. Carbin v Somerville
Supreme Court [1933] I.R. 276

In the course of inspecting the defendant's house for sale the plaintiff asked whether the house was dry and free from damp and whether the roof was in good condition. The defendant answered affirmatively to both questions though he knew his replies to be false. The house suffered from damp and the roof was faulty. The plaintiff purchased the house, and on discovering the true facts sought to rescind the contract on the ground of fraudulent misrepresentation. The defendant argued that even had the contract been so induced the plaintiff was not entitled to the relief sought because there had been delay in seeking to repudiate the contract and because *restitutio in integrum* was impossible.

Held that since the plaintiff's repudiation of the contract was made on the day she became aware of the deception there was no undue delay and that the subsequent deterioration of the house was due, not to any act of the plaintiff, but to the defendant's insistence on his right to hold the plaintiff to her bargain and the denial of the fraudulent misrepresentation he was found to have made.

FitzGibbon J.:

. . . It has been contended that even if the contract was induced by the fraudulent misrepresentation of the defendant, as I am satisfied it was, the plaintiff is not entitled to the relief claimed because she had been guilty of delay in seeking to repudiate the bargain, or because *restitutio in integrum* is impossible.

As for delay, it is admitted that upon 17 July there was a tremendous downpour of rain, which in fact penetrated into the walls of the house and caused dampness in all the rooms. The plaintiff went off at once, that same day, to the defendant's solicitor. 'In the morning I went to see his solicitor, and I told him I was deceived in the house, and I wanted to make the defendant take it back. The solicitor said that he could not promise to do that, as he could not work well with him—that is to make the defendant repair it. That same evening I went to see the defendant, between 5 and 6 in the evening. I told him that he had deceived me in the house, and I wanted him to take it back. He said he would not do that, and he denied ever having deceived me.'

From that date, 17 July 1930, until the issue of the [legal proceedings] on 1 November 1930, the plaintiff made no attempt to repair or protect the house from the effects of the weather. It is difficult to see what she should have done, or why she should have done anything. She had stated her case to the defendant, and called upon him to take back his house. Having done so, she had no right thenceforward to interfere with property which she asserted was his, and I am not aware of any principle upon which she would have been entitled to recover from him any expenditure upon the house so long as she was insisting upon her right to repudiate the contract upon the ground of fraudulent misrepresentation. The evidence of the plaintiff's architects, which is not substantially contradicted, for neither of the two architects who inspected the house on behalf of the defendant was called to give evidence for him, is that the material of which the house was constructed and the defective nature of the string course were such that the house could not be made weatherproof except by very heavy expenditure and the removal of the string course which collected the rainwater running down the external walls, and diverted it inwards. If the plaintiff was induced to purchase the house by fraudulent misrepresentation, she was entitled to repudiate the bargain provided she did so without undue delay, and she did in fact repudiate it on the very day upon which she became aware of the deception, which was the earliest opportunity she had of discovering that she had been deceived. The subsequent deterioration of the house is due, not to any act of the plaintiff, but to the defendant having insisted upon his right to hold her to her bargain and his denial of the representation he is found to have made.

We have not been referred to any decision of any court, or to any opinion of any reputable text-writer, to the effect that when a party to a contract has been induced to enter into it by fraudulent misrepresentation he loses his right to repudiate it on discovery of the fraud because the subject matter cannot be restored to the defendant in the identical condition in which it was at the date of the contract, where the alteration is due to the nature of the subject-matter itself and cannot be attributed to any act of the plaintiff. In *Adam v Newbigging* (1886) the House of Lords considered that the circumstance that the business, in which the plaintiff had been induced to become a partner by the misrepresentation of the defendants made without any fraud on their part, had become totally insolvent and worthless between the date of the contract, and the date of the commencement of proceedings for rescission, did not disentitle the plaintiff to rescission and repayment of his capital although the defendants could not recover against him for money lent and goods sold by them to the partnership during the interval. It was held unanimously that the mere deterioration of the business, though it might have been anticipated if the plaintiff had known the actual state of affairs in the beginning of 1883, could not stand in the way of the plaintiff's claim for mutual restitution, and that was a case of innocent misrepresentation only. The present defendant sold the plaintiff a defective house, by fraudulent misrepresentation as to its condition. He will get back his own defective house, which has deteriorated since he sold it through its own inherent vice, and has not been depreciated by any act of the plaintiff, who has simply refrained from spending any more of her own money upon the defendant's house in a vain endeavour to make it what he contracted to sell her . . .

Kennedy C.J. and Murnaghan J. concurred.
(See also Case 87, regarding fraudulent misrepresentation).

CHAPTER 27.

RECTIFICATION

Should the parties to a contract agree on one set of terms and that agreement is later reduced into written form which either does not contain those agreed verbal terms, or contains different terms to those agreed, the court may rectify the written document to conform to the terms verbally agreed. The court is concerned with defects not in the making of the contract but in its recording. The court will then enforce the rectified agreement. The remedy is discretionary. A mistake made by both parties, or merely known to one, is a common ground for rectification: *Monaghan County Council v Vaughan* (Case 159) and *Nolan v Graves* (Case 160).

Case 159. Monaghan County Council v Vaughan
High Court [1948] I.R. 306

The facts are given on page 143. The question arose whether rectification was the appropriate remedy in a case of mutual mistake. That court held that it was.

Dixon J.

. . . I think that the principle which is applicable here is most clearly set out in the decision in *Fowler v Fowler* (1859) where, the Lord Chancellor said:

It is clear that a person who seeks to rectify a deed upon the ground of mistake must be required to establish, in the clearest and most satisfactory manner, that the alleged intention, to which he desires it to be made conformable, continued concurrently in the minds of all parties down to the time of its execution, and also must be able to show exactly and precisely the form to which the deed ought to be brought. For there is a material difference between setting aside an instrument and rectifying it on the ground of mistake. In the latter case you can only act upon the mutual and concurrent intention of all parties for whom the court is virtually making a new written agreement.

I am satisfied that in the present case the two requirements mentioned in this passage have been fulfilled by the plaintiffs.

Gun v McCarthy (Case 72) was also a case of mutual mistake and there Flanagan J. said that he had always understood the law to be that when you seek to reform a conveyance you must first establish that there was a definite concluded agreement between the parties, but which, by mistake common to both parties, had not been carried out in the conveyance executed pursuant to the real agreement. But when the mistake is not common, he asks, by what can it be reformed? 'To reform', he continues, 'implies a previous *agreement*; but when the evidence shows that there was no agreement to which both parties assented, but only a mistake on one side, and not a common mistake, in my opinion it is impossible to support a suit to *reform*, whatever equity the party who has made the mistake may have in certain cases to rescind, the conveyance.' His Lordship here seems to be drawing a contrast between cases where the parties are *ad idem* in intention and cases where they are not . . .

For all these reasons, I consider that the plaintiffs' case for rectification has been fully established and I grant the relief as claimed . . .

(See also Case 73, regarding mistake.)

Case 160. Nolan v Graves
High Court [1946] I.R. 376

A dispute arose between the parties as regards the price of premises sold at an auction. The plaintiff claimed that the price inserted in the written contract was the correct price whereas the defendant alleged that it was higher. When the defendant refused to complete the contract at the lower price the plaintiff sued for rescission of the contract and the defendant counterclaimed for rectification and specific performance of the contract.

Held that the figure of £4,550 was inserted in the contract by mistake, and that the figure should have been £5,550. The plaintiff endeavoured to take advantage of this mistake of which she was aware. Therefore the plaintiff was not entitled to any relief. The contract would be rectified but specific performance was refused. The plaintiff could then elect whether she would, or would not, complete the sale at the true price.

Haugh J.:

. . . Accordingly, the conclusion I have come to with regard to the
contract—the offer and acceptance—was that there was a bidding that had
begun around £3,500; that it proceeded, roughly, by increases of £250; that
it reached £5,000; thereafter the bidding became slower; that it increased
by hundreds and by fifties until it reached the sum of £5,550. That figure
was repeated over and over again with monotonous repetition, as stated by
some of the witnesses, by the auctioneer, clearly and audibly, and the
plaintiff plainly intended to bid that as her offer, or as her acceptance, or
at least as her offer to the auctioneers, which, at the fall of the hammer,
the auctioneer (for the defendant) accepted. I am further satisfied that she
well knew, and at all times knew, that she had offered the sum of £5,550
for these premises, and that she sat with another bidder for some minutes,
discussing with him her purchase, and that they both knew that the final
bid was £5,550 when she and this bidder were consulting as to what each
individual house had cost her, having regard to the payment of the
auctioneer's fees and to the legal costs . . .

I have come to the conclusion very definitely that this lady went to the
table with the intention of signing, particularly after her conversation with
the other bidder—that she went to the table with the intention (begotten
of experience) to sign a contract binding upon her and binding upon the
auctioneers, for a sale for £5,550; that she saw this mistake; that she
realised its importance to her should she ever succeed in upholding it, or
making it permanent in its effect; that she, in my view, knowingly and
immediately decided to take such advantage of it as, in her lay mind, she
might think she was entitled to take.

For these reasons, I have viewed with some suspicion, and still do, the
real intention that lay behind her acts when she asked the auctioneer to
prepare this pink slip that contained more than the auctioneer's fees,
because it contained the purchase-price in detail and it also contained the
amount of the deposit. Again to her lay mind (as against the mind of a
person trained in law), it appeared that there would have been some
advantage to her, to have another permanent record, written by the
auctioneer in reference to these important matters, which she could
permanently have and which she certainly had in her possession up to the
hearing of this action.

Now, normally I would be inclined to accept her account that she
usually, or sometimes, hands her cheque-book to her creditors so that they
may fill in the body of the cheque. That may happen. Perhaps there are
some people who would do that. But I certainly view with some suspicion
her immediate doing of that act in this case, because it seemed to me to be
utterly unnecessary in the circumstances. My view is that the lady handed
that cheque to the auctioneer because she had promptly realised the
mistake made by the auctioneer in putting in a figure of £1,000 too little,
and that it seemed to her lay mind that some advantage would accrue to

her by getting him to fill in the money; it was act three, to put it down a third time: on the memorandum, on the pink slip, and again on the cheque. In my view, on the facts of this case, an innocent and very careless mistake was made by the auctioneer in the conduct of this sale. The plaintiff immediately realised that a mistake had been made and attempted to take an immediate advantage of it. She consistently followed it up on the next morning and she followed it up to some extent when she was in the hands of her solicitor until the time she asked for mere recission instead of any other relief . . .

(See also Case 48, regarding parol evidence and Case 74, regarding mistake.)

INDEX